Freedom Summer

FREEDOM SUMMER

Doug McAdam

Oxford University Press
New York   Oxford

Oxford University Press

Oxford   New York   Toronto
Delhi   Bombay   Calcutta   Madras   Karachi
Petaling Jaya   Singapore   Hong Kong   Tokyo
Nairobi   Dar es Salaam   Cape Town   ·
Melbourne   Auckland

and associated companies in
Berlin   Idaban

First published in 1988 by Oxford University Press, Inc.,
198 Madison Avenue, New York, New York 10016-4314

First issued as an Oxford University Press paperback, 1990

Oxford is a registered trademark of Oxford University Press

Library of Congress Cataloging-in-Publication Data

McAdam, Doug.
Freedom Summer / by Doug McAdam.
p.   cm. Bibliography: p.   Includes index.
1. Mississippi Freedom Project.   2. Afro-Americans-Suffrage-
Mississippi.   3. Civil rights workers-Mississippi-History-20th
century.   4. Afro-Americans-Civil rights-Mississippi.
5. Mississippi-Race relations.   I. Title.
E185.93.M6M28   1988   976.2'00496073-dc 19   88-4707 CIP
ISBN-13 978-0-19-504367-9

ISBN-13 978-0-19-506472-8 (pbk.)

We gratefully acknowledge permission to reproduce extracts
from the following books:

Sally Belfrage, *Freedom Summer.* New York: Viking Press, 1965.
Sarah Evans, *Personal Politics.* New York: Vintage Books, 1980.
David Harris, *Dreams Die Hard.* New York: St. Martin's Press, 1982.
Elizabeth Sutherland, *Letters from Mississippi.* New York: McGraw-Hill, 1965.

To Tracy

Acknowledgments

In setting out to write these acknowledgments, I can't help but think of Blanche DuBois. Like Blanche, I too have had to depend during this project on the kindness of strangers. The difference is that my strangers have not let me down. The single most important debt of gratitude I owe is to my subjects, none of whom I knew before the start of the project. This book is their story: to write it, I obviously had to have their support and cooperation. The extent to which I did was remarkable. Three hundred and forty-eight of the 556 Freedom Summer applicants to whom I sent questionnaires filled them out. This, despite the fact that they had never met me and the questionnaire itself was long and time-consuming to complete. More remarkable perhaps is the fact that all but four of the eighty-six applicants I approached about being interviewed acceded to my request. A substantial minority of them also fed and housed me as I made my way around the country conducting these interviews.

The interviews themselves were nothing short of remarkable. I expected a great deal of resistance to my request to tape the sessions. To my surprise, there was little resistance. I expected the sessions to last about an hour; they averaged nearly three. I expected my subjects to be guarded and unemotional. Instead, they were generous with their feelings as well as their recollections. In short, my respondents gave themselves to the interviews as one might hope, but could hardly expect, they would. They gave in other ways as well. Many shared highly personal letters and journals written during or immediately after the summer. Others provided archival materials collected in Mississippi. Still others made available pictures they—or others—had taken during the summer. The applicants, then, were much more than the subjects of my book. They functioned as informants, archivists, and research assistants. It is no exaggeration to say that without them there would have been no book. It is theirs as much as it is mine.

Other "strangers" bestowed a variety of kindnesses on me during the course of the project. Some of these kindnesses were financial. In 1984 I was awarded a Guggenheim Fellowship in support of the project. The award enabled me to take a semester off to complete the interview phase of the research. I also benefited enormously by a grant from the National Science Foundation (grant number SES-8309988). The grant allowed me to continue full-time work on the project during the summers of 1984 and 1985. Closer to home, the College of Social and Behavioral Sciences at the University of Arizona was extraordinarily generous in its support for this research. In the fall of 1984 I received a small faculty grant in connection with the project. More importantly, however, the following year the College awarded me a Research Professorship that again exempted me from teaching for a semester and allowed me to devote myself exclusively to the project. To all of these funding sources go my deep thanks. Without their support, I could never have hoped to undertake a project of this scope.

"Strangers" helped in ways other than financial. At the very outset of the project, Howard Zinn and Staughton Lynd—two historians who had been involved in the Freedom Summer effort—lent their endorsement to the project. Subsequently, a number of volunteers told me those endorsements strongly influenced their decision to participate in the project.

Reaching the volunteers would have been impossible without the extraordinary help I received from some 219 college and university alumni associations scattered across the country. It was they who painstakingly searched their records and supplied me with current addresses for the former applicants. To the directors and staff of these alumni associations go my deep thanks.

Gratitude is also due the directors and staffs of several research facilities that I made heavy use of during the course of the project. None of these facilities was more important than the library and archives of the Martin Luther King, Jr. Center in Atlanta. There, ably assisted by former Head Archivist Louise Cook and her staff, I discovered the original project applications that made this research possible. Nearly as important were the holdings of the State Historical Society of Wisconsin in Madison. The New Left collection there proved to be a rich source of letters and other archival materials on the summer project. My thanks to Director Richard Ermey and his staff for all the help they gave me while I was there. Finally, a very special vote of thanks goes to Ms. Jan Hillegas of the Freedom Information Service in Jackson, Mississippi. Jan came to Mississippi as a volunteer in 1964 and stayed on to help maintain the records amassed by the project. She has been there ever since, painstakingly expanding the collection at great expense to herself. What she has created is a unique collection that proved invaluable to me in my research. If it is to survive, however, it will require support beyond what Jan can provide herself. Nothing would please me more than to see this book stimulate that support.

One final group of "strangers" deserves mention as well. They are the two editors I have worked with at Oxford. Susan Rabiner was the first to express an interest in the book and it was her willingness to take the project on without so much as a sample chapter in hand that proved decisive. In addition, it was her enthusiasm and intelligent editorial guidance that saw the book through its initial draft.

Just as depressed as I was to see Susan leave the Press, was I relieved to meet and work with her successor, Valerie Aubry. Instead of grudgingly attending to a project that wasn't "hers," Valerie enthusiastically shepherded the book through the last draft and crucial production and copy editing processes. By the end, it was as much her project as Susan's. To both Valerie and Susan go my heartfelt thanks.

Besides the help of these myriad "strangers," I received much support and encouragement from friends as well. Indeed, the project began as a collaborative venture with two close friends and colleagues, Lois Horton and Victoria Rader. While each had a research focus separate from my own, they nonetheless helped to refine and extend my thinking in a number of important ways. This book bears the imprint of their contributions.

A host of other friends and colleagues have left comparable marks on the project during the past five years. Mary Rothschild, whose earlier book on the Freedom Summer volunteers made such an impression on me, graciously shared her thoughts with me in the early stages of the research. So too did the historian, Clay Carson, at a later stage in the project. More concretely, Clay also generously made available a great deal of archival materials he had collected for his exceptional book on SNCC. It was also my good fortune early in the project to meet Annie Popkin. As both a sociologist and a summer volunteer, Annie was uniquely qualified to serve as a kind of ultimate consultant to the project. This she did cheerfully and with great insight.

More conventionally, the manuscript has benefited from critical readings by dozens of colleagues. Those whose comments have found their way into the text include Al Bergesen, Carolyn Ellis, Roberto Fernandez, Neil Fligstein, Debra Friedman, David Garrow, Michael Hechter, John McCarthy, Tahi Mottl, Judy Stacey, Tracy Stevens, and Will Wright. Of these kind souls, I would like to single out Carolyn Ellis, Neil Fligstein, Debra Friedman, and John McCarthy for special thanks. It was their misfortune to slog through every last page of every last draft of the manuscript. If they look closely, they will see the imprint of their handiwork on many a page in the book.

So too will Kelly Moore, Ronelle Paulsen, Sarah Sample, Emilia Stein, and Nigel Vann. Over the past five years, this quintet has comprised the best collection of research assistants an author could ever hope for. The same can be said for the office staffs of the Sociology Departments at George Mason University and the University of Arizona. Long before any outside funding source had discovered the project, my former chair at George Mason, Joe Scimecca, had generously contributed scarce departmental resources to aid the research. Departmental secretary Peggy Gay was chief among these resources, cheerfully devoting hundreds of hours to any number of tasks associated with the research.

At Arizona, I have never received anything less than 100 percent support from the best departmental staff I have ever worked with. Administrative Assistant Sherry Enderle has worked the system, as only she can, to scrounge resources vital to the project. Georgia Zeutzius has virtually functioned as another research assistant, so often has she done work connected with the project. Finally, I owe special thanks to Jo Migliara and Barbara McIntosh for the exceptional job they have done in typing the various drafts of the manuscript. Not only did they do so quickly and accurately, but with a keen eye toward catching the grammatical errors I am prone to make.

Appropriately, the last thanks is a more personal one. As any author will tell you, writing a book is a long, emotionally draining experience. This book was no exception. What made this one all the more difficult was that it occurred during a particularly tough time in my life. The final debt of gratitude, then, is the one I owe my friends and family, whose support and love made this book possible and the tough times a lot more bearable.

Tucson, Arizona   D. M.
February 1988

Contents

Abbreviations

COFO	Council of Federated Organizations
CORE	Congress of Racial Equality
ERAP	Economic Research and Action Project
FBI	Federal Bureau of Investigation
FOR	Fellowship of Reconciliation
FSM	Free Speech Movement
HUAC	House Committee on Un-American Activities
KKK	Ku Klux Klan
LID	League for Industrial Democracy
LSCRRC	Law Students Civil Rights Research Committee
MFDP	Mississippi Freedom Democratic Party
NAACP	National Association for the Advancement of Colored People
SCLC	Southern Christian Leadership Conference
SDS	Students for a Democratic Society
SHSW	State Historical Society of Wisconsin
SNCC	Student Nonviolent Coordinating Committee
SPU	Student Peace Union
SSOC	Southern Student Organizing Committee
UAW	United Auto Workers
UFT	United Federation of Teachers
VIM	Vermont in Mississippi
WITCH	Women's International Conspiracy from Hell
WRAP	Women's Radical Action Project
YAF	Young Americans for Freedom
YPSL	Young People's Socialist League

Freedom Summer

In Search of the Volunteers

[E]very single thing that happened each day was new to me. I was being bombarded with information, bombarded with experiences . . . and my little psyche just almost cracked.[1]

You felt you were a part of a kind of historic moment; that something very profound about the whole way of life in a region was about to change; that . . . you were . . . making . . . history and that you were in some way utterly self-less and yet [you] found yourself.[2]

In terms of the kind of goals that I have in my life for social change, it was the highest possible experience I'll ever have . . . In terms of participating in history, it was the best I'll ever do, but it . . . [took] its toll on me; . . . [emotionally] it set me back . . . [Luckily] I didn't come out with any physical disabilities so, at least, physically I . . . survived.[3]

[It] was very inspirational. I mean, I think the whole thing about . . . beginning to think about what I was going to be doing as a woman and . . . what I was going to do with my life. Was I going to be a professional? Was I going to go to law school? . . . So much of what I'm in now goes back to it. So much of the work I do now goes back to my memory of that time.[4]

It totally flipped me out . . . for the first time the pieces fit . . . this felt like me . . . besides the good I think we did, it was my personal salvation as well.[5]

It was the longest nightmare I have ever had: three months—June, July and August of 1964. (Sellers, 1973: 94)

3

WHAT IS the "it" to which all these speakers are referring? What shared experiences produced such varied, yet intense, reactions in so many people? The event in question is the 1964 Mississippi Freedom Summer campaign, or, as it was simply known at the time, the Summer Project.

Spearheaded by the Student Non-Violent Coordinating Committee (SNCC), the project lasted less than three months, from early June until late August. During that time, better than 1,000 people, the vast majority of them white, Northern college students, journeyed South to work in one of the forty-four local projects that comprised the overall campaign. While in Mississippi, the volunteers lived in communal "Freedom Houses" or were housed by local black families who refused to be intimidated by segregationist threats of violence. Their days were taken up with a variety of tasks, principally registering black voters and teaching in so-called Freedom Schools.

What this capsule summary misses is the unrelieved fear, grinding poverty, and intermittent violence that beset the project. These elements combined to make the summer a searing experience for nearly all who took part. Just ten days into the project, three participants—James Chaney, Andrew Goodman, and Michael Schwerner—were kidnapped and beaten to death by a group of segregationists led by Mississippi law enforcement officers. The subsequent search for their bodies brought scores of FBI agents and hundreds of journalists to the state. Despite their presence, the violence continued. One other volunteer died before summer's end and hundreds more endured bombings, beatings, and arrest. Just as significantly, the volunteers experienced the sense of liberation that came with exposure to new lifestyles—interracial relationships, communal living, a more open sexuality—new political ideologies and a radically new and critical perspective on the United States. By all accounts, it was a remarkable summer for a remarkable group of young people. And one that would have enduring consequences for both the volunteers and the country as a whole.

At the outset, the Summer Project reflected the liberal idealism so characteristic of America in the early Sixties. Though not without tensions and contradictions, the project *did* embody the ideals of interracialism, nonviolence, and liberal/left coalition that were so much a part of the progressive vision of the era. And so it was with the volunteers themselves.

Poised on the eve of the summer campaign, project workers represented the "best and the brightest" of early Sixties youthful idealism.

Overwhelmingly drawn from elite colleges and universities, the volunteers tended to be extraordinarily bright, academically successful, politically active, and passionately committed to the full realization of the
idealistic values on which they had been taught America was based. For
the most part, they were liberals, not radicals; reformers rather than revolutionaries.

In short order, however, both the volunteers and the country were to
be dramatically transformed. As a nation we would descend in a matter
of years from the euphoric heights of the New Frontier to the domestic
unrest of the late Sixties. If Freedom Summer was a kind of high-water
mark of early Sixties liberalism, the foundations on which it rested crum-
bled soon afterward. Interracialism died amid the calls for black power
and black separatism less than a year later. Nonviolence was widely re-
pudiated, at least rhetorically, in the wake of Watts in 1965. The liberal/
left coalition failed to survive the summer. The end came in August at
the Democratic National Convention when party regulars elected to seat
the lily-white Mississippi delegation rather than the challenge delegation
that had grown out of the summer campaign.

The volunteers were no less affected by the turbulence of the era than
was the nation as a whole. The vast majority were radicalized by the
events of the mid to late Sixties. Many of them played prominent roles in
those events. Virtually none were unaffected by them.

The central theme of this book is that to fully understand the dramatic
changes experienced by the volunteers and America during this era re-
quires a serious reappraisal of the Freedom Summer campaign. For Freedom Summer marked a critical turning point both in the lives of those
who participated in the campaign and the New Left as a whole. Its significance lies both in the events of the summer and the cultural and political consequences that flowed from it. The events of the summer effectively resocialized and radicalized the volunteers while the ties they
established with other volunteers laid the groundwork for a nationwide
activist network out of which the other major movements of the era—
women's, antiwar, student—were to emerge. In short, Freedom Summer
served both as the organizational basis for much of the activism of the
Sixties as well as an important impetus for the development of the
broader counterculture that emerged during the era. This book, then,
represents a retrospective account of the Freedom Summer project and
an assessment of its impact on both the volunteers and American society
as a whole.

As straightforward as this focus is, it is quite different from the intent
with which I began the project some seven years ago. At that time, my
interest centered less on the Freedom Summer campaign or those who

participated in it, and more on the links between those participants and the later social movements of the Sixties and Seventies. A series of fortuitous events in the early 1980s prompted me to broaden the focus of my research. The story bears telling, if only to provide a bit of background for the book.

Before embarking on the project described in this book, I spent six years researching and writing a book on the origins of the modern civil rights movement (*Political Process and the Development of Black Insurgency, 1930–1970*, The University of Chicago, Press, 1982). In the course of that research I was struck by the number of references to whites trained in civil rights organizing who went on to prominent roles in the other major movements of the Sixties. I had been aware of the debt those later movements owed to the black struggle, but having myself come of (activist) age only in the late Sixties and early Seventies, I had experienced the debt as primarily one of tactics and ideology rather than of personnel. Certainly, few of the activists I knew in the early Seventies had participated in Southern civil rights organizing. But then the number of persons engaged in social action had multiplied so rapidly between 1964 and 1970 that one could hardly have expected the ranks of latter-day activists to have been dominated by the relatively small number of pioneers who had been active in the early Sixties.

If the personnel debt was not numerical, how was it to be characterized? My sense of things was that the importance of these early white civil rights activists lay in the political and cultural bridge they had provided between the Southern black struggle and the college campuses of the North and West. They were pioneers in an important diffusion process by which the ideologies, tactics, and cultural symbols of the Southern civil rights movement were introduced to the population—Northern white college students—that was to dominate activist politics for the remainder of the era. In this view, there had not been three or four discrete movements in the Sixties, but a single, broad, activist community with its roots firmly in the Southern civil rights movement and separate branches extending into various forms of activism (principally the black power, antiwar, student, and women's liberation movements).

Asserting this view was easy. Systematically studying the extent and significance of these ties was quite another matter. Nonetheless, that was the research project I was determined to tackle once the book on the civil rights movement had been completed.

Such a project, I reasoned, had to proceed from a systematic base. It would not do merely to amass anecdotal evidence of the involvement of individual activists in both the civil rights and some other movements of the period. Knowing that Tom Hayden participated in Southern civil rights activities long before his rise to bona fide movement "stardom" in the late Sixties tells us nothing about the frequency of this phenomenon. What proportion of white civil rights activists went on to pioneering roles in the antiwar movement? Student protest activity? Women's liberation? And what was it about their early civil rights experiences that disposed them to do so? These were the types of questions I hoped to answer. But to do so required systematic access to a large number of individuals who had been active in early civil rights organizing. Freedom Summer seemed to offer that access. What recommended the project as the starting point for my study was the fact that it marked the first widespread entrance of young whites into the movement. Whites, of course, had long been involved in the civil rights struggle. With but a few notable exceptions, most of the leading figures in the abolition movement had been white. During the 1930s, the white-dominated American Communist Party had sought to champion the cause of black civil rights in cases such as the one that involved the "Scottsboro boys."[6] Others, such as Anne and Carl Braden, fought the good fight through the lean years of the Forties and Fifties. A few whites, most notably Glenn Smiley of the Fellowship of Reconciliation (FOR), had been active in the Montgomery Bus Boycott. A minority of the Freedom Riders were white. But in all of these cases, the number of white participants was small. By contrast, the 1,000 or so whites who came to Mississippi for Freedom Summer represented a deluge. The sheer size of the project guaranteed me access to large numbers of white activists, *provided* I could find a list of all the summer volunteers that also included the name of the college or university (if any) each was attending at the time of the project; the only way I could think to track the volunteers in the present was to go through the alumni associations of their respective alma maters.

The search for this list came to resemble a quest for a (not so) holy grail. Fortunately my continuing work on the civil rights book occasioned numerous visits to libraries and archives throughout the South. These trips gave me the chance to inquire into the existence and whereabouts of *the* list. The bad news was that I was repeatedly told by librarians and archivists that they did not have, nor had they ever heard of, any such list. The story was the same at the Martin Luther King, Jr. Center in Atlanta. There, the head librarian, Louise Cook, said she too had never heard of any such list. She did though have a variety of other materials on the Summer Project that I was welcome to go through. True to her word, the list I hoped to find was not among these materials. Given what *was* there, however, the absence of the list hardly mattered. For there, nicely organized and catalogued, were the original five-page applications filled out by the volunteers in advance of the summer. Better still, the applications included those filled out, not only by the volunteers, but by an additional 300 persons who had applied to the project, been accepted, but for whatever reason had failed to go to Mississippi. I had serendipitously stumbled onto the makings of a kind of naturalistic experiment. Here were two groups—volunteers and no-shows—that presumably looked fairly similar going into the summer. One had the experience of Freedom Summer. The other did not.

The unexpected discovery of data on the no-shows enabled me to add two other questions to the original focus on links between movements with which I had begun the project. The first was simply the question of differences between the volunteers and no-shows *before* the summer. Were they really similar going into the summer? Or were the volunteers so different from the no-shows as to make any subsequent comparison of the two groups meaningless? The second question depended on a negative answer to the first. Assuming the no-shows *were* a defensible comparison group, *how* did the broad contours of their lives post-summer differ from the biographies of those who had participated in the project? Finally, as the study progressed, I came to regard one additional question as of equal importance to the previous three. It wasn't merely the comparison of participants and nonparticipants that was intriguing, but differences between the male and female volunteers as well. Given the clear differences in the ways men and women were raised in the early Sixties, it was simply impossible to view their participation in the project as having meant the same thing either to themselves or to others. Hence a fourth question: How did the experience of the Summer Project and the consequences that flowed from it differ for the male and female volunteers?

I have spent the past six years trying, in a variety of ways, to answer these four basic questions. To do so, however, required that I first be able to locate as many of the applicants as I possibly could. Here the original project applications came in very handy. One piece of information that had been asked of the applicants was the college or university in which they were presently enrolled. This enabled me to assemble lists of applicants to be sent to some 269 alumni associations around the country. As expected, they proved to be my single richest source of addresses.[7] There were others, however. Those applying to the project had also been asked to list the names and addresses of their parents on the application form. Notwithstanding the fact that the United States is a highly mobile society, approximately 20 percent of the parents were still at the same addresses in 1982–1983 as they had been in 1964. In turn, they supplied current addresses for 101 sons or daughters who had applied to the project. Academic directories were also searched for names that matched those who had applied to the project. Lists of applicants sharing the same undergraduate majors—another item asked of those applying—provided the basis for this search. Still other addresses were produced in a variety of idiosyncratic ways. Once contacted, many of the applicants were willing and able to supply addresses of others with whom they had stayed in touch. Friends and friends of friends put me in touch with still more applicants. So too did the publishers of at least two applicants-turned-authors. Others contacted me after hearing about my project. One even turned up as a guest at a party where I happened to be talking about my research.

The result of these varied efforts were verified current addresses for 556 of the 959 applicants for whom I had applications. Of these, 382 (of a total of 720) had been participants in the project while another 174 (of 239) had withdrawn in advance of the summer. Foreshadowing a major difference between the two groups, the percentage of no-shows I was able to obtain addresses for—73 percent—was considerably higher than the 53 percent figure for the actual volunteers. Exactly what this difference meant was to become clear only after I had started contacting the applicants.

Contact with the applicants took two forms. First, all of the applicants were mailed questionnaires (see Appendix A) asking them about their experiences during Freedom Summer, their activist histories, and the broad contours of their lives, personal as well as political, post-Freedom Summer.[8] This was the only way I could compare data on the large number of applicants with whom I was dealing.

However, I also realized that any real understanding of the complex issues I was addressing required that I talk at length to at least some of the applicants in both groups. Between August 1984 and July 1985 I did just that, interviewing forty volunteers and another forty no-shows, selected at random from among all of the applicants in each group.[9] More than half of these interviews were conducted in a hectic three-month period during the spring of 1985, during which I camped my way around the country, interviewing applicants as I went. All told, I logged 22,000 miles and interviewed forty-eight people in the course of the trip. The "sessions" lasted anywhere from two hours to two days and took place under an equally wide range of circumstances. Along the way I took part in a Native American sweat in Colorado, a bar mitzvah in Buffalo, an anti-apartheid demonstration in Washington, D.C., and a formal Japanese tea ceremony at a commune in California. By turns, I felt confused, exhilarated, depressed, and enriched by my contact with the applicants.

The end result, though, was that the trip "worked" in the way I had hoped it would. I came away with a much clearer sense of what Freedom Summer had meant to the volunteers and how it had shaped their lives in ways that clearly distinguished them from the no-shows. The somewhat superficial differences between the two groups that had been apparent in their questionnaire responses came alive in conversation. The two groups may have been similar before the summer, but they emerged from it clearly very different. Just as important, these differences were to *make* a difference, not just in the lives of the volunteers, but in the evolution of the New Left and what would come to be known as the "60s experience." Caught up in a unique confluence of biography and history, the volunteers were among the first white students to sense the possibilities inherent in the moment. Many of them climbed aboard a political and cultural wave just as it was forming and beginning to wash forward. In a sense, the remainder of this book is about that wave; its nature and course, the unique biographical and historical circumstances that produced it and the mark it left on those who tried—and in many cases are still trying—to ride it. And what of Freedom Summer? If it didn't exactly produce the wave, it certainly gave it momentum and helped fashion many of the specific political and cultural elements we associate with it. Perhaps most important, Freedom Summer created one of the major means by which this emergent Sixties culture was made available to its ultimate consumers: white, Northern college students. The Freedom Summer volunteers served as influential carriers of the new culture. How they came to play this role and the consequences, both personal and societal, of having done so is the subject of this book.

I

America on the Eve
of Freedom Summer

ALL OF our lives represent, in C. Wright Mills' (1959) phrase, the "intersection of biography and history." While we may be only dimly aware of the historical currents that are shaping our lives, we can rest assured they are. For most of us, however, the confluence of biography and history is somewhat prosaic. That is, if not seamless, there is a certain predictable match between each of us as social products and the historical era in which we grow to maturity. Who we are raised to be is relatively consistent with the broader social world we encounter as adults.

For some few others, the course and texture of the interface between their own biographies and the history of their era is less predictable. Faced with historical circumstances unanticipated by those who helped socialize them, these individuals suddenly confront new possibilities for social action and self-conception. The interplay between history and biography takes on a disjunctive quality, as the orderly progression toward adulthood is interrupted by historical events and processes. The result is often a period of thoroughgoing resocialization, as biographies and identities are modified in accordance with the newly perceived historical imperatives. Among those rare few whose biographies fit this description are many who came into young adulthood at the time of the Depression, many World War II or Vietnam War veterans, and to a less dramatic extent, the Freedom Summer volunteers.

Ignoring differences for the moment, several generalizations can be made about the volunteers. By and large, they were the sons and daughters of American privilege. They came from comfortable, often wealthy, families, some of them patrician. They applied to the project while at-

11

tending the top elite colleges or universities in the country. The volunteers had known few limits in their lives, least of all those imposed by race or class. The generally liberal, and occasionally radical, political views of the volunteers' parents stamped the volunteers as more leftist politically than most children of class privilege. Still, on the eve of the summer, they remained reformers rather than revolutionaries, liberals rather than radicals. Their narrative statements, written on the project applications, reflect a generally idealistic view of America, based on the liberal imagery characteristic of the era. The United States certainly had its imperfections, but they were less the product of flaws inherent in the system than they were remedial aberrations stemming from our failure to fully realize the humane and egalitarian values on which the nation had been founded. Neither their experiences nor their generally liberal political views prepared the volunteers for what they were to find in Mississippi. The education they were to receive there was to have profound and enduring consequences. To quote Gren Whitman, one of the volunteers, "it was simply the most important experience of my life. It really set me on a course in my life that I'm still on."[1] Such assessments remain commonplace among the volunteers, who nearly a quarter of a century later continue to view the summer as a watershed in their lives, a point in time around which to reorganize their biographies in "before" and "after" terms. It was the moment when they climbed aboard a barely discernible political and cultural wave that would later crest as the "Sixties experience," sweeping up much of their generation as it went. But the volunteers would be among the first.

Therein lies their significance. For historical currents do not irresistibly propel themselves and everyone in their path. No matter what their broader structural or ideological roots, they both carry along and are carried along by people, who are not merely the passengers of history, but its pilots as well. In the end, social history is little more than the sum of countless individual choices aggregated over time. That it appears otherwise may owe to the fact that although we can do as we choose, we can seldom choose as we please. Ordinarily, people's choices have the effect of reconfirming and reinforcing the "normal order of things." What was remarkable about the Sixties was that large numbers of people began, through their choices, to challenge all manner of longstanding social, political and cultural arrangements. This process did not proceed in random fashion, however. Instead, as in all diffusion processes, the objects of change—attitudes about the war, styles of dress, tastes in music, etc.—spread outward in ever-widening circles from an initial core of innovators. The broader societal significance of Freedom Summer lies in the stimulus it afforded this process. Through its radicalization of many of the volunteers, the project created a nucleus of political and (counter) cultural pioneers who returned to their respective colleges and communities outside the South intent on "bringing the message of Mississippi to the rest of the nation." Though it differed from volunteer to volunteer, that message variously embraced conceptions of the United States, politics, community, human relationships, and sexuality clearly at odds with mainstream values. In short order, these conceptions would attract a wide following, especially among those of the baby-boom generation. That these conceptions would, in turn, be supplanted by even more radical ones many times before the "Sixties wave" began to recede is of little importance. What is important is the role the volunteers played in the formative stages of this process.

However, to more fully appreciate this role we will want to know more about the mix of biography and history that produced it. In Chapter 2 we will take a look at the volunteers prior to their entrance into the summer project. For the remainder of this chapter, we focus on the diverse historical contexts that confronted the volunteers on the eve of the summer. It was a volatile mix.

The Demographic and Economic Context

Freedom Summer was an audacious undertaking demanding courage and confidence on the part of planners and participants alike. No doubt much of the self-assurance displayed by the volunteers owed to their generally privileged backgrounds. Class, as we are reminded each day, has its privileges. The roots of these privileges may be material, but the specific advantages enjoyed by those in the upper classes transcend their material base. Among the most important byproducts of class advantage is the psychological heritage that normally accompanies it. Of special interest here is the sense of personal efficacy or felt mastery over one's environment that often characterizes those who are economically well off. This trait is not simply a matter of class differences in socialization practices, but of actual differences in people's lived experiences. Persons in the upper classes *do* tend to have more control over their environments than those in the lower classes. Certainly they have more resources— money, education, social contacts, etc.—with which to try to shape their environments. They are thus more apt to experience their world as malleable and themselves as master of their fate, than are those who are less well off.

As the sons and daughters of middle- and upper-middle-class America, the summer volunteers benefited from the psychological heritage sketched above. But this is only half—the biographical half—of the story. Historically, the baby boom and the postwar prosperity it helped stimulate resonated well with the sense of optimism and potency that had been the volunteers' psychological birthright. In short, the psychology of class privilege and the demography and economy of postwar America produced a class and generational subculture ideally suited to the demands of a project such as Freedom Summer. To understand the dynamics of this connection, we will need to take a closer look at the baby boom itself.

During the last year of World War II, slightly more than 2.8 million babies were born in the United States, an average of roughly 233,000 births per month. Through the first six months of 1946, the number of monthly births hovered around the 1945 average. Over the last half of the year, however, the birth rate accelerated rapidly. By year's end, a record 3.4 million births had been recorded during the year. The boom was on.

Not that the boom was entirely unexpected. Given the interruption in people's lives occasioned by the war—and before that, the Depression—the sharp rise in the birth rate was plausibly interpreted as a short-term response to pent-up demand. Comparable increases in postwar birthrates in many European countries lent further credibility to this interpretation. After several years of "unnaturally" high birth rates, demographers predicted a return to the long-term trend of declining birth rates established during the Twenties and Thirties. Obviously the demographers were wrong. Although European birthrates *did* level off after a few years, the annual number of births in this country continued to soar until well into the Sixties. When at last the boom burst in 1965, the "several years" predicted by the demographers had become nineteen. In all, more than 76 million babies had been born between 1946 and 1964.

What did the baby boom have to do with Freedom Summer? A great deal. When combined with the class advantages enjoyed by most of the summer volunteers, the sheer size and extraordinary national attention lavished on the postwar generation helped produce a middle- to upper-middle-class youth subculture uniquely optimistic about the future; certain, one might even say cocky, about its own capabilities, and enamored of its "history-making" presence in the world. This self-assurance was further reinforced by the popular version of recent American history that came to be widely shared in the Fifties and early Sixties. There was a bit of "chosen people" flavor to the interpretation. We were a "can do" people, who accomplished whatever we set out to do. We had licked the Depression, turned the tide in World War II, and rebuilt Europe after the war. Our aggressive assumption of the role of democracy's policeman in the postwar era was merely an extension of this view of our own national potency. So too were two innovations of John Kennedy's early days in office; both the Green Berets and the Peace Corps embodied the special confidence and unique capabilities we had come to believe we possessed. So superior was American know-how and so noble our political mission that even small groups of Americans were bound to make a difference. The Freedom Summer project must be viewed as a reflection and product of this view of ourselves. It would certainly be hard to envision the same project arising in a generation suffused by feelings of pessimism and fatalism regarding its ability to effect change. Instead, Freedom Summer was an audacious undertaking consistent with the exaggerated sense of importance and potency shared by the privileged members of America's postwar generation.

The dynamics that set the boom in motion were largely responsible for producing these feelings. Most demographers believe that a key factor influencing family planning decisions is a couple's assessment of their future economic prospects. One of the leading proponents of this view, Richard Easterlin (1980: 39), summarizes the main thrust of the argument: "If the couple's potential earning power is high in relation to aspirations, they will have an optimistic outlook and will feel freer to marry and have children. If their outlook is poor relative to aspirations, the couple will feel pessimistic and, consequently, will be hesitant to marry and have children." Certainly, this argument offers a plausible fit with the historical fluctuations in the U.S. birth rate. So the low birth rates recorded during the early 1930s are plausibly interpreted as reflecting widespread economic fears attributable to the Depression. Conversely, the postwar baby boom is thought to mirror the widely shared feelings of optimism that greeted the end of World War II.

Just as important as the cause of the baby boom was the stimulant effect it had on the postwar economy. Not that it was the only such stimulant. America's assumption of the role of military policeman to the Free World assured a level of defense production that far exceeded previous peacetime levels. The onset of the Korean "conflict" only edged those levels ever higher. However, before the first U.S. Marines set foot on Korean soil, the economic effects of the baby boom were being felt. Demand for all types of goods and services rose sharply as the birth rate soared. As *Fortune* noted in April of 1951, "We need not stew too much about a post armament depression. A civilian market growing by the size of Iowa every year ought to be able to absorb whatever production the military will eventually turn loose." The prediction was to prove correct. As each year's birth cohort exceeded the previous one in size, the economy surged forward at an unprecedented rate. Between 1946 and 1964 the annual rise in GNP averaged 6.5 percent (U.S. Bureau of the Census, 1975: 228). Unemployment over the same period averaged 4.8 percent per year. Compare that to the 2.3 average annual percent change in GNP and average rate of unemployment of 7.5 percent between 1975 and 1986 (Council of Economic Advisers, 1987).

This economic boom only added to the feelings of optimism that had first set the birth rate soaring. Jones describes (1980: 41) a 1958 *Life* magazine cover story that nicely evokes the economic euphoria set in motion by the baby boom.

> Three dozen children were crowded onto the cover along with the banner headline: KIDS: BUILT-IN RECESSION CURE—HOW 4,000,000 A YEAR MAKE MILLIONS IN BUSINESS. Inside, the article began with another headline—ROCKETING BIRTHS: BUSINESS BONANZA—and continued chockablock with statistics and photographs about new citizens who were "a brand-new market for food, clothing, and shelter." In its first year, *Life* calculated, a baby is not just a child but already a prodigious consumer, "a potential market for $800 worth of products." Even before returning from the hospital, an infant had "already rung up $450 in medical expenses." Four-year-olds are not just sugar and spice or puppy-dog tails but rather represent "a backlog of business orders that will take two decades to fulfill."

It was in this atmosphere of widespread optimism about the future that the Freedom Summer volunteers were raised. In fact, being better off and slightly older—most of the volunteers were between twenty and twenty-two at the time of the project—than most of the postwar generation, the volunteers found their economic futures even rosier than those of their younger brothers and sisters. Being slightly older than the postwar babies, the volunteers could expect to enter job markets swollen by a boom-fed economy but not yet glutted by the boomers themselves. While job competition was to grow increasingly intense as the products of the baby boom began graduating from college in the late Sixties, prospects remained optimal on the eve of the summer project. As one volunteer remarked:

> I never really weighed going South against any risks to my future . . . career wise . . . I'd like to think that was because I was so totally committed to the struggle. You know, "I'm not into worrying about such crass shit, man; justice is at stake here." But I think it was more complicated than that. The point is, I didn't *have* to worry—or at least I didn't *think* I had to worry—about a job or ca-

reer. Man, I was getting teaching offers when I was in my second year of grad school! . . . there was this general feeling that you were invulnerable; there would always be a job for you. Jobs or material success—all that stuff—were sort of a given. So I never felt it was one or the other [a job or participation in Freedom Summer].²

It was against this backdrop of diffuse optimism that the Freedom Summer project took form. But the baby boom and the resulting boom economy shaped the psychology of the volunteers in other ways as well. It did so by creating a unique sense of generational identity and "history-making" potency, among the young. Underlying these perceptions was the experience of having participated in the first real youth market in U.S. history. Instead of waiting to grow to adulthood to occupy center stage, as most generations have to do, the postwar generation had the stage turned over to them at an early age. Or perhaps more accurately, they had a stage constructed especially for them. Initially, this stage took the form of a specialized youth (and later adolescent) market that saw children targeted as a mass consumer group for the first time in history. New products—from children's cereal to Davy Crockett coon-skin caps—flooded the market, reversing the traditional pattern of cultural diffusion in American society. "Fads used to be started by young adults and then spread up and down to younger and older people. But the fads of the Fifties, almost without exception, were creations of the children. They flowed *up*" (Jones, 1980: 49–50). If anything, the pattern intensified in the Sixties. Delighted adolescents watched in amazement as the Kennedys danced the twist—*their* dance—in the White House. The Beatles, and rock music generally, replaced adult musical styles as the nation's pop music. Hair, dress, and speech styles were increasingly dictated by the young. *Time* magazine's selection of "The Under 25 Generation" as its Man-of-the-Year for 1967 was but a formal acknowledgment of what had been apparent for years: the nation's youth had emerged as the most potent cultural and political force in the country.

The psychological effects of this world turned upside-down were twofold. First the extraordinary cultural attention lavished on the young gave them a strong sense of identity with their generation. This was especially true for the segment of the postwar generation that contributed the vast majority of the Freedom Summer volunteers. It was the offspring of the American middle- and upper-middle classes who comprised the core of the youth market in the postwar United States. It was they, or their parents, who had the discretionary income to support such a market. In turn, it was they who came to identify most closely with the distinctive youth culture that developed from that market. Whereas adolescence has (in most modern industrialized nations) typically been experienced as a kind of limbo existence sandwiched between the ordered and meaningful worlds of child and adulthood, this segment of the postwar generation found it a very different experience indeed. Far from feeling culturally marginal, the well-to-do young experienced themselves as very much at the center of everything. It was a dizzying, euphoric perception. As a student remarked to Thomas Cottle (1971: 267) in a conversation recorded in his book *Time's Children:*

> We're right at the center of everything. You remember when you're a child and your older brother is the big star, or your big sister is doing all the things? Now it's us, we're right in the center reading about ourselves in the newspaper. It's youth. Everything is youth and us.

This strong and positive identification with youth was undoubtedly crucial in developing, among the generation's well-to-do members, the capacity to act as a conscious political group. So too was its collective sense of its own potency as a cultural and political force. This was the second psychological effect of the unique position middle- and upper-middle-class youth came to occupy in postwar America. It wasn't just that the privileged among the young saw themselves as where the action was, but as the *creators* of that action.

Initially this creative force was confined to the cultural sphere. Spurred in large measure by aggressive marketing efforts aimed at the lucrative youth market, well-heeled postwar youth fashioned a distinctive culture all their own. That they were less the creators than the consumers of this culture matters little. More significant is the way they experienced this culture. Quite simply, it *felt* like theirs, as if it were their preferences that shaped musical styles, fashion trends, and speech patterns. The machinations of record executives and fashion designers were lost on them. What was not, were the "facts": John and Jackie twisting in the White House; the Beatles receiving royal honors in England; and mom having lately taken to wearing mini-skirts. *They* were reshaping the cultural landscape.

In a society where the young had traditionally exercised little influence, this was a heady experience, and one that was to have far-reaching political implications as well. With a large segment of the postwar generation sharing a sense of its own potency in the world, it would become increasingly difficult to confine their exercise of this potency to the cultural sphere. As the generation grew and matured, it was almost inevitable that its privileged members would seek to exercise their felt mastery over the world in other spheres as well. If culture, why not politics? If we can so easily reshape the cultural landscape, why not the political terrain as well? Though this vision was shared by only a small minority of the young in 1964, its adherents were certainly growing. In time, it would come to represent one of the defining themes of the era. Wini Breines (1982: xi) has expressed it nicely: "we believed we could achieve an egalitarian, free and participatory society. . . . We believed that we were going to make a revolution. We were convinced that we could transform America through our political activity and insights. We know now . . . that we were very naive." Perhaps, but as of the early Sixties there had been little in the experience of middle- and upper-middle-class youth to temper this naiveté. To that point, the world had seemed unusually responsive to their wishes. This sense of generational potency, coupled with the unbridled optimism of the period, made them prime candidates for collective political action, especially when specifically "called" to it by the political idealism of the period.

The Political Context

As historical eras recede, we tend to forget their political and social complexity in favor of a stereotypic rendering of the period. So the virulence of turn-of-the-century nativist and Klan activities are forgotten in our retelling of the history of the "Progressive Era." Similarly, popular accounts of the "conservative Fifties" often omit any reference to the progressive force of the burgeoning civil rights movement. And so it is with the early Sixties. Now often seen as part of the "turbulent" or "revolutionary Sixties, the years from 1960 to 1964 are properly regarded as a separate period in their own right.

It was a decidedly schizophrenic era, straddling the Fifties and later Sixties, politically as well as chronologically. Foreign policy continued to be dominated by the rhetoric and strategy of Fifties Cold War diplomacy. Tick off the major foreign policy events of the Kennedy and early Johnson years and you will find them of a piece with those of the Eisenhower years: the acrimonious Vienna summit during Kennedy's first year in office and the Paris summit broken off by the U-2 incident in Eisenhower's last year; the Eisenhower Administration's involvement in the 1954 coup in Guatemala, Kennedy's launching of the Bay of Pigs in April 1961; Johnson's military intervention in the Dominican Republic in 1965; Eisenhower's sending of the Marines to Lebanon and Kennedy's sending of combat troops to Vietnam; John Foster Dulles' policy of brinkmanship and Robert F. Kennedy's use of the term "eyeball-to-eyeball" to describe the nuclear confrontation during the Cuban missile crisis. Detente was unthinkable in such a climate. On foreign policy matters, the United States remained aggressively anticommunist and conservative.

On the home front, the emphasis was strikingly different. Liberal idealism flourished. Strong liberal gains in public opinion were recorded in a number of areas, most significantly, civil rights (Hyman and Sheatsley, 1964). Nor was this shift to the left merely attitudinal. Events such as the 1960 black student sit-ins, demonstrations against the House Un-American Activities Committee (HUAC), and the creation of the Fair Play for Cuba Committee clearly foreshadowed the activist impulse of the late Sixties.

The liberalization of domestic politics drew strength from a number of sources, but none was as responsible for reviving the dormant American left as the resurgence of black activism in the early Sixties. As Sarah Evans (1980: 60) has written:

> [T]he sit-in movement [1960] and the freedom rides [1961] had an electrifying impact on northern liberal culture. The romance and daring of black youth gave progressives an unassailable cause. The good guys seemed so good—Martin Luther King made them sound even better—and the bad guys seemed so horrifyingly bad. Many of those affected were former participants in the "old left" . . . who had felt intimidated and isolated by the McCarthyism of the 1950s. . . . The children of northern liberals and radicals, however, were the most likely to join the new struggle with passionate commitment.

It was a cause that meshed well with the psychology of the middle- and upper-middle-class young. Having accepted the essential goodness of the United States, young liberals were appalled to learn that there was trouble in paradise. At the same time, their general optimism prompted them to view the problem as tractable; and their sense of potency convinced them of the essential contribution they could make to the effort. Moreover, on a personal level, the "Negro struggle" gave them an exhilarating opportunity to answer the idealistic call to volunteer service so characteristic of the era. David Harris' (1982: 40) account of his decision—later reversed on threat of parental reprisals—to go South to participate in a 1963 voter registration project nicely captures the appealing naiveté of the period. "It took me half an hour to decide I was going, and another half hour in the line at the phone booth downstairs was spent waiting to call home and deliver the news. 'Freeing the Negroes of Mississippi' seemed an admirable cause and fit easily into my search for 'great things' to do."

Many other well-to-do members of a generation raised to do "great things" reacted in similar fashion to Harris. For the vast majority of Freedom Summer volunteers, the civil rights movement marked the beginnings of their own activism. For some of them, Freedom Summer was their first involvement in the movement. However, for most the Summer Project was only an extension of earlier civil rights activities. Many remember participating in "sympathy demonstrations" against Northern chain stores in the wake of the 1960 sit-ins. Others took part in the series of "Youth Marches for Integration" organized in the late 1950s. Virtually all had been active on campus in a variety of civil rights activities before heading South.

Nor were these activities the only stirrings of life on the left. Demoralized and on the defensive since the McCarthy era, the Old Left began to show signs of life as well. A series of protests were organized against the longtime scourge of the Old Left, HUAC, and its ongoing efforts to keep America safe from the "Red menace." In 1960, dozens of protesters even managed to get themselves arrested at one such demonstration in San Francisco (Heirich 1968: 38–41). Nineteen sixty-two saw the founding of Fair Play for Cuba committees in cities across the nation. Often organized by Old Leftists, the committees were designed to protest U.S. policy toward Castro's newly established regime in Cuba. Then there was the resurgent peace movement, reorganized around efforts to ban or restrict atmospheric testing of nuclear weapons. Once again veterans of the Old Left played prominent roles in the movement.

Besides their involvement in these specific activities, Old Leftists were also implicated in the resurgence of the left through the actions of their sons and daughters. Even while eschewing public activism during the McCarthy era, many of the Old Left had been quietly passing on the tenets of their political "faith" to their offspring. The early Sixties found these "Red diaper babies" coming of age and searching for ways to act on the values they had learned from their parents.

Many found the specific vehicles they were looking for in a campus political scene then awakening from the stultifying deadness of the 1950s. Those arrested at the 1960 anti-HUAC demonstration in San Francisco included a large contingent of students from the University of California at Berkeley. Among the largest Fair Play for Cuba committees were those on Eastern college campuses such as NYU and Columbia. Students were heavily involved in the burgeoning peace movement as well. Indeed, the Student Peace Union (SPU) was probably the largest student political group of the period. Sale (1973: 47) places the number of members of the SPU at around 3,000 in 1962. Successful efforts to organize student political parties at a number of schools mirrored the general upsurge in liberal/leftist activity on campus. Among these new groups were VOICE at Michigan, POLIT at Chicago, TOCSIN at Harvard, and the Progressive Student League at Oberlin. Not to be outdone, students on the political right grew more active as well during this period, with the Young Americans for Freedom (YAF) and the Young Republicans the most prominent of the conservative groups. Finally, older student groups contributed to the rebirth of student activism, even as they themselves benefited from the renaissance.

In his recent book, Maurice Isserman (1987) makes a persuasive case for the Young People's Socialist League (YPSL) as perhaps the strongest and best organized leftist student group to emerge from the political wilderness of the 1950s. By 1962 YPSL had over 800 members and a well-deserved reputation for internal discipline and superior organizing skills. But YPSL was never able to free itself from the political battles and ideological legacy of the Old Left. As a result it was soon supplanted by another organization—the renamed Students for a Democratic Society (SDS)—as the leading group in the Student left. As the moribund student arm of the League for Industrial Democracy (LID), SDS hardly seemed a likely candidate to grow to be the most influential student political group of the era. The organization began the decade with but three chapters and no more than a few hundred members (Sale, 1973: 15). But through a combination of aggressive leadership and conscious alignment with the civil rights movement, SDS was, by 1964, well on its way to attaining that position (Miller, 1987). On the eve of Freedom Summer, SDS could boast twenty-nine active chapters and nearly a thousand members (Sale, 1973: 122–123).

Typically, national political figures lagged behind the students in mirroring the leftward swing in domestic politics. John F. Kennedy represents perhaps the best example of a politician whose liberalism was more a response to the times than a deep and thoroughgoing personal philosophy. Yet in his personal style and rhetorical eloquence, Kennedy too must be credited with encouraging the rise in student activism and the general liberalization of American politics. Substantively, it remains hard to reconcile the idealism inspired by Kennedy with the policies pursued by his administration. Foreign policy during the Kennedy years was distinguished by a Cold War rhetoric consistent with that of both of his postwar predecessors as well as by Kennedy's own brand of adventurist "CIA diplomacy." Yet Kennedy himself has never been seriously criticized for his administration's aggressive embodiment of policies that came to be regarded by the left as evil incarnate in the late Sixties.

Domestically too, Kennedy's liberal rhetoric was rarely matched by concrete policy achievements. The Kennedy record on civil rights, for instance, can be read as a litany of policy failures—his long-delayed Executive Order on housing, the appointment of ardent segregationists in Southern judicial posts, his failure to propose or back significant legislative action on civil rights—only partially offset by his symbolic support for the movement.

Still, whatever his objective failings, Kennedy's subjective impact on the consciousness of American youth cannot be denied. Some observers have dismissed this impact as merely stylistic. Certainly Kennedy's youthful enthusiasm, glamorous style, and sense of humor marked him as one of our most personally appealing presidents. But Kennedy's inspirational effect on the young stemmed from a far more basic source. In his speeches and pronouncements, Kennedy confirmed youthful America's cherished image of itself as special, uniquely gifted, and collectively potent. In a peculiarly American variation on the theme of noblesse oblige, Kennedy called the "best and the brightest" of the postwar young to a more active, idealistic role in American life and politics. And they responded. A little-known event in the genesis of the Peace Corps illustrates the stimulus-response quality of this relationship. Speaking extemporaneously to a group of students at the University of Michigan during his 1960 Presidential campaign, Kennedy challenged the students with a series of questions.

> How many of you are willing to spend ten years in Africa or Latin America or Asia working for the United States and working for freedom? How many of you [who] are going to be doctors are willing to spend your days in the foreign service, and spend your lives traveling around the world? On your willingness to do that . . . will depend the answer whether we as a free society can compete. (Quoted in Wofford, 1980: 247)

The student's response was strong and immediate. Within days of Kennedy's talk, some 250 students had established an organization, "Americans Committed to World Responsibility," to help promote the idea of a Peace Corps. Two weeks later, when representatives of the group presented Kennedy with a long scroll of names of persons backing the Peace Corps plan, the group could take credit for furnishing a significant impetus to the project. But again, it had been Kennedy's ability to inspire idealism that had triggered the event in the first place. It was this ability, shown consistently during his abbreviated tenure in office, that contributed to the growing idealism and activist impulse of upperclass students in the early Sixties.

Everywhere, then, idealism seemed to have replaced the apolitical stance of students in the Fifties. When joined with the twin perceptions of optimism and efficacy, this idealism made for a potent political force; one that the Freedom Summer volunteers, as the cutting edge of this "best and the brightest" generation, found irresistible. However, favorable demographic and political circumstances were not the only components shaping the Summer Project. This irresistible generational force had also to contend with America's longstanding version of the immovable object: Mississippi.

The Geographic Context: Mississippi

Nothing in the experience of most of the volunteers could have prepared them for what they were to find in Mississippi. This was certainly not any version of America they had been raised to believe was even possible. Indeed, the very existence of Mississippi constituted a powerful challenge to virtually all aspects of the volunteers' generally sanguine view of the world. Taught to believe in the flawed but essential goodness and humanity of the American system, Mississippi stood as the living embodiment of the potential for inhumanity and injustice inherent in that system. While the volunteers remained optimistic about the prospects for significant social change, Mississippi stood as mute testimony to the changeless quality of the "Southern Way of Life." Convinced of their collective potency, the volunteers found in Mississippi a monument to the political and economic impotence of most of its citizenry. Finally, to the extent that the volunteers continued to believe in law and justice as the cornerstones of life in the United States, they could hardly have been prepared for the pattern of official lawlessness and violence that was Mississippi's heritage.

Mississippi remained an anachronism on the eve of the Summer Project. The rest of the South had been witness to a massive demographic revolution in the preceding thirty years. Set in motion by the collapse of "King Cotton," this revolution was marked by two significant trends. First, growing numbers of blacks and whites were forced to seek employment outside agricultural production. Among blacks, the decline was from a total of 915,000 farm operators as late as 1920 to only 267,000 in 1959 (U.S. Bureau of the Census, 1962). In turn, this occupational transition set in motion a significant redistribution of the South's population.

Many of the displaced agricultural workers moved out of the South (Fligstein, 1981). However, many more stayed behind and were part of a massive rural-to-urban migration within the region. So thoroughgoing was this internal migration that by 1960 the proportion of Southern blacks living in urban areas had increased to 58 percent, nearly double the figure for 1930 (Price 1969: 11). Overall, the increase in the total Southern black population was only 18 percent between 1930 and 1960. By contrast, over the same time period, the increase was 118 percent for blacks living in the urban areas of the South.

What set Mississippi apart in 1964 was how little the effects of this demographic revolution had been allowed to penetrate the state. If cotton was no longer king, someone had forgotten to tell Senator John Eastland and the score of delta planters who continued to control the state politically and economically. Part of the reason why the South's demographic revolution was so long in coming to Mississippi was the continued reliance of the state's planter elite on nonmechanized cotton farming. While neighboring states, such as Texas and Arkansas, had largely mechanized cotton farming by 1964, Mississippi planters continued to eschew modernization. The resulting demand for cheap agricultural labor not only forestalled black migration to the city, but consigned large numbers of blacks to cotton farming. In 1960, 68 percent of all blacks in Mississippi continued to live in rural areas. The comparable figure for blacks outside of Mississippi was only 39 percent. In the same year, more than a third of all black Mississippians—or twice the percentage for the rest of the South—were engaged in farming.

With rural farm employment came all the concomitants of the traditional "way of life" for black Mississippians. One of the defining qualities of that "way of life" was grinding poverty. Median nonwhite family income averaged just $1,444 in 1960, lowest in the United States, and barely a third of the average for Mississippi whites (U.S. Bureau of the Census, 1963). This meant that 86 percent of all nonwhite families in the state were living below the official federal poverty level.[3] Nor did educational statistics offer much hope of any quick way out of the economic trap that most black Mississippians found themselves in. As of 1960, the median number of years of school completed by *all* blacks over the age of twenty-five stood at just six. The comparable figure for whites was eleven years. Even more dramatic were the figures for high school completion. While 42 percent of all whites had finished at least twelve years of school, only 7 percent of the black population had managed to do so. Given the economic pressures on black families, the low levels of schooling are hardly surprising. Nor did state officials do anything to discourage the pattern. Consider that in 1964 the average state expenditure for education was just $21.77 per black pupil as compared to $81.86 for every white pupil.[4] In rural areas, especially in the Cotton Belt, the figures were often many times more skewed than the state average. North Pike County, for instance, spent $30.89 for each of its white students and a bare $0.76 per black student.[5] Worse yet was Holly Bluff, where the figures stood at $191.70 and $1.26 for each white and black pupil, respectively.[6]

No less depressing was the quality of life for Mississippi blacks on the eve of Freedom Summer. As of 1960, infant mortality rates continued to run two times higher than the rate for Mississippi whites and nearly 250 percent higher than the national average for whites.[7] Two-thirds of the 207,611 housing units occupied by blacks in the state were judged, in 1960, to be "deteriorating" or "dilapidated." Nearly half of these units—100,138—lacked piped water; two-thirds were without flush toilets.

This grim litany of impoverishment and inequality was maintained well into the 1960s through a combination of wholesale black disenfranchisement and, when necessary, white violence. The absence in Mississippi of the type of mass civil rights protest that had occurred in the other Deep South states testified to the effectiveness of the system.

Nowhere were racial restrictions on voter registration more zealously applied. The result was by far the lowest rate of black registration in the South—6.7 percent—and a number of interesting anomalies. For instance, in 1962 there were five counties in the state with black majorities and yet not a single black registrant. At the other extreme, Coahoma County boasted a white registration rate of 96 percent (Silver, 1963: 87). Such statistical anomalies reflected the utter seriousness with which the "proper authorities" sought to maintain white supremacy. And when "custom" and subtle forms of intimidation did not deter blacks from trying to register, there was always violence. Between 1882 and 1964, 539 blacks had been lynched in Mississippi (Ploski and Marr 1976: 275). The last two officially recorded lynchings to take place in the South had also occurred in Mississippi, including that of fourteen-year-old Emmett Till, killed in 1955, for allegedly whistling at a white woman. No convictions were ever returned in the case. Nor had the violence abated in the intervening years. In fact, the entrance of SNCC field workers into the state in the fall of 1961 had only occasioned more violence. One of those field workers, Bob Moses, was himself the target of an assassination attempt. It took place just outside Greenwood, Mississippi, on February 28, 1963. Howard Zinn (1965: 89) recounts the incident:

> A 1962 Buick with no license tags had been sitting outside the SNCC office all day, with three white men in it—nothing unusual for SNCC. As [the field workers] pulled away, the Buick followed. They stopped at a filling station for gasoline, and the Buick followed and circled the block. Then they headed out on the main highway toward Greenville, all three sitting in front: Jimmy Travis at the wheel, Bob Moses next to him, Blackwell on the outside. It was

about 10:30 p.m., and there was a good deal of traffic on the road. As the traffic began to thin, the Buick pulled up alongside and then came the deafening sound of gunfire. Thirteen 45-calibre bullets ripped through the car shattering the front left window, missing Bob Moses and Randolph Blackwell by inches, smashing through the window on the other side. Two bullets hit Jimmy Travis. The Buick sped off, and Moses grabbed the controls to pull the car to a stop as Travis crouched in his seat, bleeding.

Jimmy Travis survived the shooting attack. Others involved in the SNCC effort were not so fortunate. One was Herbert Lee, the first black from McComb to attempt to register to vote as part of SNCC's efforts there. The reward for his efforts: death at the hands of a Mississippi legislator named E. H. Hurst. The coroner's jury of the county labeled the killing as "justified on grounds of self defense." Another local black, Louis Allen, made the "mistake" of contradicting the jury's conclusion in "confidential" testimony to local FBI officials. "After a series of harassments, arrests on trumped-up charges, beatings and surveillance, the misery ended for Louis Allen. Three days before Allen was to leave McComb—January 31, 1964—he was found dead with half of his face scattered several feet away from his head" (Holt, 1965: 35). No arrests were ever made in connection with this case, or any of the other four "mysterious" deaths of Mississippi blacks that occurred between January 1 and May 31, 1964 (Holt, 1965: 30).

During this period, state officials were also taking measures to shore up Mississippi's "defenses" against the invading "army" of Northern volunteers expected that summer. Anne Moody (1968: 366) describes these preparations:

> [W]hite Mississippians were really preparing for . . . [Freedom Summer]. The state was in the process of tightening legislative screws to try and outlaw practically all phases of the project. Six new laws had already been enacted in the state legislature, authorizing cities to pool manpower, personnel, and equipment to assist each other in riot control. I learned . . . that an anti-invasion bill had also been introduced to prohibit entry into the state. Besides all the bills being passed, the state police force had been doubled and armed to the teeth.

Intimations of the tension building in Mississippi reached the volunteers throughout the spring in the form of ominous stories in the national press, warning of the warlike preparations being made by state and local officials. *Newsweek*, for example, carried an article in its February 24 edition describing the mobilization of Jackson's police force by its mayor, Allen Thompson. Entitled, "Allen's Army," the article read in part:

Girding for a new wave of civil-rights demonstrations this summer, Thompson is massing an impressive—and expensive—deterrent force of men and military hardware. To defend the capital city of 144,422, he is building up his young, tough, riot-trained police force from 390 to 450, plus two horses and six dogs. The force is "twice as big as any city our size," Thompson boasted last week—and it will be backed by a reserve pool of deputies, state troopers, civilian city employees, and even neighborhood citizen patrols.

With a hefty $2.2 million budget to spend, the department recently bought 200 new shotguns, stockpiled tear gas, and issued gas masks to every man. Its motor fleet includes three canvas-canopied troop lorries, two half-ton searchlight trucks, and three giant trailer trucks to haul demonstration POWs off to two big detention compounds. "I think we can take care of 25,000," the mayor said.

But the pride of Allen's Army is Thompson's Tank—the already popular nickname for a 13,000-pound armored battlewagon built to the mayor's specifications at roughly $1 a pound.

. . . The mayor insists his army is only a second-strike force designed to preserve law and order. "We have to wait," he told *Newsweek*'s Karl Fleming, "until they start trouble." But Thompson is certain trouble will come. "This is it," he said. "They are not bluffing and we are not bluffing. We're going to be ready for them. . . . They won't have a chance."

This was the world the volunteers were about to enter. Intimations aside, very few of them had any real sense of how foreign to their experience that world was. They had not yet been exposed to the grinding poverty, official lawlessness, and demeaning caste restrictions that were the daily lot of Mississippi's black population. Nor had they yet had to confront the unrelieved fear and debilitating fatalism that was the inevitable psychological byproduct of these conditions. This not only distinguished them from the local blacks, but from the extraordinary collection of young men and women who were to direct the Freedom Summer project. In many ways, it was this latter group that was to most dramatically shape the volunteers' reaction to and experience of the project.

The Movement Context: SNCC

SNCC *was* the guiding force behind the Summer Project. Technically, responsibility for planning and directing the project fell to the Council of Federated Organizations (COFO), a coalition of civil rights groups that had been formed in 1962 to coordinate voter registration efforts in the South. But since SNCC was to supply 95 percent of the staff at state headquarters, provide 90 to 95 percent of the funds for the project, and have responsibility for four of the state's five Congressional districts— CORE staffed the fifth—it was clearly in control of the project (Sellers, 1973: 96; Sutherland, 1965: 35). SNCC workers also felt that they had a kind of moral or proprietary claim on the project by virtue of the beachhead they had established in Mississippi during the period of 1961– 1964. In what remains one of the most extraordinary and sustained displays of courage and resolve in the history of American activism, a handful of SNCC field workers endured nearly three years of savage and continuous repression to challenge the most unrepentantly racist state of the old Confederacy. If Mississippi was changed in the process, so too was SNCC and the individuals who comprised its Mississippi contingent. Already evident on the eve of Freedom Summer, these changes set the volunteers and project staff on a collision course. Buoyed by their sense of optimism and idealism, the volunteers were hardly prepared for the bitterness, anger, and cynicism shared by many project staffers.

Given their experiences during the preceding three years, it is hardly surprising that the SNCC veterans were not totally sanguine in their view of Mississippi or white America in general. Perhaps the wonder is that they remained as free of anger and disillusionment as they did. Certainly the anger and bitterness had not always been there. In fact, had they looked closely enough, they might have seen, in the faith and hope of the volunteers, something of themselves some three or four years earlier. For in 1960 SNCC had been born of the same mix of optimism and idealism that the volunteers now embodied. Small wonder, for if the postwar years had been ones of hope and optimism for America generally, they had been that and more within the black community. Blacks not only shared in the general optimism of postwar America, but found specific cause for hope in what were widely perceived as cracks in the racial status quo. The evidence from postwar surveys is consistent: blacks routinely expressed more optimism regarding the future than did whites (Erskine, 1969: 148, Pettigrew, 1964: 185; Stouffer, 1955). Although there was little substantive change during the period, the symbolic politics of the postwar years raised expectations within the black community (McAdam, 1982: 108–112). There was the NAACP-engineered string of Supreme Court victories culminating in the momentous 1954 *Brown* decision that declared segregated educational facilities to be "inherently unequal" (Kluger, 1975). There was the series of widely publicized Executive Orders issued by both Truman and Eisenhower that seemed to portend still further change (McAdam, 1982: 85–86). Finally, Eisenhower's decision to send federal troops into Little Rock in 1957—the first such commitment of federal troops since Reconstruction—seemed to indicate a significant change in federal policy.

More important, this period saw the first successful mass challenge to Jim Crow since Reconstruction. The bus boycotts organized in Montgomery, Alabama (1955–1956), Tallahassee, Florida (1956–1957), and other Southern cities during this period are perhaps the most impressive evidence of the new mood among Southern blacks in the wake of the 1954 Supreme Court decision. Feelings of optimism and efficacy replaced the fatalism and grudging acquiescence to segregation that had earlier prevailed in the black community. Significantly, the pioneering activists in SNCC—and many others who took part in the early sit-ins—grew up in this atmosphere. They, no less than the volunteers, approached adulthood certain of the unique historical moment before them and convinced of their own power to take advantage of it.

The optimism and idealism inherent in this vision were clearly evident in the statement of purpose adopted at the May 1960 conference at which SNCC was founded. Wrote its author, James Lawson:

> We affirm the philosophical or religious ideal of nonviolence as the foundation of our purpose, the presupposition of our faith, and the manner of our action. Nonviolence as it grows from Judaic-Christian traditions seeks a social order of justice permeated by love. Integration of human endeavor represents the crucial first step towards such a society.
>
> Through nonviolence, courage displaces fear; love transforms hate. Acceptance dissipates prejudice; hope ends despair. Peace dominates war; faith reconciles doubt. Mutual regard cancels enmity. Justice for all overthrows injustice. The redemptive community supersedes systems of gross social immorality.
>
> Love is the central motif of nonviolence. Love is the force by which God binds man to Himself and man to man. Such love goes to the extreme; it remains loving and forgiving even in the midst of hostility. It matches the capacity of evil to inflict suffering with an even more enduring capacity to absorb evil, all the while persisting in love.
>
> By appealing to conscience and standing on the moral nature of human existence, nonviolence nurtures the atmosphere in which reconciliation and justice become actual possibilities. (Quoted in Carson, 1981: 23–24)

Later the same year, in testimony before the Platform Committee of the Democratic National Convention, one of SNCC's early leaders, Marion Barry, gave further voice to the idealism that suffused the organization at its inception. Said Barry, "the ache of every man to touch his potential is the throb that beats out the truth of the American Declaration of Independence and the Constitution. America was founded because men were seeking room to walk. . . . We are again seeking that room" (quoted in Zinn, 1965: 37). Notwithstanding the obvious public relations functions of such statements, it seems clear that the sentiments expressed were genuine. Like the volunteers four years later, the SNCC activists of 1960 could be excused for seeing the world as pliable in their hands. Fresh from their successes in the sit-in movement, the organization's members no doubt longed for new worlds to conquer.

On the eve of the Summer Project this conventional idealism and optimism survived among SNCC's Mississippi contingent, largely as rhetorical window dressing masking layers of anger, bitterness, frustration, and cynicism. What had happened? What had happened was Mississippi. The experience of confronting American racism in all its savagery for nearly three years had made SNCC's Mississippi troops immeasurably more radical. It wasn't simply the succession of unpunished attacks by segregationists that had produced this effect. Or the frustration of having achieved so few tangible victories to weigh against their sacrifices. Just as important was their growing awareness of the depths of federal complicity in Mississippi's *system* of racism. Indeed, their direct experience with the systemic quality of racism was itself profoundly radicalizing to many of Mississippi's SNCC staffers. It was no longer a matter of educating prejudiced white folk, but of dismantling an elaborate system of economic, political, and social oppression that vested interests in Washington, no less than Jackson, Mississippi, had a stake in preserving.

The disillusionment and bitterness that accompanied these realizations was thoroughgoing and acute. Both qualities are painfully evident in the following statement made by a veteran civil rights activist on the eve of Freedom Summer:

> [W]e started out hoping it would be something that would go deep into the soul of all our people, white and black, and change us so that our future could be different, richer, more open. But now—here we are hating; here we are talking about black this and black that— worse than the Mississippians with their whiteness. Is everything falling into a heap of ruins? It makes me want to cry when I remember how we colored kids started in the Movement, some of us naive, yes; but we were purehearted; some of us had mothers who had given us a deepdown security that pushed hate away. We were sort of beautiful black Galahads going forth in search of the twentieth

century's Holy Grail—the lost Grail which we must find in order for
us to live as human beings should. Well—here we are, now, and
some of us are not doing so well, are we. . . .

All I'd better say is this Movement has got my soul to aching. And
it hurts. God . . . how it hurts. (Quoted in Smith, 1964: 61–62)

As a result of their "education" in Mississippi, many of the SNCC veterans had come to question the central tenets on which the movement
and their organization had been founded; and on which the white volunteers were now being recruited to come South. Among these tenets
were those of nonviolence and the necessity for coalition with the liberal
wing of the Democratic Party. The brutality of Mississippi racism, coupled with the practice of self-defense among Southern blacks, had by
1964 seriously weakened the SNCC staff's commitment to nonviolence.
Similarly, the perceived failure of the Kennedy and Johnson administra-
tions to deliver on promises to protect voter registration workers in
Mississippi had soured many SNCC veterans on the possibility of building links to the Democratic Party left.

Perhaps the major casualty of this process of disillusionment within
SNCC concerned the doctrine of interracialism itself. "Even before the
adoption of the Summer Project, black SNCC workers had raised questions concerning the entrance during 1963 and 1964 of increasing numbers of white activists into SNCC" (Carson, 1981: 100). But during the
planning for Freedom Summer the controversy over white participation
in the movement arose again with new intensity. Accounts of planning
sessions (c.f. Carson, 1981: 98–100; Zinn, 1965: 186–189) leading up
to the project make clear the central importance accorded the issue and
the passions aroused by the debate. Zinn (1965: 186–188), for example,
describes a November 1963 conference in Greenville, Mississippi, at
which the idea for the Summer Project was first proposed:

On Friday, the first day of the session . . . there was a lively discussion on the role of whites in the movement, and several suggestions for restricting their role. On Saturday evening, with Bob Moses
chairing, the discussion started at 7:00 p.m. and ended at midnight
and, as it turned out, a good deal of this talk centered on the role
of whites. The exchange was candid and open, and revealed in a
remarkable way the complexity of feeling among those there (roughly
thirty-five Negroes and seven whites) trying desperately to escape
the bind of race, while at the same time tyrannized in varying degrees by it. . . .

Several of the people . . . discussed their inner turmoil on the
question. "I think one way and act another way. It's not rational. But

these feelings are there." Another: "These feelings are inside the Negro. Now we may feel we are all brothers. But these feelings in the Negro community cannot be ignored. . . . We must take the reality out there, that race has corrupted America tremendously. We want to change that. But in the meantime, we cannot act out in society the way we act in here."

No doubt the hostility toward whites in the movement did, as this last speaker suggested, have its roots in American racism generally. At the same time, their experiences in Mississippi could only have reinforced such feelings among the SNCC workers. How can one withstand the type of virulent racism endured by these workers without hating a bit oneself? In his capacity as staff psychologist for the Summer Project, Robert Coles had occasion to observe and interview a good many of the SNCC veterans. It is hardly surprising that among the symptoms he ascribed to the workers were those of "exhaustion, weariness, despair, frustration and rage" (1964: 308).

Finally, the logic of the project may itself have fueled the growing hostility toward whites in the movement. For the success of Freedom Summer was premised on the recognition and conscious exploitation of America's racism. The logic ran as follows: if the murders, beatings, and jailings SNCC workers had endured in Mississippi had not been enough to stir public attention, perhaps America—and, in turn, the federal government—would take notice if those being beaten and shot were the sons and daughters of privileged white America. But to even conceive, let alone act on, this plan required that Mississippi's SNCC staff acknowledge a kind of strategic dependence on the white volunteers that could only have exacerbated those normal racial tensions to be expected on such a project. Imagine the volatile emotional cross-currents the plan must have aroused among the veteran Mississippi staffers. Not only had their efforts in the state intensified their hatred and distrust of whites, but had done so without producing measurable results. Their sacrifices had merely confirmed 300 years of black political powerlessness in Mississippi. Now they were being asked to depend on the importation of 1,000 sons and daughters of white privilege—with all their naiveté and paternalism intact—to break a stalemate these veterans had been powerless to resolve. Thus, they found themselves in the distasteful position of having to exploit the very racism that they had been victims of. Faust himself could not have faced a more psychologically burdensome dilemma.

This, then, was the complex and contradictory mix of contexts that confronted the volunteers on the eve of Freedom Summer. Raised amid the generalized optimism and idealism of postwar America, the volunteers brought both qualities to Mississippi with them. There they were to experience the depths of American racism and to confront the very different world view of the project staff. Both experiences would have a powerful effect on many of the volunteers.

2

The Biographical Roots
of Activism

IF PEOPLE'S actions grow out of some confluence of
history and biography, it is essential to understand the biographical side
of the equation. In this case that means getting better acquainted with
the Freedom Summer applicants. The point is historical forces are never
felt equally by everyone in society. Rather, some combination of biographical factors render some people more susceptible to the force of
history than others. And so it was with the 1,200 individuals who formally applied to the project in the Spring of 1964.[1] Before examining
the applicants themselves, however, it is necessary to explore the events
and philosophy that gave rise to the project. For the primary factor
affecting a person's chances of going to Mississippi had nothing to do
with his or her personal biography. Instead, it was SNCC's experiences
in Mississippi and the effect of those experiences on the initial concep-
tualization, and later planning for the project, that effectively restricted
recruitment to particular types of people. That is, the SNCC braintrust
went a long way toward determining who the volunteers would be by
the strategic decisions they made leading up to the summer. More than
any other factor, those decisions were responsible for the composition of
the contingent that headed south in June of 1964.

Planning for Confrontation: The Origins of Freedom Summer

The roots of the Summer Project are to be found in the strategic stalemate that confronted SNCC's Mississippi operation in the fall of 1963.

For all the courage, hard work, and sacrifice its field workers had expended in the state since 1961, the organization had achieved few concrete victories. They had been able to persuade only a small number of prospective voters to try registering, and had succeeded in registering only a fraction of these. Three factors had combined to limit the effectiveness of SNCC's campaign in Mississippi. The first was simply the state's intransigence to any form of racial equality. The second was the absence of any aggressive federal presence in the state that might have blunted the effectiveness of state resistance. The third was SNCC's inability to generate the type of publicity that Martin Luther King, Jr. had used so effectively elsewhere in coercing supportive federal action (c.f. Garrow, 1978; Hubbard, 1968; McAdam, 1982: 174–180).

Saddled with these three impediments, SNCC found itself with few programmatic options in Mississippi. Its attempts to register black voters had been notably unsuccessful. The type of systematic campaigns that had elsewhere succeeded in desegregating lunch counters and other public facilities had long been regarded as too dangerous to undertake in Mississippi. Yet to abandon the state was unthinkable. To do so would have given segregationists a major symbolic victory and threatened SNCC's reputation as the toughest, most courageous of the civil rights organizations.

At a loss as to how to counter these obstacles, the SNCC braintrust grasped at a straw of a plan offered it by Allard Lowenstein. Lowenstein, a peripatetic Democratic Party activist and sometime college administrator, had come to Mississippi in July of 1963 to investigate the racial situation. Never one to wait for a formal invitation, Lowenstein had made himself welcome in the SNCC office in Jackson, and in the course of discussion there had offered up a suggestion that spoke to the strategic impasse SNCC found itself facing. With the state's gubernatorial election scheduled for the fall, Lowenstein proposed a protest vote to demonstrate the desire of blacks to participate in the electoral process. In the context of the dilemma confronting SNCC, the plan offered much that was attractive. There was the distinct possibility that such a campaign might generate the kind of national publicity that had thus far eluded SNCC. Second, the very effort of coordinating a statewide campaign promised to strengthen SNCC's organizational presence throughout Mississippi. Finally, the symbolic nature of the project was likely to forestall the type of violent opposition that had undermined virtually all of SNCC's previous campaigns in the state.

With few workable alternatives before them, SNCC's Mississippi staff opted for the plan. The basic idea called for SNCC fieldworkers to conduct a mock gubernatorial election among Mississippi's black population. The first step in the process took place in August with the casting of protest votes in the regular state Democratic primary. In all, some 1,000 blacks cast votes in the election, principally in Greenwood and Jackson (Carson, 1981: 97). Encouraged by the success of the primary campaign, SNCC, under the direction of Bob Moses, set about planning for the regular gubernatorial election in November. Two changes were proposed and approved for the fall campaign. First, blacks would be asked to vote, not in the regular election, but in a parallel "Freedom Vote" designed to minimize the potential for violence, and thereby insure maximum voter turnout. To give Mississippi's black population someone to vote for, a slate of "freedom" candidates was selected, headed by Aaron Henry, the president of the Mississippi NAACP, and Tougaloo College's white chaplain, Ed King. Finally, to offset the increased need for staff during the "Freedom Vote" campaign, the decision was made to import Nothern college students for the duration of the project. This decision was reached partly in response to Lowenstein's assurance that he could supply as many students as the project required. Lowenstein made good on his promise. Drawing upon contacts established during earlier administrative stints at Stanford and Yale, Lowenstein was able to recruit some 100 students to come South to help with the vote.[2]

Most arrived late in October and stayed through the November 4 conclusion of the campaign.[3] During that time, the volunteers worked with SNCC staffers in all phases of the project, from canvassing black neighborhoods and registering black voters to staging the actual election. In all, nearly 80,000 blacks cast votes in the election, testament both to SNCC's organizing skills and the electoral willingness of Mississippi's black minority.

SNCC insiders, most important, Bob Moses, deemed the project and the use of the white volunteers a success. While the presence of so many upper-middle-class whites had exacerbated racial tensions on the project, these new volunteers had also contributed a great deal of valuable labor to the effort. Moreover, their presence had also insured a great deal of favorable publicity for SNCC as well as the campaign itself. Then too, the attention lavished on the volunteers helped popularize Southern civil rights work among Northern college students. In his autobiographical book, *Dreams Die Hard*, David Harris (1982: 47–48) recalls the moral and social cachet enjoyed by the returning Stanford volunteers: "Upon their return to campus on November 7 . . . the Mississippi volunteers were greeted as heroes who had risked great personal harm for the sake of something undeniably good."

Back in Mississippi, Bob Moses wasted little time in proposing an ambitious extension of the Freedom Vote campaign. At SNCC's November 14–16 staff meeting in Greenville, Mississippi, the idea of bringing an even larger, though unspecified, number of white students to Mississippi for the summer of 1964 was raised.[4] Debate on the proposed plan was heated. Opponents used the occasion to raise the whole issue of white participation in the movement. Citing the Freedom Vote campaign as an example, several black staffers warned of the tendency of white students to appropriate leadership roles. This tendency, they argued, retarded the development of indigenous black leadership while also reinforcing traditional patterns of racial dominance and submission within the movement. Overall, though, sentiment at the Greenville meeting seemed to favor the plan. One party to the debate summarized the meeting this way:

> Considerable time was spent at Greenville discussing whether to invite a massive number of Northern whites into Mississippi for the summer. It was clear from the nature of the publicity derived from the Freedom Vote campaign that the press would respond to the beating of a Yale student as it simply would not do to the beating of a local Negro. The *New York Times* headlined its stories about the campaign with the news that Yale and Stanford students were working "for a Negro gubernatorial candidate in Mississippi." During the Freedom Rally in Jackson which concluded the campaign, TV men from N.B.C. spent most of their time shooting film of the Yalies and seemed hardly aware of the local people and full-time SNCC workers. While it was agreed by all that this was a sorry state of affairs, many contended that such publicity was essential for awakening the national conscience and preparing a climate for greater federal involvement in Mississippi. (It was noted that for the first time the Justice Department had people on hand in the *eventuality* of trouble.) It was argued that by flooding Mississippi with Northern whites, the entire country would be made dramatically aware of the denial of freedom which existed in the state and that the federal government would be inevitably faced with a crisis of sufficient magnitude that it would have to act.[5]

Ultimately, no decision was reached at Greenville, but a generally positive tone had been set that would influence future debate on the project. The debate itself was rejoined at a COFO staff meeting in December. There, objections similar to those voiced at the Greenville meeting were raised anew. Although not enough to kill the plan, these objections did persuade those in attendance to restrict participation in the Project to 100 white students (Carson, 1981: 99). SNCC's Executive Committee next took up the plan at its December 30 meeting. There, veteran SNCC staffers, such as James Forman, Marion Barry, and John Lewis gave Moses' proposal the strongest endorsement it had yet received. The committee approved a motion by Barry calling on SNCC "to obtain the right for all citizens of Mississippi to vote, *using as many people as necessary to obtain that end*" (quoted in Carson, 1981: 100; emphasis added). So committed to Barry's motion was the committee that it also agreed to send several SNCC leaders, in addition to Moses, to the January COFO Meeting to lobby for a broader mandate for the plan than the COFO staff had authorized in December. The strategy worked. At its January meeting, the COFO staff approved the basic blueprint for the Summer Project.[6]

With this last bureaucratic hurdle surmounted, planning for the project began in earnest. The need for such planning was acute. Less than five months before the start of the project little had been decided except that there would be a project. The programmatic nature of that project, however, remained a mystery, as did the source of funding for the campaign. While the project was nominally COFO's responsibility, the organization had no funds of its own to support the plan. What is more, SNCC's partners in COFO, especially the NAACP and SCLC, had been cool to the idea from the outset. CORE was more supportive, but was willing to take on only a fifth of the total project. That left SNCC with the task of arranging funding for the remaining four-fifths of the project.

Finally, there was the little matter of recruiting volunteers. How was SNCC to get word of the project to prospective applicants? How were applications to be handled? Who was to produce and distribute the forms? Who would select the volunteers? What criteria would guide the selection process? These and hundreds of other details of the recruitment process were still to be worked out. In one sense, though, the underlying rationale for the project had long since resolved the most important issue of all, that being the basic aim of the recruiting process. The fundamental goal of the project was to focus national attention on Mississippi as a means of forcing federal intervention in the state. For the project to be successful, then, it had to attract national media attention. What better way to do so than by recruiting the sons and daughters of upper-middle-class white America to join the effort? Their experiences during the Freedom Vote campaign had convinced the SNCC high command that nothing attracted the media quite like scenes of white college kids helping "the downtrodden Negroes of Mississippi." The SNCC veterans had also learned that the presence of well-heeled white students insured the conspicuous presence of federal law enforcement officials. Describing the Freedom Vote campaign, SNCC veteran, Lawrence Guyot, said:

> Wherever those white volunteers went FBI agents followed. It was really a problem to count the number of FBI agents who were there to protect the [Yale and Stanford] students. It was just that gross. So then we said, "Well, now, why don't we invite lots of whites . . . to come and serve as volunteers in the state of Mississippi?" (Quoted in Raines, 1983: 287)

In a 1964 interview, Bob Moses put the matter a bit more obliquely when he remarked that "these students bring the rest of the country with them. They're from good schools and their parents are influential. The interest of the country is awakened and when that happens, the government responds to that issue."[7] Or as James Forman, SNCC's Executive Director at the time of the Summer Project, put it more recently, "we made a conscious attempt . . . to recruit from some of the Ivy League schools . . . you know, a lot of us knew . . . what we were up against. So that we were, in fact, trying to consciously recruit a counter power-elite."[8]

The financial straits SNCC found itself in on the eve of the project served to reinforce the strategic decision to recruit at elite colleges and universities. The organization simply lacked the resources to subsidize the participation of the summer volunteers. With little support forthcoming from SCLC or the NAACP, SNCC was forced to underwrite the project on a budget that was never adequate to its basic operation, let alone an ambitious undertaking such as Freedom Summer. At least three times during the first quarter of the year, staff members missed paychecks because of the organization's precarious financial situation.[9] An extended discussion at the May 10 Executive Committee Meeting indicated that the financial crisis remained acute barely three weeks before the onset of the project. At that meeting, Courtland Cox asked that a special account be established to differentiate monies set aside for the Summer Project from ordinary operating funds. Prathia Hall responded that the absence of any such funds made the question of any "special account" moot. She then went on to inform the committee that "our debt [is] presently growing and [costs] incurred [during the Dick] Gregory tour [are] still due."[10]

Faced with such severe financial constraints, SNCC would have been hard pressed to pay the volunteers even had strategic considerations argued for doing so. In the end, the strategic and financial imperatives of the project combined to convince project organizers to pitch their recruiting appeals to those who could bear the costs of a summer in Mississippi. Practically, this translated into a recruitment campaign geared to the nation's elite colleges and universities. Schools, such as Stanford, Harvard, and Princeton, offered project recruiters large numbers of students who not only could pay their own way, but whose social and political connections fit the public relations aims of the project.

The actual recruitment of volunteers was coordinated by Friends of SNCC chapters or other civil rights groups on campus. Starting some-time in March, descriptive literature and project applications were sent to these groups for distribution to all prospective applicants. Shortly thereafter, completed applications began flowing into the central project office in Jackson, where they were screened and evaluated. With the ar-rival of each new batch of forms, the success of SNCC's recruiting ef-forts became all the more apparent. The narrow recruiting net fashioned by project organizers had caught exactly the type of applicants the SNCC high command had been after.

The Applicants: A Profile

The information from the applications provides a broad-brush portrait of the Freedom Summer applicants. There are three components to this portrait: the applicants' background characteristics, motives for applying, and what might be called their "social relationship" to the Summer Project.

Background Characteristics

No doubt the single most salient characteristic of the Freedom Summer applicants is the comfortable, if not elite backgrounds from which they were drawn. If it was the intention of project organizers to attract the sons and daughters of well-to-do America, the data presented in Table 2.1 clearly indicates they succeeded in doing so.

In 1960, median family income in the United States was $5,660 (U.S. Bureau of the Census, 1961). For the applicants' families, the compara-ble figure, $8,417, was nearly 50 percent higher. The latter figure takes on even greater significance when we recall the class background of the families that were to house many of the volunteers in Mississippi. In 1960, median nonwhite family income in Mississippi was just $1,444 (U.S. Bureau of the Census, 1963). That meant that some of the least privileged persons in America were to play host to the offspring of some of the most privileged. This clash of class backgrounds was to produce some of the most poignant and eye-opening moments of the summer for both volunteers and residents alike.

The privileged character of the applicants makes sense, given two fea-tures of SNCC's recruiting efforts. First, SNCC's policy requiring the volunteers to be self-supporting encouraged the class bias noted above. Secondly, SNCC's stress on recruiting at elite colleges and universities

Table 2.1   1960 Median Family Income for the Freedom Summer
Applicants and the Total U.S. Population[a]

	Freedom Summer Applicants		U.S. Population (in thousands)	
	%	No.	%	No.
Under $1,000	0	(0)	6	(2,513)
1,000–1,999	0	(0)	7	(3,374)
2,000–2,999	0	(0)	8	(3,764)
3,000–3,999	3	(7)	9	(4,283)
4,000–4,999	7	(20)	11	(4,958)
5,000–5,999	14	(37)	12	(5,564)
6,000–6,999	15	(40)	11	(4,827)
7,000–7,999	19	(50)	9	(3,872)
8,000–8,999	10	(28)	7	(2,991)
9,000–9,999	9	(23)	5	(2,190)
10,000–14,999	18	(48)	10	(4,728)
15,000–24,999	5	(13)	3	(1,491)
25,000+	1	(2)	1	(575)
Total	101	(268)	99	(45,128)

[a] The original project applications contained no question on family income. Instead, median family income was estimated by substituting the comparable 1960 figure for the census tract in which the applicant's parents (or in some cases, the applicant) lived in 1964.

also favored the well-to-do over the average student. Again, the figures show clearly just how much emphasis SNCC placed on recruiting at high-status colleges and universities. While 233 schools contributed applicants, the majority of students who applied came from the top thirty or so schools in the country. Elite private universities, such as Harvard, Yale, Stanford, and Princeton, accounted for nearly 40 percent of the total. In fact, those four schools alone contributed 123 of the 736 students who applied to work on the project. An additional 145 applicants were drawn from among the dozen most prestigious state universities—including Berkeley, Wisconsin, Michigan—in the country. All told, then, students from the nation's highest ranking public and private colleges and universities made up 57 percent of the total applicant pool.

The class advantages that account for the elite educational backgrounds of the volunteers may also help to explain the relatively small numbers of blacks who applied to the project. Less than 10 percent of the applicants were black. Project organizers *did* make some effort to recruit black volunteers, even setting aside money for fellowships. But clearly the central emphasis in recruiting was antithetical to widespread black participation.

For one thing, SNCC's avowed intention of bringing large numbers of whites to Mississippi for the national media they would guarantee no doubt discouraged some blacks from applying. More importantly, the locus of recruitment efforts virtually insured the underrepresentation of blacks on the project. In 1961–1962 blacks made up only 2.9 percent of all undergraduates at colleges and universities in the United States.[11] To the extent that project recruitment centered here, the small percentage of blacks on the project makes sense.

A bit more surprising is the relatively large number of women who applied to the project. Forty-one percent of all applicants were female. This represents a slight overrepresentation of women among the applicants when compared to their proportion among all college students. In 1964, women comprised only 39 percent of all undergraduates.[12] Then, too, it must be remembered that the women applicants had come of age during one of the more romanticized and traditional eras of gender socialization in this country's history (Hewlett, 1986). For them to have even applied required a level of rejection of traditional sex roles not demanded of the male applicants.

Every geographical region of the country contributed applicants to the project. However, some contributed more than others. Those regions that were overrepresented on the applications include the Great Lakes, Mid-Atlantic, and Far West. In fact, applicants from the three largest states in those regions—Illinois, New York, and California—made up nearly half (46.3 percent) of all prospective volunteers. By contrast, the states of the Mountain and Western Plains regions contributed relatively few applicants. The closest thing to a surprise in these data is the fact that better than 11 percent of those who filled out applications were from the South. The suprise is muted somewhat by the realization that a near majority of the Southern applicants were black.

Given the preponderance of college students among the applicants, their average age—23.2—is a bit higher than might be expected. The fact that nearly 20 percent of the applicants had already completed their undergraduate education (though many were still enrolled as graduate students) helps account for the slightly older age of the applicants. However, even among the applicants who were undergraduates, the age distribution was weighted toward the upper end of the college age range. Seniors and juniors outnumbered freshmen and sophomores by nearly two to one. So even if colleges and universities were the locus of recruitment efforts, it is clear that other factors—perhaps including age or class standing—affected a student's receptivity to these recruitment appeals.

Taken together, these various bits and pieces of information yield a reasonably coherent portrait of the applicants. The central theme of that portrait is one of biographical availability. For all the social-psychological interpretations that have been proposed to account for the conspicuous role of students in social protest (c.f. Block, Hann, and Smith, 1969; Feuer, 1969; Flacks, 1971; Keniston, 1968; Lewis and Kraut, 1972), there may be a far more mundane explanation. Students, especially those drawn from privileged classes, are simply free, to a unique degree, of constraints that tend to make activism too time consuming or risky for other groups to engage in. Often freed from the demands of family, marriage, and full-time employment, students are uniquely available to express their political values through action. Certainly, this view is consistent with the information we have on the applicants. Only 22 percent of those who applied held full-time jobs, and nearly 70 percent of this group were teachers out of school for the summer. The rest of the applicants were spared the need to work during the summer by virtue of their advantaged class backgrounds. The same story applies on a personal level. Barely 10 percent of the applicants were married, more often than not to another applicant. Less than 2 percent were parents.

Attitudes and Values

Availability may be a necessary prerequisite for involvement in a project like Freedom Summer, but it certainly does not insure participation. After all, the type of freedom enjoyed by the applicants can be exercised in a variety of ways. Only when that freedom is joined with particular attitudes and values does the potential for activism exist. In the case of the applicants, what were some of these attitudes? What motives underlay their decision to apply to the project? At a broader social-psychological level, who were the applicants?

By way of a general answer to these questions, the applicants were exactly who we would have expected them to be, given the era in which they were raised and the class advantages most of them enjoyed. To the extent that they were drawn from that privileged segment of the American middle and upper-middle classes who came of age in postwar America, they shared in the generalized optimism, idealism, and sense of potency that was the subjective heritage of their class and generation.

The applications help complete this portrait. One open-ended question on the application asked the prospective volunteers to explain why they wanted to work in Mississippi. Their answers furnish a fascinating glimpse of the applicants *before* the onset of the project and their immersion within the embryonic New Left. The following excerpts capture the dominant tone of the applications:

As Peter Countryman said at the Conference on Racial Equality held at Pomona in February, "The only thing necessary for the triumph of evil is for the good men to do nothing." . . . I have always known that discrimination was wrong and that *now* is the time to overcome these obstacles. . . . Until we do all that we stand for in democracy and Christianity is negated, mocked while such oppression exists. . . . I can not sit by idly, knowing that there is discrimination and injustice, knowing that there is terror and fear, while I do nothing.

I want to work in Mississippi this summer because . . . there is a great deal of work to be done and . . . just as great [a] need for workers. . . . But more than that, I feel that I *must* help. There is so much to do, so many barriers between men to be broken, so much hate to be overcome. I think that this is most acutely true of Mississippi, where barriers of ignorance, fear and hate are only now beginning to be effectively attacked. I want to contribute what I can to the effort so that we might at long last build a truly colorblind [sic] society "with liberty and justice for all."

A century ago, the proclamation of emancipation was signed. A decade ago, the desegregation of schools was ordered. Today, the Negroes of Mississippi still await their emancipation from the bondage of manifold segregation. No longer, though, are they resigned to accept the injustice of their political and economic, social and educational thralldom. Now they are impatient and will act.

Now I, too, am impatient and will act, because for too many years I have been passively waiting. In endless discussion I have philosophized about the essence of man, and attempted to establish fundamental principles of moral action. With the untroubled detachment of a self-proclaimed liberal, I patiently suffered the rebukes of James Baldwin and the laments of Pete Seeger. Next year in the insulation of a graduate school, I begin the lengthy study of medicine, dedicated to the alleviation of human suffering.

Such ethical and intellectual dedication, without any bodily commitment, rings hollow, however, and is surely of no avail in the struggle against intransigent injustice in Mississippi. The time for empathy without action is long past. I am impatient and will act now.[18]

What strikes the reader first about these statements is the depths of idealism they express. Indeed, that idealism is so passionately stated that it occasionally sounds naive and a bit romanticized. That it does may tell us as much about the lack of idealism in contemporary America as it does about any lack of sophistication on the part of the applicants. In any case, what is more important than *our* reaction to the statements is, first, the consistency with which these views were expressed, and second, what they tell us about the applicants. These were deeply idealistic individuals, dedicated to achieving equal rights and human dignity for all. What sets the applicants apart from a good many others who espouse similar values was their optimism that these values could be realized through a kind of generational mission in which they shared. Wrote one applicant:

> I no longer can escape the tension, the spirit, the anxiety that fills my heart and mind concerning the movement in the South. It is impossible for me to deny the fact that the fight against racial prejudice, intolerance, ignorance—the fight for Civil Rights—is the most significant challenge and the most crucial war my generation will ever be called to fight.

Another considered:

> [T]he Civil Rights Revolution to be one of the most important events in this country since the American Revolution nearly two centuries ago . . . this movement is like a thunderstorm in the midst of . . . a partched [sic] and arid wasteland. My generation has a responsibility to insure that this "thunderstorm" does not end but remains a lasting "shower" to keep this country "green" for *all* Americans.

Still another remembered John F. Kennedy's challenge

> to "ask not what your country can do for you, but what you can do for your country." Surely, no challenge looms larger than eradicating racial discrimination in this country. It will not be easy. But SNCC's program should make a sizeable dent in the problem. I want to do my part. There is a moral wave building among today's youth and I intend to catch it![14]

So the applicants' idealism was informed by a sense of generational potency that made them extremely optimistic about the prospects for social change. One even referred to the need "to solve the racial question, so we can move on to eliminate hunger and poverty in America."[15] Never let it be said that the applicants lacked either imagination or confidence!

These quotes also say something about the ideological diversity of the applicants on the eve of the Summer Project. Clearly, their perceptions of the world were not being filtered through a single dominant interpretive frame (Snow, et al., 1986). Their narrative statements predate the emergence of the mass New Left and the dissemination of its political perspective throughout mainstream youth culture. So unlike activists in the late Sixties, for whom the "correct" *political* analysis became de rigueur, the Freedom Summer applicants display a remarkably eclectic mix of world views and reasons for wanting to go to Mississippi. In fact, many of the answers on the applications make no mention of larger political issues or motivations. As Elinor Tideman Aurthur told me in the course of her interview:

> [D]uring that period [prior to Freedom Summer] I was . . . apolitical . . . I was into the humanities, and culture . . . and literature. I was kind of impatient with my father and his involvement with social causes. I felt that was dead . . . I wanted to write . . . I didn't have the confidence to write but I saw myself as a writer, and I did not do anything political.[16]

Another put it this way: "Politics? What the hell was that? I didn't know for nothing about politics . . . I was going to spend my summer 'helping Negroes' . . . sort of a domestic Peace Corps number."[17]

Those applicants whose statements evidence the least political orientation to the project fall into one of two groups. The first are teachers or education majors whose primary motivation for applying represents a simple extension of their occupational roles or future career plans.

> As a part-time instructor of English Composition for both remedial and average students at The George Washington University, Washington, D.C., I have become increasingly aware of the problems of cultural deprivation and lack of basic skills which prevail today. My teaching experience has given me insights into the actual limitations of students who have emerged from inadequate cultural backgrounds or have not had sufficient training for college; this experience has, however, revealed both the need and possibilities for guidance and remedial work. Moreover, I have become more and more aware and disturbed by the inability of students to think critically or even differently about the world around them. Thus, within the context of the Mississippi Project, I would hope to be able to narrow the educational and cultural gaps, as well as to encourage responsible action and critical thinking among the residents of Mississippi.

> I have been working in the NSM [Northern Student Movement] tutorial program here in New Haven for the past six months. That experience has convinced me of two things. First, that I want to be a teacher and secondly, that we will never be able to achieve true racial equality in this society until we improve the educational preparation of our negro [*sic*] students. Working with SNCC in Mississippi will hopefully contribute to the goal while also giving me valuable teaching experience. . . .[18]

Religion + Resume experience (career boost)

The second group of "nonpolitical" applicants consists of persons whose reasons for applying appear to be primarily religious. For them the project represented an extension of the social gospel in action or, reflecting the existential theology of the day, an opportunity to bear "personal witness" to the idea of Christian brotherhood. One applicant put it this way: "Christ called us to *act* in the service of brotherhood, not just talk about it. I'm tired of talking. Mississippi is my opportunity to act."[19]

The widespread salience of religious motives among the applicants may surprise some readers unfamiliar with America's longstanding tradition of church-based activism. From religious pacifists to Quaker abolitionists to Catholic settlement workers, much of America's activist history has had deep roots in the church. With its ministerial leadership and strong ideological ties to Southern black theology, the civil rights movement merely continued this tradition. It is hardly surprising, then, to find religious sentiments being voiced by many of the volunteers.

Among the more political applicants, a kind of conventional patriotic rhetoric was more often invoked than a radical leftist analysis. Many applicants cite a desire to "honor the memory" or "carry out the legacy of John F. Kennedy" as their principal reason for applying. Another sounded particularly Kennedyesque when he said that he was attracted to the project "by a desire to enhance the image of the United States abroad, thereby undercutting Communist influence among the underdeveloped nations of the world."[20] Still others cite everything from the Constitution, the Emancipation Proclamation and the 1954 Supreme Court school desegregation decision to legitimate their participation in the project.

Conventional leftists and socialists were not absent from the ranks of the applicants; they simply were no more dominant—and perhaps less so—than the other three groups. Statements such as the following appear only rarely in the applications:

> Not only do I agree with SNCC's ends, I am also very much in accord with the methods by which those ends are to be achieved. Marx finished his *Manifesto* by calling for the workers of the world to unite. SNCC has either intentionally or unintentionally followed his advice. The fight for freedom has become a struggle for unity—the haves against the have nots. This is not a struggle to be engaged in by the mere liberal, but the zealot, for the liberal can't be counted on to make the sacrifices required. Instead, it must be a conflict of the disenfranchised against the appressors [*sic*] for rights and freedoms which have been denied not merely since . . . the landing of the first slave ship on the eastern seaboard, but since the beginnings of recorded history. I have rejected my "birthrights" and voluntarily identified with the suppressed classes.[21]

The impression that one gets from reading the applications, then, is one of healthy ideological diversity. All four of the groups identified here seem to have been present in roughly equal numbers in the ranks of the applicants. What is interesting is that these ideological differences mask a common source of inspiration for whatever values the applicants espouse. Regardless of ideological stripe, the vast majority of applicants credit their parents with being the models for their actions. Fifty-nine of eighty applicants interviewed explicitly acknowledged the positive role that either or both of their parents played in shaping the values that prompted them to apply. Only nine described their applying as part of an ongoing conflict with conservative or racist parents. In fact, in some cases the act of applying seems to have been an attempt by the applicant to please rather than antagonize their parents. When asked how her parents reacted to her decision to apply to the Summer Project, Judy Michalowski reported that, "My father was thrilled . . . if he could have cast me in any particular role, that's how he would have cast me. And I'm sure that approval had a lot to do with my applying."[22] Even in less extreme instances, it seems clear that parental values were motivating the applicant and, in some cases, being used by them to force reluctant parents to support their decision. The interviews turned up numerous examples of this dynamic, including the following two:

> I grew up in a politically conservative family. The only thing was that my parents were Christians; they were Episcopalian and they raised us with very strong Christian beliefs and in my case I took them very seriously so that . . . when I wanted to go to Mississippi and had to have my parents' permission, my father was caught in the bind that he didn't want me to go but to refuse me permission was to contradict everything he had taught me. . . .[23]

> They didn't want me to go in the worst way. They were scared; very scared and . . . yet they were in this terrible predicament. Here I was doing what, after all, in a sense they had raised me to do . . . so this was something that they couldn't . . . criticize.[24]

This, then, is one case in which the popular view of the Sixties activist is *not* consistent with the evidence. Far from using Freedom Summer as a vehicle for rebellion against parents, the applicants simply seem to be acting in accord with values learned at home. This finding is consistent with most previous research on the roots of student activism (c.f. Block, Hann, and Smith, 1969; Flacks, 1971; Keniston, 1968).

Social Relationship to the Project

Were freedom from adult responsibilities and sympathetic attitudes enough to account for the applicant's decision to apply to the project? Or were there ways in which concrete social ties served to "pull" people into the project? The answer to this last question would appear to be "yes." The image of the activist as a lone individual driven only by the force of his or her conscience applies to very few of the applicants. Rather, their involvement in the project seems to have been mediated through some combination of personal relationships and/or organizational ties.

Organizationally the applicants were a very active group. Only 15 percent of the prospective volunteers reported no group memberships, while 62 percent list two or more. The percentage of volunteers listing various types of organizations is shown below:

Civil rights organization	48%
Student club or social group	21
Church or religious group	21
Socialist or other leftist organization	14
Democrat or Republican party affiliate	13
Academic club or organization	13
Teachers organization	10

Not surprisingly, the highest percentage of memberships are to civil rights groups. Within this category, CORE or Friends of SNCC chapters account for better than half of all the affiliations. Given that SNCC and CORE supplied 100 percent of the field staff for the Summer Project, it seems reasonable to assume that membership in one of their chapters would have insured a certain knowledge of and loyalty to the project.

The remaining organizational categories mirror the ideological diversity touched on above. Each of the four informal divisions discussed in the previous section correspond to one of the next six largest organizational categories. Twenty-one percent of the applicants were members of church or religious groups. Fourteen percent belonged to leftist organizations. Thirteen percent included Republican or Democratic party organizations—such as the Young Democrats—among their affiliations. Finally, 10 percent were active in one (or more) of a variety of teacher's organizations.

The real importance of these organizations lies not so much in the ideological divisions they reflect as in the role they played in drawing the applicants into civil rights activity *before* Freedom Summer. One volunteer described her initiation into the Movement in this way:

> [The] Church was very important to me. I was studying to be a minister at the time that I went to Mississippi and actually that is how I got involved in it [Freedom Summer] because I went to Beaver College which was an all female institution, wanting to be a missionary eventually, got involved in the YWCA there and was sent on a voter registration drive, which Al Lowenstein headed, in Raleigh, North Carolina . . . he . . . told us about the Mississippi summer project and after having my eyes opened by the whole Raleigh experience I knew I wanted to go.[25]

Two other applicants told virtually identical stories involving a church-sponsored trip to a black mission in Biloxi, Mississippi, and an UFT (United Federation of Teachers) organized tutoring program in the Bronx.[26]

For the vast majority of applicants, then, Freedom Summer did *not* mark their initial foray into the civil rights movement. Instead, through a variety of sponsoring organizations, some 90 percent of the applicants had already participated in various forms of activism. Not that the nature of their involvements was in all cases terribly significant. Most of the applicants had confined their activities to such safe forms of participation as "on-campus civil rights organizing" (36 percent) or fund-raising (10 percent). But it is not the intensity of these earlier involvements as much as the fact that they took place that is significant. Extremely risky, time-consuming involvements such as Freedom Summer are almost always preceded by a series of safer, less demanding instances of activism (McAdam, 1986). In effect, people commit themselves to movements in stages, each activity preparing the way for the next. The case of the volunteer, who engaged in voter registration work in Raleigh, North Carolina, prior to Freedom Summer illustrates the process. While in Raleigh, three very important things happened to her. First, she met activists she had not known previously, thus broadening her range of movement contacts. Second, talking with these activists and confronting segregation firsthand clearly deepened the volunteer's understanding of and commitment to the movement. Finally, at the level of identity, the week in Raleigh allowed her to "play at" and grow more comfortable with the role of activist. As the research on identity transformation suggests, it is precisely such tentative forays into new roles that pave the way for more thoroughgoing identity change (Bem, 1972). Playing at being an activist is usually the first step in becoming one. As a result, the volunteer left Raleigh knowing more people in the movement and more ideologically and personally disposed toward participation in the Summer Project. As she herself said, "the trip to Raleigh really laid the foundation for Mississippi . . . I don't think I would have even applied to the project otherwise."[27]

So most of the applicants were already linked to the civil rights movement either through the organizations to which they belonged or their own modest histories of civil rights activism. But what about their links to one another? How extensive were the ties *between* prospective volunteers on the eve of the summer? The presumption, of course, is that an individual would have found it easier to apply had they known someone else who had done so.

Fortunately, one question on the application allows for a very conservative estimate of the extent of such ties. That question asked the applicant to "list at least ten persons who . . . would be interested in receiving information about your [summer] activities." These names were gathered in an effort to mobilize a well-heeled, Northern, liberal constituency who might lobby Washington on behalf of protection for civil rights workers as well as other changes in civil rights policy. Judging from the names they listed, most of the applicants seem to have been well aware of this goal. The names most often provided by the applicants were those of parents, parents' friends, professors, ministers, or other noteworthy or influential *adults* with whom they had contact. On occasion, however, the applicant also included another applicant in their list of names. Just how often was surprising.

Exactly a fourth of the applicants listed at least one other prospective volunteer on their applications. What makes this figure impressive is the fact that the intent of the question was not to have the applicants identify other applicants. That 25 percent did so suggests that the personal ties between the applicants were extensive. Interviews with the applicants confirm this impression. Forty-nine of the eighty applicants said they knew at least one other applicant in advance of the summer. And their accounts make it clear that these ties were important in their decision to apply to the project. Several even described their decision to apply as more a group than an individual process. As one volunteer put it:

> [T]he group that went down to Raleigh . . . were from Cornell, Dartmouth, Amherst, BU [Boston University], Yale . . . and I just felt that I was with a very special group of people and I wanted to be with them for as long as I could and we would sit up at night talking about whether we would go down [to Mississippi] and [then] we communicated with each other after that Raleigh experience . . . [and] talked each other into going.[28]

Together, the bits and pieces of information presented above yield a fairly coherent portrait of the Freedom Summer applicants. The central themes embodied in this portrait are those of "biographical availability," "attitudinal affinity" and "social integration." Raised by parents who espoused values consistent with the project, the applicants found themselves disposed to participate on attitudinal grounds. Then too, their freedom from family and employment responsibilities (the latter owing largely to their privileged class backgrounds) made it possible for them to act on their attitudes and values. Finally, a combination of organizational ties, personal links to other applicants, and their own histories of activism served to pull the applicants into the project even as their values were pushing them in that direction.

Following Through: Overcoming the Obstacles to Participation

Applying and actually taking part in Freedom Summer were two very different things. Roughly a quarter of all those who applied to the Project never made it to Mississippi. Between April and June, the typical applicant had to overcome at least three obstacles if he or she were to participate in the project. Project interviewers had to be convinced that the applicant was the type of person they were looking for. Skeptical or overprotective parents had to be induced to countenance the venture. Perhaps most important, self-doubts and fears had to be conquered or at least successfully managed.

For most of the applicants, a formal project interview was the first of the hurdles they were to encounter. Exactly how many of the prospective volunteers were interviewed is not known. A reasonable guess is that most of those who applied from schools with strong links to the project were interviewed. This guess accords with the little bit of data available on the interviews. Of the eighty applicants interviewed, fifty-one remember being interviewed. The twenty-nine who apparently were not interviewed tended to come from schools that sent very few—and often only one—person to Mississippi. Invariably, the applicants from schools such as Stanford, Oberlin, and Berkeley were interviewed. So too were applicants who lived near enough to one of these schools to enable them to be interviewed there.

The actual interviewing was done by a variety of people. On occasion SNCC staffers handled the sessions. Most of the interviews, however, seem to have been conducted by Friends of SNCC personnel or sympathetic faculty members. The interviews were typically held on campus and lasted anywhere from fifteen minutes to two hours.

Perhaps the most interesting aspect of these sessions concerns the type of things the interviewers were looking for in questioning the applicants. To alert the interviewers to the issues they deemed important, project organizers sent each of them a three-page memo, dated April 14, entitled, "Guidelines for Interviewing."[29] Less than a page of the memo was given over to a listing of eight "criteria which should guide the Mississippi Project interviewers." The bulk of the memo, however, dealt with the single issue that clearly troubled project organizers the most. That was the issue of paternalism or insensitivity on the part of the volunteers. Citing the case of a student active in the Freedom Vote project, the memo warned of the dangers of "students . . . who came to Mississippi with fixed ideas about what they wanted to do and what they hoped to achieve." The ideal volunteer was one who understood that "his role will be to *work with* local leadership, not to *overwhelm* it. . . . A student who seems determined to carve his own niche, win publicity and glory when he returns home can only have harmful effects on the Mississippi program." Thus the principal charge given the interviewers was weeding the troublesome "mavericks" out from the ranks of the "good soldiers." How the interviewers chose to carry out this charge is examined later in the chapter. For now it is enough to know that no more than seventy or so of the applicants were formally rejected by project organizers, and many of these simply because they were underage or had applied too late to be integrated into the project.[30] Thus, while the interview may have been a stressful hurdle for some of the applicants, it appears to have been a fairly easy one to surmount.

Encounters with skeptical or protective parents were another matter. This was especially true in the case of applicants under the age of twenty-one, who were required to obtain parental permission in order to take part in the project. This requirement granted the parents of all underage applicants ultimate say over whether their son or daughter went South for the summer. The available evidence suggests that as many as 15 percent of all parents chose to exercise this control. Even some applicants over twenty-one decided to forego the project because of strong parental opposition. Rather than risk serious problems with their parents, they simply decided not to go. In all, a quarter of the no-shows attribute their withdrawal from the project to opposition from parents.

Finally, the applicants had their own fears and worries to contend with. Applying to the project in February or March was one thing. Remaining committed in the face of the ominous warnings of violence coming out of Mississippi in May and June was quite another. Typical of the tone of these warnings was a piece written in early June by the nationally syndicated columnist, Joseph Alsop. In part it read:

> A great storm is gathering—and may break very soon indeed—in the State of Mississippi and some other regions of the South. The southern half of Mississippi, to be specific, has been powerfully reinvaded by the Ku Klux Klan which was banished from the state many years ago. And the Klan groups have in turn merged with, or adhered to, a new and ugly organization known as the Americans for the Preservation of the White Race.
>
> Senator James O. Eastland has managed to prevent infiltration of the northern part of the state where his influence predominates. But Southern Mississippi is now known to contain no fewer than sixty-thousand armed men organized to what amounts to terrorism. Acts of terrorism against the local Negro populace are already an everyday occurrence.
>
> In Jackson, Mississippi, windows in the office of COFO (Council of Federated Organizations, under whose auspices the civil rights workers were coming to Mississippi) [are] broken almost nightly. Armed Negroes are now posted at the office each night. The same is true in other Mississippi cities. (Quoted in Lomax, et al., 1964: 9–10)

In the face of such warnings—and Alsop's was only one among many—it was the rare applicant who did *not* experience qualms and second thoughts about his or her decision. The wonder is that so many of the applicants resolved these doubts in favor of the project. Not all of those who applied did so, however. As the project got underway, there were those who simply could not bring themselves to make their way to Mississippi.

The Survivors: Distinguishing Volunteers from No-Shows

Confronted by these various hurdles, roughly a quarter of the applicants fell by the wayside prior to the start of the project. Can these no-shows be distinguished from those who did make it to Mississippi? Are there specific factors that account for the different courses of action taken by those in each group? The answer is yes. Expressed in terms of the three broad factors touched on earlier in the chapter, it appears that going or not going to Mississippi had more to do with the applicants' biographical availability and social links to the project than to any apparent differences in attitude between the volunteers and the no-shows. What is more, it would seem that the impact of these factors is closely related to the three major hurdles—staff rejection, parental opposition, and applicant fears—already noted.

Background Characteristics

Perhaps the most striking finding about background characteristics concerns the relative absence of significant differences between the two groups. The volunteers and no-shows appear as essentially alike on a long laundry list of variables that includes: race, social class, type of neighborhood (urban, suburban, rural) home region, type of college, and major in school. While these factors may have affected the decision-making process of particular applicants, they did not differentiate the two groups.

The only two background factors that did distinguish the volunteers from the no-shows were age and sex. Specifically, those applicants who were either under twenty-one or female were more susceptible to parental opposition than those who were older or male. The female applicants also seem to have encountered more opposition from project staff and interviewers than did the male applicants. The follow-up questionnaires and interviews help explain the dynamics of these processes.

Age   It would seem reasonable to assume that young people are more available for activism than older persons. But clearly there is an age below which this simply is not true. Below a certain age, parental control limits one's availability for activism, even in the absence of adult responsibilities such as family or full-time employment. In the case of Freedom Summer, this informal barrier to activism was made official by SNCC's decision to require all applicants under the age of twenty-one to obtain parental permission. This requirement spelled the end of at least one applicant's involvement in the project barely minutes after she had applied to go. She explains:

> I heard a SNCC person speak . . . [about the Freedom Summer Project] at . . . [school] and was absolutely mesmerized. It was like I now had a mission in life. I remember filling out the application and racing back to my dorm to call my parents, thinking, of course, that they would be as thrilled with my "mission"as I was. So what happens?! My mom starts crying. Then my dad gets on and starts yelling about how he's not paying $2,000—or whatever my tuition was—for me to run off to Mississippi; that I'm there to get an education and that if I have anything else in mind he'll be glad to stop sending the check. End of discussion.[31]

In general, SNCC's implementation of a parental permission requirement made age one of the key factors distinguishing volunteers from

Table 2.2   Reasons for Not Attending Freedom Summer, by Age

	All No-Shows	By Age		
		18–19	20–21	22+
Parental opposition	25%	46%	32%	8%
Other priorities (i.e., summer school)	23	8	24	29
Biographical constraints (i.e., marriage, pregnancy)	19	12	13	29
Fear	16	15	16	17
Other activism	7	4	8	7
Miscellaneous reasons	7	4	8	7
Don't remember	3	12	0	3
	100%	101%	101%	100%

no-shows. The volunteers, for example, averaged nearly two years older than the no-shows.[32] The overriding impact of age is perhaps better reflected in the answers the no-shows gave to an item on the follow-up questionnaires asking them why they did *not* go to Mississippi (Table 2.2). Nearly half of all 18- to 19-year-old no-shows cited opposition from parents as the reason they did not participate in the Summer Project. This was nearly double the percentage for all no-shows and six times the comparable figure for those who were over twenty-one years of age. Regarding the Summer Project, the attitude of the older applicants toward their parents was expressed succinctly by one volunteer. "They weren't particularly thrilled by my decision to go, but, hell, I was 23 at the time. (laughing) What were they going to do; ground me? cut my allowance?"[33]

Sex   The number of women who applied to the Summer Project was surprising, both in view of the composition of the undergraduate population in 1964, and the strength of traditional barriers to women's participation in projects such as Freedom Summer. Certainly, the dangerous, unchaperoned, interracial, and political character of the project posed more of a threat to traditional conceptions of femaleness than maleness. For the male applicant, participation in a project like Freedom Summer could be seen as functionally equivalent to any number of other traditional challenges that were available to young men as part of the process of "becoming a man," "seeing the world," or "testing one's mettle." There were no similar precedents available to the female volunteers to legitimate their participation in the project. Unlike young men, it really was not expected or accepted that college-age women would expose themselves to adventures of a potentially dangerous nature. In a letter written shortly after the summer, the mother of one of the female volunteers described how a Congressman had tried to convince her and her husband to cut short their daughter's participation in the project. He had told her "husband . . . to go and get her immediately. He said if he were 20 years younger he'd go himself, but a girl . . . emphatically 'no.' "[34]

Similarly, the traditional sexual double standard—alive and well in mid-Sixties America—made a young woman's involvement in an unchaperoned project, such as Freedom Summer, much more problematic than it was for a young man. Finally, America's near phobic preoccupation with even the most insignificant contact between white women and black men posed a serious obstacle to female, but not male, involvement in Freedom Summer. The following incident, related by Judy Michalowski in one of the interviews, suggests just how real this latter obstacle was in the early Sixties.

> [T]here was a black fellow who worked in the cafeteria. . . . The night before the [1963 Civil Rights] march [on Washington] I was out in my parents' front yard with my boyfriend at the time and this fellow drove by and stopped 'cause he recognized me and he said something to me and it took me two seconds to place who he was . . . and then I was friendly to him and this boyfriend of mine practically attacked him . . . the police came. There was a huge altercation and the whole time I kept saying, "I know this guy! There's no problem" . . . but everyone else assumed the worst.[35]

Needless to say, this type of casual contact between a white male and a black, male or female, would never have precipitated such an incident. Based on the interviews, it seems clear that these factors did indeed constitute a set of barriers to female participation in the project. Especially potent was the combination of the sexual double standard and the taboo concerning contact between white women and black men. One interesting form of archival evidence helps to illustrate this point. As part of the interview process, the interviewer was supposed to forward a written report to the SNCC office summarizing their evaluation of the applicant. Many of the "interviewer reports" from these sessions have been obtained from collections around the country.[36] They are important for what they reveal about the way project staff viewed the applicants on the eve of the summer. On the issue of gender differences, these reports support one very simple conclusion: the substance and tone of the interviewer's comments differ depending on the sex of the applicant.

One difference concerns the amount of attention given the issue of sex in the interviews. Rarely, if ever, does the issue seem to have been discussed in the interviews with male applicants. Quite the opposite is true in regard to the sessions with female applicants. The following excerpt from a report on a female applicant is typical of a number that could be cited:

> _____ _____ was in on the interview and asked her how she'd deal with a Negro man who came up to her on the street and asked to sleep with her. She said she might. I asked her what she'd do if I told her, as a staff member, that sexual activity would endanger everyone, and not to do it. She said she might go ahead and do it anyhow.[37]

The applicant in question was rejected for work on the project. Given the very real Southern phobia regarding contact between black males and white females as well as the need for discipline on the project, this seems a reasonable decision. The more basic question is, why were these issues more often raised with female, and not male, applicants? Was it because the issue of interracial sexuality was more explosive when it came to white women than white men? Or does the different emphasis in the interviews perhaps also reflect the more general influence of a traditional sexual double standard that made sex less acceptable for a woman than a man? There is no clear answer to this question. What is certain is that the whole issue of sexuality posed a threat to female but not male participation in the project.

Other evidence of a kind of sexual double standard are the frequent references to physical appearance that show up on the reports for female, but not male, applicants. Two examples will serve to illustrate the general tone of these comments:

> This girl is uncommonly ugly with an almost piggish look to her. EEEECH!
> She has long blond hair and is frankly a knock-out.[38]

Other than a single reference to the "frailness" of one of the prospective male volunteers, the interviewer reports on male applicants are totally devoid of references to physical appearance. There is no evidence that female applicants were rejected on the basis of their physical appearance. What the comments do suggest, though, is that the female applicants were being delivered a contradictory set of signals about the issue of sexuality on the Summer Project. At the same time they were being warned of the dangers of sex in Mississippi, they were also being physically evaluated in a way their male counterparts were not. The potential for conflict inherent in these messages would soon be realized in Mississippi.

Finally, the following interviewer report hints at a kind of generalized sexism that was also to surface in Mississippi:

> This girl presents problems. She is a photographer; graduate of Radcliffe '61, works doing odds and ends as she takes pictures. Is interested in doing documentary films as a profession. She is a trained typist, but hates to do this type of work. Has had some experience in civil rights, BUT didn't "like" working for NAACP because she walked in to help and found fifteen girls typing and the room filled with smoke . . . the girl flatly refuses to do clerical work. When pushed to the wall she said she'd do it, but not more than half the summer. . . . She says she wants to "work with people" and "learn something from the summer," and that she won't be able to do either if she works in an office. . . . RECOMMENDATION: *DEFINITE REJECTION*[39]

One of the applicants I spoke with described her interview experience as similar to that of the woman discussed above.

> Officially I'm sure they [the project staff] thought I had withdrawn from the project. But . . . that's not what happened. I've always felt that they *rejected* me . . . the whole interview was so hostile and sexist. I wouldn't have known to call it that at the time, but that's certainly what was going on. I remember the gal who was interviewing me asking if I'd be willing to do clerical work. I said, "sure, but I'd like to work on voter registration too." At that point she launches into this harangue about how "we need dutiful foot soldiers," and "you've got to accept project discipline," blah, blah, blah . . . the whole tone was, "they also serve who sit and type!" I mean, I can't believe they were putting the same questions to the guys.[40]

While the *general* issues of project discipline and staff authority seem to have been a central concern in *all* of the interviews, the *specific* questions regarding acceptance of work assignments appear to have been asked of the female applicants far more often than their male counterparts. The impression that one is left with is that the project staff had a narrower vision of women's role in the project than the one they applied to male applicants. Given the prevailing attitudes toward women and work in early Sixties America, such a vision is hardly surprising. The application of this vision, however, represented yet another obstacle to women's participation in the project. Applicants subjected to interviews such as those described above were very likely to withdraw or be rejected

Table 2.3   Status on the Summer Project by Sex

	All Applicants	Rejects	No-Shows	Volunteers
Male	59%	48%	52%	62%
Female	41%	52%	48%	38%

in advance of the summer. That all the factors discussed here had the practical effect of reducing the likelihood of female participation in the project is suggested by the data given in Table 2.3. Certainly the fact that the no-show and reject categories boast the highest percentages of women suggests that female applicants faced more obstacles to participation in the project than their male counterparts.

Attitudinal Differences

There appear to be very few attitudinal differences between volunteers and no-shows. Nothing in the narrative statements of the two groups suggest that those who went to Mississippi were any more idealistic, optimistic, or committed to the aims of the project than those who stayed home. Rather, *all* of the applicants—participants and no-shows alike—emerge as highly committed, articulate supporters of the goals and values of the summer campaign. The logic of the application process virtually assured this outcome. To apply, interested parties had to seek out and obtain a five-page application from a campus representative of the project. The applicant then had to fill out the form and in many cases submit to a formal interview by the campus coordinator of the summer project (or traveling SNCC staffer). In short, applying to the project required considerable effort on the applicant's part, no doubt insuring a kind of self-selection in the application process. Presumably, only those with considerable commitment to the project would have been willing to expend the time and energy required to apply.

Another possibility is that the two groups did not so much differ in their basic orientation or commitment to the project, as in their reasons for applying. Fortunately, the open-ended question on the application asking applicants to explain why they "would like to work in Mississippi" allows us to test this possibility. A comparison of the answers given by the volunteers and the no-shows, however, fails to turn up any real differences in motivation between the two groups.[41]

There was, however, one striking attitudinal difference between the volunteers and no-shows that bears closer examination. This difference is captured in Table 2.4. In their statements, the volunteers were far more

Table 2.4   Ideological Reference Group by Status on the Summer Project

	Volunteers	No-Shows
Teachers	12%	5%
Church	13	8
Socialists/Leftists	13	8
Liberal Democrats	8	4
Civil rights movement	11	5
No discernible group	43	70

likely to explicitly align themselves with a specific ideological community or reference group than were the no-shows. Some examples of these types of "aligning" statements follow:

> "If I'm to continue *calling myself a Christian,* I must act NOW to put my abstract conception of brotherhood into practice."

> "*All of us in the movement* must join forces if the summer project is to succeed."

> "*In my groups of future teachers* I make it a point to ask each of them, 'Why do you want to go into education?'" (Emphasis added)[42]

The significance of these statements stems from the sense of support that the majority of volunteers derived from their identification with one of the ideological communities listed in the table. If there is strength in numbers, then the sense that one's actions are supported by many other teachers, Christians, etc., must surely have had a positive effect on those applicants who identified with one of these groups. On the other hand, those applicants who did *not* identify themselves with any larger community may well have found it harder to make good on their applications. Deprived of the sense of support *and* obligation that comes with membership in or identification with any community, the applicant may have lacked the necessary strength or motivation to go to Mississippi. Certainly this lack of identification is more characteristic of the no-shows than of the volunteers.

Social Relationship to the Project

It may be that the contrast sketched above is as much a social-structural as an ideological one; that is, that identification with a particular community grows out of and depends on strong social ties to that community. In other words, the larger percentage of volunteers expressing an ideological affinity for various groups may also indicate stronger links to those groups, links that, in turn, served to pull the volunteers into the project in greater numbers than the no-shows. Certainly this interpretation fits the avaliable data. On all the measures cited earlier, the volunteers emerge as more closely tied to the project than the no-shows. For example, the volunteers belong to a significantly greater number of organizations than the no-shows. Two-thirds of the participants, but only 52 percent of the withdrawals, belong to two or more organizations.

As Table 2.5 indicates, it is not simply the number but also the *type* of organizations that distinguish volunteers from no-shows. Volunteers tend more often to be members of explicitly political organizations than do the no-shows. Especially significant, given the focus of the Summer Project, is the difference in the percentage of each group belonging to civil rights groups. Similar percentage differences are evident in regard to all the other categories of political organizations. The same holds for the other two types of organizations—religious and teachers—with strong ideological links to the project. By contrast, the no-shows were drawn disproportionately from the ranks of social or academic organizations. The significance of this contrast owes to the different levels of pressure the two groups were likely subjected to as a result of the organizations they were involved in. Their more extensive ties to groups with strong links to the project meant that the volunteers were probably exposed to

Table 2.5   Percentage of Participants and No-Shows Who Belong to Various Types of Organizations

Type of Organization	Volunteers		No-Shows	
	%	No.	%	No.
Civil rights organization	50	(347)	40	(96)
Socialist or other Leftist organization	15	(107)	9	(24)
Democratic or Republican party organizations	13	(91)	11	(26)
Other political organizations	16	(108)	12	(29)
Church or religious groups	22	(150)	18	(43)
Teachers organizations	12	(80)	6	(15)
Student club or social organization	20	(140)	24	(56)
Student government	8	(57)	9	(21)
Student newspaper	6	(43)	7	(17)
Academic club or organization	12	(81)	16	(37)

more pressure or encouragement to make good on their applications than were the no-shows.

This latter point would seem to apply as much on the level of informal relationships as it does to memberships in formal organizations. That is, the volunteers also had stronger and more extensive ties to other project participants than did the no-shows. In fact, no other item of information on the applications proved to be a better predictor of participation in the project than this (see Appendix B). Project participants listed more than twice the number of volunteers as those applicants who withdrew from the project. Conversely, the percentage of no-shows listed by the volunteers was two and one-half times fewer than those given by the no-shows.[43] The follow-up interviews helped confirm the impression that personal ties served to pull many of the applicants into the project. Twenty-nine of the forty volunteers interviewed said they were friends of others who applied and subsequently went to Mississippi. Only ten of the forty no-shows fit this description.

A comparison of the civil rights histories of the volunteers and no-shows yields one last piece of evidence consistent with the profile sketched so far. Both groups were asked to list on their applications any previous civil rights activities in which they had been involved.[44] As expected, participants had significantly higher levels of prior involvement than the no-shows. Moreover, a closer look at the data show that as the level of prior activity rises, the gap between the two groups widens.

Together, the findings reported here offer a consistent picture of the Freedom Summer volunteers. Stated simply, the volunteers enjoyed much stronger social links to the Summer Project than did the no-shows. They were more likely to be members of civil rights (or allied) groups, have friends involved in the movement, and have more extensive histories of civil rights activity prior to the summer. The practical effect of this greater "proximity" to the movement would have been to place the volunteer at considerable "risk" of being drawn into the project via the application process. Having applied, the volunteer's close ties to the civil rights community would then have served another function. Given the extended time commitment expected of Freedom Summer volunteers and the highly publicized dangers of the campaign, it seems reasonable to assume that individual applicants—even highly committed ones—would have considered withdrawing from the campaign prior to the summer. What might have discouraged applicants from acting on these fears was the presence of strong *social* constraints discouraging withdrawal. If one acted alone in applying to the project and remained isolated in the months leading up to the campaign, the social costs of withdrawing from the project would not have been great. On the other hand, the individual who applied in consort with friends or as a movement veteran undoubtedly risked considerable social disapproval for withdrawal. One can also stress a more positive interpretation of the same process. In the months leading up to the summer, well-integrated applicants were no doubt encouraged to make good on their commitment through the reinforcement and sense of strength they derived from other applicants. As one volunteer explained, his relationship with another applicant was "probably the key to me making it to Mississippi . . . [he] and I just sort of egged each other on . . . I'm pretty sure I wouldn't have made it without him and probably that was true for him too."[45] Whichever interpretation one chooses, it is clear from the data that participants *do* differ significantly from no-shows in the extent and strength of their social links to the project.

Those applicants who finally made it to Mississippi, then, were an interesting and very special group. They were independent both by temperament and by virtue of their class advantages and relative freedom from adult responsibilities. They were not children, however, but young adults whose slightly older age granted them an immunity from parental control not enjoyed by the no-shows. Owing to the formidable obstacles the female applicants faced, the volunteers were disproportionately male. Academically, they numbered among "the best and the brightest" of their generation, both in the levels of education they had obtained and the prestige of the colleges and universities they were attending. Reflecting their privileged class backgrounds as much as the prevailing mood of the era, the volunteers held to an enormously idealistic and optimistic view of the world. More important, perhaps, they shared a sense of efficacy about their own actions. The arrogance of youth and the privileges of class combined with the mood of the era to give the volunteers an inflated sense of their own specialness and generational potency. This message was generally reinforced at home by parents who subscribed to values consistent with those of the project. Finally, the volunteers were already linked to the civil rights community. Whether these links took the form of organizational memberships, prior activism, or ties to other applicants, the volunteers benefited from greater "social proximity" to the project than did the no-shows. In fact, nothing distinguishes the two groups more clearly than this contrast. Biographical availability and attitudinal affinity may have been necessary prerequisites for applying, but it was the strength of one's links to the project that seem to have finally determined whether one got to Mississippi or not.[46]

3

Freedom High
THE SUMMER OF '64

FOR MOST of the volunteers, Freedom Summer began not in Mississippi, but at the Western College for Women in Oxford, Ohio. There, in mid-June, the National Council of Churches sponsored two, week-long orientation sessions for volunteers accepted for work in Mississippi. The first session was held June 14–20 and was tailored to those who were to work in voter registration. A second session, for Freedom School teachers, was held the following week.

If the volunteers had expected a languid, leisurely week in the early summer freshness of rural Ohio, they were to be disappointed. The intensity that was to mark the entire summer was very much in evidence at Oxford. It is interesting that the volunteers interviewed have retained so few specific memories of orientation or of the summer itself. They seem to attribute this to the fact that the events in question occurred nearly twenty-five years ago. In contrast, they usually have very detailed memories of events *prior* to the summer, such as when and how they heard about the project in the first place. Possibly the reason for the lack of specific memories is simply the pace of events that summer. Things happened too quickly to allow time for the reflection required to commit specific events to long-term memory. The volunteers were feeling, seeing, experiencing too much.

Some of the intensity of the experience owed to the specific activities planned for the week. The volunteers were subjected to a daunting schedule of general assemblies, section meetings, and work groups. The general assemblies brought all the volunteers together to hear what amounted to broad orientation sessions on Mississippi or some aspect of the movement. Sometimes staff members spoke at these assemblies; more often, it was invited speakers from outside the project. Established civil right leaders, such as Bayard Rustin, Vincent Harding, and James Lawson, spoke. So too did native Mississippians, trying to give the volunteers a better understanding of their state. Jess Brown, one of only three civil rights lawyers in the state, apprised the volunteers of the "unique" quality of Mississippi justice. Long-time state civil rights leader, Aaron Henry, gave a short history of the movement in Mississippi. Even the Justice Department dispatched a representative to the orientation. In a sobering and, for many, radicalizing session, John Doar warned the volunteers not to expect federal protection while in Mississippi. "Maintaining law and order," he argued, "is a state responsibility" (quoted in Belfrage, 1965: 22). In the weeks to come, the volunteers would have ample opportunity to see just how Mississippi exercised that responsibility.

Section meetings were more focused planning groups involving twenty to thirty people who were expected to be engaged in the same type of work during the summer. Work groups were smaller still, consisting of between five and ten people who would actually be working with one another in Mississippi. What these smaller groups lacked in drama and emotional intensity, they made up for in relevance. It was here that the volunteers met and got to know their fellow project members and were trained in the basics of their work assignments.

The power of orientation, however, derived less from this mix of planned sessions as from the informal aspects of the experience. For many of the volunteers it was the beginning of an intensely stressful, yet exhilarating, confrontation with traditional conceptions of America, community, politics, morality, sexuality, and, above all else, themselves. What the volunteers were beginning to experience at Oxford was, to use Peter Berger's term, "ecstasy," that giddy, disorienting sense of liberation that comes from "stepping outside . . . the taken-for-granted routines of society" (1963: 136). It was not so much a case of the volunteers *choosing* to take this step, as being compelled to do so by virtue of their contact with a project staff that had itself become more radical and alienated as a result of three long years of struggle in Mississippi. If ever a group embodied the risks and rewards of an "ecstatic" way of life, it was the SNCC veterans. The volunteers were clearly fascinated by them and drawn to the way of life they represented. One volunteer interviewed by Sarah Evans (1980) "claimed that the first night of the orientation session in Oxford changed her life 'because I met those SNCC people and my mouth fell open' " (quoted in Evans, 1980: 70). In a letter home, another volunteer, Margaret Aley, described the SNCC staff in equally glowing terms:

I've never known people like them before; they are so full of heart
and life. They are not afraid to show their emotions, they cry when
they are sad; they laugh and dance when they are happy. And they
sing; they sing from their hearts and in their songs they tell of life,
struggle, sadness and beauty. They have a freeness of spirit that I've
rarely seen. But I think that's because they don't worry about maintaining the status quo. When we arrived here Saturday, I had a feeling that I didn't belong . . . [Now] somehow I feel like I've found
something I've been looking for for a long time. I feel like I've finally
come home. I now have no doubt that I belong here.[1]

Ruth Steward put the matter a bit more succinctly. In a letter to her parents, she explained that "you can always tell a CORE or SNCC worker—
they're beautiful."[2] What these statements betray is a growing identification with the activist community and with a way of life that would later
be dubbed the "counterculture."

Other aspects of the orientation sessions also reinforced this sense of
identification. For many, the legions of reporters and television camera-
men swarming over the campus had that effect. Their presence communicated a sense of "history-making" significance that was intoxicating.
Not that the hypocrisy and sensationalism of the media was lost on the
volunteers. This too was a part of the radicalizing process they were undergoing. In her beautiful book describing the Freedom Summer experience, another volunteer, Sally Belfrage (1965: 23–24), wrote of how the
media

followed us into the classrooms and dormitories, around the lounges,
out along the paths. They asked people to sing that song again for
the American public. There was footage, yardage, mileage of every
face in the place. "At the beginning it made me feel important," a
boy from Utah said at lunch. "But they have a way of degrading
everything they touch." "It's because we need them more than they
need us," his neighbor returned, "and they know it." "It's just their
job," commented a third. "Well, I feel unclean," the boy from Utah
said.

Degrading or not, the volunteers' letters home are filled with entreaties
to parents to "save the *Life* magazine picture for me," or to "watch CBS
tonight; I may be on." Degrading or not, the media attention clearly reinforced the volunteers' sense of their own and the project's importance.

More than anything else, however, it was the volunteers' growing appreciation of the dangers inherent in the project that had the greatest
impact on them. If they had not realized the extent of these dangers before orientation, they certainly did by the time they left Ohio. This was

no accident. In planning the sessions, one of the overriding goals had been to overwhelm the volunteers with the savagery and violence of life in Mississippi. It was hoped that by doing so, the staff might be able to persuade the naive or those with lingering doubts to stay home. So in session after session, staff members recounted the litany of horror they had seen in Mississippi. In turn, the volunteers duly recorded these sessions in their journals or letters home. Margaret Rose wrote:

> Last night's objective narration of facts is shot to hell by a breakdown in my defensives against fear and intimidation. The straw to break the back was the narration of a white leader here (a face mangled by scars) about a near death experience on the road coming up here. Fifteen guys in 3 cars ran them off the road (normal) and all in the car experienced the intent of the group: murder. It was somehow absolutely clear. A car full of leaders. Too good to pass over. One man, an exchange professor from Pakistan in a Mississippi university, happened to say he was a foreigner and had a passport. Some small doubt cross [sic] the minds of one of the 15. Somehow the mood shifted. They did not murder. He said we could expect this kind of encounter. He means it.[3]

Another volunteer wrote:

> There is a quiet Negro fellow on the staff who has an ugly scar on his neck and another on his shoulder where he stopped 45 slugs. . . . Another fellow told this morning how his father and later his brother had been shot to death. . . . I'd venture to say that every member of the Mississippi staff has been beaten at least once and he who has not been shot at is rare. It is impossible for you to imagine what we are going in to, as it is for me now, but I'm beginning to see. (Quoted in Sutherland, 1965: 7–8)

Role playing sessions and lessons in how to protect oneself if attacked only underscored the growing fear the volunteers were feeling. A volunteer described the general response to one such session: "John Strickland [a volunteer] stood ashen, staring at the lad curled up on the ground. Like the rest of the crowd, he was silent. Their eyes stayed riveted to the frozen tableau of a violence that till that moment had existed for them only in grade-B movies and tabloid spreads" (Sugarman, 1966: 29).

But no planned simulation could ever have dramatized the dangers of Mississippi life more forcefully than the real life event that took place in Neshoba County, Mississippi, on June 21, just as the second group of volunteers were arriving at Oxford, Ohio. Less than twenty-four hours after arriving in Mississippi, one in the first group of volunteers, Andrew

Goodman, climbed into a station wagon with staff members James Chaney and Michael Schwerner, and drove off to investigate a church bombing near Philadelphia, Mississippi. They never returned. Arrested in the afternoon on traffic charges, the three were held until the evening, and then released into the Mississippi night. It was the last time they were seen alive. Their burned-out station wagon was found near Bogue Chitto Swamp the next day. But it was not until August that the bodies were discovered beneath an earthen dam near Philadelphia: Chaney's showed signs of a savage beating, and Goodman's and Schwerner's, single gunshot wounds to the chest.[4]

Back at Oxford, news of the disappearance reached the volunteers during a general assembly. Sally Belfrage (1965: 11–12) describes the scene:

> There was an interruption then at a side entrance: three or four staff members had come in and were whispering agitatedly. One of them walked over to the stage and sprang up to whisper to Moses, who bent on his knees to hear. In a moment he was alone again. Still crouched, he gazed at the floor at his feet, unconscious of us. Time passed. When he stood and spoke, he was somewhere else; it was simply that he was obliged to say something, but his voice was automatic. "Yesterday morning, three of our people left Meridian, Mississippi, to investigate a church-burning in Neshoba County. They haven't come back, and we haven't had any word from them. . . ." Then a thin girl in shorts was talking to us from the stage: Rita Schwerner, the wife of one of the three. She paced as she spoke, her eyes distraught and her face quite white, but in a voice that was even and disciplined . . . Rita asked us to form in groups by home areas and wire our congressmen. . . . We composed telegrams, collected money and sent them, and tried to rub out the reality of the situation with action. No one was willing to believe that the event involved more than a disappearance. It was hard to believe even that. Somehow it seemed only a climactic object lesson, part of the morning's lecture, an anecdote to give life to the words of Bob Moses. To think of it in other terms was to be forced to identify with the three, to be prepared, irrevocably, to give one's life.

Word of the disappearance did, in fact, force the volunteers to confront the possibility of their own deaths. Some, like Stuart Rawlings, did so dispassionately:

> What are my personal chances? There are 200 COFO volunteers who have been working in the state a week, and three of them have already been killed. I shall be working in Forrest County, which is reputedly less violent than Neshoba County. But I shall be working

on voter registration, which is more dangerous than work in Freedom Schools or Community Centers. There are other factors which must be considered too—age, sex, experience and common sense. All considered, I think my chances of being killed are 2%, or one in fifty.[5]

Others expressed their fears more emotionally. "The reality of Mississippi gets closer to us everyday. We know the blood is going to flow this summer and it's going to be our blood. And I'm scared—I'm very scared."[6] In the face of these fears and mounting parental pressure a few of the volunteers did leave for home. The vast majority, however, stayed. And with the decision to stay, their commitment to the project and attachment to the "beloved community" grew as well. By week's end the combination of fear, history-making media attention, exposure to new lifestyles, and sense of political mission that suffused the project had produced for many the type of transcendent, larger-than-life experiences that would bind them to the movement for years to come.

June 25

It happened today. . . . We were all watching the CBS TV show—about 100 of us . . . Walter Cronkite told how the whole country was watching Mississippi. And then the television was singing our freedom song, "We shall overcome, we shall overcome. . . ." So we all joined hands and sang with the television. We sang with all our hearts—"justice shall be done . . . we shall vote together . . . we shall live in freedom . . ." and then someone said, "Everyone hum softly," so we hummed, and a Negro by my side spoke . . . "You know what we're all doing. . . . We're moving the world. We're all here to bring all the people of Mississippi, all the peoples of this country, all the peoples of the world . . . together . . . we're bringing a new revolution of love, so let's sing out together once again now, everybody hand in hand. . . ." "Deep in my heart, I do believe. Oh . . . we shall overcome some day." Stunned, I walked alone out into the night. Life was beautiful. It was perfect. These people were me, and I was them. Absolutely nothing came between us, as our hearts felt the call to work toward a better world . . . I felt that I could and would devote my life to this kind of revolution. Alleluia.[7]

June 20

We just saw off two chartered bus-loads . . . of kids headed south. It was an incredibly moving experience. The buses pulled up and all belongings were piled aboard. But the kids refused to follow them, and we all stood in a large circle along side one bus and sang "We Shall Overcome"—SNCC-style—i.e. with arms crossed, holding hands. Then the departing kids got aboard, and along [sic] period of farewells through the windows began. All this time, black clouds were

massing on the horizon. The sky was angry and threads of lightning
flashed occasionally: it seemed like a bad omen. Finally, the bus
motors started up and the buses began to move forward. Kids were
hanging out the windows kissing and hugging their friends from the
moving bus. It was a strange [combination] of children headed for
summer camp and soldiers going off to war. Finally the buses gathered speed and left us behind. Wordlessly, as if pulled by some
strong magnet, we silently formed a circle and, joining hands, sang
"We'll Never Turn Back" very slowly and solemnly. Afterwards, we
broke up silently and moved apart. Overhead, the . . . sun . . .
burst . . . through the clouds.[8]

June 30

Friday evening the conference met for one last time as a whole.
After discussing security regulations, Bob Moses . . . got up and
spoke to us. He spoke of his fears and his weariness, of the burden
he carries because of the workers who have been killed in Mississippi
and because he knows that the probability is great that more will be
killed. . . . He shared with us his burden of having to send us in
knowing that he was sending some of us to our death.

The group was very still as each person watched his leader bare
his soul to the group. When Bob finished, a girl's voice rose up singing . . . "They say that Freedom is a long, long struggle." Slowly
the voices in the room joined in. We stood with our arms around
each other and we sang for each other. I stood between a boy I knew
from Morehouse and a girl I knew from Carleton. And I felt the boy
reach across behind me and hold the girl as well as me. I felt his love
go through me whom he knew and loved to a girl he did not know
well but whom he loved also. On the other side of this girl stood a
woman who had taught at Spèlman whom I knew and loved and
who gave her love to this girl she did not know. . . .

The group sang in one voice, each individual singing not for
himself but for the group. Tears ran down many faces. . . . As I
sang . . . I knew better than ever before why I was going to Mississippi and what I am fighting for. It is for freedom—the freedom to
love. It is something that no one can have until everybody has it.[9]

In the vernacular of the movement, the volunteers had had their first
taste of "freedom high."[10]

Buoyed by that high, the volunteers left Oxford and headed South.
Some traveled by car, but the majority went by bus. One of the volunteers interviewed said that the bus ride down was "the only time during
the entire summer I had a chance to step back and reflect on what was
happening."[11] Afforded the same opportunity, another volunteer, Paul
Cowan, recorded the following thoughts:

[I]t is one o'clock and our bus, inconsequential to whoever observes it, is traveling down a Tennessee road, far into the country. I have always thought that between the hours of one and three a.m. America comes closest to realizing her promise. There is a true unity between all her travelers sharing, for the particular night, a lonely vigil, a personal responsibility for their land. But it was at this hour six days ago that Mickey, James and Andy disappeared on the frontier of Mississippi. And it was Americans who apparently captured them, men who speak the same language, sing the same anthem, fight in the same wars as those of us on this bus. We all inhabit the same night in the same land, but somehow that is not enough.[12]

By whatever means the volunteers traveled, neither the fears activated in Oxford nor the media were ever far behind. Both grew more active as the volunteers reached the state.

Last Saturday four of us took the long ride from Oxford to Memphis in a small Corvette which was rigged with a mike so a CBS sound car behind us could record our profound thoughts as we went into battle. . . . I felt quite relaxed during most of the 14 hour drive. Mississippi seemed very remote! At midnight we pulled up to a Howard Johnson's Motel just a few miles from the border . . . the feeling that we were in enemy territory swept in on me.

Sunday morning after the dead sleep of exhaustion, I awoke with fear gripping my gut. I had a hard time forcing down breakfast. At 10 a.m. we left for . . . Ruleville. When we got to the state line, the camera car told us to stop at the side of the road while they went to set up a shot at the big sign that welcomes tourists to the Magnolia State. Waiting there as cars streamed past with their occupants craning their necks to look at us, we got quite spooked. We finally got the go-ahead but then had to go back past the sign for a second run. (Quoted in Sutherland, 1965: 36)

Those volunteers who entered the state without benefit of a media escort had their share of anxious moments as well.

My eye moved once more to the mirror, once more to the road ahead, once more to the shivering needle of the speedometer. Once more I eased to fifty-five, and for the first time I was beginning to feel the tension in my neck. The car approaching moved out of the overheated light and turned out to be a green Ford pick-up truck. Two white men wearing wide, straw farmer's hats studied our license and squinted at us as the truck whooshed past. As I read my mirror, the man next to the driver turned and watched us move away. (Sugarman, 1966: 37)

By and large, however, the volunteer's entrance into Mississippi proved a bit anticlimactic. "Hell, off what we'd heard at Oxford, I figured there'd be road blocks or something. It was a bit disappointing."[13] Having made it behind "enemy lines," some of their initial fears drained away, and the volunteers began to size up their new environs. For those raised in the big cities of the North and West, it could be a strangely beautiful world, heightening the ecstatic state they were already in.

> The countryside is magnificent. Along sides of the road red clay banks tower up to 10 feet and over them drap [sic] long green vines. There is a special vine with round leaves that grows over everything else. The panorama thus looks rounded and makes the environs feel like a stage set for a fantasy.[14]

> Flat, endless Delta land of cotton, straight two-laned road, monotony, with only an occasional miserable shack to interrupt a landscape that was a visual forever. . . . A very few of them had flower gardens and a little tree, attempts at brightness, but by most the cotton grew to the door and the houses simply sagged as though about to melt into the ground. Shimmering in the heat mirage, they looked utterly insubstantial and invented. Dark men and women lazed on the tilting boards that were porches, or hacked at the dry dirt . . . SAVE OUR REPUBLIC! said a billboard, IMPEACH EARL WARREN! alone among miles of the pale, heat-colored earth, where the little plants grew, not a foot high. Another billboard shouted KILLS 'EM FAST! KEEPS 'EM DYING! and only abreast of it could you see the smaller print above, advertising a boll weevil pesticide. At a cross-roads, pointers to towns named Savage, Coldwater, Alligator. . . . There was nowhere that litter of neon, billboards, and gas stations, the identical sleep-and-eateries that negate distance and make American highways so much the same as each other; the country was foreign, resembling Spain or Syria or anywhere where heat and poverty combine to overwhelm attempts at the streamlined. Only at the outskirts of Greenwood did the asphalt widen, lines straighten, and ads for the Holiday Inn flash out America again. (Belfrage, 1965: 31–32)

Only in the larger towns and cities did the volunteers find hints of the America they knew. The downtown commercial districts and prosperous white neighborhoods of places like Jackson, Hattiesburg, Greenwood, and Biloxi bore at least some resemblance to places they had known before. But it was not in white Mississippi that they would be living.

> [W]e crossed the tracks, and for a block or two the wiry, cheesy commercial atmosphere remained but as a cheap exaggeration of itself;

then the pavement bellied out and sidewalks disappeared or fell away in broken pieces: Niggertown. Rows of shanties perched on stones and bricks and jammed together in precarious asymmetry. . . . The hot, end-to-end living sent the people out into the streets, where children, watched by parents on the porches, roamed barefoot. . . . (Belfrage 1965: 33)

As bleak as the landscape was, the reception accorded the volunteers was warm and celebratory.

Batesville welcomed us triumphantly—at least Black Batesville did. Children and adults waved from their porches and shouted hello as we walked along the labyrinth of dirt paths and small wooden houses. . . . We had been warned to expect fear and hostility, but we were immediately invited to live and eat in Negro homes and to speak in Negro churches. For many local citizens, our coming was a religious event; I found it difficult to be cynical. Sometimes when we pass by, the children cheer. (Quoted in Sutherland, 1965: 42–43)

The volunteers arrived in Mississippi in two waves. The first took place June 20 to 21 as the 250 voter registration workers who had attended the first orientation fanned out across the state. A week later, some 300 Freedom School and community center workers arrived fresh from the second orientation. These two groups formed the backbone of the thirty-two principal projects staffed by COFO (see figure on facing page). The projects were located in all five of Mississippi's Congressional districts, CORE having charge of those in District 4; SNCC the rest. District boundaries represented more than organizing devices. They also helped define natural geopolitical units with very different potentials for violence. Relatively speaking, the safest spots in the state were in the Fifth Congressional District. Here the majority of projects were located in Gulf Coast towns dependent on the tourist trade. At the opposite extreme was District 3. Especially dangerous was the southern half of the district, where a history of racial violence and Klan strength limited COFO activity to a small operation in Natchez and a beleaguered project in McComb. Over the course of the summer, the McComb area would suffer more than two-thirds of all the bomb attacks directed at the Summer Project (Harris, 1982: 61).

The size of the projects varied as much as the danger associated with each. The largest projects might have as many as fifty workers assigned to them. As an example, Stuart Rawlings listed forty-nine volunteers in Hattiesburg as of July 4. The breakdown of these volunteers was as follows: twenty-one Freedom School teachers, twenty voter registration workers, five community center personnel, and three office workers.[15]

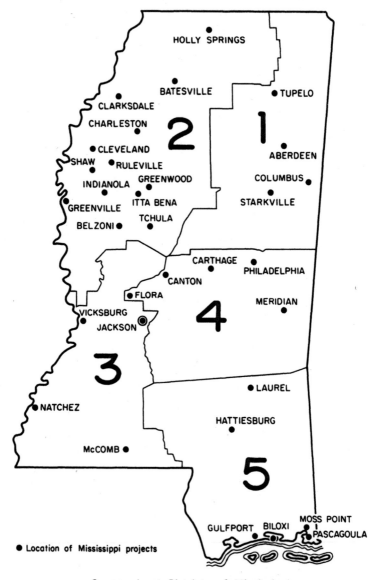

HOLLY SPRINGS

BATESVILLE • TUPELO

CLARKSDALE
CHARLESTON 2 1

CLEVELAND ABERDEEN

SHAW RULEVILLE
INDIANOLA GREENWOOD COLUMBUS
ITTA BENA STARKVILLE
GREENVILLE TCHULA
BELZONI

CARTHAGE
PHILADELPHIA
CANTON
FLORA MERIDIAN
VICKSBURG 4
JACKSON

3

LAUREL

NATCHEZ HATTIESBURG

McCOMB

5

GULFPORT BILOXI MOSS POINT
PASCAGOULA

• Location of Mississippi projects

Congressional Districts of Mississippi

Principal Local Freedom Summer Projects (From Sutherland, 1965: 66)

Other projects, however, were staffed by as few as two volunteers.[16] Neither was the number nor personnel composition of the projects set for the entire summer. Volunteers came and went while both the total number of projects and workers rose between June and August. The ranks of the 550 early arrivals were supplemented by an estimated 400 to 450 additional volunteers who continued to arrive in the state until well into August. Whenever possible, the new arrivals were given a brief weekend orientation in Jackson, and then assigned to whatever project was in need of their services.[17] In this way, personnel attrition was offset by a steady stream of newcomers. Still, there were probably never more than 600 or so volunteers in the state at any one time, only slightly more than the number of workers who began work in June.

The same general pattern holds true for the number of projects. An August 25 accounting by the communications office in Jackson showed twelve additional projects in operation besides the thirty-two identified earlier.[18] For the most part, these new projects represented small operations spun off from the largest ones. Appendix C provides information on the size, project composition, and level of activity of all forty-four of these projects.

Appendix C also hints at the relative importance of the three principal components of the Summer Project. These were (1) voter registration, (2) the Freedom Schools, and (3) the community centers. Only two of the forty-four projects failed to have a voter registration program. Thirty of the projects organized Freedom Schools and twenty-three staffed community centers. The vast majority of the volunteers, however, were assigned either to teach in the Freedom Schools or to do voter registration work.

Voter Registration

Voter registration was the cornerstone of the Summer Project. This is not to say that it was necessarily the most important part of Freedom Summer. However, it did supply the strategic impetus to the project. It was the success of the Freedom Vote campaign in the fall of 1963 that led SNCC and COFO to approve Bob Moses' plan for an even more ambitious political project the following summer. Originally, the plan was simply to use large numbers of white students—à la the Freedom Vote—to register as many black voters as possible. However, as long as the state Democratic party was effectively closed to blacks, it was unclear how beneficial the simple registration of voters would be. To address the problem, SNCC spearheaded the establishment of the Mississippi Freedom Democratic Party (MFDP) at a meeting held in Jackson on April 26, 1964. The MFDP then selected and ran a slate of candidates in the June 2 Democratic Primaries for Senator and three House seats. Not surprisingly, all four of the MFDP candidates (Fannie Lou Hamer, Victoria Gray, John Houston, and the Rev. John Cameron) were soundly beaten. So, following the primary, they obtained and filed the necessary number of signatures to be placed on the November ballot as independents. The Mississippi State Board of Elections rejected these petitions. Thus stymied, the SNCC/MFDP leadership returned to the strategy that had served them so well the previous fall. If they were to be shut out of regular electoral politics in the state, they would conduct a mock election to challenge the Mississippi Delegation to the August Democratic National Convention to be held in Atlantic City.[19]

For the volunteers, this meant they would be involved in two parallel tasks: persuading blacks to attempt to register as official voters and "freedom registering" voters on behalf of the MFDP. Freedom registration forms could be filled out in the applicant's home; official registration meant a trip to the courthouse. That made the latter process the much more difficult of the two. Neither, however, was easy.

> Canvassing is very trying, you walk a little dusty street, with incredibly broken down shacks. The people sitting on porches staring away into nowhere—the sweat running down your face! Little kids half-naked in raggy clothes *all* over the place—this is what you face with your little packet of "Freedom Forms". . . . Unfortunateley [sic], Freedom registration is terribly [sic] remote to these people. I almost feel guilty—like I'm playing for numbers only; . . . you walk up to a porch, knock on a door and enter into another world. . . . The walls are inevitably covered with a funeral hall calendar, a portrait calendar of President Kennedy, old graduation pictures. Maybe a new cheap lamp from Fred's dollar store.
>
> You meet an afraid, but sometimes eager, curious face—one which is used to . . . saying "Yes Sir" to everything a white man says. . . . You see their pain, the incredible years of suffering etched in their worn faces; and then if you convince them to sign you leave. You walk down the deteriorating steps to the dirt, to the next house— the next world and start in on your sales pitch again, leaving behind something which has broken you a little more. Poverty in the abstract does nothing to you. When you wake up to it every morning, and come down through the streets of it, and see the same old man on the ground playing the accordian [sic], the same man selling peaches out of [a] basket to [sic] heavy for his twisted body, the same children, a day older—a day closer to those men—after this everyday, poverty is a reality that is so outrageous you have to learn

to . . . become jaded for the moment—or else be unable to function.[20]

I work in voter registration. . . . On a normal day we roll out of bed early in the morning. We may have slept in the Freedom House, or in the home of some generous and brave farmer. . . . We study the map of the county, decide where we will work for the day. We scramble for breakfast and hit the road.

The work is long and hot. We drive from farmhouse to farmhouse. I have averaged almost 200 miles a day in the car. The roads are in despicable condition . . . where the pavement stops the Negro sections are likely to begin. And if there is not even gravel on the roads, we can be reasonably sure that we are in a "safe" neighborhood. Such is not always the case, though, and more than once we have been cursed and threatened by someone for knocking on a white man's door.

When we walk up to a house there are always children out front. They look up and see white men in the car, and fear and caution cover their expressions. Those terrified eyes are never quite out of my mind; they drive me as little else could. Children who have hardly learned to talk are well-taught in the arts of avoiding whites. They learn "yassah" as almost their first words. If they did not, they could not survive. The children run to their parents, hide behind them. We walk up, smile, say howdy, and hold out our hands. As we shake hands I tell them my name. They tell me their names and I say Mr. ———, how do you do. It is likely the first time in the life of this farmer or housewife a white man has ever shaken hands with them, or even called them "with a handle to their names." This does not necessarily bode well with them; they are suspicious. Chances are they have heard about the "freedom riders" passing through. The news is usually greeted with mingled fear, excitement, enthusiasm and gratitude. But the confrontation is more serious and more threatening. They think, if Mr. Charlie knew . . . , and they are afraid. They have good reason to be. . . . Many . . . are sharecroppers, who must turn over a third to a half of the year's harvest to a man who does not work at all, but who owns the land they till. They may be evicted, and have often been for far less serious offenses. Nearly everyone black in Mississippi is at least a year in debt. The threat of suspended credit and foreclosure is a tremendous burden.[21]

But the work could be rich and rewarding as well.

I have met some of the most amazing, great people among my canvassees. Out of nowhere, seemingly, come little old women with so much warmth and wisdom that I almost cry. . . . Yesterday, around

7 p.m. I marched up on the steps of a dark little falling apart house. Mrs. Brotherns—the lady of the house . . . invited me in. . . . She was already registered, but her husband was not. He was a beautiful man of about 59, great masses of graying hair and completely beardless face. He was crippled with arthritis and thus could not write and could not read either. . . .

It was really quite beautiful. Just then it began to pour and the pageant continued inside—in a small dark room, lighted only by a brief flame in the fireplace, where Mrs. Brotherns was cooking dinner. The three adopted children sat on the floor and read from their school books or counted . . . bottletops, while the two old people looked on with love. The whole scene was from another century—especially because the little boy had a self-made bow and arrow, bent from a stick and tied with some cord. He proudly shot an arrow into the bushes across the street as I watched.[22]

One day when I was canvassing I met Mr. Brown. I told him my name is Ann. He said yes, Miss Ann, pleased to meet you. He is a young Negro teacher in the all-Negro Temple High School and of course he had no contact with white people before, except as Mr., Mrs., "Massa,"—well, I said, please call me Ann . . . there was nothing so beautiful as the rest of the conversation. At every opportunity he had, he said Ann—he didn't just say Ann—he rolled the name around his tongue, savored the taste and sang it, listening to the echo in the back of his mind. He played with the word as a child would play with a new and fascinating toy, as a person would delight in the ecstasy of a new-found love. And that conversation has left a mark on me. I hear the name—a loved word—the start of something so big, so beautiful, so new. (Quoted in Sutherland, 1965: 49)

Whether the volunteers were trying to persuade someone to register or signing up people for the MFDP, canvassing represented only the first step in a larger process. Having persuaded someone to attempt to register, there was still the matter of a trip to the courthouse. For blacks, this was a momentous and potentially dangerous act, a public challenge to the established order, and an invitation to violence or economic reprisals. For the volunteers it was a further test of their powers of persuasion.

At about 9:30 [A.M.] two of us COFO workers drive to the houses of three or four people who want to register to vote. The car's driver is usually a local man who has volunteered to take people to the courthouse. I, or another COFO worker, would knock on the door, be invited in, and then ask how does the applicant feel. Usually he says "fine," but then offers some small excuse for not going—meeting some unexpected guests, doing chores, etc. At this point I often ignore the excuses and . . . ask, "Well, how long will it take to get ready? We can pick someone else up and be back for you in about ten minutes. Will that be enough time?" . . . All their excuses usually disappear after this question, and they say they can be ready in about five minutes. I wait at the house and we all drive to the courthouse.[23]

The fact that about 17,000 blacks traveled to the courthouse attests to the persistence of the volunteers and the extraordinary courage of those attempting to register (Carson, 1981: 117). Although only 1,600 of the completed applications were accepted by state registrars, the lonely trips to the courthouse proved to be a major step toward the democratization of voting in Mississippi and throughout the South. The many instances of delay, obstruction, and harassment of the applicants were duly recorded by the volunteers, thus providing the evidence for several important voter discrimination suits. In addition, the inequities uncovered over the course of the summer helped to dramatize the need for legislation and therefore to generate momentum on behalf of the 1965 Voting Rights Act.

Just as important as these formal political consequences was the effect this activity had on the black community. For its part, the white community observed the registration attempts with something more than benign indifference. In many communities, newspaper editors did their share for the old order by printing daily lists of those attempting to register, thereby making the names of the registrants available to anyone who might be inclined to take offense at such a brazen act of defiance. Historically, the publication of such lists had been enough to deter all but the most courageous, or craziest, blacks from trying to register to vote. But as more and more people donned their Sunday best for the trip to the courthouse, a curious thing happened: the daily newspaper lists of those registering to vote were transformed from an effective means of social control into a vehicle for gaining prestige in the black community. As one volunteer proudly noted in a letter home, "in Panola County now the Negro citizens look with pride at their names in the *Panolian;* they point out the names of friends and neighbors and hurry to the courthouse to be enlisted on the honor roll" (quoted in Sutherland, 1965: 87–88).

In the case of the MFDP, the act of registering voters was only the first step in a long process that eventually took black Mississippians and some of the SNCC leadership to the Democratic National Convention and later to the halls of Congress. The road there wound through the same tiered primary process the party regulars were subject to. The process began at the precinct level where all registered voters were free to participate in the election of delegates to a county convention. At the county convention, representatives to a district convention were chosen. The process was then repeated at several district conventions and finally the state convention, with the state delegates electing representatives to attend the National Convention in Atlantic City. The volunteers were involved every step of the way. Not only did they freedom register 80,000 prospective voters, but they served as precinct organizers as well (Carson, 1981: 117). In this capacity, they attended the precinct, county, and district conventions. Their accounts capture the excitement generated by the proceedings:

> The day before yesterday I went to a precinct meeting in one of the poorer sections of town. It was a very moving experience: about 40 people came, which was far above the expectations of the people who had been canvassing that area; many of them came up after the meeting which was probably the very first experience in their life of democratic procedures, their first inkling of the possibility . . . of any kind of action, and shook our hands, saying "God Bless You." . . .[24]

The delegate selection process reached its climax on August 6 at the state convention in Jackson. There sixty-eight people (including four whites) were elected to represent the disenfranchised voters of Mississippi at the Democratic National Convention in Atlantic City. One of the few volunteers lucky enough to attend the convention described the scene:

> From the floor of the State Convention of the Mississippi Freedom Democratic Party: This is the most exciting, moving, and impressive thing I have ever had the pleasure of witnessing—let alone be a part of.
>
> Miss Ella Baker presented a very stirring keynote address. . . . Right after Miss Baker's speech, there was a march of all the delegates around the convention hall—singing Freedom Songs, waving American flags, banners and county signs. This was probably the most soul-felt march ever to occur in a political convention, I felt, as we marched with a mixture of sadness and joy—of humility and pride—of fear and courage, singing "Go Tell It on the Mountain," "Ain't Gonna Let Nobody Turn Me Round," and "This Little Light of Mine." You would just . . . have to be here to really feel . . . what this means to the people who are here. (Quoted in Sutherland, 1965: 212–214)

A few of the volunteers would travel on to Atlantic City to support the convention challenge. For most of the volunteers, however, the state convention marked the end of their involvement in the summer's political program. It had been a powerful experience, one marked by personal discovery as well as political education. The lessons learned, skills developed, and identities formed in the process would affect the evolution of the New Left for years to come.

Freedom Schools

In planning for the Summer Project, the SNCC staff was smart enough to realize that the oppression of Mississippi's black population depended on more than restricting access to the political system. An elaborate array of caste restrictions and institutional inequities also contributed to the maintenance of the racial status quo. Among these was Mississippi's separate but clearly unequal school system. As noted in Chapter 1, state educational expenditures in 1964 averaged $81.66 per white student and $21.77 for each black student. The fact that Mississippi was one of only two states without a mandatory education law merely underscored the lack of importance accorded public education. So too did other bits of evidence. At the time of the fall cotton harvest, many of the black schools in the delta were routinely closed to take advantage of the cheap source of labor the students provided. Within the classroom, curriculum content was carefully controlled. State-selected textbooks glorified the "Southern way of life" and made no mention of significant achievements by black Americans. In some districts, school superintendents even forbade the history of the Reconstruction period from being taught in the black schools. The Freedom Schools were an effort to counter the obvious inequities and insidious political messages inherent in this system.[25]

The chief architect of the Freedom Schools was veteran SNCC field secretary Charlie Cobb. Drafted in the fall of 1963, Cobb's proposal called for the establishment of Freedom Schools "to provide an educational experience for students which will make it possible for them to challenge the myths of our society, to perceive more clearly its realities, and to find alternatives, and ultimately new directions for action" (quoted in Carson, 1981: 110). To put the necessary curricular flesh on the bones of Cobb's proposal, the National Council of Churches sponsored a March, 1964 meeting in New York City. There, educators, clergy, and SNCC staff members hammered out a basic curriculum for the schools emphasizing four principal topic areas: (1) remedial education, (2) leadership development, (3) contemporary issues, and (4) nonacademic curriculum (Rothschild, 1982: 95). This basic framework was modified again following the appointment of Staughton Lynd, a history professor at Spelman, as director of the Freedom School program. In a mimeographed packet sent out just before the start of the Summer Project, the prospective teachers were informed that "the kind of activities you will be developing will fall into three general areas: (1) academic work, (2) recreation and cultural activities, (3) leadership development" (quoted in Holt, 1965: 103). In effect, the second and third topic areas designated in the original proposal had been lumped together under the single heading of "leadership development." Judging from the letters and journals written by the teachers, most projects adhered to this modified framework in organizing their Freedom School programs.[26] Most offered a variety of basic courses in "leadership development," or what came to be known as the core curriculum. This consisted of courses in the history and philosophy of the movement, current events, and black history. "Academic work" was represented by nearly as many courses as there were students interested in taking them. Offerings ranged from basic remedial courses in reading and math to a variety of specialized classes in such topics as French, science, dance, and debate. Finally, a variety of "recreation and cultural activities" served to round out the Freedom School program. Among the most notable of these activities were the establishment of student-run newspapers on several projects and the writing and performing of an original play by the students in the Holly Springs project.[27]

By any standard, the Freedom Schools were a success. Where project staff had hoped to attract 1,000 or so students, between 3,000 and 3,500 showed up.[28] This in the face of a lack of facilities, the fears of black parents, and considerable violence directed at the schools. In McComb, seventy-five students showed up for classes the morning after a bomb leveled the church that had been serving as their school. Classes were held on the lawn in front of the smoldering church while younger children played in the ruins. In the small town of Harmony, the volunteers and townspeople set to cleaning up and repairing four abandoned school buildings to be used as classrooms.

> Then the sheriff came with about six white men, who were introduced as the "Board of Education." If they weren't Klan men, then they were at least Citizen Council [a more moderate segregationist group] people. God, they hated us . . . they told us we should not use it [the school building]; it is county property. We told them it was private property. We are getting a lawyer and will fight in court. Meanwhile . . . we will teach in a nearby church and outside. (Quoted in Sutherland, 1965: 114)

Predictably, the court ruled in favor of the "Board of Education." Undaunted, the community erected its own school/community center.

Everyday this week . . . the men of the community hammered and poured cement. At noon, about 7 or 8 women all gathered at the center with fried chicken, fish, salad, gallons of Kool-Aid, and apple turnovers, and served them to the men, we teachers, and each other. It is a thing of beauty to see us all work together. . . . We are a living repudiation of the "too many cooks" theory. It should be up by Saturday, or at latest Tuesday. (Quoted in Sutherland, 1965: 115)

Eventually construction was finished and classes were held in the new building, if only for the final week of the summer.

In the classroom, the volunteers discovered most of the frustrations teachers have always faced. Overcrowding was frequently a problem:

It became evident quite early that we were going to have many more than the expected 75 students. We called Jackson and got a promise of more teachers—at full strength we will have 23. This was when we expected 150 students. On registration day, however, we had a totally unexpected deluge: 600 students! . . . After a while, as they were coming in, it changed from a celebration to a crisis. This is 26 students per teacher—much better than the local or usual ratios, but still not enough . . . to do all we want to in six weeks. (Quoted in Sutherland, 1965: 94)

Complaints about a lack of "educational standards" or "academic discipline" were common as well:

The . . . class tends to degenerate into discussion of anything from standards of Negro beauty to the Marxist view of private property. . . . They are eager to argue, in some ways less eager to learn; some days ago I was attempting to give some minimal account of certain facts, when one of the more brilliant and remarkable pupils, but somewhat headstrong, declared that no offense, but, all this was rather boring, and it would be better if other people got a chance to speak, and if we could have discussions. I often think of the difficulties which . . . we will (for these schools will be continued all year) have in making the transition from this school to one where solid academic discipline must be imposed.[29]

Add to this list the problems of absenteeism, staff dissension, and teacher "burn-out," and one might well be describing the generic teaching experience. But there was a difference. The volunteers also experienced the emotional rewards reserved for those teaching students who are there voluntarily and who are being taken seriously for perhaps the first time in their lives.

I can see the change. The 16 year-old's discovery of poetry, of Whitman and Cummings and above all else, the struggle to express thoughts in words, to translate ideas into concrete written words. After two weeks a child finally looks me in the eye, unafraid, acknowledging a bond of trust which 300 years of Mississippians said should never, could never exist—I can feel the growth of self-confidence. (Quoted in Sutherland, 1965: 97)

The atmosphere in the class is unbelievable. It is what every teacher dreams about—real, honest enthusiasm and desire to learn anything and everything. The girls come to class of their own free will. They respond to everything that is said. They are excited about learning. They drain me of everything that I have to offer so that I go home at night completely exhausted but very happy in spirit because I know that I have given to people. . . . Every class is beautiful. The girls respond, respond, respond. And they disagree among themselves. I have no doubt that soon they will be disagreeing with me. At least this is one thing that I am working towards. They know that they have been cheated and they want anything and everything that we can give them. I feel inadequate to the task of teaching them but I keep saying to myself that as long as I continue to feel humble there is a chance that we might all learn a whole lot together.[30]

In talking to the volunteers today it is clear that they *did* learn a lot from their experience as teachers. Some became more politically radical as a result of the courses they taught or the discussions they had with other teachers. Others altered their career plans because of the satisfaction they had derived from teaching. The schools, then, had an impact beyond the students; the teachers, too, were taught.

Life in the Black Community

While not discounting the time and energy the volunteers expended on their jobs, it may well be that work was the least demanding part of their summer experience. After all there was a certain familiarity about their work assignments. Many of those who taught either were studying to become teachers or had taught before. Those with no teaching experience had at least spent years going to school as students, so the classroom was hardly a foreign place to them. As for the voter registration workers, 76 percent had participated in some form of civil rights organizing prior to the summer.[31]

Very few of the volunteers, however, had had experiences that prepared them for life in the black community. For one thing, few had ever lived in rural areas. Their letters capture a kind of bemused appreciation of the new experiences this afforded them.

> Man, like I don't even believe what I just did. You really had to be there to appreciate it. I took a bath. But no ordinary bath 'cause there's no running water. No, we take this bucket out in the back yard and fill it with water warmed over a fire. It's pitch black so we shine Mr. Clark's truck lights on the bucket. Then I strip down naked and stand in the bucket to wash. That is the way you take a bath around here. (Quoted in Sutherland, 1965: 42)

> [T]here are several [chickens] and several roosters. Roosters have this habit—one sits by the window and at dawn melancholically crows in a refrain reminiscent of a man falling off a cliff. The dog outside is just thrilled by this and barks his approval. The rooster thinks about this for a while—then to show he's no party-pooper he lets go again. This sends the dog in to sheer ecstasy. A little while later they pal it up and do a duet. By this time I usually wake up for the third time convinced that someone is being murdered at the foot of my bed.[32]

More significant and more sobering than the volunteers' introduction to rural life was their exposure to "the other America." The publicity accorded Michael Harrington's 1962 book of the same name may have made the volunteers intellectually aware of poverty, but their class advantages had insulated them from any real experiential understanding of the problem. No such comfortable distance was possible in Mississippi. The volunteers' generally optimistic, idealistic upbringing had not prepared them for the underside of the American dream.

> This was the most appalling example of deprivation ever seen by any of us who were canvassing. Upon approaching the house, we were invited on the porch which was strewn with bean shellings, rotten cotton sacks, pieces of a broken stove, and other assorted bits of scrap. . . . On a drooping cot to our right as we came in the door lay a small child (six months old). The child's eyes, nose, and mouth were covered with flies. Not being able to stand such a sight, I tried to chase them away only to be met with the reply of the mother of the child. "They will only come back again."
> The whole house seemed diseased, rotten, and splitting at the seams with infection. Nevertheless, the people knew what we were coming for, and the forms were filled out without our asking. . . . This is a scene that was burned into all of our minds and which will make quiet sleep impossible.[33]

One day has passed in Shaw and the other America is opening itself before my naive, middle-class eyes. The cockroaches draw patterns across the floor and table and make a live patchwork on the bed. Sweat covers my skin and cakes brown in my joints—wrist, elbow, knee, neck. Mosquito bites, red specks on white background.

The four-year-old grandson is standing by my side. I wonder how our presence now will affect him when he is a man?

I saw other children today who bore the marks of the Negro in rural Mississippi. One had a protruding navel the size of the stone he held in his hand. Several had distended stomachs.

Is America really the land that greets its visitors with "Send me your tired, your poor, your helpless masses to breathe free"?

There is no Golden Door in Shaw. (Quoted in Sutherland, 1965: 54–55)

These images had a powerful impact on the volunteers, especially those whose upbringing had failed to provide them with even an ideological awareness of the problem. One especially sheltered volunteer, raised in an upper-middle-class suburb of Chicago, remembers "crying myself to bed at night [in Mississippi]. . . . I was just seeing too much, feeling too much. Things weren't supposed to be like this. I was just a mess. I just remember feeling sad, guilty and angry all at the same time."[34]

In the face of these feelings—especially the guilt—the warmth, openness, and acceptance the volunteers felt from the black community was both confirming and confusing at the same time. Confirming because it communicated a kind of redemptive forgiveness that assuaged the guilt many of the volunteers were feeling; confusing because they didn't feel they deserved the special attention they were receiving. It all added up to a rich welter of feelings that left a good many of the volunteers overwhelmed. In a letter to her parents, Pam Parker struggled to communicate all she was feeling:

I am starting to ramble because there is so much in my head and heart that I want to say but cannot. It has been a big week filled with so much enthusiasm and love that I feel overwhelmed. The girls I work with . . . have accepted me completely. They have told me this in a way they have responded in class, and some have told me this directly in their essays they have written me or in actual conversations. . . . This abundance of love and gratitude and acceptance makes me feel so humble and so happy.[35]

Even today this jumble of emotions is evident in the former volunteers' recollections of the summer. Elinor Tideman Aurthur movingly recalled the daily lunchtime ritual at the Freedom School where she taught.

[T]he women from the church everyday would bring food for all the teachers. . . . I used to look forward to it so much, and the fact that they would give this to us everyday, you know, was just wonderful . . . they had fried chicken and deviled eggs and potato salad. . . . They would spread it out on the table and they would, it was so nice [starts to cry] . . . it was so touching . . . to be cared for . . . that [way] . . . I felt like I belonged; I felt like they liked me and they wanted me to be there and I, it was so healing, you know, knowing what the divisions were . . . and yet somehow you can heal . . . I don't mean to say that they idealized us . . . because I don't think they did, but I think there was a kind of love . . . and a kind of compassion for us that they showed. It was a daily demonstration of love and acceptance . . . they were feeding us; they were giving us nourishment.[36]

For many of the volunteers, the most immediate purveyors of this love and acceptance were the families that housed them. Sally Belfrage (1965: 36) describes her introduction to her summer hostess: "[Mrs. Amos] hadn't planned to house summer volunteers, but Cora Lou's guest immediately became to her another child . . . she hugged me, fed me fried chicken and cornbread and installed me in the back bedroom."

Midway through the summer another volunteer described her "home life" to her mother:

I have become so close to the family I am staying with—eleven people—that Mrs. H. finally paid me a great compliment. She was introducing me to one of her Negro women friends and said, "This is Nancy, my adopted daughter!" I baby-sat for her one night and in general we have become very close friends. She is a beautiful mother. My favorite picture of her is sitting peacefully in a summer chair with her 2-year old baby girl in her lap; the baby, sucking her bottle, with one hand inside her mother's dress resting on her bosom. It is such a human sight; such love oozes from this house I can't begin to explain. (Quoted in Sutherland, 1965: 48)

The hospitality of the local families was all the more touching for the risks they ran in housing the volunteers. Sheltering the "invaders" was grounds for harassment, dismissal from a job, or worse. David Gelfand relates an incident that took place while he was living with a prosperous black family in Meridian:

[D]uring the five or six days I was there, there had been numerous . . . threatening phone calls and his [the black homeowner's] wife was quite upset about it. And one morning he came and woke me up. I was sleeping on the couch in the living room. And we had put a single piece of hair on Scotch Magic Tape across the hood, so you always checked before you got in the car. And the tape was broken. He had checked it. And the carport was right next to the kids bed-room—ages four to twelve . . . And so he said, "okay, let's not do anything but release the emergency break and roll it out to the road." And we did that and then opened the hood. And there were four sticks of dynamite tied [to] . . . the ignition coil.[37]

On occasion the volunteers were reluctantly asked to leave following incidents such as this. More often than not their hosts responded with a resiliency and toughness that impressed the volunteers. In his journal, Gren Whitman recounted the following early-morning encounter with the woman in whose house he was living:

I am writing this at 6 A.M. Just now coming down the hall from the bathroom, I met Mrs. Fairley coming down the hall from the front porch carrying a rifle in one hand [and] a pistol in the other. I do not know what is going on . . . [All she said was] "You go to sleep; let me fight for you."[38]

Nor was this volunteer's experience unique. In their journals, letters, or interviews, many of the volunteers recounted similar incidents.[39] For a group not raised around guns, it was yet another eye-opening aspect of the summer, and one that would lead a number of the volunteers to re-think strongly held pacifist convictions.

Besides their "home lives," the volunteers took part in other aspects of black community life. Many volunteers went to church either on their own or with the families they stayed with. For many it was their first real church-going experience. As such, it often proved to be a learning experience for everyone involved.

Today we went to church. It is the only social event around here, and I enjoy it very much. It is a very spontaneous sort of meeting— the music comes from whomever feels like singing. But I admit it felt a little awkward when the lady standing next to me asked what religion I was and I said I was an agnostic, and she asked if we bap-tized or sprinkled in our church?[40]

Even among the volunteers who regularly attended church or temple in the North, few had any experiences that prepared them for the sights and sounds of the rural black church. The cool cerebral propriety of Reform Judaism or the liberal Protestant denominations common to the volunteers—Unitarian, Quaker, Methodist—contrasted sharply with the sweaty immediacy of the Southern black Baptist tradition.

This tradition was also very much in evidence at the weekly mass meetings, held to generate support for the voter registration drives. Part religious revival, part political rally, the mass meetings were also a social event of the first order. They were an occasion for rekindling the faith of the veterans and attracting new recruits to the cause. They were also a time to celebrate an exuberant and immediate community, the likes of which most of the volunteers had never before seen.

The meeting had begun . . . with freedom songs and Brother Williams, who led a prayer and delivered a short pep-talk. An old man in shirtsleeves, he communicated with the soul of the crowd, arousing their enthusiasm, laughter, or indignation in a Southern patois so impenetrable that it took me half the summer to make out all the words. Biblical verse was stirred in liberally. "Of one blood He made all nations," Brother Williams would quote. "So if those people are so separate, who all these bright [light] Negroes?" The crowd would sway with reaction, in tune with him as they never were with a Northern speaker of either color. "Seem to me the white man done hisself some integratin' at night." . . . "There's a law 'gainst shooting' deer," he would say, pausing. The audience knew what was coming. "There's a law 'gainst rabbit." "Yes, yes," some voices answered. "There's a law 'gainst possum." "That's right." ". . . but it's always open season on Negroes!" They would laugh wryly, as they always did, as though the joke were new. Brother Williams, winding up to a shouting finish, would finally threaten, "If you don' register to vote you goin' to hell, that's all they is to it!" Then he would lead them in a hymn. . . . The moral came through the music and the people gave themselves the message of the meeting. Words could never rival its effectiveness, but there had to be words. [SNCC veteran] Stokely [Carmichael] spoke to them that night, grabbing the tension already built up and manipulating it to give them courage. "We've got a lot to do this summer," he told them. "While these people are here, national attention is here. The FBI isn't going to let anything happen to them. They let the murderers of Negroes off, but already men have been arrested in Itta Bena just for threatening white lives." He urged, cajoled, and ordered them down to Martha Lamb, the registrar of Leflore County and sole judge of the test she administered. Some had been there before, some of them more times, literally, than they could count. "What do we have to do?" Stokely asked. His audience knew. "REGISTER!" they shouted.

There were more songs, and finally we stood, everyone, crossed arms, clasped hands, and sang "We Shall Overcome." Ending every meeting of more than half a dozen with it, we sang out all fatigue and fear, each connected by this bond of hands to each other, communicating an infinite love and sadness. A few voices tried to harmonize, but in the end the one true tune welled up in them and overcame. It was not the song for harmony; it meant too much to change its shape for effect. All the verses were sung, and if there had been more to prolong it, it would have been prolonged, no matter how late, how tired they were. Finally the tune was hummed alone while someone spoke a prayer, and the verse struck up again, "We shall overcome," with all the voice, emotion, hope, and strength that each contained. Together they were an army. Across the room I saw Clara; she had somewhere found a yellow dress to wear. There were tears on her cheeks. (Belfrage, 1965: 52–53, 55)

Nothing embodied the power and appeal of the black community better than the mass meetings. And perhaps no aspect of the summer made so profound or lasting an impact on the volunteers as those sweaty nights in Mississippi's black churches. One volunteer remembers

finding myself in those churches. The thing I remember more than anything is the sweat. It was . . . so therapeutic. I was literally thawing out . . . loosening up, letting go. It was just so different from the way I had been raised; you know, to be proper and demure and all that. . . . It [the release] was just a great feeling. This whole stiff, uptight way I'd been raised felt like it was melting away.[41]

In contrast to the sterile propriety of their Northern upbringings, the immediacy and strong communal base of the black community attracted many of the volunteers. However positive this attraction was, it served only to reinforce the growing sense of alienation from white America that many of the volunteers were beginning to feel. The anger and guilt triggered by the oppression and poverty they were witnessing was already pushing many in this direction. Now what one volunteer termed the "warm, womb-like" appeal of the black community was pulling them in the same direction.[42] There were more profane pulls operating on the volunteers as well.

For every volunteer who fondly remembers church services or prayer meetings, there is another who will wax poetic about the "incredibly funky joints I hung out in that summer."[43] It is as if the traditional tension in the black community between the sacred and the profane are encoded in the volunteer's recollections. The "profane" memories, however, are no less powerful for being voiced a bit more reluctantly. They, no less than the "sacred," capture the exhilarating sense of discovery and adventure that came with the volunteers' exposure to a more sensual way of life. In the interviews, several of the volunteers struggled to describe this way of life and their reaction to it.

[I]t was a constantly sensual experience . . . I mean . . . I was young and impressionable and not very experienced sexually . . . I don't know, it was . . . transporting . . . having sex in a field in the countryside where all you see are stars and I don't know, it just blew my mind. I don't know how to describe it . . . I was frightened by it and awed by it.[44]

[I]t was a real romantic trip. It was heavy and Faulknerian and I was, you know, over-intellectualizing it all, I suppose. But it was really affecting—the kudzu [a vine common to the South] and the heat and the blackness of the black people and the whiteness of the white people, really very pale skin . . . it was so intense.[45]

Later this same volunteer described a typical evening's social routine in Mississippi:

We frequently . . . [did] not eat until very late and [then we'd] go to a little place called Bodina's Cafe and have beer and chicken . . . and greens and grits and stuff and then dance . . . all this great stuff on the juke box . . . and we danced in the back and we drank a lot of beer by the quart. It was great . . . and a lot of it was very intense. A lot of romances . . . very sort of free that way.

The theme of sexual liberation runs like a subterranean current through the volunteers' letters, journals, and interviews.[46] It was not yet the full-blown ideology of "free love" that was to take hold a few years later; social action and personal—including sexual—liberation were still seen as incompatible by many. Instead it was a discrete, often tentative experimentation that anticipated the explicit connection between personal and political liberation made later in the decade.

Although the extent of sexual activity on the Summer Project might surprise some people, its occurrence has previously been discussed by a number of authors (c.f. Evans, 1980; Harris, 1982). Neither the fact nor extent of this activity, however, seems especially surprising when one considers various aspects of the project. Perhaps the most important of these was simply the ideology espoused within SNCC, emphasizing the notions of freedom and equality. The project was held to be the living embodiment of that ideal; the "beloved community" that would serve as a model of what a true egalitarian society was to be like. The members of that community were expected to be free; free from the restraints of racism and consequently free to truly love one another. For many volunteers, then, interracial sex became the ultimate expression of this ideology, conclusive proof of their right to membership in the "beloved community." As Harris (1982: 67) observed, "the coupling was considered not so much license as one more small expression of a liberation that was taking place on all fronts."

The physical proximity of the volunteers to one another also made sexual experimentation that much more likely. The manner in which the volunteers were housed played a large part in this. Try as they might, project organizers were unable to place all the volunteers in private homes. Given the risk attendant to playing host to one of the "outside agitators," this was hardly surprising. To accommodate the overflow, a number of projects housed the remaining volunteers in the project offices, or in separate "Freedom Houses." Theoretically, only male volunteers were to be housed in this fashion, but the pace of project activities and the multiple uses to which the houses were put soon rendered this arrangement unworkable. Instead, a steady stream of volunteers—female as well as male—passed through the houses at all hours of the day and night. Said one volunteer:

> You never knew what was going to happen [in the Freedom Houses] from one minute to the next. . . . I slept on a cot . . . on a kind of side porch . . . and . . . I'd drag in some nights and there'd . . . be a wild party raging on the porch. So I'd drag my cot off in search of a quiet corner . . . [only to find] an intense philosophical discussion going on in one corner . . . people making peanut butter sandwiches—always peanut butter . . . in another . . . [and] some soap opera . . . romantic entanglement being played out in another. . . . It was a real three-ring circus.[47]

Another recalled the "kind of manic adrenaline high you felt living in the . . . [Freedom House.] You just never came down . . . you never were alone long enough to come down. . . . There was always a million people around."[48] When combined with the frequently electric atmosphere of the houses, the presence of so many people made romantic and sexual entanglements almost inevitable. As David Harris (1982: 67) wrote: "the pace was frantic and adrenaline leaked into all aspects of freedom house life. Among other things, being on the battlefront together led to a level of heterosexual experimentation unavailable in the more regulated college circles from which the COFO workers hailed."

The presence of white women and black men on the projects made such entanglements all the more likely. The reason was simple. Each represented the ultimate sexual taboo for the other. This meant two things. First, that members of both groups would be intensely curious about one another. And second, that the project's ideology of racial liberation would create pressures to challenge these taboos as vestiges of a racist society. Both tendencies were, of course, played out on the project. It seems clear from the interviews that the heaviest volume of sexual activity during the summer involved black men—both locals and project staff—and white women. There was also considerable activity between the white male and female volunteers, but a great deal less so involving white males and black females, and black males and black females. This latter point resulted in serious tensions within SNCC, the repercussions of which will be discussed later. For now, however, it is important to emphasize the powerful dynamics promoting relationships between the white females and black males. Evans (1980: 79) explains:

> For black men, sexual access to white women challenged the culture's ultimate symbol of their denied manhood. And some of the middle-class white women whose attentions they sought had experienced a denial of their womanhood in failing to achieve the cheerleader standards of high school beauty and popularity so prevalent in the fifties and early sixties. Both, then, were hungry for sexual affirmation and appreciation.

As one of Evans's subjects said, "in terms of black men, one of the things I discovered . . . [was] that physically I was attractive to black men whereas I never had been attractive to white men" (quoted in Evans, 1980: 79).

Finally, the danger, tension, and sense of exhilaration the volunteers felt in putting their bodies on the line served as an important aphrodisiac in Mississippi. The relationship between these feelings and sex is nicely captured in the following event recalled by a volunteer working out of Starkville, Mississippi:

> I remember one incident. . . . We were just having a normal kind of meeting in a little corner grocery store . . . and [the police] . . . drove up, a lot of cops, dogs, the whole thing . . . [and they] could have decided to beat the hell out of all of us or shoot us . . . it was . . . the real psychological moment of truth . . . and that moment could have gone either way . . . everybody was very afraid. . . . They told us to break up the meeting and instead we stood our ground . . . outside this little store [and] began to sing and . . . the psychological balance of power . . . [shifted] in our favor and they left. It was moments like that you felt . . . practically an erotic feeling . . . it was sexual in a certain way; you felt so close . . . you loved everybody in that place at that moment. In fact, there was a woman there . . . who I had been after all summer long . . . [but] she had been very cool. . . . The point of the story is that, in fact, I didn't sleep with her that night, but she said, "sure, let's do it." . . . It was a symptom of everything that was happening.[49]

On one level the function of sex in situations such as this can be seen as simple tension release. From the volunteer's account, however, it is clear that it was much more than that. Indeed it would be hard to think of a more sexually potent mixture of feelings than those of tension, fear, excitement, danger, and uncertainty. Add to that the close emotional bond created by external threat and you have all the ingredients for intense sexual attraction. So intoxicating were these feelings that there were even some volunteers who deliberately courted situations that were likely to produce them. In his journal, Stuart Rawlings describes one volunteer who "[walked] through a white neighborhood singing freedom songs at the top of his voice."[50] Another admitted that he "used to cruise through the white section of town at night. . . . Some of it was just wanting to be defiant. . . . But secretly . . . I loved the danger too."[51]

All was not transcendent community and sex under the stars, however. There was a reason why SNCC veteran Cleveland Sellers described Freedom Summer as the "longest nightmare of my life" (Sellers, 1973: 94). The volunteers left Mississippi with their share of scars as well. Perhaps the most frequent source of these scars was the volunteers' confrontations with White Mississippi.

Confrontation with White Mississippi

During the course of the summer, COFO compiled a running chronology of "hostile incidents" (reproduced in Appendix D). The list is twenty-six mimeographed pages long and covers everything from threatening phone calls to the disappearance of the three workers. Oddly, instead of being viscerally powerful, the list is curiously unaffecting. The sheer number of incidents simply overwhelms the reader, leaving one emotionally numb to the specifics of any given incident. A summary of violence during the summer has much the same effect. So that the following statistics:

4	project workers killed
4	persons critically wounded
80	workers beaten
1000	arrests
37	churches bombed or burned
30	black homes or businesses bombed or burned[52]

fail to inform in an emotional sense. To gain some empathetic understanding of these events, one really has to read the volunteers' own accounts of them. Only then does one begin to appreciate the combination of shock, anger, disillusionment, and fear the volunteers felt in the face of the violence and terror they were witnessing.

> I really cannot describe how sick I think this state is. I really cannot describe the feeling in my stomach when I hear a typical story of injustice. . . . I cannot describe the real courage it takes to stay down here. I cannot describe the fears, the tensions and the uncertainties of living here. When I walk I am always looking at cars and people: if Negro, they are my friends; if white, I am frightened and walk faster. When driving, I am always asking: black? white? It is the fear and uncertainty that is maddening. I must always be on guard. . . . When confronted with a crisis, then the action is clearly defined. But when I do not know what to expect, but always know to expect something, then the tensions mount and I think of courage and of how deep my commitment has to be, and I think of getting the hell out of this sick state. I live day to day. I wake up in the morning sighing with relief that I was not bombed, because I know that "they" know where I live. And I think, well, I got through that night, now I have to get through this day, and it goes on and on. Even as I write this letter we are told that our office might be bombed by an anonymous voice, "to get rid of it once and for all." (Quoted in Rothschild, 1982: 59)

> Yesterday while the Mississippi River was being dragged looking for the three missing civil rights workers, two bodies of Negroes were found—one cut in half and one without a head. Mississippi is the only state where you can drag a river any time and find bodies you were not expecting . . . Negroes disappear down here every week and are never heard about. Things are really much better for rabbits here. There is a closed season on rabbits when they may not be killed. Negroes are killed all year round. So are rabbits. The difference is that arrests are made for killing rabbits out of season . . . Jesus Christ, this is supposed to be America in 1964.[53]

> Tonight the sickness struck. At our mass meeting, as we were singing "We Shall Overcome," a girl was shot in the side and in the chest. We fell to the floor in deathly fear; but soon we recovered and began moving out of the hall to see what had happened. . . . When I went out I saw a woman lying on the ground clutching her stomach. She was so still and looked like a statue with a tranquil smile on her face. I ran to call an ambulance. (Quoted in Sutherland, 1965: 119)

While the presence of so many reporters in the state muted the violence to a degree, there was still no shortage of celebrated atrocities. In

Greenwood a local activist, Silas McGhee, was shot in the head while he sat in his car out in front of a local club. Three volunteers raced him to the hospital only to be told they couldn't bring him in because they didn't have shirts on. They had taken their shirts off to bandage Mc-Ghee's head.[54] On the evening of July 8, the front wall of the McComb Freedom House was destroyed by eight sticks of dynamite. Miraculously, the workers sleeping inside sustained only minor injuries.[55] In Hattiesburg, two days later, five voter registration workers (including a rabbi visiting from Ohio) were attacked and severely beaten by two local men armed with lead pipes.[56] And so it went, day in and day out, an endless string of incidents that lent a brutal and frightening texture to the volunteers' lives.

Had the volunteers been in their home states, they would invariably have turned to the police for protection from such incidents. Obviously, this was not practical in Mississippi. Often the police were implicated in the very incidents they were called to investigate. For instance, it turned out that Neshoba County Deputy Sheriff Cecil Price had coordinated the kidnapping and murders of Chaney, Goodman, and Schwerner. Even acting in their official capacity as law enforcement officers, the police spared few opportunities to harass or terrorize the volunteers. The following two affidavits filed by project volunteers recount typical incidents:

> On July 9, 1964 Mary Lane, George Johnson and I accompanied Phillip Moore to the Greenwood Police Station. His purpose was to swear out a warrant against one of the local whites who had beaten him on the street. While Moore was thus occupied in another room, Miss Lane (Negro), Johnson (white) and I waited in the station room. There were three officers present—Desk Sergeant Simpson, Officer Logan and another unidentified officer. Logan was not in uniform—evidently off duty.
>
> Logan took a long knife out of his pocket and started to sharpen it, [directing] a running stream of threats at the three of us. He asked Johnson how he liked "screwing that nigger" (indicating Miss Lane). Then he said, while sharpening the knife: "sounds like rubbing up against nigger pussy." He poked the knife up against my ribs a few times; then he held it out toward me, told me to put my hand on it and asked: "Think it's sharp enough to cut your cock off?" Then he looked at Officer Simpson and said "You'd better get me out of here before I do what I'd like to do." At no time did Simpson or the other officer make any move to restrain him or protect us.
>
> Shortly thereafter, he walked over behind the desk and took out a pistol from his trousers pocket. He brandished it in our direction and

spun the chamber, then tucked it in his shirt front. He walked over to the door. Miss Lane was standing about eight feet from the door in front of him with her back turned to him. He took out his gun again, pointed it at Miss Lane for a few seconds and put it in his pants pocket. Then he opened the door with his left hand and simultaneously reached out and gave Miss Lane a shove with his right fist, knocking her several feet across the room. He swore at her; then Officer Simpson joined in and told Miss Lane: "Nigger, you get your ass away from that door." Miss Lane refused to move, explaining that she wasn't in the doorway, especially since Logan had knocked her practically across the room. Both the officers shouted threats at her, threatening to throw her in jail if she didn't move.

We went out about 15 minutes later and found that the tires of my car had been slashed. We went back in and reported the vandalism to the police but to no avail. (Quoted in Belfrage, 1965: 126–127)

I pulled over and stopped, even though I heard no siren and had no definite knowledge that the following car contained police . . . and waited until the man in the car arrived. He came up to the truck and told me to get out. I asked for identification. He didn't show me anything, but told me to get out of the truck. I got out . . . and he and I walked to his car. Eric also got out and we received a . . . lecture while he was writing a ticket for speeding. . . . A highway patrol car arrived. . . . A third car then pulled up, which was unmarked and contained one man not in uniform. We could tell he had been drinking because of his actions and because we could smell the liquor.

After a short interchange between him and the first man, the first man left and the third man took me back to the car of the highway patrolman. He opened the car and told me to get inside. I got inside and sat on the back seat. He told me to move over and got in. All the doors and windows were shut. He said, "I can't kill you, but you know what I'm going to do to you." I answered, "No, sir." At this time he pulled his gun out of his holster and started to hit me on the head with the gun butt. I put my hands up to protect my head and rolled into a ball on the seat. Over a period of about a minute he hit me about four times on the head and about eight to ten times on the left hand. He also hit me about three times on the left leg, twice on my right hand, and once on my left shoulder. All of this was with the gun butt. . . . Three of them then went up to Eric. They had a conversation with Eric which I could not hear and one of the men raised a gun and struck Eric, knocking him down. He got up and was knocked down again. I had been sitting in the car through all of this. I felt the blood on my face and on my arm. The man who had beaten me then came back to the car and sat down in the back seat. He picked up a flashlight and hit me across the mouth with it. I then rolled into a ball again and he put the gun to my temple and cocked it. He said, "If you move, I'll blow your brains out."[57]

Arrest often held a special kind of terror for the volunteers. As generations of Mississippi blacks had learned, there was virtually no end to the physical and psychological brutality Southern jailers could inflict upon a prisoner. In this the volunteers achieved equality. The police accorded them the same treatment.

> Upon entering [the] cell block we were taken to "nigger bull pen." Then [we] were shoved inside and officers said, "Here they are, get'em boys." This is very unusual practice for whites to be put into the Negro section. The Negroes expressed confusion and fear. They were moved to beat us. Five minutes later, two officers took us into a white cellblock. This was about 12:30 A.M. Wednesday. At the white cell, the officers tried to incite white prisoners to take out their aggressions on the volunteers. ("It's wooping [sic] time.") The officers left and white prisoners gathered about. R——— opened a conversation with one, and eased some of the tension. At this point, a Mexican spoke up and R——— spoke to him in Spanish to help develop a rapport. After several minutes, a Mississippian announced that he hated all niggers and nigger-lovers and that COFOers were there to be beaten by the whites. However he was going to let us go.
>
> We lay down and listened to the argument, that lasted about three hours, on whether or not to beat us up. Sporadically, police officers and trustees would enter argument, attempting to incite white prisoners to "do justice." Morning arrived without real incident.
>
> About 10 A.M. officers took us out of the cell into fingerprinting rooms. As they were fingerprinting and [taking mug shots of] me, the officers told ——— sordid stories about brutality that had been imposed upon fellow COFOers since the day before . . . and that a fellow white girl worker had been brutally raped and was on her death bed. At this point R——— fainted. Upon awakening, the back of his head bleeding, we both were escorted to the lobby where attorneys from COFO in Jackson were waiting. . . . Local police refused to return personal papers, mainly handwritten notes, and denied they had even taken them. . . . In a subsequent interview, FBI agents expressed no interest in the mental harassment which occurred during the 12 hours spent in jail. . . . When taken to jail, R——— had been told he was being arrested on a vagrancy charge. The following morning the sheriff said there were no charges.[58]

Even when nothing happened, the possibility that something might could turn an evening alone in jail into an exhausting experience. In a letter home, William Hodes described his feelings during just such an evening.

> So there I was: alone in a Southern jail. First thing I did was check the layout of the cell in case I had to protect myself. I pulled the mattresses halfway off the beds so that I wouldn't hit any sharp corners as I went down. I planned to stay on one of the beds in the corner, so that I could get between two beds and a wall, and make myself hard to get at, except maybe by kicking. I was very jumpy, and was terrified at every door slam, phone call, and particularly key ring jingle jangle. My pulse was . . . over a hundred the whole three hours or so that I was in jail. . . . Then I was sure they would suddenly decide to drop charges and put me out into the hostile night. That would be really bad, because I knew that trouble was brewing all over the city. I could see the big police wagon outside my cell window, all ready to go. Cops with gas masks and sheriffs with rifles jump into cars and zoom off. I heard dogs barking, police dogs. I figured that I would refuse to leave the station until they gave me a phone call: "You didn't let me have one when I came in, so you might as well give it to me now," I imagined myself saying. Could I hit a cop to get rearrested, or would that beating be worse than the possibility of getting caught by a mob? You can see why my pulse wasn't normal. . . .
>
> I went home to bed, absolutely exhausted. The mental strain of being in there alone was just too much. While I slept, the office was shot into.[59]

The cumulative effect of these confrontations with the enemy was to wear the volunteers down. As the summer wore on, the physical and emotional strain grew progressively worse. "Fear *can't* become a habit," wrote one volunteer to a friend (Belfrage, 1965: 195). But in fact it had. The quality of Mississippi violence—random, savage—necessitated the habit. It was a means of survival. But it was achieved at the cost of physical and psychological exhaustion. Writing late in the summer, Sally Belfrage (1965: 195) acknowledged that "there are incipient nervous breakdowns walking all over Greenwood." Tensions within the projects only added to the strain.

The (Not So) Beloved Community

Given the dangers and difficult living conditions—heat, overcrowding—the volunteers were exposed to, a certain level of tension within the projects was inevitable. In an August 6 letter to her parents, Pam Parker put the matter in sharp relief:

> I am tired, as are most of the other people on the project. We live in an atmosphere of tension caused by outside pressure but intensified by our own [tensions]. . . . I don't think that this problem is particularly unique with our project. . . . One of the boys from the Atlanta group who came to Mississippi stopped by Holly Springs yesterday. He said that one of their hardest problems was the tempers within the group flying at one another. Imagine the frame of mind you would be in after a few days of traveling around the counties, never knowing when the sheriff might decide to stop you and find something to arrest you on or when a car or truck might begin to follow you and attempt to push you off the road. Add to that coming home to crowded living quarters and peanut butter and jelly sandwiches, if there is any bread left when you come in late at night. Also add dusty roads all day long and very hot, humid days. These are the conditions under which [we] work.[60]

The ordinary range of tensions produced by these conditions, however, were supplemented by two other sources of conflict that were to have important ripple effects well beyond Mississippi. In fact, in Mississippi they were little more than undercurrents of tension against the generally harmonious backdrop of the "beloved community." Later, however, the seeds planted in Mississippi and elsewhere would ripen into two very open, very bitter conflicts that would dramatically reshape the face of the New Left and the structure of American society more generally. These conflicts, separately and in combination, centered around the volatile issues of race and sex.

Racial Tensions on the Project

In pure form, the "beloved community" was envisioned as a collection of truly color-blind, loving individuals. Try as they might, the Summer Project would never measure up to this ideal. To begin with, save for a handful of foreigners, all of the volunteers had been raised in an America profoundly shaped by racism. For nearly 350 years the political economy of the Colonies, and later United States, had depended on the labor provided by imported black slaves. To justify the forced enslavement of this population, a thoroughgoing ideology of racial superiority had slowly evolved to become one of the fundamental cornerstones of American popular consciousness. Having been shaped by that consciousness, the volunteers could hardly help but carry the traces of racism to Mississippi with them. They were not so much color-blind as supremely desirous of *appearing* color-blind. The project staff too had been exposed to American racism since birth. But their nightmare experiences in Mississippi during the previous three years had moved them well beyond the attitudes embraced by the volunteers. Many of the staff members had long ago dismissed the practicality of the "beloved community" as an organizational model for civil rights work. Rather than denying racial differences, their experiences in Mississippi had encouraged them to emphasize them. The racial tensions that surfaced during the summer reflect the very different and increasingly incompatible psychologies of staff and volunteers.

At the same time, the racial dynamics of the project only served to exacerbate the conflicts that had already been developing. The immediate sources of tension during the summer were varied. One important source had less to do with the volunteers than it did with white America's reaction to the project. The extraordinary media attention paid the volunteers merely confirmed the depths of American racism. It wasn't black Mississippians or even the abstract concept of civil rights that concerned white America but simply the safety of its sons and daughters. One little remembered incident early in the summer served to place this hypocrisy in sharp relief.

Following the disappearance of the three workers, President Johnson ordered several dozen FBI agents and 400 Navy personnel to Mississippi to aid in the search. In and of itself, this action confirmed the cynicism of the SNCC veterans. No such measures had been taken in the wake of the eight civil rights-related slayings recorded in Mississippi earlier in the year. The worst was yet to come, however. At the height of the search for the three workers, fisherman pulled two mutilated and badly decomposed bodies out of the Mississippi River. There was a brief flurry of media interest in the corpses until it was established that the bodies were not those of the volunteers. The two victims, Charles Moore and Henry Dee, quietly joined the ranks of Mississippi's anonymous black martyrs. Apparently there was nothing newsworthy about the brutal murder of two black men in Mississippi. While the SNCC staff was willing to exploit this hypocrisy and the media attention it insured, it could only have intensified their own anger and hatred toward whites. As the fair-haired objects of all the attention, the volunteers were convenient scapegoats. Not that the volunteers were always innocent victims in the unfolding racial conflict. For their part, a good many of the volunteers brought a kind of "missionary" attitude to the project that only aggravated existing tensions. Hints of paternalism and insensitivity show up with great frequency in the volunteers' letters and journals.

The coordinator—the only Negro among us, left me with mixed feelings. She was practicing openness and full respect for others' ideas and genuine listening, but somehow seemed more to be going through the exercise than [making] a full-hearted commitment. She is not overly literate and showed failings in organization.[61]

The COFO student leader of our project is unfathomable in his ability to not get things done—completely unorganized. The local leadership . . . will be cold to us. This would seem bad, but in reality it is fine with me because I'm on my own in effect, and I've taken on an informal position of leadership.[62]

Several times I've had to completely re-do press statements or letters written by one of them. It's one thing to tell people who have come willingly to Freedom School that they needn't feel ashamed of weakness in these areas, but it's quite another to even acknowledge such weaknesses in one's fellow workers. Furthermore, I'm a northerner; I'm white; I'm a woman; I'm a college graduate; I've not "proven" myself yet in jail or in physical danger. Every one of these things is a strike against me as far as they are concerned. I've refused to be ashamed of what I cannot change; I either overlook or purposely and pointedly misinterpret their occasional thrusts of antagonism. (Quoted in Sutherland, 1965: 202)

It was almost as if some of the volunteers had come to believe the view put forth by the national media; that it was *they* who had come to save the Mississippi Negro. One black volunteer remembers his white counterparts as "generally a good bunch, but there were . . . a few who just came in and wanted to take over. Their attitude was 'okay, we are here, your troubles are over. We are going to put your house in order.' "[63] One volunteer who fits this description recalls the tension that ensued as a result of his "insensitivity":

[The black project director] and I absolutely drove each other crazy because I didn't understand him [and] he didn't understand me. I had all these skills and, you know, worked eighteen hours a day. ———— was real laid back and, of course, was being courted by the local women . . . and I was self-righteous as hell about all this. . . . So I was always after him about being immoral, irresponsible. . . . Hell, he was probably [overwhelmed] . . . by these college kids from the north. I mean, how the hell was he going to compete with that? . . . I just moved in and took over. I mean I wasn't trying to supplant him, I just did. I had absolutely no sensitivity to what that might have been doing. . . . And the more I took over, the more ———— withdrew. [It was] . . . this vicious cycle.[64]

Other blacks reacted to such paternalistic displays with less equa-
nimity and more overt hostility. Sexual interaction often served as a
vehicle for generalized aggression against female volunteers. Volunteers
were subjected to angry tirades or long racial harangues. There were even
isolated incidents of real psychological terror being inflicted on the summer workers. In his journal, Ronald de Sousa described an incident in
which three black workers took a single white volunteer out on a lonely
country road at night and "staged an elaborate show of . . . sell[ing]
him to the Klan for 2000 dollars. They apparently managed to make it
look sufficiently realistic so that the boy was really frightened."[65] While
such occurrences were rare, the hostility that lay behind them was not.
And while most of the volunteers and staff struggled successfully to overcome and manage the tensions created by this hostility, those tensions
nonetheless served as a disturbing undercurrent on the project all summer long. The beloved community was not so beloved after all. Within
a year it would cease to exist at all.

Sexism on the Project

Unlike the overt racial tensions that surfaced during the summer, any
serious concern over sexual discrimination stayed well beneath the surface. It is not that various forms of sexism did not occur, only that
they went unchallenged and largely unrecognized by the female volunteers. As one volunteer, Jan Hillegas, put it, "sexism was not something
that . . . had been made conscious to me at the time, but looking back
on it [Freedom Summer], that's . . . what it was."[66]

The two principal forms that sexism took during the summer involved the issues of sexual politics and discrimination in work. On the
sexual front, women were subjected to considerable harassment and a
clear double standard in sexual behavior. In her interview, one volunteer captured the dilemma nicely.

> It really was your classic "damned-if-you-do, damned-if-you-don't"
> situation. If you didn't [have sex], you could count on being ha-
> rassed. If you did, you ran the risk of being written off as a "bad
> girl" and tossed off the project. This didn't happen to the guys.[67]

In fact, a number of women *were* asked to leave the project for
behavior that was considered unbecoming a project member.[68] The
accounts of these incidents, however, always betray more than a hint
of sexual double standard. In his journal, Ronald de Sousa described
how "some people found it very hard to conform to the necessary discipline . . . in particular one girl was sent home last weekend after

various incidents involving breaches of discipline in the field of social and public etiquette."[69] Not denying the importance of maintaining project discipline in a situation as volatile as Mississippi, it nonetheless remains hard to understand how a female volunteer could have violated "social and public etiquette" without the help of a male. Yet, there is no evidence that any man—staff or volunteer—was removed from any of the projects for sexual (or any other) reasons.

Nor was this double standard evident only in regard to the volunteers. Miriam Cohen Glickman remembers it being applied to project staff, as well.

> I remember huge tensions in the SNCC staff. . . . A lot of it was on who dated who. I remember . . . all these black guys were dating the white volunteers and then one of the black girls . . . had one date one night with a white guy. And I heard that the next morning four black . . . male SNCC staff were over at her house chewing her out.[70]

Apparently it was all right for the male staff and volunteers to be sexually active, but not female staff members. Indeed, a small number of male project staff and volunteers seem to have practiced a form of sexuality that bordered on sexual harassment. One volunteer who was serving as project director for a time remembers having to intervene in one such situation:

> [W]e ran into a problem [with] . . . a white guy; tattooed and kind of a rough character. . . . He was predatory. We had [this] situation: a very attractive woman volunteer came down and he started leaning on her . . . he wanted to get into her pants and he was telling her that she had to [do something]. I forget what the hell it was she had to do, but it involved going some place with him. And it would have been for several weeks. And she didn't want anything to do with this, but it was putting her in a tremendous bind . . . [because] he was physically threatening.[71]

As regards black males, the situation was even more explosive. Their very presence in Mississippi put the white female volunteers "at the center of an emotionally shattering crossfire of racial tensions that [had] been nurtured for centuries" (Poussaint, 1966: 401). Their status as the ultimate sexual symbol of a racist society made the female volunteers targets of a great deal of anger and hostility masquerading as normal sexual attention. Nothing less was at stake in their encounters with black males than the repudiation or reinforcement of racism. This created yet another emotionally and politically charged dilemma for the female volunteers. They could either reject the black male's advances and risk being labeled a racist, or they could go along at considerable physical and psychological cost to themselves.

This is not to say that the female volunteers were always the victims of sexual aggression by black males. Although this may have been the most common dynamic, it was far from the only one. Like the black males on the project, the white female volunteers were bedeviled by complex and often contradictory desires that often prompted them to initiate sexual activity. Some, like a volunteer quoted earlier, found sexual validation in her relations with black men that had been denied by white males. According to SNCC staffer, Mary King (1987: 464), a number of the female volunteers also "found themselves attracted by the sexually explicit manner of certain black men in the local community and also on the SNCC staff. . . . [This] sudden exposure to the sexual frankness of some of the black men meant that a few of . . . [the female volunteers] fluttered like butterflies from one tryst to another." No doubt others encouraged or initiated sexual relations simply because they wanted to experience the forbidden fruits or stereotypic joys of interracial sex. For others, sex became a vehicle for expressing other less sexual needs. According to Rothschild (1979: 481), "sleeping with black men was a way to 'prove' their [the white females] 'commitment' to black and white equality; some women tried to demonstrate their liberalism in that way. It has also been suggested that white women expiated their 'guilt' about racism by sleeping with black men." The point is the white female volunteers were not exclusively passive in their sexual orientation during the summer. They, no less than the black males on the project, had a need to come to terms with the charged emotional legacy of black male/white female relations that was, and remains, such an integral part of racist America. Sex was merely one of the principal means for achieving this.

The imprint of sexism was also clearly evident in the very different work assignments given to the male and female volunteers. Overwhelmingly, the women were employed as Freedom School teachers, clerical workers, or community center staff. The bulk of the "really important political work" was left to the males. It is important to emphasize that these divisions reflect more than simple sex differences in preferences for work assignments. Table 3.1 compares the preferred and actual work assignments of male and female volunteers.

Reflecting the overall importance of the Freedom Schools and voter registration to the project, it is not surprising that the vast majority of volunteers—male and female alike—were concentrated in these two areas. More revealing is the much greater disparity between the preferred and

Table 3.1   Preferred and Actual Work Assignments for Male
and Female Volunteers[a]

	Females				Males			
	Preferred		Actual		Preferred		Actual	
	%	No.	%	No.	%	No.	%	No.
Freedom Schools	48	(68)	56	(196)	37	(80)	33	(151)
Voter registration	22	(31)	9	(31)	32	(69)	47	(212)
Community centers	20	(29)	22	(79)	8	(18)	8	(38)
Communications	6	(9)	4	(15)	9	(19)	4	(17)
Research	4	(6)	6	(21)	5	(11)	4	(16)
White communities	0	(0)	3	(10)	6	(12)	4	(18)
Legal	0	(0)	b	(—)	3	(6)	b	(—)
	100	(143)	100	(352)	100	(215)	100	(452)

[a] The volunteers were asked on the applications to rank order their preferences for summer work assignments. Their actual work assignments were reported on a list of all applicants accepted as of May 30, 1964. This list was copied from the original, which is contained in the archives of the Martin Luther King, Jr. Center in Atlanta, Georgia.
[b] Applicants accepted for legal work were not included in the list from which these percentages were calculated.

actual work assignments given the female volunteers. It is clear that the project staff had a narrower and less political vision of women's, as opposed to men's, role in the project. Part of the logic underlying this vision is entirely understandable. Many on the project staff felt the mere presence of white women on the project was sufficiently threatening to the white community; to have them canvassing door to door was to only court disaster. The overall safety of the project would be better served, it was felt, by placing the women in less visible teaching and clerical positions.

The net effect of this policy was to reproduce traditional sex and work roles on the projects. The men would leave every morning and go off to work while the women stayed around the (freedom) house and cared for the children (students). Then "when they [the mostly male voter registration workers] came home you were to be out of the kitchen; . . . they were tired and they had driven long distances and worked under greater pressure."[72] In the same vein, Sally Belfrage's description (1965: 101–102) of a typical day in the Freedom House begins to sound suspiciously like that of that underappreciated jack-of-all-trades, the everyday housewife.

> It was impossible to be alone. All the other deprivations, the total lack of recreation, relaxation or release, might have been supportable if only there had ever been a chance to be alone. . . . Inside there

were never less than two or three dozen people and children and staff, with constant interruptions and distractions, accumulations of tensions and numbers . . . that one wants a colored marker to make a poster—try to find one but they've all disappeared, the children took them; simultaneous discovery that most of the rest of the office supplies have disappeared as well; nag the man who promised weeks ago to build me a shelf with a lock; a field secretary arrives from Tallahatchie and sits on my desk—talk about what it was like; four children have a battle about who got hold of the book each one wants first—mediate and dry the tears, find a coloring book for the injured party; someone feeling bossy shouts about the children cluttering up the office with their coloring—discuss it, calm it down; a volunteer must go out this minute and hasn't time to see to the mimeographing of some leaflets for canvassing—find Matthew Hughes and give him the stencils; Samuel T. Mills, in an excess of helpfulness, has refilled the air cooler with water so full that it overflows—protect the books and papers being sprayed, mop up the puddle, stop people stepping in it, give Samuel something to do; . . . a voter registration worker has just found a place for the next mass meeting—add it to the big schedule at the top of the stairs . . . someone arrives from the field and has to have his shirt laundered because he's due for an interview with the FBI—wash it or find someone to . . . someone says all the typewriters are broken except the one I'm using and he has a historically important report to get out—give him the typewriter and continue the letter by hand; a volunteer cries that he can't find his spare pair of pants, which were right here last night, he used them as a pillow—see if they have been mixed up with the clothes for local distribution . . . Monroe strides in and denounces me because the library is in such a mess and I never do any work—explain about crowds and arithmetic textbooks, and find out if possible what's really bothering him.

But it was not simply that the female volunteers did different jobs than the males, but that the jobs they tended to do were seen as less important than those the men did. The major distinction here, of course, was between the Freedom School teachers and the voter registration workers. One of the voter registration workers characterized the difference in this way:

> I remember the voter registration workers being different from the Freedom School people. The voter registration workers were predominantly male . . . [and] adventurous, and they really wanted to do the nitty, gritty [work]. The Freedom School people tended to be women and I think . . . with some exceptions . . . tended to be more protective of their persons. . . . So they'd go to a Freedom

School and they'd teach the kids about black history. I think it was a very important part of . . . that summer . . . and yet it wasn't the same kind of, if you want, macho adventurism that I was into.[73]

Not surprisingly, Linda Davis, a former Freedom School teacher remembers things a bit differently:

There was very much a sense [that] . . . voter registration activity was where it was at. And since we had chosen teaching, we were sort of shoved to the side. . . . You know, here [were the] . . . guys running out . . . being macho men . . . you know, "we're going to go out and get our heads busted and we'll come back to here where you nurse us . . . and otherwise service us and send us back out again."[74]

For all the differences between these two views, there is agreement on one fundamental point: when compared to the voter registration workers, the Freedom School teachers were second-class citizens. And to the extent that women were predominantly teachers, they shared unequally in this second-class status. Just as women's work has traditionally been undervalued in society at large, so did it tend to be on the projects.

Reinforcing the reproduction of work and sex roles on the project was a kind of macho competitiveness that pervaded the project, equating status with arrests endured and beatings absorbed. For example, in a letter home, a volunteer who had recently been knocked down while canvassing reported that he was "proud to see my name finally get into . . . the official record of the day's harrassments."[75] Another, upon learning that two members of his project had been severely beaten, admitted that he "felt a sudden envy toward" both of them. "You see," he explained, "when we come down here for the summer, our friends at home all expect us to get beat up or at least have something exciting happen to us. If we have no incidents, our egos suffer no end."[76] This equation of status with violence made voter registration all the more attractive to many male project members. Voter registration was where it was at. Not only was it political and therefore important relative to the "nonpolitical" work the women were involved in, but its highly visible character made it dangerous to boot. These two qualities made voter registration "naturally" a man's, as opposed to a woman's, job.

The difference between these subtle forms of sexism and the racial tensions noted earlier is that the sexism never generated the overt hostility that the racial dynamic did. To the extent that they were recognized at all, these hints of sexism produced little more than a vague sense of resentment on the part of female staff and volunteers. Elinor

Tideman Aurthur remembers feeling that the voter registration workers "were on the front line; . . . they were the ones who were really
in danger and we were the . . . rear support system and I remember
being content to be part of the rear support system, but that there was
also a sense in which I didn't like it."[77] What their summer experiences
had given the female project members was a vague, as yet unnamed,
awareness of sexism that was to play a major role in helping crystallize
an emerging feminist perspective among women in the New Left. It
also gave the volunteers an ideological framework ideally suited to the
construction of this perspective. The basic elements of radical feminism—with its stress on self-determination, community, and empowering
the powerless—were already encoded in the rhetoric and practices of
SNCC to which the volunteers were exposed during the summer. So
the legacy of Freedom Summer for the women's liberation movement
was not simply a matter of negative experience, but positive proscription
as well.

It was perhaps no coincidence then, that the first public feminist
critique to surface in the New Left was written by two female Freedom
Summer participants less than ten weeks after the close of the project.
The critique was one of thirty-seven position papers prepared for a
November SNCC staff retreat at Waveland, Mississippi. By now the
details of the paper and its presentation at Waveland are well known.
The two authors, longtime SNCC staffers Mary King and Casey Hay-
den, submitted the paper anonymously, fearing that it might invite hos-
tility and ridicule from the male staff. Their fears proved well founded.
King (1987: 450) recalls the reception the paper was accorded:

> When the document on women was distributed informally at the
> meeting, the reaction to the anonymous position paper was one of
> crushing criticism. I had been right about the ridicule. People
> quickly figured out who had written it. Some mocked and taunted
> us. . . . As Bertha Gober's freedom song went, I felt as if I'd "been
> 'buked" and I'd "been scorned."

" 'Buked" and "scorned" as they might have been, King and Hayden's
tentatively voiced feminism was not extinguished by the reception given
the paper. A year later they would once again raise the issue, this time
in a memo aimed at "other women in the peace and freedom movement." The second time around King and Hayden would find a much
more receptive audience.

All things considered, it had been a remarkable summer for a remarkable group of people. As it drew to a close, the volunteers found
themselves exhausted and exhilarated in equal measure. There simply

had been no letup in intensity from the time they had arrived at Oxford. For the better part of two months they had been subjected to one emotionally draining experience after another. They had confronted their own mortality, experimented with new lifestyles, reveled in transcendent community, known terror, lived in poverty, felt the sting of racial hostility, and experienced the development of a radical new political consciousness. Theirs was an interesting dilemma. As much as they wanted the psychic barrage to stop, so too did they want the "high" to continue. In letters home the volunteers acknowledged the strong and conflicting feelings they were having:

> All I have to do is sit and the world piles in on me. I would like something simple, to go swimming once, or see a movie, or walk in a field, or go for a drive without having to look out the back window or just to sit somewhere cool and quiet with a friend. Only once might work. . . . I'm simply exhausted. I yell at everybody. No, I don't yell at anyone at all, I only think I do, but I can't. Madness, a constant agitation, unrest. It could all be explained by fatigue. . . . But there's a strange mechanism at work on us at night . . . when the children are gone, the chicken eaten, the mass meeting over, then there are still all of us left to egg each other on, everyone full and fed up with it but somehow longing for the next disaster. . . . All I've got is a fabulous depression, split in two—I can't bear another moment of it but it's impossible to believe that it can end in three weeks. How can I leave? How can I leave people I love so much? What made me think I could accomplish anything in this length of time? There's nowhere else I want to be. (Belfrage, 1965: 195–96)

The volunteers resolved this conflict in very different ways. At least eighty decided to stay in Mississippi indefinitely.[78] While there had been little encouragement from SNCC to do so and no official mechanism set up to retain people, these volunteers were not ready to leave in August. Their letters home reflected both their resolve and the anguish they were causing their families.

> I have been here nearly two months. I know the drudgery, the dangers, and the disappointments. I know what it's like to eat meatless dinners, to be so exhausted you feel as though you will drop, to have five people show up at a meeting to which 20 should have come. Yet I also know what it's like to sing, "We Shall Overcome" with 200 others till you think the roof will explode off the church. I know what it's like to see the organization which you have nurtured come to life and begin to function and create. I know what it's like to have a choir of little girls sing out, "Hi, Ellen," as I walk down the road and envelop me in their hugs.

Only now that I know these things can the decision to stay be mature and meaningful.

Furthermore, maturity does not develop from facing a familiar routine from year to year. Maturity comes from having to face new situations, from making new decisions, from coming to terms with a new world. . . .

This summer is only the briefest beginning of this experience—both for myself and for the Negroes of Mississippi. So much of it will seem pointless if it ends now, or if it is taken up again in two years. A war cannot be fought and won if the soldiers take twelve-month leaves after every skirmish. . . . I have considered your parental qualms; really I have. But I'm afraid they cannot counterbalance the feelings of my duty here.[79]

Many people, including those who supported my going to Mississippi as part of the Summer Project, and those who believe that the Summer Project has been an important thing, have expressed shock and disapproval at my decision to go back to Mississippi, and have attempted to dissuade me from returning. I have been amazed at this response.

There is a certainty, when you are working in Mississippi, that it is important for you to be alive and to be alive doing just what you are doing. And whatever small bit we did for Mississippi this summer, Mississippi did ten times as much for us.

I guess the thing that pulls me back most are the people who made us a part of their community. People I knew in Mississipi could honestly and unselfconsciously express affection in a way that few people I know in the North are able to do. They did not have to be "cool" or "one up" or "careful." . . . In Mississippi I have felt more love, more sympathy and warmth, more community than I have known in my life. And especially the children pull me back. (Quoted in Sutherland, 1965: 225–226)

The majority of the volunteers *did* go home. However, for many the decision to do so was just as wrenching as it had been for those who remained behind.

August 6
I had a very hard time . . . convincing myself that I should leave Mississippi. . . . It is so necessary that people stay, especially northern white students. Holly Springs has so much potential and could really develop into something much greater than it already is if there are the right leaders here. I would love to be a part of making the Freedom School into a real ongoing concern with the adults and kids of the community doing most of the teaching and leading themselves. However, I have come to realize that there is still a great

deal that I need to learn. I feel that I still have a lot of growing up to do. But most of all I see what this kind of life can do to you and I think that I need a rest and a change of environment to prepare myself for a life-long commitment wherever I might be needed.[80]

Even harder than the decision to leave was the painful sense of dislocation many of the volunteers felt once they were out of Mississippi. They had arrived in the state in groups, buoyed by the exhilarating sense of community they had felt at Oxford. Now they trickled out of Mississippi one by one, alone and exhausted, without ever having an opportunity to process or come to grips with all they had seen and felt. If Oxford had oriented them to life in Mississippi, nothing prepared them for life after Mississippi. For many the transition was rough. Barely three weeks after writing the previous letter, Pam Parker struggled to express how she was feeling:

> I have been putting off writing my concluding thoughts on my experiences in Mississippi because I have been unable to sort out my thoughts and feelings since leaving. I will try to at least give you a picture of the reactions of one girl on entering the free, white world of her past once again. No one can go through an experience such as Mississippi without coming out changed. I do not believe that many of those who spent their summer in Mississippi will be able to go back to their old way of living.
>
> I am out of Mississippi and glad to be out for a while. I have always loved to take walks at night but never have I felt so grateful for the opportunity to take peaceful walks as these last few days. I could sit for hours on the porch of our friends' place in New Hampshire, soaking in the peacefulness and the quiet of the countryside. I feel so relaxed . . . but I am not relaxed, not completely. I wonder if I will ever relax fully again. . . .
>
> I have found that instead of Mississippi seeming distant from my life, it and all that it exemplifies in a magnified form of our society has become unbearably real to me.[81]

She was not alone in what she was feeling. On the very same day, another volunteer in another state echoed her sentiments: "I've felt depressed since I've returned. I don't know how much is personal, and how much it is a reaction to that place and the people I've left behind, and a heightened awareness of so much that is wrong up here" (quoted in Sutherland, 1965: 231). Contrast the underlying tone of these two letters with that expressed in a third letter written the same day by a volunteer who had stayed on in Mississippi:

We were sitting on the steps at dusk, watching the landscape and the sun folding into the flat country, with the backboard of the basketball net that is now netless sticking up into the sunset at a crazy angle. Cotton harvesters went by—and the sheriff—and then a 6-year-old Negro girl with a stick and a dog, kicking up as much dust as she could with her bare feet. As she went by, we could hear her humming to herself, "We shall overcome." (Quoted in Sutherland, 1965: 117)

The psychic and geographic distance from Mississippi was great indeed. Even greater was the gulf between the volunteer's summer experiences and their previous lives. Bridging that gap would prove difficult for many, impossible for some. For many the old adage, "you can always go home," would prove a lie. For some of the volunteers there would be no "going home" except in a geographical sense. They had simply seen and felt too much to ever experience their world in the same way again. They had been changed in some very fundamental ways. The extent and significance of these changes would become apparent over the next few months.

4

Taking Stock
THE IMMEDIATE IMPACT
OF FREEDOM SUMMER

THERE IS an ignorance about Freedom Summer in contemporary America that bears no relationship to the impact the project had at the time. Nor can this ignorance be traced to any lack of attention accorded the project in 1964. Other than the year's Presidential campaign, it was certainly the nation's top news story that summer. But the nation's collective memory proved short, especially when confronted by the rush of events that followed close on the heels of the project. In quick succession, Freedom Summer was supplanted in the public's mind by a series of dramatic events that rendered it all but forgotten only a few months later. The Gulf of Tonkin incident, the Free Speech Movement, Lyndon Johnson's landslide election, Selma, Watts, the escalating war in Vietnam; each, in turn, took center stage in an ever-escalating cascade of events from which we have yet to recover. The Sixties, as a psychological rather than chronological experience, had begun.

The pace of social, political, and cultural change during these years quickly relegated important events of the previous year to the shadowy recesses of some distant and anachronistic past. Amid mounting protests against the war, few in 1966 remembered Johnson's landslide election of two years earlier. Could Watts really have happened just six months after the triumphal Selma-to-Montgomery march? In similar fashion, Freedom Summer came to be lost in a kind of historical backwater, relegated to the tail-end of another era, more a part of the Fifties than the Sixties. In a narrow sense, this view is correct. Freedom Summer *did* precede the solidification of the highly politicized "counterculture" most white Americans associate with the Sixties. At the same time it had as much to do with bringing that counterculture into existence as any other single event during the era. There is a reason why Wini Breines (1982: 18) and other historians of the New Left date the beginnings of "The Movement" from 1964. On the one hand, this view reflects a white, middle-class bias. One of the underlying themes of this book is that the roots of the Sixties experience are firmly embedded in the civil rights movement and therefore are considerably older than 1964. White America may have discovered the movement in 1964, but it had been developing since at least 1955. Still, the diffusion of activism and the development of an activist subculture among white students were critical processes in the evolution of the Sixties experience. The significance of Freedom Summer lies in the central role it played in these processes. In this sense, David Harris (1982: 49) would appear to be on target when he argues that "[n]o single event marked the course of that decade more fully than the 1964 Mississippi Summer Project."

The project's importance owes to the impact it had on the major parties to the campaign. For its part, SNCC emerged from the summer as an organization in crisis. Although Freedom Summer had been the most ambitious and arguably the most successful campaign in SNCC's history, it had also aggravated tensions and conflicts that had been building within the organization for several years. The result of the crisis was a stalemate between competing factions and the effective suspension of the main philosophic tenets on which the organization had always operated. This included the tenet of interracialism. It would take several years before whites were formally barred from the organization, but the summer marked the end of SNCC's efforts to encourage white participation.

Ironically, the move to restrict the role of whites in the movement coincided with a resurgence of student activism attributable to the Summer Project. Most of the volunteers left Mississippi politically radicalized and intent on carrying on the fight in the North. In turn, their example and the attention and status accorded the volunteers on campuses throughout the North triggered a sharp increase in student activism. The separatist trend within the civil rights movement, however, restricted access to the movement at precisely the time more and more white students were seeking to play an activist role. They were forced, as a result, to seek out other targets for their activism. The proliferation of other issues—student rights, the Vietnam War, sexism, etc.—after 1964 owes, in part, to this process.

Finally, the summer had a subtle, but important, impact on the country as a whole. After all, the volunteers were not the only ones to go

South that summer. In a very real sense, the entire country had visited Mississippi courtesy of the national news media. And given the editorial tone of most of the coverage, many of those who visited vicariously came away with a generally favorable view of the civil rights movement, college students, and activism in general. This view was reinforced by the parents of the volunteers and the scores of doctors, lawyers, ministers, and other influential adults who spent some time in Mississippi during the course of the summer. Thus, by undermining the popular view of the political left and activism evident during the McCarthy era, the Summer Project subtly paved the way for the events of the later Sixties.

The Radicalization of SNCC and the Collapse of the Beloved Community

For most of the volunteers, Freedom Summer ended with their departure from Mississippi. However, for SNCC and the MFDP there remained the matter of a trip to Atlantic City. Early in August, the sixty-eight MFDP delegates (forty regular delegates and twenty-eight alternates) and members of the SNCC high command began arriving at the Democratic National Convention in New Jersey. The SNCC/MFDP contingent had come prepared to challenge the seating of the regular Mississippi delegation. By now the story of the confrontation between the MFDP and the Democratic Party left is well known.[1] But it is a story worth retelling, both for its inherent drama as well as the lessons SNCC and the burgeoning New Left were to draw from it.

Initially, the SNCC leadership's purpose in organizing the MFDP was largely symbolic. Much like the Freedom Vote campaign the previous fall, Mississippi's delegate selection process afforded the SNCC braintrust another opportunity to demonstrate the willingness and desire of Mississippi's black population to participate in the state's political process. As the project gained momentum, however, the possibility of unseating the regular Mississippi delegation began to be taken seriously. Expressions of support from as many as twenty-five Democratic members of Congress and nine state party delegations served to raise expectations as the convention approached.[2] Still, on the eve of the convention, the SNCC leadership knew its best chance of unseating the regular Mississippi delegation was likely to come from bringing the issue to the full convention rather than through any official action of the Credentials Committee. As the official body charged with reviewing the credentials of all state and territorial delegations, the Committee was home to a good many party regulars whose interest lay in seeing that the proceedings went smoothly. Therefore, they were not likely to countenance the divisive challenge of some ragtag band of maverick upstarts from the lowly state of Mississippi. For the MFDP the problem was that even a floor fight over the issue required a minority report from members of the Credentials Committee. This prompted the MFDP forces to adopt a dual strategy at the Convention. First, they sought support from state delegations through an intensive lobbying campaign. Second, they made a strong and emotionally powerful appearance before the Credentials Committee. The highlight of the appearance was Fannie Lou Hamer's emotional account of being savagely beaten in jail following her arrest for participating in voter registration activities. At one point, she recounted how her jailers had forced several black prisoners to beat her:

> The first Negro began to beat, and I was beat until he was exhausted. . . . After the first Negro . . . was exhausted, the State Highway Patrolman began to beat. . . . I began to scream, and one white man got up and began to beat me on my head and tell me to "hush."
> One white man—my dress had worked up high—he walked over and pulled my dress down and he pulled my dress back, back up. . . . All of this is on account we want to register, to become first-class citizens, and if the Freedom Democratic Party is not seated now, I question America. . . . (Quoted in White, 1965: 279)

Hamer's electrifying testimony moved even the hardened party regulars on the Committee, as well as a national television audience, which responded with a flood of telegrams in support of the challenge. It began to look as if the moral force of the challenge might actually prevail. Almost unbelievably, the MFDP was poised to play David to the Mississippi Dixiecrat's Goliath.

What the MFDP leadership had underestimated was the lengths to which Lyndon Johnson and his supporters would go to block the challenge. Fearing the erosion of Southern support, the Johnson forces were determined to do whatever was necessary to insure that the regular Mississippi delegation was seated. Toward that end, Johnson ordered the FBI to place the SNCC/MFDP convention forces under surveillance. FBI Director J. Edgar Hoover responded by tapping the phones in SNCC's Atlantic City office.[3] The White House let it be known that the seating of the MFDP delegation would damage the vice-presidential prospects of Hubert Humphrey. This move was probably directed at Joseph Rauh, the MFDP's chief counsel and long-time Humphrey supporter. In turn, Humphrey's staff pressured Rauh to urge moderation and compromise on the MFDP delegation. Walter Reuther, Rauh's immediate superior and the President of the United Auto Workers (UAW) flew in for a bit of backstage arm twisting of his own. He threatened to pull all the UAW's money out of Mississippi should the MFDP persist in its challenge.[4] According to Rauh, Johnson supporters even threatened individual Committee members. Later he told an interviewer that one black supporter was informed "that her husband wouldn't get a judgeship if she didn't leave us, and the Secertary of the Army told the guy from the Canal Zone that he would lose his job if he didn't leave us" (quoted in Romaine, 1970: 335–336).

In the end, the pressure worked. Support for the challenge evaporated in the Credentials Committee and the MFDP forces were left to consider a rather weak compromise proposal: two at-large convention seats and a promise that the whole matter of racial exclusion would be reviewed prior to the 1968 convention. When moderate civil rights leaders such as Martin Luther King, Jr. and Bayard Rustin joined the chorus of those calling for acceptance of the compromise, the delegates' sense of betrayal and isolation was complete.

The delegates overwhelmingly rejected the compromise. Fannie Lou Hamer summed up the feeling of most when she said, "we didn't come all this way for no two seats!" (quoted in Carson, 1981: 126). That was not quite the end of it, though. Using credentials borrowed from sympathetic delegates from other states, a contingent of MFDP members gained access to the convention floor and staged a sit-in in the Mississippi section. The sight of black Mississipians being carried from the convention floor by uniformed, white security officers was but the ultimate ironic denouement to Freedom Summer.

The convention challenge represented the high-water mark for SNCC. The challenge capped what had been an exhilarating but enormously draining and ultimately debilitating summer for the organization. It was not just that the staff was exhausted from months of nonstop effort, or that the challenge itself had failed. From the outset, James Forman and others in SNCC's inner circle had cautioned that the chances of the challenge succeeding were slim. Instead the effects of the summer cut to the very heart of the organization, calling into question its raison d'être and undermining the very philosophy on which it had been based. The principal components of this philosophy were nonviolence, integration, and an existential politics of moral suasion. There had always been opposition to each of these tenets within SNCC. But consensus within the organization continued to favor all three up to and during the Summer Project. The effect of the project, however, was to destroy this consensus once and for all. All three of these fundamental organizing principles came under increasing attack.

Freedom Summer and the Failure of Moral Suasion

In rejecting the compromise offered at the convention, the MFDP delegation was merely acting on reservoirs of frustration and suspicion that had been building within the SNCC/MFDP leadership toward Northern liberals and civil rights moderates for some time. But it was Freedom Summer and the abortive challenge that served to crystallize these feelings. According to SNCC's Executive Director, James Forman (1972: 395–396),

> Atlantic City was a powerful lesson, not only for the black people from Mississippi but for all of SNCC. . . . No longer was there any hope . . . that the federal government would change the situation in the Deep South. The fine line of contradiction between the state governments and the federal government, which we had used to build a movement, was played out. Now the kernel of opposites— the people against both the federal and state governments was apparent.

Following the Convention, Forman's conclusion came to be almost universally shared within SNCC, thus creating a real tactical problem for the organization. As radical an organization as SNCC had always been, its modus operandi had remained but an aggressive variation on the "petition the masters" strategy. Its approach depended upon the federal government's willingness to respond to "moral suasion," albeit of a forceful sort. Events in Mississippi had undermined SNCC's confidence in such a strategy. But it was the convention challenge that foreclosed this strategic option once and for all. In the eyes of the SNCC leadership, the Northern liberal elite had finally shown its true colors; moral force had proven no match for raw political power.

It was one thing to come to this conclusion, quite another to know how to act on it. Having based their entire operation on a politics of personal witness, the SNCC leadership faced enormous obstacles in trying to devise a new tactical agenda. If moral suasion had not worked, what would? Stokely Carmichael's call for "black power" some two years later was as much a rhetorical symbol of the organization's failure to resolve this dilemma as it was a real solution to the problem. In the face of impotence, one boasts of potency.

Ironically, then, it was Freedom Summer and the MFDP challenge—

the crowning glory of SNCC's existential style—that exposed the limits of the approach and left the organization in a quandary as to how to proceed. Efforts to resolve the dilemma would embroil the organization in almost continuous controversy for the remainder of its short life.

The Abandonment of Nonviolence

Events in Mississippi also served to renew debate within the organization over the usefulness of nonviolence as both tactic and philosophy. Actually, some of this rethinking was stimulated by the demonstrated failure of moral suasion in Mississippi. If, in fact, the federal government could not be persuaded to do what was morally right, if they were not going to protect civil rights workers from violence, then nonviolence might well be a luxury SNCC could ill afford. Tactically, nonviolence made sense only if it restrained the violence of one's opponents or induced government officials to intervene on behalf of the demonstrators. In Mississippi, neither objective was achieved. There had certainly been no shortage of violence on the part of white supremacists, and, from SNCC's point of view, federal officials had done little to constrain that violence. If that was what they could expect, perhaps it was better to meet force with force.

The Summer Project supplied another impetus to this debate as well. The SNCC braintrust had always argued that nonviolence was more a tactical than a philosophical necessity in the Deep South, insofar as the use of violence would precipitate the wholesale slaughter of blacks. In Mississippi, however, the SNCC leadership encountered a local black population that relied on armed self-defense as the ultimate response to supremacist violence. This tradition had a strong impact on many within SNCC. Another of the SNCC veterans, Julian Bond, discusses this impact.

> There was a big debate in SNCC once about carrying guns, whether or not we should carry guns, and two or three of the guys from Mississippi said, "This is all academic. We been carrying guns. I got mine here."
>
> The rest of us were shocked: "We can't carry guns. We're nonviolent."
>
> Guy said, "Don't tell me I can't carry my gun. I been carrying this for a year or more." Guy had a little automatic.
>
> Almost everybody with whom we stayed in Mississippi had guns, as a matter of course, hunting guns. But, you know, they were there for other purposes, too.
>
> This old guy, Hartman Turnbow, I remember him. He used to

carry an army automatic in a briefcase, and it's funny to see a man
who looks like a farmer and is dressed like a farmer in coveralls and
boots and, let's say, an old hat, with a briefcase. And he opens the
briefcase and nothing's in it but an automatic. (Quoted in Raines,
1983: 267)

Figures like Hartman Turnbow provided a powerful, and no doubt psychologically attractive, alternative to those within SNCC who were
frustrated by the apparent ineffectiveness of moral suasion as a strategy
for social change.

To the extent, then, that Freedom Summer came to represent the
failure of this approach for many in SNCC, it increased the attractiveness of force or self-defense as an alternative strategy. According to
James Forman (1972: 375), "The Mississippi Summer Project . . .
confirmed the absolute necessity for armed self-defense—a necessity that
existed before the project but which became overwhelmingly clear to
SNCC people during and after it." Although generally accurate, Forman's statement would seem to exaggerate the degree of consensus within
SNCC concerning the issue of nonviolence. The drift was clearly in the
direction Forman indicates, but the issue continued to generate considerable debate and controversy within the organization. These debates
contributed to the organizational paralysis SNCC was beginning to experience. So too did one other issue.

The Exacerbation of Racial Tensions

Of all the effects that flowed from the Summer Project, none was more
important than the exacerbation of racial tensions within SNCC and
the resultant pressure on whites to leave the movement. Two sources
for these escalating tensions were the paternalism and insensitivity of
certain of the white volunteers and staff resentment of the attention
lavished on the summer workers. But there were other strains as well.
One of these was simply numeric. SNCC had always been a tight-knit,
predominantly black organization of no more than 100 people. With
the addition of the eighty to ninety volunteers who stayed on after the
summer, the SNCC staff suddenly swelled to 180, half of whom were
white (Evans, 1980: 89). The sudden influx of so many new staff—
virtually all of them white—threatened to undermine the organization's
delicate numeric and racial balance. Under more stable circumstances,
the veteran staff might have been able to adapt to the newcomers, but
when coupled with the other strains the organization was experiencing,
the transition to a new order proved too difficult to negotiate.

The gender composition of the newcomers posed yet another problem for the organization. The majority of volunteers who stayed on apparently were white women.[5] Exactly why this was so is not clear. It meant, though, that the sexually explosive mix of race and gender survived the summer. So too did the tensions and jealousies this combination inevitably produced. These strains tended to drive a wedge between black men and black women as the latter reacted with anger and bitterness at what they interpreted as rejection and a denial of their femininity. In her book, *Personal Politics*, Sarah Evans (1980: 88) tells of an incident:

> [S]oon after the summer [in which] some black women in SNCC confronted black men with the charge that "they could not develop relationships with the black men because the men didn't have to be responsible to them because they could always hook up with some white woman who had come down."

In turn, the white women experienced a great deal of hostility from black female staff members. One of the volunteers who stayed on after the summer remembers

> feeling lonely almost immediately. It was tough because we had had such a big project [approximately forty volunteers] and now there were only 6 or so of us around all the time . . . and I just never was able to connect . . . with the two black women on our project. . . . They just seemed to hate me. . . . It was probably the sex thing, but I never got close enough to find out.[6]

Although little acknowledged, the "sex thing" seems to have functioned as one of the most powerful pressures encouraging the expulsion of whites from SNCC. This is really not surprising when one realizes the broader power dynamics of the whole sexual issue. It was not simply sexual jealousy that motivated the black female staffers but fears of political usurpation as well. Sexual or romantic relationships granted the white female volunteers unique access to some of the most influential black males within SNCC. In turn, this access threatened to eclipse the political stature and influence that the black female staffers had struggled long and hard to achieve. They responded to this perceived threat with hostility and anger, their actions adding to the growing racial tensions that buffeted SNCC during and following the summer. Although officially the organization remained integrated for another two years, the egalitarian ideal of the "beloved community" died with the Summer Project.

Under the weight of these issues, SNCC emerged from the summer as an increasingly fragmented organization, divided along racial, ideological, and class lines. These lines of division tended, however, to coalesce in two distinct positions within the organization. One wing of SNCC came to be known as the "structure" faction; the other as the "freedom high" faction. The structure faction felt that SNCC needed to move beyond the improvisational politics of moral suasion to mobilize political power through an increasingly structured organizational program. The structure faction also tended to take a hard line on the issues of nonviolence and integration. Nonviolence might be defensible as long as SNCC was relying on the power and influence of others—federal officials, the media, Northern liberals—to make changes and restrain segregationist violence. But as soon as the emphasis shifted to building an indigenous power base, SNCC had to be prepared to defend its program against the backlash it was likely to provoke. The presence of large numbers of whites in the organization might also prove incompatible with the goal of building a power base among blacks. Not only did whites tend to introduce racial tensions into the organization, but they also inhibited the development of leadership among local blacks. Thus, by emphasizing power politics rather than moral suasion, the structure faction moved perceptibly in the direction of separatism and self-defense.

The "freedom high" faction, on the other hand, represented a kind of ultimate extension of the anarchic, existential politics traditionally practiced by SNCC. Whether the association was accurate, Bob Moses came to symbolize this faction and its distrust of centralized organization and top-down leadership. In its place, Moses and his supporters would have substituted an informal network of organizers, each responding to the needs of the community in which he or she was working. In this, the freedom high faction remained largely faithful to SNCC's long-standing style of operation. The image was still that of a band of existential radicals who, by the force of their example, would catalyze people into action. This stress on the individual as organizer also resonated with SNCC's traditional emphasis on interracialism and nonviolence. There was a particular color-blind quality to the freedom high image of the activist. Presumably, the ability "to go where the spirit say go and do what the spirit say do," was as available to whites as blacks.[7] Violence also seemed somehow incompatible with the image of the organizer as moral exemplar. Camus' existential rebel did not fight so much as bear witness.

In the fall of 1964 these two positions were not yet sharply delineated. Rather, they represented two schools of thought—emergent and inchoate—around which people gradually came to rally. The broad contours of these positions began to emerge at an October 10 staff meeting in Atlanta and the November retreat at Waveland, Mississippi. Forman's earlier characterization of SNCC as "a band of brothers, a circle of trust," seemed faintly anachronistic as the SNCC staff argued long and often over issues ranging from sexism in the organization to decision-making policy. The SNCC staff were hardly strangers to heated debate and self-criticism. What marked these meetings as unique were not the passions aroused, but the failure to achieve any real consensus about the future direction of the organization. If anything, the meetings merely exposed the divisions that had developed within SNCC while doing little to resolve them. The organization was effectively in limbo with neither the structure nor freedom high faction having enough leverage to dictate a coherent course of action.

Eventually, the remnants of the structure faction would take control of the organization, but in the two years it would take for this to happen, SNCC would lose its organizational momentum and its vanguard position within the civil rights movement. Just as important, it would forfeit its preeminent position in the burgeoning New Left. The organization's increasing hostility toward whites, coupled with its own internal crisis, would foreclose the possibility of massive Northern student involvement in SNCC at precisely the moment when Freedom Summer was awakening those students to the appeal and possibility of civil rights activism. How different the New Left and the 1960s might have looked had SNCC been in a position to use the momentum of the Summer Project to expand its already strong links to Northern colleges and universities. Instead, their exclusion from SNCC and the civil rights movement forced students to search elsewhere for activist alternatives. The eventual "shape" of the New Left would owe much to this process. The volunteers were, in many cases, at the forefront of this process.

The Volunteers and the "Lessons of Mississippi"

Notwithstanding all the political turbulence, the Sixties were not simply about politics. Nor were they exclusively about experimenting with new lifestyles. What made the era unique was the combination of these two emphases. Personal transformation came to be wedded to political and social change as a rhetoric of liberation suffused the New Left and the later counterculture. Only after 1968 or 1969 did the cultural and political components of the "Sixties experience" diverge. Thereafter, the political left came to be more exclusive and sectarian while elements of the counterculture—dress and hairstyles, music, drug usage—diffused through a wider public. But early on, the two impulses were clearly joined.

Much of the significance of Freedom Summer derives from the impetus it furnished this process of fusion. For most of the volunteers, the "lessons of Mississippi" were as much personal as political. Returning North, they carried with them the seeds of a new culture, equally attuned to personal and political change as necessary components of a broader transformation of American society. In effect, the twin themes of political and personal change received early expression in Mississippi and the volunteers came away clearly committed to both.

Political Radicalization

Above all else, the volunteers became more political as a result of their experiences in Mississippi. In their interviews the volunteers returned to this theme over and over again. Said Heather Tobis Booth, "It [the summer] had an enormous effect on me . . . it made me really feel [that] I want to do this kind of thing for the rest of my life."[8] Another said, "The summer moved me light years beyond where I had been politically . . . I went from being a liberal Peace Corps-type Democrat to a raging, maniacal lefty."[9] Yet another put it even more succinctly, "I *became* political in Mississippi. I began to see the world strictly in political terms."[10]

The sources of this radicalization were numerous. Chief among them were the events of the summer. Given their advantaged and generally sheltered backgrounds, it would be hard to imagine the volunteers *not* being powerfully affected by the things they saw in Mississippi. Those who had been raised in leftist homes may have been ideologically familiar with the concepts of oppression and inequality, but few of the volunteers had ever experienced them directly. But it wasn't the discrimination alone—the "colored only" drinking fountains and KKK billboards—that made such an impact; the volunteers had expected those things. It was the depths of the problem and the broader implications of what they saw. It was the poverty of black Mississippi and what that said about the inherent goodness of America. It was the endemic quality of official lawlessness and the blatant contradiction it posed to their "law and order" upbringings. But perhaps what shocked the volunteers most was the depths of federal complicity in maintaining Mississippi's system of segregation. If the SNCC veterans had grown increasingly dubious of Washington's commitment to civil rights, the majority of volunteers arrived in Mississippi with generally positive images of the federal government. It was the redneck farmer, Southern sheriff, and

Dixiecrat politician who were the enemy. For many, the events of the summer upset this simplistic distinction between "good guys" and "bad guys." All too often, the "good guys" were linked to the "bad guys" in ways that were no less disturbing for their subtlety. In a long essay written during the summer, a volunteer named Brian Peterson attempted to delineate these connections.

> The Klansman-assassin at the local gas station has close connections with the local sheriff, who in turn has connections with the legislature and governor, who in turn have connections with Congress and the President. The implications of this aren't always clear: the FBI will find the murderers of Schwerner, Chaney and Goodman, but they won't find out who killed the six other Mississippi Negroes since January and they won't interfere with the constant police brutality.
> Similarly, the Negro sharecropper is bossed by a plantation manager, who is employed by the local bank to run the land it owns, this bank is controlled by a bank in Memphis, which is largely owned by a bank in Chicago or New York. (Other large owners of sharecrop land include life insurance companies, most notably Metropolitan of New York, and Northern universities, most notably Harvard, that citadel of liberalism.) Thus the highest financial (and intellectual) levels of this country have a direct interest in exploiting the Negro sharecropper and seeing to it that he does not gain political power by which he could end that exploitation.[11]

A sign on the wall of many of the Freedom Houses put the matter of federal complicity in Mississippi a bit more ironically. The sign read:

> There's a street in Itta Bena called FREEDOM
> There's a town in Mississippi called LIBERTY
> There's a department in Washington called JUSTICE

Though the volunteers lagged behind the SNCC veterans, they too were beginning to redefine who the enemy was. The radicalizing effect of Freedom Summer is reflected in the answers the volunteers gave to one item on the follow-up questionnaire. They were asked whether their estimate of various branches or agencies of the federal government was raised, lowered, or remained unchanged as a result of their experiences in Mississippi. Their answers are given in Table 4.1. The direction of change in the volunteers' perceptions is the same for all branches or agencies of government. Overwhelmingly, the volunteers report Freedom Summer lowering their opinion of federal officials.

Their strongest criticisms were reserved for the FBI and the contacts

Table 4.1 Effect of Freedom Summer on the Volunteer's Perception
of Various Branches or Agencies of Government

	President		Congress		Justice Dept.		FBI	
	%	No.	%	No.	%	No.	%	No.
Lowered estimate	42	(81)	40	(77)	50	(98)	73	(143)
Raised estimate	12	(23)	9	(18)	26	(51)	6	(12)
Estimate unchanged	46	(87)	51	(98)	24	(46)	21	(42)
Total	100	(191)	100	(193)	100	(195)	100	(197)

they had with individual agents. Time and again, FBI agents called to investigate violence against the projects either never showed up or were uncooperative or hostile when they did. The worst of the incidents recounted during the interviews was one provided by David Gelfand, a volunteer who had been severely beaten on August 21, 1964, near Laurel, Mississippi. As bad as the beating was, the failure of the FBI to take action during the attack, to pursue the investigation following the attack, or to cooperate in the prosecution of those involved was even more damning to Gelfand:

> The bottom line was the federal government never did anything. . . . [It] was another interesting fiasco with the FBI . . . we had been assured by our local congressman, Ogden Reed . . . that the local FBI in Jackson and Laurel would be very cooperative . . . [it] turned out [that] the head of the Laurel FBI was . . . related to the [local] sheriff and this Klan guy. . . . I wound up totally disenchanted with the FBI and the Justice Department.[12]

Nor was the FBI seen as some anomaly in relation to an otherwise responsive federal government. The entire federal establishment came in for criticism. At the height of the summer one volunteer took angry aim at a variety of targets:

> Coming from lunch the other day to the COFO office we noticed a hush unusual for the place. A boy in a bloody shirt was reporting a brutal beating via phone to the FBI. . . . The FBI will "investigate" and no more.
> Where is the USA? It is a violation of FEDERAL LAW to harass voter registration workers. Where are the Federal Marshals to protect these people? How do the Negroes defending "democracy" in Viet-

nam feel about the defense that democracy gets in Mississippi?
(Quoted in Sutherland, 1965: 147)

Others singled out specific targets for criticism. By its timidity and re-
luctance to aggressively prosecute civil rights violations, the Justice
Department earned the enmity of many volunteers. So too did Lyndon
Johnson and his supporters for the tactics they employed at the Democratic Convention in Atlantic City. Said one volunteer, "the convention
challenge was kind of a last straw for me. . . . When I went to Mississippi I was a Kennedy Democrat. After Atlantic City I didn't really
feel like I had . . . [a party]."[13] Other liberal standard bearers came
in for criticism as well. Marion Davidson remembered "complaining to
[then Attorney General] Robert Kennedy that our mail was being
opened. His response was formal and . . . cold . . . and it was clear
that he didn't care all that much and [that he] couldn't really do anything about it."[14] Wouldn't do anything about it is probably closer to
the truth. Based on evidence uncovered by the late Senator Frank
Church's Select Committee on Government Intelligence Activities, we
now know that Kennedy himself authorized wiretaps on Martin Luther
King Jr.'s home and several SCLC offices.[15] Finally, another volunteer
described as "shocking and depressing" a meeting he had during the
summer with yet another hero of the Democratic left.

> [A] group of us . . . were sent for a few days to Washington to
> lobby among senators and congressmen . . . for some immediate ac-
> tion on their [Chaney, Goodman, and Schwerner] disappearance and
> [on] the more general question [of civil rights]. . . . Paul Douglas
> [D-Ill.] was still a senator in those days . . . he was this sort of lib-
> eral hero of mine but this was a very disillusioning meeting. . . . I'll
> never forget this, he said, "you young people want to play you're
> great and . . . [that] this is a wonderful thing you are doing, but,"
> he said, "the main thing," and he'd repeat this over and over again,
> "is watch out for the Commies." . . . that word is indelible in my
> memory; it was like something [from a] comic book . . . very sad
> and very disillusioning.[16]

Consistently, then, their encounters with federal officials left the
volunteers frustrated and disillusioned. This was especially true for
those whose political socialization had been fairly conventional.[17] The
government they had been led to believe was powerful and essentially
just was proving itself to be cowardly and amoral in its dealings with
segregationists. For many, this contrast was profoundly radicalizing.
Long-time SNCC staffer, Mary King, describes the effect the summer
had on many of the volunteers: "there were certain feelings of betrayal,

particularly, I suspect, this was true for the white kids involved, the feeling that you couldn't count on your own government. A sort of suspension of values, almost, that the things I had grown up believing were constants; were just of dust" (quoted in Sinsheimer, 1983: 139).

Another source of radicalization for the volunteers was their interaction with the project staff. There was even a phrase—the "SNCCizing of the volunteers"—to describe this process. Several volunteers touched on it during their interviews.

> Lots of the volunteers sort of sat at the feet of the SNCC guys, and it was the [SNCC] guys, not the girls. It was sort of pathetic, everybody trying to out SNCC each other. But it was also hard not to. They [the male SNCC staffers] were tremendously charismatic . . . very forceful and frankly, their rap made sense. It was hard not to start seeing the world through their eyes.[18]

> It's hard to say this now, but I wanted to be like them [the SNCC staff]. Not to the point where I started to talk and dress like them; some of the others almost become [sic] like groupies . . . I mean politically, I wanted to be like them. . . . More than anything else I guess I admired their courage and their commitment to political *action*.[19]

This latter point is especially important. It was not simply that the volunteers had their political *attitudes* changed by their experiences in Mississippi. Indeed, a good many of the volunteers arrived in Mississippi with a relatively sophisticated and sometimes radical political view of the world. This was especially true of the sizeable number of volunteers whose parents had been socialists or communists. Even these "red diaper babies," however, found their politics changed by the experience.

> Well, I wouldn't say I was politicized by it [Freedom Summer]. I had always been political, but in what strikes me now as a very detached, academic sense. . . . Shit, I could debate Trotsky's position against Lenin when I was ten! . . . I was the classic arm chair radical . . . smug, self-congratulatory . . . I always prided myself on having the "correct analysis." . . . But I didn't become an *actionist* until Mississippi. I came to see that you could talk till you were blue in the face, but at some point, if you were really committed to the stuff, you had to *act* on what you were saying.[20]

Heather Tobis Booth described the political legacy of the summer for her as "the positive impulse to action."[21] So it was not only the attitudes of the volunteers that were changed by the summer, but their willingness to act on those attitudes. This is not a trivial point. When we speak of the Sixties as a "political" era, we are really making a statement about the level of political *action* during the period rather than the content of political attitudes per se. In this sense, the most important legacy of Freedom Summer may lie in the "positive impulse to action" it furnished the New Left. While collective action had been more or less continuous among blacks since 1955, and especially 1960, the predominantly white Northern colleges and universities had remained very quiet over the same period of time. While there were stirrings of political life before the summer, the dramatic upsurge in campus activism corresponded with the return of the volunteers to school in the fall. The confluence is no coincidence. Freedom Summer had served as a kind of activist "basic training" for some 1,000 people, nearly all of whom returned North following the summer. With them went not only the ideological "lessons" of Mississippi, but the desire to *act* on those lessons. The radicalization of the volunteers, then, had important behavioral as well as attitudinal implications. It was the former that was to prove so important in the emergence of an activist subculture in the North. The volunteers were among the first activist role models for an entire generation.

Personal Liberation

The impact of Freedom Summer on the volunteers was not exclusively political. If it had been, the volunteers presumably would have had little trouble returning to the lives they were leading prior to the summer. In fact, this transition proved difficult for most of the volunteers. For some, there was no desire to even attempt it. They had been changed in too fundamental a sense to think about resuming their previous lives. Two processes were at work here. The first was an outgrowth of the political radicalization the volunteers had undergone. Their experiences in Mississippi had led them to see the world in more starkly political terms than they had previously. In turn, this heightened political awareness made them more critical of American society and the lives they had led before. But this was only half the story. Even as the volunteers were rejecting certain aspects of their previous lives, they were embracing new images of the world and of themselves. Mississippi had exposed them to a way of life and a vision of community that most of the volunteers found enormously appealing. The trick now was to recreate this alternative way of life and community in the North. On the personal front, then, Freedom Summer moved the volunteers in two directions: away from various aspects of mainstream society, and toward an alternative vision of America and of themselves.

Alienation from Mainstream Society

For many of the volunteers the immediate effect of the summer was to leave them feeling disoriented, depressed, and alienated. Having spent eight to ten weeks isolated from mainstream white society, it was inevitable that the volunteers would have some trouble readjusting to life outside of Mississippi. Some of the difficulties were of a temporary, even humorous, nature. One volunteer remembers "almost missing how much I stunk in Mississippi . . . it was this kind of earthy badge of courage or something. When I got back home I remember [being] . . . depressed by all the sterility."[22] Another spoke of how, on returning to New York City, he found himself monitoring white passengers on the subway more closely than black because of the distrust of whites he had developed in Mississippi.[23] These adjustments were fleeting, but there were others that suggested more basic changes in the values and attitudes of the volunteers. Their summer in Mississippi had put considerable distance between themselves and the privileged worlds they had previously inhabited. To the extent that the perceived superiority of any world depends on its insularity, the Freedom Summer experience was bound to raise questions and plant doubts in the minds of the volunteers. There were other worlds, other ways of life out there; and the view from those other worlds did not necessarily confirm the assumptions the volunteers had previously taken for granted. Late in the summer, Ellen Lake wrote home challenging her parents' objections to her plan to stay on in Mississippi. She wrote:

> You speak of losing focus from spending a year in Mississippi; but what kind of focus do I have? All of my nineteen years I have shuttled between Westchester, Martha's Vineyard, the Virgin Islands, summer camp and Radcliffe—how can I help but gain a new perspective from Mississippi?[24]

While provocative, this "new perspective" was also confusing and generally alienating. In the interviews, more than half of the volunteers acknowledged some degree of estrangement from their previous lives immediately following the summer. For Pam Parker, these problems began the day she left the project to begin a vacation with her parents. She describes what happened:

> my folks had a station wagon and they were all in the front seat and I was in the back seat lying down . . . we were driving up in New Hampshire and I totally freaked out that we were going to crash . . . there had been one civil rights worker killed on our project in an

automobile accident [Wayne Yancy] and . . . that was intense dealing with his death . . . so I always thought that [my freaking out]
was a reaction to the pressure and fear of being in Mississippi and
then having come out and things having lightened up, I . . . [could
finally let] this fear . . . come up. . . . [But] a couple of years ago
I realized that that probably was not the case, that more likely . . .
what had happened to me was that I was confronting the reality of
going into northern white society with all its deadness and that I
was on a subconscious level feeling the fear of dying and being a
walking zombie.[25]

Several months later Parker was featured in a documentary done by a
local television station in Philadelphia on two of the returning project
workers. The segment on her featured sunny, upbeat shots of her stroll-
ing around the grounds of her parents' large home in the rolling horse
country of eastern Pennsylvania. Against this idyllic visual backdrop,
however, her voice-over narration provides a somber, chilling contrast.
The last line of the segment captures the mood nicely. "I feel," she says,
"like . . . a marginal person. I am not happy nor comfortable in white
society any longer nor am I fully comfortable in Negro society, and I
know, at least for myself, it's been a very lonely, isolated year because of
this."[26]

Other volunteers recalled similar difficulties in adjusting to life after
Mississippi. Len Edwards remembers

not [being] in control of my emotions for at least a year [afterward],
I was consumed by what I had seen; what [I] had been exposed
to . . . and had a very difficult time . . . relating to people. . . .
Here I am . . . [coming] out of this very intense summer and then
suddenly I'm back reading law books again and sitting with guys
drinking beer and they want to talk about how the Cubs are doing
and talk b.s. and talk about girls and somebody casually says, "well,
what was happening down there in Mississippi?" . . . And I started
talking and I said about two sentences and I started crying; I just
burst out crying and it wasn't just . . . a little trickle down the
cheek . . . I just sobbed . . . I had other times that were bad. I
remember dating a girl . . . and she asked me about it once and
the same thing happened to me and she didn't know what to do . . .
and I didn't know what to do . . . it was embarrassing, but I
couldn't control myself.[27]

The confusion and alienation the volunteers were feeling spilled over
into all aspects of their lives. Some felt estranged from their parents,
either because they viewed them as somehow morally culpable for the

situation in Mississippi or because they had come to redefine their parents' lifestyle as amoral or excessive. After returning home late in the summer, one of the volunteers expressed her new-found reservations in a letter to a friend:

> Coming out of Mississippi and into the "civilized white" world was hard. It was like cultural shock or something. Like I didn't feel like talking to anyone. I was in a kind of daze . . . I don't know quite what I am saying except that I am against much of what my family stands for. I realize that four families could live comfortably on what my father makes—comfortably Miss. Negro style . . . He's worked for what he's got. But it hurts me.[28]

The interviews afforded a certain historical perspective on the long-term effect of Freedom Summer on the volunteers' relations with their parents. They made it clear that, in most cases, whatever conflict the summer precipitated was only temporary. For at least four of the volunteers, however, the summer marked the beginning of a prolonged or even permanent estrangement between volunteer and parents.[29]

In other cases, it was the volunteers' school or career plans that came to be questioned. The doubts started well before the summer ended. The alienation the volunteers were feeling is clearly evident in their letters home.

> Hell, Ollie, I'm scared to death to leave this place next month . . . what am I going to do with myself. I really think that I've changed on what is important in life and what I want to do in life. What am I going to do sitting in the halls of Chicago reading taxation and corporation cases when I hear that one of the people I have lived with and fought with and loved has been shot?[30]

Another wrote to inform friends that she would not be going on to graduate school in the fall as she had originally planned.

> Maybe the immediacy of the sufferings and dangers here *is* overwhelming me and blurring out the essential "larger view," but I can simply no longer justify the pursuit of a Ph.D. When the folks in Flora have to struggle to comprehend the most elementary of materials on history and society and man's larger life, I feel ashamed to be greedily going after "higher learning." And when I feel the despair of youngsters who can't even get through high school because cotton planting prevents them, I almost feel ashamed of my college diploma. And when I reflect on the terrors and deprivations in daily lives here, I cannot return to the relative comforts and security of student life. (Quoted in Sutherland, 1965: 228)

Those who did return often found themselves at a loss socially and academically. Writing nearly a year after the summer, the parents of one volunteer described the change they had witnessed in their daughter.

> It's been an unhappy year for her at college. She didn't want to go back. It had lost its meaning, but she'd promised her father. She's having trouble with identification and relating to others. She graduates this June and doesn't know what she wants to do. Our very normal, bright, young child has changed.[31]

Finally, Freedom Summer precipitated religious crises for a number of Christian volunteers. In some cases the crisis stemmed from a general sense of betrayal on the part of the volunteer. One remembers the summer as the point at which "I started questioning everything . . . I was never told about this [the situation in Mississippi] in my history classes, and in my family. [I wondered] what else haven't I been told. . . . I used to wear a cross and I ripped it off and said 'this is it' . . . I had it with religion."[32] For others, the crisis was a specific response to the "good Christian" reception accorded the project by members of the volunteers' own congregations.

> We had to raise a certain amount of money—300 or 500 dollars, something like that—and I knew there was no way I was going to get it from my parents . . . so I went to him [her minister] and asked if he would make an announcement to the congregation . . . he said "no" and proceeded, in the sleaziest way to [try to] talk me out of going. . . . I was just stunned. His whole rap seemed to be "good Christians don't rock the boat." I figured either he was nuts or Christ was a bad Christian.[33]

On all fronts, then, the volunteers were feeling the alienating effects of the summer. Their experiences in Mississippi seriously undermined the volunteers' faith in the American political system and undercut their relationships to church, school, and family. This wholesale rejection of mainstream values and institutions created a dilemma for the volunteers. If they could no longer incorporate their lives into mainstream society, what alternative identities and forms of community were they prepared to substitute? Freedom Summer had provided them with the broad contours of an answer.

The Roots of the Counterculture

If the volunteers had gone South with the idea of integrating Mississippi into the rest of American society, the alienation they felt at the close of the summer had soured many of them on this goal. Instead, they sought to reproduce in the North the way of life and identity they had discovered in Mississippi. Ronald de Sousa wrote that

> people in the movement . . . do not live on myths. . . . If nothing were achieved in the field of civil rights proper, the movement would still be the best thing in America today. For it frees those that are in it first and foremost. *They* already *have* the "beloved community" and they rightly see the aim of the movement to be the inclusion of the whole of America into *this* community, not the integration of themselves into the rest of America as it is now. Our aim is indeed miscegenation, more profoundly so than they think.[34]

One of the leaders of the French student movement of the Sixties, Daniel Cohn-Bendit, once said that the function of revolutionaries was to create "an experiment that . . . breaks with that society, an experiment that will not last, but which allows a glimpse of a possibility . . ." (quoted in Breines, 1982: 30). What many of the volunteers glimpsed in Mississippi was a way of life, a form of community, and a vision of themselves far more exhilarating and engaging than any they had known before. Here was high moral purpose, adventure, and rich community all rolled into one. The close of the summer project brought an end to all these, and left the volunteers depressed and wanting more.

> The whole experience was such a high . . . it really was like taking acid for the first time . . . coming down was so hard; you didn't want it to end. . . . I was so . . . naive, [but] I really did think we represented the wave of the future; some new way of life or something . . . it was just up to us to create it . . . just like . . . with the drugs; you were supposed to turn others on.[35]

Another volunteer put it this way:

> I mean we really came back feeling that. . . [we] had been part of a new world . . . a new community, a new society . . . that was being born and you know all these people . . . and there were networks of people all over the place and . . . you really did feel very much a part of a movement . . . and you really felt you *belonged* to [it].[36]

This feeling of belonging or membership in something larger than themselves was stressed by many of the volunteers as the most important legacy of Freedom Summer. Said Marion Davidson, "It [Freedom Summer] totally flipped me out . . . for the first time all the pieces fit . . .

this felt like me . . . besides the good I think we did, it was my personal salvation as well."[37] Another remembers feeling that "you were part of a . . . historic movement . . . you were . . . making a kind of history and that you were . . . in some way utterly selfless and yet [you] found yourself [in the process]."[38] These recollections accord with statements made by other volunteers during the summer. Margaret Aley, for instance, wrote that she felt "like I've found something I've been looking for for a long time. I feel like I've finally come home. I now have no doubt that I belong here."[39]

The volunteers had discovered a powerful sociological truth: the most satisfying selves we will ever know are those that attach to communities and purposes outside of our selves. Having experienced these selves, the volunteers were not about to give them up. To preserve them, they knew they had to recreate in the North the form of community that had given rise to these identities in the first place. The volunteers' attempts to do so provided a crucial impetus to the rise of the Sixties counterculture. There were, of course, many other influences—America's "Beat" subculture, watered down Eastern philosophies, the "mod" movement in England—woven together to form a cultural patchwork. But in discussions of the roots of the counterculture, the impact of the civil rights movement (and specifically Freedom Summer) is rarely acknowledged. While the *political* links between the civil rights and the other major movements of the era have long been acknowledged, the *cultural* ties between the "beloved community" and the counterculture have not. On reflection, the influences seem obvious.

Perhaps the most important cultural contribution of Freedom Summer was the early behavioral expression it gave the link between personal liberation and social change. It was this connection as much as anything that gave the decade its distinctive style and ideological tone. This is not to say that the necessary conceptual link between personal and social transformation was first made during Freedom Summer. James Miller's (1987) impressive account of the rise of SDS makes it clear that this connection was present, in germinal form, within the organization from the very outset. And by the time of the drafting of the Port Huron Statement in 1962, the link between the two was explicit and powerful.

Still it was one thing to assert the connection in the abstract; quite another to effect this ideology in one's own life. Before Freedom Summer the connection had been made almost exclusively at a theoretical or rhetorical level. What defines Freedom Summer as an important moment in the evolution of the New Left and the Sixties counterculture is the practical expression it gave to theory. The ideology of liberation came to be *applied* personally as well as politically over the course of the summer.

The volunteers came to believe it was just as important to free *them-selves* from the constraints of their racial or class backgrounds as it was to register black voters. *They* became as much the project as the Free-dom Schools they taught in. A stress on self-awareness and personal lib-eration suffused the project. Later both elements would be incorporated as important behavioral cornerstones of the counterculture. Conformity was out; experimentation and personal liberation were in. What makes Freedom Summer so interesting is that this behavioral transition appears to have occurred quite spontaneously over the course of the summer. Certainly it was nothing the project staff had intended from the outset. On the contrary, concern for appearances and respectability were clearly evident at the beginning of the summer. At orientation, the volunteers were lectured on "matters of decorum and social etiquette." Male volun-teers were required to shave mustaches and beards before departing for Mississippi. Sexual activity was discouraged, in no uncertain terms. Over the course of the summer, however, this concern for appearances gradu-ally succumbed to the rhetoric of personal liberation. Appearances and respectability themselves came to be seen as trappings of a middle-class mentality that the volunteers had to transcend if they were ever to be free. Toward the end of the summer this emerging attitude was expressed in almost defiant terms by one volunteer:

> The roads are clay and dusty. Red dust that kicks up when the breeze passes. It gets into your clothes and your hair. The red mud on the side of the road left over from yesterday's rain storm clogs your shoes and somehow leaves stains on your pants. But somehow none of this matters when you are welcomed into a person's home and talk to him about registering for the vote. . . . And so clothes cease to be a real concern. "Image" ceases to be a real concern. If it ever was. In spite of the National Council of Churches' advice, we crap on the clean, antiseptic, acceptable, decent middle-class "image." It is that decency that we want to change, to "overcome." It is that decency which shuts these "niggers" in their board shacks with their middle-class television antennas rising above tar paper roofs. So crap on your middle class, on your decency, mister Churches man. Get out of your god-damned new rented car. Get out of your pressed, proper clothes. Get out of your unoffensive, shit-eating smile and crew-cut. Come join us who are sleeping on the floor. . . . Come with us and walk, not ride, the dusty streets of Gulfport. . . .
> (Quoted in Sutherland, 1965: 198)

The emergence on the project of a general ideology of personal libera-tion was paralleled by the appearance of many of the specific cultural elements that were later associated with the counterculture. Among these

were communal living, a more liberated sexuality, interracial relationships, and a distinctive style of speech and dress. Each bears at least passing mention.

Communal Living   By 1966 or 1967 every self-respecting university
town or "student ghetto" had its "Peace House" or other communal resi-
dence. Of course, the practice of group living was already well established among American college students. The system of Greek houses
common to most colleges and universities were only the most visible man-
ifestations of the practice. Houses based on religious preference or academic specialty were also common. So too was the practice of sharing an
off-campus apartment or house with several other students. As the baby
boom cohorts began to swell college enrollments in 1963 and 1964, the
pressure to maintain or expand these group living arrangements grew as
well.

What differentiated the Peace or other such houses from these other
communal forms was their avowedly political nature. These houses were
not primarily a means of sharing expenses or advancing one's career
through fraternal contacts but carrying out a politically "meaningful" experiment in communal living. David Harris' (1982: 159) description of
one such house captures the flavor of these experiments:

> Cooley Street formalized its collective existence and began calling
> itself the "Peace and Liberation Commune," pooling all money . . .
> in a common pot from which we all drew as we needed it. We were
> exuberant about the change and honestly thought we had invented
> the political unit of the coming age. The Sixties were, among other
> things, a time of "experiments," and the Peace and Liberation Com-
> mune was ours.

The Freedom Houses of Mississippi were clearly the model for these
communal experiments. Like explorers on some countercultural spice
trade, the volunteers brought the practice back with them from Mississippi. One volunteer remembers, "never intending to live any other way
[after Mississippi] . . . when I went off to grad school in the fall I ad-
vertised [in the school paper] for people interested in starting . . . what
I grandly called Freedom House North [laughing]."[40] And so the practice spread. What makes it interesting is that, like all the other cultural
elements touched on earlier, communal living had a logical, even necessary, relationship to the Summer Project. In the North, however, the
practice became less a matter of practical necessity than ideological
expression.

In Mississippi the potential for white violence and retaliation against "integrationists" was so great as to discourage all but the hardiest souls from housing the volunteers. As a result it was simply impossible to accommodate everyone in single-family houses. The Freedom Houses were used to offset the deficit. At the beginning of the summer, then, these houses bore no particular ideological or countercultural significance. By the end of the summer, however, the general ideological change mentioned earlier had transformed the houses—at least in the eyes of the volunteers—into the structural and symbolic expression of the link between personal and political change. The houses had come to be seen, not only as organizational vehicles for pursuing political change, but settings within which self-awareness and liberation could be achieved as well. It is this conception of the Freedom House, then, that is carried northward. To those who adopted the practice in the next few years, it was nothing less than a countercultural badge or symbol of one's commitment to liberation, both personal and political. The form may have remained the same, but the function served by the houses bore no relationship to the original purpose intended for the Freedom Houses.

It is also interesting to speculate on the relationship between the Freedom Houses and the emphasis on self-awareness and personal liberation that emerged during the summer. Quite simply, personal liberation does tend to become intensely political, or at least publicly relevant, in any communal setting. The demands of coordinating the lives and diverse personalities of the ten, twelve, or fifteen residents of the Freedom House almost certainly encouraged, if it did not precipitate, the impulse to self-criticism so evident on the project. Debbie Louis (1970: 68), herself a participant in the movement during this period, has expressed this point nicely.

> [T]he communal living was also a *discipline,* and one of the hardest to achieve because it required a kind of giving, an ability to criticize oneself and an objectivity difficult for many people to achieve. Most of all, this kind of interrelating meant each learning to be open and honest, and to accept the honesty of others . . . involvement on this level required a painful self-examination as well as the alteration of social values and *self*-image that few outside such conditions of struggle ever find necessary to undergo. It is hard to be honest with oneself, let alone lay oneself bare to others.

It may be, then, that the demands of living in the Freedom Houses or their Northern equivalents contributed to an emerging awareness and concern for issues of personal politics within the New Left. If so, like the houses themselves, this concern quickly transcended its functional origins. While the success of the projects depended on self-awareness and criticism, these traits came to be valued within the New Left as ends in themselves. Once again function gave way to form.

Styles of Speech and Dress   Much the same can be said for the styles of speech and dress the volunteers tended to adopt in Mississippi. Both had their origins in the conscious, and entirely sensible, efforts of SNCC's pioneering field secretaries to adopt the speech and dress style of rural blacks as a means of "relating to the people." By the time the volunteers arrived at orientation, the "SNCC uniform" was well established as standard issue in the organization. It was foreign to all but a few of the volunteers, however, as the detailed descriptions of staff dress in letters and journals suggest. One such account borders on ethnographic description:

> The male staff members tend all to dress alike in a similar "country style." It takes some getting used to, I must say. The standard outfit consists of blue denim pants and a long-sleeve [sic] work shirt (usually blue). A heavy denim jacket or bib-overalls appears to be optional.[41]

Blue jeans and a work shirt are hardly exotic dress for anyone who grew to adolescence in the mid to late Sixties, but for the majority of volunteers, raised amid the stylistic propriety of the Fifties and early Sixties, this was anything but normal dress. Before the summer, most of the male volunteers appear to have favored chinos or other dress slacks for everyday wear. Among their age peers, only "greasers" or working class kids wore blue jeans. But over the course of the summer, most of the male volunteers took to wearing jeans. In his autobiography, long-time SNCC member Cleveland Sellers (1973: 82) recalls how after only a few days in Oxford, a good many of the volunteers had begun to "emulate Bob [Moses'] slow, thoughtful manner of speaking," while others rushed downtown to purchase bib overalls, Moses' variation on the SNCC uniform.

As Sellers suggests, speech was another matter on which the volunteers proved impressionable. It was not simply the speed or cadence of speech that they tended to emulate. Just as evident was the conscious or unconscious adoption of movement vernacular, that mixture of rural phrases and urban street slang the volunteers found so appealing. In reading the volunteers' letters and journals, it is fascinating to observe the greater frequency with which certain words or phrases appear over the course of the summer. As the summer progressed, the volunteers were more likely to be "freedom high," rather than exhilarated, by the day's events. Instead of speculating about something, several volunteers were more prone to "reckon." In describing the aftermath of a confrontation in Itta Bena, a twenty-year-old Harvard undergraduate reported ecstatically that "three of the white cats who bothered our guys have been picked up by the FBI. You dig it—they are in a Southern jail."[42] In her interview, another volunteer recalled how "everyone, but especially the guys, got in to talking like the SNCC [staff] . . . I mean by the end of the summer we were all 'diggin' this and 'messin with' that . . . it was pretty funny. I remember my parents freaking out; they thought I had set my education back years!"[43]

One of the most fascinating aspects of the cultural revolution of the Sixties was the reversal of the traditional direction of cultural transmission. Instead of some elite dictating styles of dress or music in top-down fashion, cultural style came increasingly to be influenced by a kind of "trickle up" process of cultural diffusion. Speech was no exception to this pattern, with young urban blacks usually serving as the arbiters of style. The influence of Black English on American English was, of course, nothing new. The distinguished linguist, J. L. Dillard (1972, 1977) has argued convincingly that Black English has been an important source of linguistic innovation in America since the very earliest days of the slave trade. What marked the Sixties as distinctive was the *extent* to which the larger culture—and especially the youth counterculture—embraced the speech patterns of Black America. Freedom Summer and the speech patterns taken home by the volunteers contributed to this receptivity.

Sexual Experimentation The sexual atmosphere that pervaded the Summer Project led to a great deal of sexual experimentation during the summer. Nearly half of the volunteers interviewed described the summer as their first experience with the kind of open sexuality that came to characterize the era. Clearly they liked it. Barry Clemson recalled that he

> was much shyer and less experienced than most of my peers about . . . women. So that, you know, the whole sort of new view about open sexuality, of Freedom Summer, was . . . clearly an attraction for me . . . it was, for me, the first time of real sexual experimentation. During my time in Mississippi, I slept with more different women than I had up to that point.[44]

A female volunteer concurred:

> [Later on] sex became very problematic; I'm talking around '69, '70, somewhere in there . . . it was like the whole rhetoric of sexual liberation was used . . . in a kind of predatory way. It's like men had figured out it was a good line . . . but Freedom Summer never

felt like that . . . to me. It was all too new . . . it was the most open, adventurous sex I've ever had.[45]

As David Harris (1982: 67) has written, "the coupling was considered not so much license as one more small expression of a liberation that was taking place on all fronts." Like a concern for appearances and middle-class respectability, sexual inhibition was something that had to be overcome. To be truly "free," politically as well as personally, the volunteer had to work through their sexual "hang-ups." While not all of the volunteers subscribed to or practiced this doctrine (a third of those interviewed said they refrained from sex that summer), those who did returned North with a new *political* conception of sexuality that quickly became one of the cornerstones of the New Left and later counterculture. Freedom Summer was important for the early expression it gave this connection between political and sexual liberation.

Interracial Relationships The most explicit connection between sex and politics made during the summer centered on the many interracial relationships that developed on the project. These relationships represent one final example of a cultural element whose specific ideological connection to the project did not stop it from becoming an important component of the larger counterculture. In Mississippi, interracial relationships were the ultimate expression of the type of social and political revolution the volunteers hoped to help spark. This is not to say that all such liaisons that took place that summer were born of pure and principled motives. On the contrary, the dynamics underlying these relationships were complex and as likely to be harmful to one or both parties as not. Nonetheless, they were consistent with, and probably inevitable, given the project's ultimate goal: racial equality.

In the North, such relationships were stripped of much of the specific political significance they had in Mississippi. Instead, they became a more general symbol of the counterculture; an experience—one of many—that distinguished those who were liberated from those who were not. The Freedom Summer volunteers were among the first to be so liberated. Indeed, it was their example that helped establish the ideological salience of interracial relationships within the emerging counterculture.

Thus, while the SNCC staff was going through a process of soul-searching and stock-taking following the summer, a good many of the volunteers were experiencing their own personal adjustment crises. This was not the way it was supposed to be. From the beginning, the volunteers had been told—contemptuously by the SNCC staff and hopefully by parents—that they could always "go home." Unlike the black SNCC staff, the volunteers were supposed to be able to leave Mississippi and return to mainstream white society without much difficulty. This presumed that the volunteers would leave Mississippi the same as when they entered. Many did not. They had been changed by the political and personal "lessons" they had learned in Mississippi. Those lessons had the effect of moving them away from the institutions and identities they had previously organized their lives around, and toward an exciting new world they had only glimpsed during the summer. Their choice was either to rejoin mainstream society, often with considerable difficulty, or act on the lessons of Mississippi. Most of the volunteers chose the latter course. In so doing, they found an America newly receptive to the messages they brought back with them. America, too, had been affected by Freedom Summer.

Freedom Summer and the Liberalization of American Society

Successful social movements almost always occur in the context of a certain receptivity or vulnerability to protest on the part of those in power. Many examples of this tendency can be found in the literature on social movements and revolution. Skocpol (1979), for example, has shown that the Chinese, Russian, and French revolutions were preceded by major regime crises in all three countries. Similarly, Schwartz (1976) argues that a period of political instability preceded the rise of the Populist movement in the post-Civil War South. Or to take a contemporary example, the Moral Majority has not been successful simply because conservatives grew tired of "permissiveness" and organized against it. In part, it has succeeded because of a more general mobilization of conservative political sentiment in American society coupled with the legitimating sponsorship of Republican officeholders.

The New Left benefited from a similar process in the early to mid-Sixties. Then, however, the political drift was clearly in a more liberal or leftist direction. The result was that officeholders and the society at large were unusually receptive to or at least tolerant of the New Left for a period of time. Any serious attempt to account for this tolerance must make mention of Freedom Summer. This is not to deny the important trends in this direction prior to the summer. But if Freedom Summer was a response to those trends, it served also to magnify and extend them. It wasn't only the volunteers, SNCC staff, and residents of Mississippi who were affected by the events of the summer. American society shifted leftward in the wake of the project.

Reminders of McCarthyism

Much of the significance of Freedom Summer owes to its role as a political and cultural bridge between two relatively coherent eras which
have been inaccurately termed the Fifties and the Sixties. In point of
fact, the political and cultural Fifties extended into the chronological Sixties, just as the "Sixties experience" overlapped the chronological Seventies. One of the notable ways in which the political and cultural legacy
of the Fifties lived on into the early Sixties was in the lingering after-
effects of McCarthyism. Though muted somewhat, the near phobic preoccupation with Communism that had characterized the McCarthy years
was still very much in evidence in the early Sixties. These were, after all,
the years of the U-2 spy incident, fallout shelters, and the Cuban missile
crisis. The House Un-American Activities Committee (HUAC) remained a powerful political force in this country, and the threat of being
labeled a communist remained a potent deterrent to any leftist associations. In this atmosphere, activism of any sort seemed risky; associated in
the public mind with shadowy figures engaged in disreputable and
vaguely traitorous goings-on.

Freedom Summer helped change all this. This is not to say that at
summer's end Americans were prepared to welcome communists in their
midst. It is more accurate to say that Freedom Summer muted the association between activism and un-American activity in the minds of the
general public. The legitimacy, or at least tolerance, that leftist activism
had enjoyed during the Thirties had been partially restored. This transformation was crucial to the full flowering of the New Left. Had America and its leaders remained as fearful of leftist activism as they had been
in the Fifties, it is questionable whether as many people would have become active in the face of the stigma attached to movement participation.

What was it about Freedom Summer that abetted this transformation?
Various episodes or aspects of the project served to reconcile certain influential segments of American society to the necessity and promise of
activism. Much of the credit for this change must go to SNCC and the
courage of its leaders.

The Lawyers' Guild Controversy

Just how salient America's preoccupation with Communism remained
on the eve of the summer was made clear by the so-called Lawyers'
Guild controversy. At the height of planning for the summer, Jack
Greenberg, Director of the NAACP Legal Defense and Education Fund,
threatened to withdraw the considerable legal resources of his organization if the National Lawyers' Guild were allowed to participate in the

Bob Moses, architect and guiding spirit of the Freedom Summer project.
Copyright © 1964, Steve Schapiro, Black Star.

James Forman (with pipe), executive secretary of SNCC, in front of a group of volunteers at orientation in Oxford, Ohio, June 1964. Copyright © 1964, Steve Schapiro, Black Star.

Practicing nonviolence at orientation. A group of volunteers assumes a protective position against the imaginary assault of a segregationist mob. For many, such exercises would come in handy later that summer. *Copyright © 1964, Steve Schapiro, Black Star.*

John Doar, head of the Civil Rights Division at the Justice Department, spoke at orientation to warn students not to expect federal protection while in Mississippi. *Copyright © 1964, Steve Schapiro, Black Star.*

Many of the volunteers remember being angered or shocked by Doar's remarks. Here a female volunteer challenges Doar's statements. Copyright © 1964, Steve Schapiro, Black Star.

Much of the impact of orientation came from the education the volunteers received at the hands of the COFO staff and local Mississippians. Here Len Edwards (*center*) and other volunteers get a briefing from Charles McLauren (*left*) and other members of the project staff. *Copyright © 1964, Steve Schapiro, Black Star.*

Waiting for the buses that would take them to Mississippi, a group of volunteers and staff link arms. *Copyright © 1964, Steve Schapiro, Black Star.*

Saying goodbye at the close of orientation. Copyright © 1964, Steve Schapiro, Black Star.

The charred remains of the Mt. Zion Baptist Church near Philadelphia, Mississippi. It was to this site that the three project workers—Chaney, Goodman, and Schwerner—came on June 21 to investigate the burning. *Wide World Photos.*

After leaving the site, the three were arrested and later that night released into the waiting arms of a white mob. The workers' burned-out
station wagon was found the next day, but it would be August before
the bodies of the trio were recovered. *Copyright © 1964, Steve Schapiro,
Black Star.*

Rita Schwerner, widow of one of the murdered workers, impressed many of the volunteers with her quiet courage. At Oxford, she told a second group of volunteers that the disappearance of the three workers only made it more important that the project go forward. *Copyright © 1964, Steve Schapiro, Black Star.*

Armed Mississippi police were a presence throughout the summer, sub-
jecting volunteers to the violent intimidation tactics used against blacks
all year long. *Copyright © 1964, Steve Schapiro, Black Star.*

Canvassing for voters was tedious, time-consuming work. Here volunteers attempt to persuade a group to register. *Copyright © 1964, Steve Schapiro, Black Star.*

For all the drama associated with the project, the days were generally
routine. Here a volunteer leads a Freedom School class (*right fore-*
ground), while a construction project and picnic go on around him.
Staughton Lynd Collection, State Historical Society of Wisconsin.

A volunteer leads a Freedom School class. Project organizers expected 1,000 students, but ended up with at least 3,000. *Staughton Lynd Collection, State Historical Society of Wisconsin.*

A relaxed moment on the project. Four volunteers stand in front of the project office, decorated with a campaign poster for Victoria Gray, the Mississippi Freedom Democratic Party (MFDP) candidate for the U.S. Senate. *Sandra Adickes Collection, State Historical Society of Wisconsin.*

Holding posters depicting Schwerner, Chaney, and Goodman (*from left to right*), MFDP activists demonstrate in front of the Democratic National Convention hall in Atlantic City, New Jersey, August 1964. *Copyright © 1964, Bob Adelman.*

project. Long suspected of having a history of "communist association," the National Lawyers' Guild was an organization of leftist lawyers who had offered to help with the flood of legal work expected to arise during the summer. Needing all the help it could get, project planners had gratefully accepted the offer. It hadn't taken any particular courage to do so. What did take courage was holding firm in the face of the red-baiting that accompanied the controversy. SNCC came under a great deal of pressure to reverse its position and bar the Lawyers' Guild from participation in the project. By its refusal to do so, SNCC moved the American left decisively away from the preoccupation with communism that had prevailed in the Fifties and toward the ideological stance that was to characterize the Sixties. Instead of being "soft on communism," as some of its critics charged, SNCC simply saw the issue as irrelevant. As James Forman (1972: 383) put it, "we decided that the so-called fights of the Thirties and Forties were not really our fights, although some tried to impose them on us." The white New Left adopted much the same stance. Even many in the Old Left who had been exasperated by SNCC's stance on the issue were moved to change their minds as the decade wore on. Writing in 1970, the liberal journalist Pat Watters (1971: 305–306) offered the following "confession" of his own:

> Through the Mississippi Summer . . . many liberals, black as well as white, expressed genuine concern, worry over whether, indeed, the taint of communism had attached itself to the movement. . . . The very language of the concern sounds quaint now, only six years later—a mark of how far the nation has been able to move from the political straitjacket of Communist phobia, mostly thanks to the young, whose model in dismissing the Communist issue as irrelevant was SNCC. We talked seriously in 1964 . . . about whether there had been "infiltration," or even—dread thought!—"a takeover" . . . the consensus was that no "takeover" or even real infiltration had occurred, but that SNCC was endangering the reputation of the movement by refusing to deny it, or even to discuss the question. This was the most exasperating thing of all—their stubborn insistence that if a person believed in integration and was willing to work with them, even risk his life, his past or even present political persuasion, made no difference. We had not ever encountered such an attitude; it took me a long time, years, to realize that it was the essence of real civil libertarianism and to understand how deep into doctrinaire acceptance of Cold War repression I was in 1964.

SNCC's resolve in the face of this "repression" helped render it ineffective and establish a legitimacy for activism that the left hadn't enjoyed since the Thirties.

Red-Baiting Mississippi Style

The crude, vitriolic attempts of segregationists to red-bait the project also served to undermine the legitimacy of the whole issue of "communist infiltration." Lest they be identified with the racially tinged anticommunism of their Southern brethren, liberal cold warriors moved to soften their own anticommunist rhetoric or otherwise distance themselves from the issue. As a result, the issue began to take on a distinctly Southern and racist cast that undercut its credibility elsewhere in the country. Statements such as the following editorial that appeared in the July 30 Jackson *Clarion-Ledger* helped to regionalize the issue:

Mississippi Invasion

A thousand college students from the North are reported to be invading Mississippi this summer in order to engage in a Negro voter registration drive. It is unbelievable that a thousand college students would do this of their own volition. Those who know the ways of propaganda, especially of a Communist nature, probably correctly suspect that idealism of some college youngsters has been taken advantage of by some very hard boiled left-wingers and Communists who know exactly what they want to do—stir up trouble in the South.

It is interesting to note how, within almost hours after the disappearance of the first three civil rights agitators in the South, there were parades in Washington, Boston, in the federal courthouse in Chicago and in many other places across the land, demanding that federal troops be sent into Mississippi.

If preparations had not been carefully made a long time ago for such demonstrations, they could not have come about so speedily.

This newspaper a long time ago pointed out that it is a deliberate attempt by Communist forces in the United States to stir up racial strife in this nation. The ultimate aim is, we believe, a black revolution. This invasion of Mississippi this summer is, in our estimation, part and parcel of this plan.

These young people who have gone to Mississippi have been attending training schools which can be described as nothing short of inflammatory in their instructions to these young people. The naive inexperience of these youngsters has been preyed on and they have been stirred up by tales of horror and violence that simply don't exist in Mississippi.

Entirely aside from the arrogance and the holier-than-thou attitude of these college students, who are going to Mississippi with no knowledge of the Negro problem or how to handle the situation, the really serious aspect of this invasion of Mississippi is the fact that this is part of an over-all scheme to destroy the United States by way of a racial revolution.[46]

For its part, SNCC did its best to discredit the issue by widely circulating prime examples of racially motivated red-baiting directed at the organization. So on June 18, a mimeographed letter from SNCC's Executive Secretary, James Forman, was mailed to thousands of "friends of SNCC" throughout the country. Enclosed with Forman's note was a sample of the "viscious propaganda" then being directed at the Summer Project. It took the form of a letter from a local chairman of the National States' Rights Party to SNCC's Chairman, John Lewis:

Mr. Lewis: June 16, 1964

It is to the credit of the majority of your race in the Dayton area that they had enough good sense to stay away from your Communistic race-mixing attempt on Sunday, June 14th. They are beginning to wake up to the fact that it is immoral, unjust, stupid, against the Laws of Nature (each to his OWN KIND), and absolutely Communist-dictated!

For your information, we had observers at your Communistic "song-fest" and were kept regularly informed as to the actions and general stupidity, not only of members of your race, but also of the morally rotten outcasts of the White race that went with you. These "White Negroes" are the rottenest of the race-mixing criminals. All race-mixers will some day be brought to justice for their crimes against humanity and all future generations, and, since race-mixing is morally more CRIMINAL than MURDER, it would give me great satisfaction if I were selected to sit on such a jury.

You are right about one thing—this is going to be a long, hot, summer—but the "heat" will be applied to the race-mixing TRASH by the DECENT people who do not believe in racial mongrelization through racial prostitution, which is in violation of all concepts of justice, decency, and Common Sense. When your Communist-oriented GOONS get to Mississippi, I hope they get their just dues as infiltraters [sic] of an enemy power, which they will be in FACT.

Charles J. Benner
Chairman, Unit 42
National States Rights Party[47]

When associated with racial demogoguery of this extreme sort, the credibility of the "communist issue" suffered, as did those who espoused it. Accordingly, public figures became increasingly reluctant to speak out on the issue. While it was understood that politics often made for strange bedfellows, few national politicians cared to be associated with the likes of Charles J. Benner. Thus discredited, the issue of "communistic infiltration" failed to tarnish the project's image.

The Media and Mississippi

In a June 1964 Gallup poll, the American public identified civil rights as the "most important problem confronting the country" (Gallup, 1972: 1894). The results had been the same in the two previous Gallup polls dating back to the May 1963 demonstrations in Birmingham, Alabama. The national media had made civil rights the top news story in the country. Northern journalists covered events in the South much as war correspondents would, and it was clear in this "war" whom they regarded as the "good guys" and the "bad guys." This was true long before Freedom Summer, but the onset of the project created a story angle that intensified media and audience interest in the struggle: the sons and daughters of American privilege, enroute to Mississippi to join the fight for Negro freedom. The media, in turn, played the story for all it was worth. The sub-headline to the July 25 *Saturday Evening Post* story on Freedom Summer captures the flavor of much of the reporting. It reads: "AT THE RISK OF THEIR LIVES, HUNDREDS OF NORTHERN STUDENTS ARE CHALLENGING THE HEART OF THE DEEP SOUTH." The headline of a June 25 front-page story in the *San Jose Mercury* put it even more succinctly: "THEY WALK IN FEAR, BUT WON'T GIVE UP." The "they" of course, referred not to Mississippi's black population, or the SNCC staff, but to the Northern volunteers, who were described in glowing terms in virtually every major article written on the project. The *Saturday Evening Post* article quoted an M.I.T. staff psychiatrist as saying volunteers were "an extraordinarily healthy bunch of kids, mentally and physically. There aren't a lot of starry-eyed idealists here." Readers of a July 13 *Newsweek* article learned that despite differences, the volunteers "had much in common. They are scared and brave all at once. They are bright. They are energetic." A *Look* magazine article dated September 8 reported that the volunteers "looked disturbingly like the kids next door."

These lead articles in America's major newsmagazines were supplemented on a daily basis by a steady stream of stories on Mississippi in local newspapers throughout the country. In addition to wire service stories reporting events in the state, these papers ran profiles on, or printed letters written by, the hometown volunteers. The form of these "human interest" stories varies little from paper to paper. The following example nicely captures the style:

Stuart Rawlings III in Civil Rights Fight

by
Joan Woods, Society Editor

Friends of Stuart Rawlings III, son of the junior Mr. and Mrs. Rawlings, will be interested to learn he will leave today to take part in a summer long civil rights movement in Mississippi.

It comes as no surprise that the Stanford student will devote his vacation to such a cause. Three years ago he traveled to Africa to participate in the Operation Crossroads program and last year he worked in the slums of Lima, Peru, and the towns in the Andes.

Hispanic American studies are his main interest along with economics, and he will do graduate work in that subject or in law when he completes his senior year next summer. Eventually he hopes to go into international relations.

During the past week Stuart has been undergoing a training program in Ohio with 200 other students from Stanford, Yale, Harvard, Princeton, Sarah Lawrence and Vassar. They will be part of a group of 1,000 who will tutor Negroes to enable them to pass voting tests for the November elections.

The historic undertaking is being sponsored by the National Council of Churches and the Congress of Federated Organizations which is composed of CORE, the NAACP, the Student Non-Violent Coordinating Committee and the Southern Christian Leadership Conference of the Rev. Dr. Martin Luther King, Jr.

"We're very proud of him," Kay Rawlings, a former president of the Junior League, told us yesterday, "but of course we're scared to death. They're prepared to face anything."

The young man will keep his parents in touch with developments by means of a diary which some day he hopes to publish.[48]

Much of the credit for orchestrating the media event that Freedom Summer became must go to SNCC. There was nothing accidental in this. SNCC had planned from the outset to exploit the project's built-in news value. For instance, all who filled out the original project applications were required to provide the staff with the names, addresses, and frequency of publication of their "hometown and city and college or college-area newspapers." They were also asked to list any "specific press or broadcast media contacts you have made in preparation for working in the Mississippi Summer Project."[49] Finally, they asked each volunteer to send with their completed applications four formal photographs of themselves for use by the Communications Office in Jackson.

SNCC's intention had been to use these materials and information to coordinate a disciplined media campaign that kept all hometown and college newspapers (and other media outlets) apprised of their Johnny's or Susie's experiences in Mississippi. Let Johnny be beaten on the streets of Itta Bena and the dedicated folks in the Communications Office would see to it that the folks back home would be reading about it in a matter of days. The same would happen were Susie to find herself in jail for violating Greenwood's antipicketing ordinance.

Ultimately, the pace of events and the logistics of the project made it impossible to sustain this media blitz. Some of the need for such a campaign had also been eliminated by the kidnapping of the three workers in June. No longer was there a need for SNCC to write stories to send to the media; reporters were already there en masse covering the story themselves. Accordingly, the efforts of the Communications Office were increasingly directed toward insuring an efficient and timely flow of information to the assembled media. The provision of this service earned the office and the project the goodwill of the media, a goodwill that couldn't help but be reflected in the coverage afforded the project. Robert Beyers, then, as now, Director of Public Information for Stanford University and the main coordinator of the Communications Office during his month as a volunteer, describes the workings and ultimate effect of the office:

> What we had going for us was credibility, and I wanted to make absolutely sure that we kept it. One of the things we did was to attach a level of . . . reliability to every piece of information . . . we gave out. We would say to somebody, "we have a report from two people we think are reliable [that] churches [are] burning at X and Y streets and their reliability is such that we think it's about 60% to 70% . . . that that's happened. But the local fire department denies that there's any fires. I can tell you with 100% certainty that we are dispatching four people in a car to go down and see what's there and take pictures." And that won us enormous friends with the press.[50]

While the Communications Office was shaping the media's coverage of the project through its role as an information clearinghouse, the volunteers were busy taking over one of the primary functions originally envisioned for the office. At the urging of the SNCC staff, many of the volunteers prepared accounts of their experiences in Mississippi for publication in hometown newspapers. Many of these accounts had the quality of personal dispatches from a war zone. For example, in a July 22 story entitled "Ordeal in a Dixie Jail," Margaret Aley described the harrowing five days she and a group of six other volunteers spent in jail in Greenwood. She concluded her story with a brief account of the "trial" the seven volunteers received when they were finally released from jail.

> On Monday, while our attorney was seeing the Federal judge in Oxford, we were all hustled into the city court here, given what they call a trial, and convicted, and sentenced to 30 days in jail and fined $100 each.
>
> There was something disturbing about it all, beyond the kangaroo court atmosphere and procedure, and finally I realized what it was—a grim irony: behind the judge stood the American flag.
>
> You get the oddest feeling of remoteness from the rest of the world down here. In Mississippi, only Mississippi seems real. California seems so far, far off, almost as if it were a memory out of another life.[51]

From SNCC's point of view this coverage was hypocritical, focused as it was on the volunteers and not Mississippi per se. They, of course, were right; but from a broader historical perspective, this coverage served a very important purpose. By representing the first major instance of leftist activism since the Depression as a form of principled "missionary work" by the "best and the brightest" of American youth, the media helped set the stage for what was to follow. One of the volunteers, Andy Schiffrin, explains:

> That summer . . . legitimized political action on a large scale in a very confrontational . . . way . . . so you could go out there and . . . demonstrate . . . [and] you weren't wrong to do it . . . the Civil Rights Movement that summer . . . was a very important . . . media event in most of the country. There [were] . . . large numbers of people and a lot of publicity . . . as opposed to . . . the anti-HUAC demonstrations or Fair Play for Cuba or labor unions which had been completely discredited by the media . . . if you look at how much media attention came out of the . . . summer . . . I think it did help create a new climate . . . that legitimized counterculture political activities; political activities that were not in the mainstream and that was an important thing to happen at that time because of the . . . mindset that people had [been in].[52]

Activism had been reclaimed as a normal and legitimate part of American life; and the media had played an important role in the reclamation project.

The extent and generally favorable editorial tone of the media's coverage also helps account for the influence wielded by the volunteers upon their return to the North. Their stature as "returning heroes" or role models had less to do with their actions in Mississippi than with the publicity attached to the campaign. It was the media that granted them celebrity status, a status that in turn gave them a great deal of political and cultural cachet among their age peers back home. Without that cachet, the volunteers could never have hoped to play the central role they did in the development of the activist subculture. The volunteers may have carried the "lessons of Mississippi" North with them, but it was the media that established the credibility of lessons and carriers alike through their response to the project. Representatives of professions other than journalism had a hand in this process as well.

Doctors, Lawyers, and Ministers

The volunteers were not the only ones to visit Mississippi during the summer of 1964. Between May and September another 650 persons came to assist the project in various ways. These "auxiliary forces" were made up of three principal groups. The largest was the contingent of 400 ministers, priests, and rabbis assembled by the National Council of Churches to minister to the spiritual needs of the volunteers.[53] This group formed the basis of what was to become the Delta Ministry, a highly successful volunteer ministry that served Mississippi for nearly twenty years after the project. Next there were the 150 or so volunteer lawyers, under the direction of SNCC field secretary, Hunter Morey, who negotiated their way through Mississippi's legal thicket on behalf of the volunteers.[54] Finally, the Medical Committee For Human Rights dispatched some 100 personnel—including doctors, nurses and psychologists—to treat the various physical and emotional injuries suffered by project participants.[55]

While they were obviously sympathetic to the project to begin with, the visiting professionals had their sympathies deepened by what they saw in Mississippi. Despite their relatively short stays in the state, they managed to see a lot. The clergy, in particular, were spared none of the violence directed at the other project participants.

> This morning as five of us—two local Negro girls, one white COFO boy, a white rabbi from Ohio, and I—were returning from voter registration work, we were attacked by two local white men. We were walking along a railroad track, when their truck stopped. They got out and came toward us with two iron bars, each over a foot and a half long. I started to run. . . . The younger of the two white men came right up to me and started to beat me on the head and

shoulders with his iron bar. . . . Meanwhile, the older man was beating my two friends with his iron bar. Dave Owen, the other COFO worker, had . . . assumed the non-violent position, but he had been hit in parts of his head and shoulders. The rabbi had forgotten all about the non-violent position, and when he fell he did not pull in his knees or guard his head. The older white attacker beat him severly [*sic*] on the head and shoulders. . . . As I returned to the top of the bank, the rabbi was kneeling and blood was streaming from wounds on his eye and the back of his head. The attackers had gone back to their truck. I helped the rabbi to his feet and the five of us moved on down the track trying to get to a nearby Negro church . . . then the same truck came up unexpectedly behind us. . . . The younger man leaped from the cab with his iron bar and said, "I'm going to wup 'em again." The rabbi was standing up in a daze and bleeding profusely. . . . The man raised his bar and hit the rabbi again. . . . The man then returned to the cab of the pickup truck and they sat. We crossed the street heading toward the church as quickly as we could. While helping the rabbi, I noticed that he was growing weaker from loss of blood. . . . We [made it] . . . to the church and then went to a Methodist hospital . . . the rabbi was . . . in such a terrible condition that we weren't sure of the extent of his injuries.[56]

Even those most detached of professionals, the doctors, found it hard to retain their composure in the face of the conditions they witnessed. Perhaps the best example of this involved an expert pathologist, Dr. David Spain, called in to conduct an independent examination of James Chaney following the discovery in August of the bodies of the three missing workers. Although nominally sympathetic to the project, Spain had remained uninvolved prior to his visit to Mississippi. Once there, however, he was gradually moved to abandon his stance of professional detachment. By the time of his examination, it was all he could do to keep himself under control. His anger was directed as much at a Mississippi medical establishment that had conspired to keep news of Chaney's injuries from reaching the public, as it was at the killers themselves. In Spain's own words:

I could barely believe the destruction to these frail young bones. In my twenty-five years as a pathologist and medical examiner, I have never seen bones so severely shattered, except in tremendously high speed accidents or airplane crashes.

It was obvious to any first-year medical student that this boy had been beaten to a pulp.

I have been conducting examinations of this type for a quarter century, but for the first time I found myself so emotionally charged

that it was difficult to retain my professional composure. I felt every
fiber in my own body shaking, as I involuntarily imagined the scene
at the time this youngster received such a vicious beating to shatter
his bones in this incredible manner.

I felt like screaming at these impassive observers still silently
standing across the table.

But I knew that no rage of mine would tear their curtain of silence. I took off the green surgical smock they had given me, thanked
them for their cooperation, and left the room as fast as I could. I
went straight to the hotel, dictated a report of my gruesome findings,
and left immediately for the airport.

I felt an irrational, immediate urge to get out of Mississippi the
fastest way possible. The first plane out went the wrong way from
New York—to New Orleans—but I felt an indescribable relief when
I boarded it and flew—I guess you could say . . . fled—from Jackson.
(Quoted in Spain, 1964: 49)

Finally, a good many of the lawyers who visited the state came away
radicalized as well. It was not the specific legal subterfuges they encountered, nor the contempt citations they received that did the trick, but
rather the wholesale disregard for the rule of law that characterized the
state. As young and generally idealistic lawyers, the travesty of Mississippi justice offended them deeply. At the end of the summer one lawyer expressed his outrage at what he had witnessed in a telegram to a
member of the Democratic Credentials Committee in Atlantic City.

To: Gov. Lawrence, Credential [sic] Committee
      Democratic Convention
      Atlantic City, New Jersey

I have just spent a week in Mississippi as a volunteer attorney
with the Lawyer's Constitutional Defense Committee. This week I
appeared in court in Laurel, Mississippi, the home of Senator
Collins, on behalf of white and Negro COFO workers who were
beaten by local white people. The complaints were dismissed. I personally witnessed an assault upon a white COFO worker engaged in
voter registration on August 17. From personal observations I know
there is no justice in Laurel or personal safety in Mississippi. The
state of Mississippi is a police state rivaling Nazi Germany. Today,
August 22, COFO workers in Laurel were assaulted and fired upon.
I urge you to seat the Freedom Democratic Party.

                              Edward I. Koch, Democratic Dist. Leader
                              1st Assembly District
                              Manhattan, New York[57]

As the name on the telegram indicates, the lawyers and other professionals who volunteered their services in Mississippi were not without influence of their own. They hardly constituted a random sample of all Americans. Instead, they were young, idealistic, and generally ambitious representatives of society's most respected professions. As such, they were opinion leaders in their own right. Returning North, they now added their influential voices to those of the volunteers and members of the media in calling for broad political and cultural changes in American society. They were joined in this call by one final group: the parents of the volunteers.

Change on the Home Front

For every volunteer who went to Mississippi, there were usually two parents at home anxiously attuned to events in Washington and Mississippi. Typically, this resulted in the political reeducation of three people rather than one. Not being in Mississippi themselves, the parents were ordinarily not affected to the extent their sons or daughters were. Judging from the interviews, however, it seems safe to say that the political attitudes of most parents became more liberal as a result of the summer. One volunteer spoke for a number of others when he said, "I think it [Freedom Summer] opened their eyes a lot too. They had always been . . . 'good liberals' . . . but very cautious. . . . [But] they got really into it that summer, writing letters; the whole bit. . . . My mother still refers to that summer as her political 'coming out' party."[58]

Given the nature of their experiences that summer, it is not surprising that the parents found themselves radicalized a bit in the process. For one thing, events in Mississippi encouraged this result. The deaths of Chaney, Goodman, and Schwerner, the arrests or beatings of their own sons and daughters, the failure of the Justice Department to protect the workers; these and a host of other events pushed the parents in this direction. However, more important than the events themselves was the way many of the parents reacted to them. They did so, not in private, apolitical ways, but by engaging in political action of their own. Often prodded by memos from SNCC, the parents beseiged their elected representatives and the Justice Department with letters and phone calls demanding protection for the civil rights workers. For instance, shortly after the disappearance of the three workers, all parents of volunteers received a five-page memo from COFO headquarters in Atlanta detailing the failure of the federal government to respond to the disappearance of the three workers. In part the memo read:

Immediate action is needed by all those concerned with the safety of the Mississippi Summer Volunteers. Unless the President and the Attorney General can be convinced of the need for Federal protection of civil rights workers in Mississippi, the events of Philadelphia are almost certain to be repeated over and over again in the next two months.

We are asking all parents to use their influence in the coming week to pressure President Johnson and Attorney General Kennedy into a commitment to protect workers *before* violence occurs, instead of waiting until the worst has happened before they offer their help.[59]

Specifically, the parents were asked to disseminate the information contained in the memo to "local papers and radio and TV stations" and to "contact the President, Attorney General, and your own state and national representatives [to] demand immediate Federal protection for *all* people in Mississippi." Better yet, they could "organize friends and relatives to make the same demand."[60]

Many of the parents went the COFO leadership one step better. They organized themselves into various support groups with names like "Parents Emergency Committee for Federal Protection of Students in the Mississippi Summer Project," "Parents Mississippi Emergency Committee" and "Parents Summer Project Support Organization."[61] How many of these organizations sprang up and what proportion of all parents were affiliated with them is not certain. What is clear from the fragmentary records of these groups is that they were not merely paper organizations. The largest of the groups were associations of many parents actively engaged in lobbying, fund-raising, and a variety of educational efforts. Appendix E includes materials produced by one such committee composed of parents from New York, New Jersey, Maryland, Massachusetts, and Washington, D.C. These records show that in the first week of the summer the group had already: (1) completed a mailing to all parents of volunteers, (2) issued a press release and held a press conference to urge stronger protective measures for civil rights workers, and (3) lobbied extensively in Washington on behalf of the Summer Project. Nor did that mark the end of the group's efforts. As the summer wore on and the initial fears of wholesale violence dissipated somewhat, the group shifted its efforts to fund-raising and educational campaigns. Indeed, this and several other parents' groups remained in existence well after the summer ended. For instance, the California-based Parents Mississippi Freedom Association finally disbanded on September 22, 1966, after nearly two-and-a-half years of continuous operation. During that period of time it was estimated that they raised nearly $60,000 to support the work of SNCC as well as other civil rights groups.[62]

The final important point about the parents—both in and out of these groups—is that like the doctors and lawyers who visited Mississippi, they did not represent a random cross-section of the American public. If theirs were the sons and daughters of privilege, they were the source of that privilege. They were drawn from the middle and upper-middle classes, were extremely well educated, and possessed strong links to the "powers that be." When the aforementioned California parents group was trying to decide whether a meeting with then governor, Pat Brown, would be of any real value, they simply had a friend of his on the committee call him up and ask him.[63] Nationally, the volunteers' parents included Arthur Schlesinger, Jr. and Congressman Don Edwards (D.Cal.). The lists of references the volunteers were required to include on their applications read like a Who's Who of the era. Besides Messrs. Schlesinger and Edwards, the list includes such notables as Eugene Rostow, Arthur Goldberg, Kingman Brewster, Bill Moyers, William Sloan Coffin, Herbert Marcuse, U. N. Ambassador, Sidney Yates, Rep. Phillip Burton (D-Cal.), and many others. As Len Edwards wryly observed: "part of the big impact of the . . . [summer] was that [the] upper-middle-class parents who sent their kids down there . . . no way they were going to let something happen to their kids. They were pushing every button . . . they knew; and they knew a lot of very big buttons!"[64] As a group, the parents enjoyed unique access to the media, to educators, and to the halls of government. In turn, they used this access, not just to protect their children, but to voice their increasingly liberal views on Mississippi, civil rights, and the role of activism in American life. In speaking out, these parents reinforced their own growing radicalism even as they were changing the minds of others. With obvious pride, Stuart Rawlings recalled his father's courage in speaking out in very conservative circles:

> [A]t the end of his day's work he would go to the Pacific Union Club in San Francisco which . . . was really Goldwater conservative, and he would face the people there who had read about me . . . in the San Francisco Chronicle. . . . A lot of them did not think that I was doing a very good thing. . . . He turned some minds around . . . some of [his friends] supported him and he began to . . . develop a sense of pride [in] what I was doing.[65]

In countless encounters like this one, the ripple effects of Freedom Summer spread outward from Mississippi in ever-widening circles. The

SNCC staff, the volunteers, their parents, friends, and other relatives, the general public; each in turn felt the effects of the Summer Project. Nor were these effects narrowly political, only changing attitudes on Mississippi or civil rights generally. Most important, the American attitude toward activism had begun to change. Dire warnings of Communist infiltration had failed to deter the volunteers. Fears of wholesale violence had proved exaggerated. Parents who had opposed their children going to Mississippi were now singing a different tune. Writing toward the end of the summer, Phillip Hocker's mother found that "being a hero's mother in a small town is an odd experience. . . . It's the greatest thing that's [sic] happened to mothers since Sigmund Freud."[66]

All of this was in marked contrast to the reminders of McCarthyism that greeted the project. Freedom Summer had helped move America decisively out of the McCarthy era. The stage was now set for the "Sixties." To many observers, the era commenced at Berkeley in the fall of 1964. The Freedom Summer volunteers were conspicuous by their presence.

5

Applying the Lessons
of Mississippi

THE VOLUNTEERS who fanned out from Missis-
sippi following the summer were a changed lot. Politically they had become more radical as a result of their experiences in Mississippi, and personally they found themselves attracted to an embryonic counterculture
stressing community and an ideology of personal liberation. Returning
North, most of the volunteers had every intention of acting on the personal and political lessons they had learned in Mississippi. Their capacity
to do so, however, varied greatly, depending on the social circumstances
in which they found themselves. For those volunteers who had graduated the previous spring or who returned either to full-time jobs or to
colleges that lacked an activist subculture, the transition out of Mississippi was particularly difficult. They found little or no social support
or organizational vehicles to sustain the politics or way of life they had
enjoyed during Freedom Summer.

The majority of returning volunteers were not so isolated. Instead
they returned, usually in clusters of ten, fifteen, or twenty, to the major
colleges and universities that had contributed the majority of the volunteers in the first place.[1] So Harvard absorbed nearly twenty-five returning volunteers. Stanford, Yale, and Berkeley received just as many.
Michigan, Wisconsin, Princeton, and Chicago welcomed back only
slightly fewer. These clusters of workers constituted a loose network of
experienced activists. Moreover, because of the media attention accorded their summer activities, the volunteers returned to school to find
themselves regarded as conquering heroes by the small but growing
activist subcultures on their respective campuses. These subcultures were
to provide the immediate audience and vehicle for acting on the lessons

of Mississippi. The first campus to receive the "good news" was the University of California at Berkeley.[2]

The Free Speech Movement and the Rise of the Student Movement

The significance of the Free Speech Movement in the evolution of the New Left has long been recognized. A major chronicler of the movement, Max Heirich, describes it "as the first of a new genre of conflict on American campuses." He adds that "the Free Speech controversy set the tone for an entire college generation's confrontation with authority. Some of the conflicts that ensued grew directly from the influence of Berkeley; others arose independently but adopted . . . the Berkeley style" (1968: 1). New Left historian, Wini Breines (1982: 12), concurs:

> [The] FSM [Free Speech Movement] was critical because, as the first major white student rebellion, it laid down the terms for many others during the rest of the Sixties. The ideas, demands, and experiences at Berkeley were enunciated time and again, and may serve as a characteristic scenario by which to understand the politics of the early student movement. FSM forced the white student movement's attention and focus back to the northern campuses.

As such, "the Free Speech Movement was politically the first and most important white student demonstration of the 1960s" (Breines, 1982: 23). This much is well known. What has never been fully appreciated is the extent of the links between Freedom Summer and the Free Speech Movement. It is impossible to know whether the Free Speech Movement would have occurred in the absence of Freedom Summer. What is certain is that for most of the leaders of the Berkeley revolt, the movement was seen as an extension of the civil rights struggle and the Summer Project in particular. The tactical, ideological, and personnel imprint of Freedom Summer was everywhere evident in the events at Berkeley. A review of those events makes the extent of that imprint clear.

The initial focus of the controversy was a twenty-six-foot section of sidewalk at the Bancroft and Telegraph entrance to the Berkeley campus that, over the years, had come to serve as the spot where campus political groups set up tables to solicit funds and distribute literature. Beginning in the fall semester, the university administration sought to ban these activities from this location. A coalition of twenty-two campus groups protested the new regulations and, after a series of unsatisfactory compromises by the administration, set up tables in defiance of the ban. The result of this September 30 protest was the suspension of eight students and a ten-hour sit-in in the Sproul Hall Administration Building. The following day, October 1, brought the return of the tables and the arrest of Jack Weinberg for distributing materials for CORE. However, before police could remove Weinberg from campus, the police car was surrounded by hundreds of students protesting his arrest. The sit-in continued for thirty-two hours before an agreement was reached between protest leaders and University President, Clark Kerr. Negotiations between the movement and the administration on how to implement the agreement foundered over the next two months and were finally broken off when Kerr announced his intention to proceed with plans to suspend four protest leaders. His action precipitated an all-night sit-in, December 2–3, in Sproul Hall. It ended only after 783 students were arrested on orders from Governor Pat Brown.

Following an ugly incident at a special convocation called by Kerr, in which protest leader Mario Savio was dragged from the stage, an outraged faculty met and voted overwhelmingly to urge an end to restrictions on campus political activity. Meeting later in the month, the University of California Regents followed suit by adopting provisional rules granting students the same rights of political action and expression as ordinary citizens. The Free Speech Movement had won.

But what of Freedom Summer? How had the Summer Project shaped events at Berkeley? First, the majority of Berkeley's returning volunteers took part in the movement. Of the twenty-one volunteers known to have returned to Cal for the fall semester, twelve show up on the list of those arrested in connection with the December 2–3 sit-in in Sproul Hall.[3] Moreover, two of the returning volunteers played central roles in the unfolding conflict. Steven Weissman emerged as one of the principal strategists of the Free Speech forces.[4] But it was Mario Savio, in his role as principal spokesperson for the movement, who emerged from the conflict as the first white activist "star" of the Sixties. In a movement that, in best SNCC fashion, publicly eschewed leaders, it was Savio who attracted the lion's share of media and administrative attention. It wasn't simply his eloquence and integrity as a speaker; more significant was the catalytic role he played at the outset of the conflict and at various critical junctures in the unfolding drama. It was Savio who led 300 protesters into Sproul Hall on September 30, in what turned into the initial sit-in of the conflict. The next day it was Savio who transformed the capture of the university police car into a "focused rally" by climbing atop the car and addressing the crowd (Heirich, 1968: 114). Later that same day, it was Savio who assumed the role of point man in the negotiations with the administration when he climbed down from the police car and left to present the movement's "demands" to University Chancellor Edward Strong (Heirich, 1968: 119). After those negotiations failed to produce any agrement, it was Savio who again led a group of protesters into Sproul Hall for a second sit-in. When an agreement was finally reached the next day, Savio was one of nine student leaders to sign it. Moreover, it fell to Savio to return to the beleaguered police car to announce the agreement and urge the remaining demonstrators to go home. When the agreement collapsed two months later, it was Savio at his impassioned best who urged the crowd assembled for the December 2 rally to once again occupy Sproul Hall. In what became a classic of New Left oratory, Savio exhorted his audience to take action against the "corporate mentality" that pervaded the Administration.

> We have an autocracy which runs this university. It's managed. We were told the following: "If President Kerr actually tried to get something more liberal out of the Regents . . . why didn't he make some public statements to that effect?" And the answer we received from a well-meaning liberal was the following: he said, "Would you ever imagine the manager of a firm making a statement publicly in opposition to his Board of Directors?" That's the answer.
>
> I ask you to consider: if this is a firm, and if the Board of Regents are the Board of Directors, and if President Kerr in fact is the manager, then . . . the faculty are a bunch of employees and we're the raw material. But we're a bunch of raw material that don't mean . . . to be made into any product, don't mean to end up being bought by some clients of the university. . . . We're human beings.
>
> And that brings me to the second mode of civil disobedience. There is a time when the operation of the machine becomes so odious, makes you so sick at heart, that you can't take part; you can't even passively take part, and you've got to put your bodies upon the gears and upon the wheels, upon the levers, upon all the apparatus and you've got to make it stop. And you've got to indicate to the people who run it, to the people who own it, that unless you're free, the machines will be prevented from working at all. (Quoted in Heirich, 1968: 199–200)

Finally, it was Savio's attempt to address the special convocation held on December 7 and his bodily removal from the stage that precipitated the outraged faculty vote of December 8 that foreshadowed victory for the Free Speech forces. At every critical point of the unfolding conflict,

Savio was clearly center stage. If he emerged as the "first among equals" in the Free Speech cadre, it was because he was acknowledged as such by all the major parties to the conflict. His was a leadership position that was not created—though it certainly was enhanced—by the media.

How did Savio come to occupy center stage in the movement? Certainly, he had not distinguished himself as a leader in campus politics prior to the fall. Those who had been prominent in civil rights activism at Berkeley during the 1963–1964 academic year included people like Art Goldberg, Mike Miller, Malcolm Zaretsky, Betty Garman, and Bob Wolfson.[5] Indeed, Savio had only been marginally recommended for participation in the Summer Project by his interviewer, a veteran Bay Area civil rights activist who had worked with Mario prior to the summer. Her report to SNCC follows:

> Mario Savio—Univ. of California—I worked with him earlier this year in Friends of SNCC! he then got diverted into an abortive tutorial project which folded six weeks after it had begun. Generally what I have to say about him is this: not a very creative guy altho [*sic*] he accepts responsibility and carries it through if you explain to him exactly what needs to be done; not exceedingly perceptive on the movement, what's involved, etc.; not very good at formulating notions with which one moves into the Negro community . . . this in relation to the planning sessions we had on the collapsed tutorial program . . . was more interested in "getting the thing into operation" than in discovering purposes for which that kind of a program be established . . . in the end the program was formulated (altho not only because of his thinking cause he did not really play that much of a leadership role) in terms of helping the poor kids in the ghetto get through school easier . . . hardly my idea of why to establish tutorials and related programs. On the other hand I think that he's a grad student (tho can't remember) and probably would be of good use in the freedom schools depending upon what subject he's in (math? . . . can't remember, again). Can't decide if I were picking people if I would choose him . . . probably he would be one of those "average" people who I'd want to see the results of the interview, reference forms, etc. . . . before making a judgment.[6]

"Not very creative," "not exceedingly perceptive"—hardly the description one would have offered of Savio at the height of the Free Speech controversy. How do we reconcile this portrait with Savio's actions during the Berkeley movement? Perhaps it was just an unfair and inaccurate characterization of Savio on the part of the interviewer. At least one volunteer who knew Savio before and after the summer suggests otherwise:

No way he ever would have . . . stepped forward [during the Free
Speech Movement] if it hadn't been for Mississippi. Part of it was
confidence. He was really a pretty shy guy [but] . . . Freedom
Summer tended to boost you; you felt like you had been there and
you knew what you were talking about . . . that seemed to happen
to him [Savio]. . . . But more than that it was moral outrage . . .
I think. Off of what he saw in McComb, there was just this . . .
total commitment to the [civil rights] movement . . . and no stupid
bureaucratic rules were going to get in the way. There was this
single-mindedness of purpose and moral certainty that just pushed
him . . . and it came from Mississippi, I think.[7]

A case can be made then, for Freedom Summer as the crucible within
which much of the leadership of the Free Speech Movement was
forged. Just as important as the leadership, however, was the application
of tactics and ideologies learned during Freedom Summer to the events
at Berkeley. Tactically, the "Free Speech Movement was the first example of participants in . . . [the civil rights] movement using what they
had learned on their own behalf" (Breines, 1982: 24). A good many
tactics employed in Mississippi were practiced by the Free Speech
forces. There was, of course, the sit-in. That we now regard the sit-in
as a kind of obligatory feature of any serious demonstration obscures the
fact that black students reclaimed it as a tactic only four years prior to
the conflict at Berkeley. It is a measure of the Free Speech forces' identification with the civil rights movement, then, that the sit-in was the
principal tactic employed during the events at Berkeley. Including the
capture of the police car, there were five major sit-ins over the course
of the three-month conflict.

Other aspects of the unfolding drama also bore the tactical imprint of
Freedom Summer. Decision making in the movement reflected SNCC's
often anarchic, consensual style. Catch phrases repeated often in Mississippi, such as "one man, one vote," and "let the people decide," surfaced again at Berkeley as the Free Speech forces sought to practice
SNCC's brand of participatory democracy.

During at least one of the sit-ins, "freedom classes" were set up as an
alternative to regular university fare. Heirich (1968: 201–202) describes the scene on the night of the climactic December 2–3 sit-in:

Inside Sproul Hall, a myriad of activities went on through the afternoon and evening. The FSM had announced that they would conduct a Free University inside Sproul Hall. Each floor of the building
was devoted to à different kind of activity so that people could locate

themselves by preference for how they would spend their time. There was a study hall, a discussion area, a sleep area, and square dancing and movie areas . . . Joan Baez sang and led folk singing. A Peace Corps trainer conducted a Spanish class in one area of the building, a Sociology faculty member discussed the theory of conflict in relation to . . . the Free Speech issue, a Quaker addressed a class on civil disobedience. Spirits were high.

In the exuberant, free-form quality of these activities, Berkeley's Free University resembled nothing so much as a transplanted version of Mississippi's Freedom Schools. Freedom songs learned in Mississippi were routinely sung at the major Free Speech demonstrations (c.f. Heirich, 1968: 72). Reconstructing the events of October 1 from live tapes made by radio station KPFA, Heirich (1968: 127) makes it clear that the songs were a part of the movement from the very beginning. "When the new tape begins," he writes, "the seated demonstrators are singing 'We Shall Overcome,' which seems to have become their theme song, *expressing their sense of unity with the civil rights movement*" (emphasis added).

More than any specific tactical parallels or the leadership exercised by the former volunteers, it is this more general identification with the civil rights movement that provides the strongest and most significant link between the Summer Project and the Berkeley movement. Certainly, at the outset of the controversy, the leaders of the Free Speech Movement saw their protest "as an extension of either vicarious or actual involvement in the struggle for civil rights" (Mario Savio quoted in Draper, 1965: 5). Specifically, they believed that the restrictions on political activity imposed by the administration were the result of conservative pressure by local opponents of the civil rights movement. As one leader of the Free Speech forces said shortly after the denouement of the conflict, "Obviously, this ruling was directed against the civil rights movement, no matter what kind of language it was clothed in. . . . The only groups that were doing any kind of effective proselytizing or fund-raising were the civil rights groups and the socialist groups; the civil rights groups have impact" (quoted in Heirich, 1968: 62). In an interview marking the twentieth anniversary of the movement, another of its leaders, Bettina Aptheker, echoed this view. Said Aptheker, "the FSM arose because we were trying to organize for civil rights. In 1964 the southern power structure had by no means decided to give up segregation, and the power structure in the northern states was in collusion. That's why we were cut off" (quoted in Dellabough, 1984: 18). In another recent interview, Mario Savio stressed an even closer connection between Freedom Summer and the Free Speech Movement. "The Movement," said Savio,

> was a direct outgrowth of white student involvement in the civil-rights movement of the very early 1960s. In the summer preceding the FSM, the summer of 1964, a number of students from western and northern campuses—including myself—took part in the Mississippi Freedom Summer. . . . When we came back to school in the fall of 1964, the administration sent letters out to the heads of the various political and social action organizations . . . and those letters said that from then onward there would be no such activity on the Berkeley campus. For us it was a question: whose side are you on? Are we on the side of the civil-rights movement? Or have we now gotten back to the comfort and security of Berkeley, California, and can we forget the sharecroppers whom we worked with just a few weeks before? Well, we couldn't forget. (Quoted in Barker, 1984: C3)

The immediate concern of the Free Speech forces, then, was the elimination of all procedural restrictions that threatened their effectiveness as *civil rights* organizations. For example, in a debate held during the September 30 sit-in in Sproul Hall, Savio argued against an administration proposal that would have required nonstudents to obtain permission to speak seventy-two hours prior to their appearance. "The issue," he said,

> is freedom of speech. . . . Why 72 hours for non-students and no time for students? Let's say, for example—and this touches me very deeply—let's say that in McComb, Mississippi, some children are killed in the bombing of a church. . . . Let's say that we have someone who's come up from Mississippi . . . and he wanted to speak here and he had to wait 72 hours in order to speak . . . everybody will have completely forgotten about those little children because, you know, when you're black and in Mississippi, nobody gives a damn . . . 72 hours later and . . . the whole issue would have been dead. (Quoted in Heirich, 1968: 92–93)

But if the initial impetus to action was conceived narrowly in terms of the civil rights movement, over the course of the conflict the FSM leaders began to apply the lessons of Mississippi to their own situations. This change is reflected in several statements made by Savio toward the close of the conflict at Berkeley.

> Last summer I went to Mississippi to join the struggle there for civil rights. This fall I am engaged in another phase of the same struggle,

this time in Berkeley. The two battlefields may seem quite different to some observers, but this is not the case. The same rights are at stake in both places—the right to participate as citizens in democratic society and the right to due process of law. Further, it is a struggle against the same enemy. In Mississippi an autocratic and powerful minority rules, through organized violence, to suppress the vast, virtually powerless, majority. In California, the privileged minority manipulates the University bureaucracy to suppress the student's political expression. That "respectable" bureaucracy masks the financial plutocrats; that impersonal bureaucracy is the efficient enemy in a "Brave New World." (Quoted in Rothschild, 1982: 181)

The people are all cut off from one another and what they need is a spark, just one spark to show them that all these people around them, likewise, are quite as lonely as they are, quite as cut off as they, quite as hungry for some kind of community as they are. . . . Free speech was in some ways a pretext. . . . Around that issue the people could gain the community they formerly lacked. (Quoted in Breines, 1982: 26)

Savio and the other volunteers had brought back with them the political critique and vision of community they had acquired in Mississippi. The FSM was but the first attempt to apply both to targets in the North. The ideological critique of the "multiversity" voiced by the Berkeley protesters was soon picked up by students all across the country. So too was the FSM's attempt to apply SNCC's organizational style to campus politics. By means of the Berkeley controversy, the political and personal lessons of Freedom Summer had been successfully transplanted to the North. The "revolution beyond race" was underway. In the months following the events at Berkeley, student movements developed at numerous other schools.[8] Consciously modeled on the FSM, Freedom Summer volunteers were to play central roles in several of these dramas.[9] A former volunteer recalls the beginnings of student protest activity at Michigan State.

I remember having mixed reactions to Berkeley [FSM]. On the one hand it was almost electrifying . . . coming out of Mississippi with all these ideas and all this energy and not knowing what to do with it and they [the FSM] were . . . showing the way. . . . At the same time I remember feeling a little . . . envious that they were seen as the vanguard. . . . I think a certain feeling of competition was involved in the organization of our . . . [movement]. A number of us knew Mario [Savio] from Mississippi and I think that was part of it.[10]

Thus, besides the tactical and ideological lessons learned in Mississippi, personal ties among the volunteers played a part in the rapid expansion of campus activism. Just as important was the hero's welcome accorded the returning volunteers by the activist subcultures on most campuses. Here again, the role of the media in enhancing the stature of the Mississippi veterans has to be acknowledged. If the fall of 1964 saw the "birth of the student movement," the media played midwife to the process. It was not simply that the volunteers returned from Mississippi more willing and able to play leadership roles in campus politics. In many instances they were thrust into that role by virtue of the notoriety they had acquired through participation in the Summer Project. One of the no-shows recalled the reception the volunteers received upon their return to school in the fall. He confessed that he had always

> counted . . . [not going to Mississippi] as one of the great regrets of my life. But it was hardest, I think, when they [the volunteers] came back to school . . . [in the fall]. It was like they were returning war heroes. There were stories in the school newspapers; they spoke in classes; *they sort of took over [the campus chapter of] CORE . . . almost by acclamation.* And some of them hadn't even been active the previous spring.[11] (Emphasis added)

Several of the volunteers remembered the cachet their status as returning volunteers granted them on campus and in activist circles more generally. Elinor Tideman Aurthur recalled feeling that

> I had paid my dues . . . I felt that any place I went from Berkeley to Brooklyn . . . that I qualified [as an activist] . . . everybody knew about the summer project and everybody wanted to ask me what it was like and . . . I was an authority, an instant authority on the civil rights movement.[12]

By virtue of being the only volunteer to return to the University of Pittsburgh, another of the Mississippi veterans enjoyed a kind of exclusive celebrity status. "When I got back," he recalls, "I got re-involved in . . . [campus politics] and there was a little bit of the returning war hero stuff . . . especially . . . in my case because I was the only one . . . I am not pleased to admit [this], but I played into [it] a bit."[13] Barry Clemson remembered being recruited to run for student body president because of the stature he had acquired as a returning "civil rights hero."[14]

The combination, then, of their own radicalization and the reception accorded them by other student activists transformed the volunteers into a kind of political vanguard in the year or so following their return. Not only had their experiences in Mississippi sharpened and extended their political analysis, but the notoriety they gained through participation in the project made others unusually receptive to their views. As such, the volunteers often found themselves in the forefront of efforts to apply the lessons of Mississippi to other targets. In doing so, the volunteers were merely acting on the injunction, voiced often by SNCC veterans, to organize in their own communities and against the sources of oppression in their own lives. The initial target of these efforts were the colleges and universities the volunteers were attending. In short order, however, other issues arose that commanded the attention of the volunteers and the New Left generally. Of immediate concern was the escalating war in Southeast Asia.

The Antiwar Movement

Formal U.S. involvement in Vietnam was already fourteen years old when the volunteers left for Mississippi. In May of 1950, President Harry Truman first authorized aid to the French in Vietnam. However, it was President Eisenhower who first sent military personnel to the country, dispatching 350 advisers in May of 1956. In turn, that most glamorous of cold warriors, John Kennedy, increased the number of U.S. servicemen in Vietnam by some 16,000.[15] Nonetheless, American involvement in the war remained limited on the eve of the Summer Project. To the extent that Americans were aware of the war at all, they regarded it as something remote and of only peripheral concern. On May 27, Gallup released the results of a national survey showing that two-thirds of the American public had either "not followed" or had no opinion concerning the United States "handling [of] affairs in South Vietnam." Opposition to the war was largely confined to old-line pacifists and lone iconoclasts. Students and others in the New Left had yet to really "discover" the war as an issue. As with so many aspects of the "Sixties experience," however, the year 1964 was to mark a crucial change in this regard. While Lyndon Johnson still enjoyed popular and congressional support for his stepped-up war effort, awareness of and opposition to the war grew dramatically late in the year. In a November 18 poll, a national sample listed the "international situation—specifically Vietnam" as the problem they "would . . . most like to have President Johnson deal with now that he has won the election." Eleven days later a nationwide Gallup poll showed that only 35 percent of the American people felt the "United States is handling affairs in South Vietnam as well as could be expected." Fifty percent thought we were "handling affairs there badly."

Some of this increased awareness and opposition can be attributed to external events. On August 4, Congress overwhelmingly approved the Tonkin Gulf resolution, paving the way for a much wider war. Monthly draft calls rose sharply. So did the number of U.S. combat troops in Vietnam. By December, 23,000 Americans were fighting there. Even before the passage of the Tonkin Gulf resolution, however, opposition to the war among the young was on the rise. Freedom Summer and the resulting radicalization of the volunteers was to play an important role in the process. Pat Watters (1971: 308–309) remembers the "startlement" he felt at seeing his first antiwar poster. "It was in the COFO headquarters in Jackson during . . . Freedom Summer." In light of the volunteers' experiences in Mississippi, the groundswell of antiwar sentiment within the project was hardly surprising. For politically sophisticated and increasingly critical young people, the parallels between aggression against blacks in Mississippi and Vietnamese in Southeast Asia were too obvious to ignore. By summer's end, a good many of the volunteers were drawing these parallels in their letters home. Eight days after the passage of the Tonkin Gulf resolution, Ellen Lake wrote her parents that:

> For the first time in my life, I am seeing what it is like to be poor, oppressed, and hated. And what I see here does not apply only to Gulfport or to Mississippi or even to the South. . . . The people we're killing in Viet Nam are the same people whom we've been killing for years in Mississippi. True, we didn't tie the knot in Mississippi and we didn't pull the trigger in Viet Nam—that is, we personally—but we've been standing behind the knot-tiers and the trigger-pullers too long.[16]

No less than six of the volunteers interviewed trace their opposition to the war to Freedom Summer. Several recalled the circumstances surrounding their "conversion" in great detail. One volunteer remembers coming out against the war following the shooting of Silas McGhee in Greenwood.

> A group of us were waiting at the hospital and Silas' family comes in including one of his brothers, or a cousin or something; and this guy is huge; and he's in uniform. Turns out he's on leave from the Army! . . . That was it. I remember thinking that any war in which blacks are fighting Asians for the benefit of whites while their brothers are being murdered back home is not worth supporting.[17]

Another attributes his opposition to the war to insights gained in teaching his Freedom School classes. "Here we were talking about self-determination in the classes and I began thinking . . . about what the hell we were doing in Vietnam."[18]

So a good many of the volunteers left Mississippi with a new-found critical awareness of the war based on the contradictions it posed to the ideology of the civil rights movement. This marked the volunteers as among the earliest critics of the war within the New Left. Moreover, their status as returning heroes made them especially influential spokespersons within the emerging antiwar movement. As opposition to the war escalated sharply in the wake of the first bombing raids over North Vietnam in February, 1965, the volunteers found themselves in the forefront of protest activities. Volunteers were among the first to refuse induction. One who did so was Bruce Maxwell. Maxwell coupled the burning of his induction papers with an application for conscientious objector (CO) status that stressed the war's incompatibility with his work in the civil rights movement.

> The freedom movement in the South, of which I am a part, is trying to destroy what is destroying humanity in the South. I also realize that the U.S. military is destroying humanity all over the world, for instance, it is trying to prevent a free election in Vietnam. . . . Now the U.S. government is saying to me: "Join the world's largest force of destruction or go to jail and sacrifice your future effectiveness in the freedom struggle in the South." Now I have never wanted to fight a CO battle because that is not the most effective way I can function in humanity's struggle for freedom, but since fate sees fit to have me drafted, I cannot stand before God willing to destroy humanity for two years or six months and still claim that I am a valid part of the people's struggle for freedom when I return to the South.[19]

The impact of the volunteers and the civil rights movement was also evident in the Spring 1965 "teach-ins," which marked the first mass demonstration of student opposition to the war. The teach-ins "constituted an academic equivalent of its Southern model, the sit-in. Thousands of students sat through all-night marathons learning the history of Vietnam, of Asia, of American intervention, and debating the morality of American foreign policy" (Evans, 1980: 158). The first use of the tactic took place March 24–25 at the University of Michigan, and bore the clear imprint of the Summer Project. The first mention of the idea apparently came at a March 11 meeting of some fifteen Michigan faculty members intent on demonstrating their opposition to the war. A number of different options for doing so were discussed, including one put forth by the young sociologist, William Gamson. Thomas Boettcher (1985: 423) an historian of the Vietnam War, takes up the story:

Gamson had been a member of CORE in the Boston area when a school boycott there had been organized. To occupy the time of Boston students not attending normal classes, a "Freedom School" had been organized to teach black history and civil rights. Gamson recounted the details of this experience to his associates, who quickly locked onto it as a constructive and significant form of protest to American policy in Southeast Asia.

But planning demonstrations and having them succeed are two very different things. Fortunately, the University of Michigan was blessed with one of the largest contingents of Freedom Summer veterans of any school in the country. These veterans joined with the professors and other student leaders in mobilizing an impressive turn-out at the March 24–25 event. "Within two weeks of the University of Michigan events, teach-ins had been conducted on dozens of college campuses" (Boettcher, 1985: 424). And in most of these cases, former volunteers played important roles in the planning and execution of the subsequent teach-ins.[20]

By the summer of 1965, what had a year earlier been a barely audible whisper of dissent had grown to a full-throated chorus of protest over the escalating war. This chorus was made up of many voices. Socialists or other leftists spoke out against the war on narrow ideological grounds. Old-line pacifist organizations, such as the War Resisters League or the American Friends Service Committee, lent their collective voice to the growing chorus. So too did a wide variety of student groups, religious as well as political. Finally, iconoclastic public figures, such as Senators Wayne Morse of Oregon and Ernest Gruening of Alaska, added much needed visibility and legitimacy to the growing movement. But the returning volunteers were among the earliest, loudest, and most influential critics of the war.

Nor was it only those volunteers who returned to college who went on to play pioneering roles in the antiwar movement. Radicalized by their experiences in Mississippi and angered by the bombing of North Vietnam, two school teachers from New York City, Sandra Adickes and Norma Becker, organized the Teachers Committee for Peace in Vietnam. The Committee's first act was to publish a full-page ad in the May 30 *New York Times* addressed to "Our PRESIDENT, A Former Teacher." Listing 2,700 signers, the ad expressed strong opposition to the war and ended with a plea to the President "to stop the bombings immediately and initiate a peaceful settlement in Vietnam."[21] At a time when off-campus criticism of the war was still rare, the Committee's ad was a powerful rejoinder to those who were inclined to write off all opposition to the war as the work of "student radicals." As such, the ad marked an important momer.. in the mobilization of moderate opposition to the war. The Committee went on to establish itself as a fixture in the New York City antiwar community, publishing newsletters, cosponsoring demonstrations, and encouraging the formation of similar organizations elsewhere.[22]

Among those volunteers who remained in Mississippi or were otherwise affiliated with SNCC, several were in the forefront of efforts to link the war publicly to the issue of civil rights. Some, like Bruce Maxwell, sought to do so through individual acts of conscience. Others within SNCC pressed the organization to come out officially against the war. Among the most aggressive advocates of this position was former volunteer Gren Whitman, who had become a SNCC field secretary at the close of the Summer Project. Whitman explains the events leading up to SNCC's January 1966 release of its official antiwar statement:

> I agitated to have the subject [of Vietnam] introduced as an agenda item at a staff conference at Atlanta's Gammon Institute in November, 1965. . . . After a statement was approved, I wrote a first draft and circulated [it] throughout the organization. Only a handful of comments were returned. With these comments, Bill Mahoney, Charlie Cobb, and I repaired to a Hunter Street bar . . . and hammered out the final version. This included reference to Sammy Young, [a] staff worker murdered in December, 1965, an event which had a profoundly deep . . . effect upon the staff.[23]

Released January 6, the statement offered a ringing indictment of the war, stressing once again the parallels between U.S. policy in Vietnam and Mississippi.

> We believe the United States government has been deceptive in its claims of concern for the freedom of the Vietnamese people, just as the government has been deceptive in claiming concern for the freedom of colored people in such other countries as the Dominican Republic, the Congo, South Africa, Rhodesia, and in the United States itself.
>
> We, the Student Nonviolent Coordinating Committee, have been involved in the black people's struggle for liberation and self-determination in this country for the past five years. Our work, particularly in the South, has taught us that the United States government has never guaranteed the freedom of oppressed citizens, and is not yet truly determined to end the rule of terror and oppression within its own borders. . . .
>
> The murder of Samuel Young in Tuskeegee, Alabama, is no different than the murder of peasants in Vietnam, for both Young and

the Vietnamese sought, and are seeking, to secure the rights guaranteed them by law. In each case, the United States government bears
a great part of the responsibility for these deaths.

Samuel Young was murdered because United States law is not
being enforced. Vietnamese are murdered because the United States
is pursuing an aggressive policy in violation of international law.
The United States is no respecter of persons or law when such persons or laws run counter to its needs and desires. . . .

We are in sympathy with, and support, the men in this country
who are unwilling to respond to a military draft which would com-
pel them to contribute their lives to United States aggression in Vietnam in the name of the "freedom" we find so false in this country. . . .

We recoil with horror at the inconsistency of a supposedly "free"
society where responsibility to freedom is equated with the responsibility to lend oneself to military aggression. We take note of the fact
that 16% of the draftees from this country are Negroes called on to
stifle the liberation of Vietnam, to preserve a "democracy" which does
not exist for them at home.[24]

Ironically, even as SNCC was being heavily criticized in liberal circles for its statement, the Pentagon released figures strongly supporting
the organization's view of the links between racism at home and in
Vietnam. During 1965, 24 percent of all American soldiers killed in
Vietnam were black (Jones, 1980: 110). Such figures only deepened
the former volunteers' commitment to the antiwar effort.

Perhaps the most important contribution of the Freedom Summer
veterans to the growing movement against the war came with the founding of The Resistance in the spring of 1967. Conceived of as a small
vanguard organization dedicated to aggressive noncooperation with the
war effort, The Resistance was to grow into one of the few effective and
influential national antiwar groups. The organization had its roots in
informal conversations that took place during the summer and fall of
1966 between several Mississippi veterans. Among those involved were
three persons—Dennis Sweeney, Mary King, and Mendy Samstein—who
had been in Mississippi during the summer of 1964 and a fourth, David
Harris, who had worked there briefly in October of the same year. Harris
(1982: 145), who would later serve a prison term for his Resistance
activities, describes the group's origin:

In July [1966], Mendy Samstein, a white former SNCC staffer
Dennis [Sweeney] had worked with in McComb, visited him and
Mary [King] for a week. Samstein had been traveling around the
country talking with "movement people" about what to do now.

Eight of us gathered in the tiny room at the top of the Channing Street house's stairs.

Mendy's starting point was the tail end of the Mississippi Project. Like Dennis, he agreed with SNCC's decision to urge whites to return to their own communities to organize "against their own oppression" there. Also, as for Dennis, just what that meant for him was still up in the air. The most likely options were the war and the draft. The "We Won't Go" petitions had been a step in the right direction, but the government could easily dismiss the threat of students protected by deferments. The rest of his talk was mostly questions. What if white students organized on a wholesale basis and refused their privilege, forcing the government to draft the middle class just like everyone else? If those draftees also refused to be inducted, wouldn't the government be forced to incarcerate thousands or be discredited? Politically, might that not be more than Vietnam policy could bear? The first draft-card burnings had already taken place at several demonstrations in New York. Why not extend that civil disobedience on a broad scale?

Eventually that is exactly what the organization did, at its peak counting forty-six affiliated groups or individuals as part of the national Resistance network.[25] Many Freedom Summer veterans joined the network. Among those who did were Staughton and Alice Lynd. Staughton, who had directed the Freedom School program during the Summer Project, captured the essential link between the former volunteers and The Resistance in his description of the impulse that had given rise to the group. He described it as a decision by "people who really knew where it was at, like those who had been under fire in Mississippi . . . [to] create a moral equivalent of Mississippi for the anti-war movement" (quoted in Evans, 1980: 180). In both its personnel and guiding philosophy, then, The Resistance bore the mark of the Summer Project.

Finally, so too did the Vietnam Summer Project, "the largest organizing effort the New Left ever attempted" (Rothschild, 1982: 183). Consciously modeled on Freedom Summer, the Vietnam Summer Project took place in 1967. As with Freedom Summer, the goal of the project was to promote political action and "self-determination" on the part of local citizens. The only difference was that in 1967 the issue around which the citizens were to organize was the war rather than civil rights. Toward that end, 200 national and 500 local staff worked full-time coordinating the efforts of some 20,000 local volunteers. "All of the major national office organizers were veterans of the southern civil rights movement" (Rothschild, 1982: 184). A good many of these were Freedom Summer veterans, as were a number of the local staff. Although the project failed to produce the network of permanent local projects its organizers had envisioned, it nonetheless contributed to the growing public awareness and opposition to the war. Thus, three years after Freedom Summer the project was still being used as a model for New Left activism; and in their capacity as Vietnam Summer staff, the volunteers remained in the forefront of antiwar organizing. Rothschild (1982: 182) would seem to have been on target when she wrote that "the growing peace movement reaped the major benefit of the volunteer's political apprenticeship in the South." Everywhere one finds evidence of the decisive impact—ideological, organizational, tactical, and in personnel—of Freedom Summer on the growth of organized opposition to the war.

The Women's Liberation Movement

At the same time the interracial civil rights movement was winding down and student and antiwar activism were heating up, the seeds of the third major movement of the period were being nurtured in these other struggles. As Sarah Evans (1980) has documented, the genesis of women's liberation took place in the civil rights, antiwar, and student movements during the years 1964–1967. Once again, the influence of Freedom Summer is everywhere evident in this incubation process. Not only does the project mark the ostensible beginning of the process, but it also contributed many of the specific figures who later figured so prominently in the movement's emergence. As such, Freedom Summer serves as one of the few unifying foci in a process that was otherwise highly decentralized and chronologically diffuse. To understand the importance of the Summer Project, we will need to follow this process forward from Mississippi.

As noted in Chapter 3, the subtle and not-so-subtle forms of sexism that pervaded Freedom Summer generated little overt criticism during the summer itself. However, it did expose female volunteers and staff to the glaring contradiction between the civil rights movement's ideology of equality and the lived experience of inequality. It was the growing awareness and resentment of this contradiction that eventually precipitated the decisive break between radical feminists and the male New Left. The 400 female veterans of Freedom Summer were among the first to experience this contradiction; not surprisingly they were among the first to raise tentative voices against it.

Two who did so were Mary King and Casey Hayden, the authors of the position paper on the status of women in SNCC that was presented at the SNCC staff retreat held at Waveland, Mississippi in November

1964. The paper detailed the many ways in which women were relegated to second-class status within the organization. The specific examples discussed by King and Hayden—"the automatic relegation of women to clerical work, exclusion of women from decision-making groups" could as easily have applied to the female volunteers as the staff members (quoted in Evans, 1980: 86). The fact that the paper was presented anonymously tells us a lot, not only about the tentativeness of the author's critique, but their expectation that the paper would invite hostility and ridicule by the male staff. They were right. As noted in Chapter 3, the paper received only scant and generally negative attention at the retreat (King, 1987: 450).

Whatever discouragement the authors felt at the rebuff of their paper, they were not inclined to let the issue die; or perhaps the persistence of the conditions they were writing about served to keep it alive. In any case, King and Hayden returned to the issue in November 1965 when they drafted and circulated "a kind of memo" addressed to "a number of other women in the peace and freedom movements" (Hayden and King, 1966: 35). Like Mario Savio and others in the student movement, Hayden and King drew upon their experiences in the South and the analogy of black oppression to explain their own second-class status. They argued that, just like blacks, women

> seem to be caught up in a common-law caste system that operates, sometimes subtly, forcing them to work around or outside hierarchical structures of power which may exclude them. Women seem to be placed in the same position of assumed subordination in personal situations too. It is a caste system which, at its worst, uses and exploits women. (Hayden and King, 1966: 35)

In writing the article, Hayden and King hoped simply to generate a greater awareness of a problem that had gone generally unrecognized to this point. They lamented the fact that "nobody is writing, or organizing or talking publicly about women, in any way that reflects the problems [of] . . . women in the movement." They hoped that at least "we can start to talk with each other more openly than in the past and create a community of support for each other." Much more than that, they concluded, was unrealistic. "Objectively," they conceded, "the chances seem nil that we could start a movement based on anything as distant to general American thought as a sex-caste system" (Hayden and King, 1966: 36). What Hayden and King had underestimated were the number of women with a history of leftist activism whose experiences made them receptive to the issues they were raising. This became clear when, one month after the Hayden-King memo appeared, angry women walked

out of a national SDS conference in Champaign-Urbana, Illinois, to
protest the lack of attention to various issues they were trying to raise.

The walkout marked the first time that the "women's question" had
been raised publicly at a major gathering of the New Left. Although
the women's liberation movement, as an organized entity, was still a
year-and-a-half away, voice had been given to the ill-defined, inchoate
feelings of many women activists. Among those groping to express those
feelings were a number of Freedom Summer veterans, Hayden and King
being only the most prominent of these. In addition, at least a half dozen
other volunteers were involved in the walkout and discussions at the
December 1965 SDS conference.

Over the next eighteen months, these and a good many other female
volunteers helped nurture the emerging feminist perspective, even as
they continued to organize against the war and in support of students
and black civil rights. In the summer of 1966, Cathy Cade and Peggy
Dobbins helped organize a course on the sociology of women—a novel
offering at the time—as part of the New Orleans Free School. In December of the same year, Heather Tobis helped put together a "women's
workshop" at a "We Won't Go" conference held at the University of
Chicago. A month later, Jane Adams (1967) published an article in
New Left Notes entitled, "People's Power: On Equality for Women."
Sue Thrasher remembers discussing the status of women while serving
on the national staff of the 1967 Vietnam Summer Project. That same
summer, Heather Tobis taught a course on women at the Center for
Radical Research in Chicago.

As yet, however, there existed no organized movement to link these
actions. They existed in a kind of vacuum, important as early expressions of a subterranean feminism, but lacking any overall coherence or
continuity. One volunteer remembers the years between Freedom Summer and the organized beginnings of the women's liberation movement as

> a lonely period really. After 1965 or so, there was really no place
> [for whites] in the [civil rights] movement . . . and SDS had
> grown so large, so factionalized . . . and really cut-throat competi-
> tive that . . . I think a lot of women—including me—just got really
> turned off.[26]

The accumulated anger and alienation these women were feeling surfaced with unprecedented force at the National Conference for New
Politics (NCNP). Held in Chicago over Labor Day Weekend, 1967,
the Conference was an attempt to rebuild some semblance of coalition

among the increasingly fractious elements of the New Left. Instead, the meeting turned into three days of divisive confrontations that only accelerated the process of factionalization already underway.

The psychic centerpiece of the conference was a running attack on white radicals by the black separatists in attendance. In her description, Evans (1980: 197) captures the confusing and destructive emotional crosscurrents at work at the conference.

> Black power was at its zenith. Separatism had meant for whites that they could only admire and emulate from a distance the black movement, which remained the touchstone of "true radicalism." When whites met with blacks again at the NCNP they seemed desperate to receive validation from them. Black delegates in turn needed to unleash their fury at American racism on the whites at the conference. For both, these pressing emotional needs proved far stronger than the desire for a strategic alliance. The politics of moralism reached new heights as the moralism of middle-class guilt clashed head on with the morality of righteous anger. Black delegates shouted: "Kill Whitey!" as they repeatedly insisted that they should cast 50 percent of the conference vote and occupy half of the committee slots though they constituted about one-sixth of the convention. In addition they demanded from this audience full of Jewish radicals a resolution condemning Zionist imperialism. Each time the conference capitulated to black demands, the majority of whites applauded enthusiastically in apparent approval of their own denunciation.

Preoccupied by their confrontation with the black separatists, white males reacted to the issues raised by the women participants like so many harried fathers. With but a few exceptions, resolutions introduced by women were either ignored or greeted with hostile condescension. The breaking point was reached when a male participant reportedly patted Shulamith Firestone on the head and told her to "move on little girl; we have more important issues to talk about here than women's liberation" (quoted in Evans, 1980: 199). Furious, a group of women met the following week in Chicago to brainstorm about the ways women might go about organizing a movement of their own. Present at the meeting were several Freedom Summer veterans. The immediate result of the meeting was a paper addressed "To the Women of the Left" in which the authors argued that "it is incumbent on us, as women, to organize a movement for women's liberation."[27] Like the Hayden and King memo of two years earlier, the new paper found a responsive audience among New Left women. Already politicized by their own experiences and the informal discussions of the previous two years, these women reacted to news of the debacle at the NCNP much as the authors of the paper had.

> It was as if the NCNP had broken a dam. As the women who met in Chicago moved from hope to the conviction that they could build a movement for the liberation of women, the new flood of self-conscious feminism flowed into the channels left by seven years of movement activity. Through a network of personal friendship, organized media, and events the word spread until within a year there was hardly a major city without one or more "women's liberation groups," as they called themselves. (Evans, 1980: 201)

In the majority of these cities, former volunteers were in the forefront of the initial organizing efforts. This was especially true for the earliest women's liberation groups. In Chicago, for example, Heather Tobis and Jo Freeman were central to the movement from the outset.[28] In New York City, Mississippi veteran Pam Parker Allen joined with Shulamith Firestone to call the initial organizing meeting. Two other Freedom Summer volunteers, Kathie Sarachild and Peggy Dobbins were among the half dozen or so women who answered the call. Several months later Dobbins broke with the group to found Women's International Conspiracy from Hell (WITCH), one of the earliest and most militantly active groups in the movement. At the same time, Cathy Cade, herself a former volunteer and close friend of Dobbins, was acting as the prime mover of the early movement in New Orleans. In Berkeley, Lisa Mandel was among the dozen or so founding members of the initial women's liberation group. Pat Hansen and a recently transplanted Pam Parker Allen played the same role in the first such group to form in San Francisco. When Bread and Roses was organized in Boston in 1969, another volunteer, Annie Popkin, was among its first members.

Even in cities where no Freedom Summer veterans were active, the emergence of a women's liberation group often owed to their influence. In founding the first such group in Washington, D.C., Marilyn Salzman Webb drew upon the insights and inspiration of Heather Tobis (and a non-volunteer, Sue Munaker) during several visits to Chicago. Tobis played much the same role in the genesis of the first women's group at San Francisco State. Women's liberation came to the school only after hours of conversation between Tobis and the group's organizer, Sharon Gold. Kathie Sarachild was also instrumental in the founding of two early movement groups. She helped spread the "gospel" of women's liberation to Boston when she visited two women, Nancy Hawley and

Myra Levenson, who went on to serve as catalysts of the early movement there.

> Finally, in the South, long-time activists in CORE and SDS in Gainesville, Florida, read the *New Left Notes* accounts of the women's caucus at the 1967 SDS Convention and of the subsequent formation of women's liberation groups. Judith Brown and Beverly Jones wrote a paper in response to the SDS women, arguing strongly for an independent movement for female liberation. Their collective did not begin, however, until Judith Brown had attended a meeting of feminists at Sandy Springs, Maryland, where she immediately formed close bonds with two New York women—Kathie Sarachild and Carol Hanish. She returned to Gainesville and organized a women's caucus out of the SDS chapter (Evans, 1980: 210–211).

Time and time again, then, we find former volunteers playing key roles in the establishment of the earliest groups in the women's movement. Moreover, the presence of these Mississippi veterans in the movement provided a wealth of personal ties that served to draw other volunteers into women's liberation once the movement was underway. The experiences of two former volunteers help to illustrate this process. Miriam Cohen Glickman was encouraged to join the movement by the girlfriend of someone she had worked with in Mississippi.[29] Another got involved

> at the urging of a friend I had met in Mississippi. She said, "why don't you come over—my women's group is meeting." And I thought, "Oh geez, just what we need." . . . It's embarrassing to admit, but I basically bought the male line that raising the women's thing would only divert our attention from the "really important" issues like the war, capitalism, what have you. . . . So the only reason I went was because of our friendship. . . . Of course, when I did, I was hooked.[30]

Whether as pioneering organizers or skeptical recruits, the vast majority of the women who had gone to Mississippi did eventually get involved in the women's movement. Nearly half of the female Freedom Summer volunteers indicated on their questionnaires that they had been "very involved" in the movement. Another 27 percent reported their involvement as "moderate." Not surprisingly, the presence of so many of the volunteers—especially in the role of organizers—gave the movement a decidedly Freedom Summer "feel." That is, the volunteers' experiences in Mississippi proved to be a major influence in shaping the ideology, tactics, and organizational structure of the emerging movement.

Organizationally, the movement approximated the autonomous, local cell-like structure of the Summer Project. At the heart of this organizational structure was a singular emphasis on community. Above all else, the women's liberation groups were to be communities in which the values of the movement were put into practice. Disenchanted with the size, impersonality, competitiveness, and rising tide of factionalism in the male-dominated New Left, the volunteers sought to recreate in the new movement the spirit and form of the "beloved community" they had known in the South. It was this spirit that "hooked" many of the volunteers on first contact with the women's liberation movement. As one volunteer put it, "when those meetings began, I felt like it was almost like being back in the South . . . the feeling was that feeling, you know" (quoted in Evans, 1980: 203). Annie Popkin put it this way: "The civil rights movement had a . . . personalized politics; a community, a vision of human connection and humanity. All those things for me [were] . . . there again in the women's movement."[31] Chude Pamela (Parker) Allen stressed the same connection during an emotional reminiscence at a twentieth reunion of Freedom Summer veterans:

> What I remember about Mississippi was the love I felt . . . from everyone. There was this openness and acceptance of you as a person that I've never really felt since, not even in the women's movement, *even though that's what we were trying to recreate.*[32] (Emphasis added)

Statements such as these betray a strong organizational connection between Freedom Summer and the earliest women's liberation groups. The influence of the Summer Project can also be seen in the central ideological premise of the new movement. "The personal is political" is a lesson the female volunteers first learned during Freedom Summer. A part of this learning was purely experiental. Whether fending off unwanted sexual advances, or coping with parental disapproval, the volunteers had come to know the intimate connection between their personal lives and political choices. This connection was further reinforced by the general emphasis on self-discovery and personal liberation that gradually suffused the Summer Project. As noted in Chapter 4, the project came to be as much about the personal exorcism of racial bias as the registration of black voters. In the women's liberation movement this emphasis assumed even greater importance. Self-awareness and personal liberation were no longer a part of the activist project, but for many, virtually the *whole* of the project. In this case, however, it was the effects of gender, rather than racial, socialization that had to be rooted out and overcome. Those who decried the broader political impotence of this emphasis failed to appreciate that the immediate goal of most movement groups was personal rather than institutional change.

This emphasis did not owe to any lack of analytic sophistication on the part of the pioneering feminists. Quite the contrary, the early movement was dominated by veterans of the New Left—many of them Marxists—whose political analysis was as sophisticated as any in activist circles. It certainly wasn't ignorance that prompted movement pioneers to turn the programmatic emphasis away from such abstractions as "modes of production" or "institutionalized sexism." Both were important, to be sure, but regarded by most in the movement as necessarily secondary to the more immediate goals of consciousness-raising and the development of "sisterhood."

To accomplish these goals, movement organizers devised and refined the technique of consciousness raising (CR). Even here, the influence of Freedom Summer is evident. As Mary Rothschild (1982: 187) has argued, "the experiential basis" for CR may have come from the teaching methods practiced in the Freedom Schools. In SNCC's confrontational, consensual meeting style, the volunteers were exposed to yet another possible model for the CR group. The fact that a former volunteer, Kathie Sarachild, is widely credited with pioneering the CR technique, only lends credence to those who stress its roots in the Summer Project (c.f. Carden, 1974: 64).

As with the student and antiwar movements, then, the burgeoning women's movement drew heavily on the ideology, tactics, and form of organization of the Freedom Summer project. But the volunteers constituted the project's most important and enduring contribution to all three movements. It is impossible to read the journalisic histories of the New Left without being struck by the number of references to the Mississippi veterans. They appear as so many commandos in a subterreanean army surfacing two, three, four, or more years after the summer to fight the good fight in yet another time and place. In a culture—the New Left—that forgot its heroes and its past almost as quickly as it created them, the volunteers represent a rare source of continuity. Therein lies their importance. Not only did they carry the personal and political lessons of Mississippi North with them, but they were among the earliest to apply those lessons to the issues—student rights, the war, and sexism—that would dominate left politics for the remainder of the decade.

The No-Shows and the Volunteers: A Comparison

Obviously, the Freedom Summer veterans had a strong influence on the evolution of the New Left. But what about the volunteers themselves? What were their lives like during the remainder of the decade, and to what extent did the personal and political decisions they made during this period reflect the continuing influence of their experiences in Mississippi? Answers to these questions, especially the last one, necessitate a comparative look at the lives of the volunteers and the no-shows between 1964 and 1970. Going into the summer the biographies of the two groups looked very similar. The question is, do the two groups continue to resemble one another after the project? The answer is not nearly so much as they did before. After 1964, the biographies of the volunteers diverge from those of the no-shows.

Political Differences

In describing what he hoped the Summer Project might accomplish, Bob Moses often spoke of an annealing process by which Mississippi would be brought to a state of "white heat" as a precondition of changing it. For the most part, Moses and the rest of the COFO leadership accomplished what they set out to do. Mississippi *did* experience a searing crisis that summer that dramatically changed the state. In many ways, though, the analogy is as apt when applied to the volunteers as to the state itself. In the "white heat" of that Mississippi summer, many of the volunteers experienced their own annealing process. They too were changed, politically above all else. The most immediate consequence of this process was the transformation of many of the volunteers from conventional liberals into leftist radicals. Having been denied (or spared) the annealing process, most of the no-shows emerged from the summer with their liberalism intact. Thus, while both groups appear to have shared a common political orientation going into the summer, they most assuredly did not by summer's end.

Information furnished by the two groups on the follow-up questionnaires provides an interesting confirmation of this divergence. Individuals in both groups were asked to define their political stance, immediately before and after Freedom Summer, using a ten-point scale ranging from "1" for radical left to "10" for radical right. There was no difference in the way the two groups characterized their political orientations prior to Freedom Summer. Both groups scored in the 3.5 range. Just how much the volunteers perceived themselves to have been radicalized by

Mississippi is reflected in their assessments of their political position at the close of the summer. The average post-Freedom Summer score given by the volunteers is nearly a full point lower than the pre-summer figure. Nearly two-thirds of all the former volunteers felt they had moved further to the left as a result of the experience. By contrast, the no-shows' characterization of their political stance following the summer shows only a slight change from their position on the eve of the project.[33] While most of the no-shows interviewed claimed to have followed the events in Mississippi closely, they apparently were not radicalized by doing so.

In some ways this attitudinal comparison trivializes the political impact of the volunteers' experiences in Mississippi. For it wasn't anything as narrow as their attitudes that changed, as much as it was the way they saw and interpreted the world. It was the salience of politics or political concerns that was enhanced for the volunteers as a result of the summer. Indeed, for many of the volunteers, politics became the central organizing force in their lives. Everything else—relationships, work, etc.—got organized around their politics. One of the volunteers captured this idea nicely when he described his life following the summer as

> a set of episodes; it had a kind of political continuity to it . . . but the geographic or occupational focus might shift . . . because these kind of normal concerns—education, career, occupation—were totally incidental in my life. [They get] slotted in as a necessary kind of nuisance; it's something that didn't provide a framework, a guiding thread; in fact, it was repulsive to think of them as providing guiding threads to one's life. There was so much more at stake.[34]

A few of the applicants who did not go to Mississippi seem to have adopted similar perspectives later in the decade. However, it was the volunteers, to a much greater extent, who made politics the central feature of their lives. While the liberal/left views of the no-shows disposed them to a more active role in the movements of the Sixties than the general public, their activism remained subordinate to the rest of their lives. One no-show put it succinctly when she said, "I did my bit. I marched against the war. I did a sit-in or two. I was in a CR group . . . the usual stuff . . . *But it wasn't my life*"[35] (emphasis added).

This difference in orientation was immediately evident at the close of the project. When asked what they did following the summer, nearly a quarter of the volunteers, but only 8 percent of the no-shows, reported that they worked full-time as activists. If we count the Peace Corps as a form of activism, the figure jumps to nearly 30 percent. Having defined themselves as activists, a good many of the Mississippi veterans had a strong need to confirm that identity through action. Describing that period in her life, one of the volunteers observed that "you learned too much [in Mississippi] to go back to what you were doing before . . . part of what you learned was that you were part of the struggle . . . so I went looking for [struggles] to be part of."[36]

By contrast, the no-shows continued on the fairly conventional paths they had been on before the summer. Two-thirds returned to school in the fall. Another 15 percent began (or continued) full-time employment. For many of the volunteers, however, the overriding importance of politics coming out of the summer had stripped these pursuits of their previous significance. This was especially true of higher education, which many of the volunteers had come to regard as irrelevant or, worse yet, as part of "the system." One volunteer expressed it this way. "How could I go back? It turned out my beloved Harvard was one of the biggest landholders in all of Mississippi!"[37] Those volunteers who did return to school brought this more critical view of the university to the student movements they helped organize in the fall. For some, however, the critique was enough to keep them away altogether. Others stayed away, not because they viewed school as inherently evil, but because they had found something more worthwhile to do with their lives. Said Jan Hillegas, "I had had the intention of going on to grad school in social work, but once I got involved in civil rights, that seemed like the thing to stay in."[38] Whatever their motives, the volunteers forsook school in large numbers. Only about half returned to college in the fall. For many, the movement would be their career.

Just how much the volunteers organized their lives around activism is clear from information provided on the follow-up questionnaires. While many of the no-shows were active as well, as a group they were no match for the Freedom Summer veterans. Following the summer, 90 percent of the volunteers as compared to two-thirds of the no-shows claim to have remained active in the civil rights movement. But the forms of activism the volunteers tended to be involved in were more demanding than those practiced by the no-shows. In addition to the volunteers who stayed on in Mississippi after the summer, at least nineteen others served as SNCC or CORE staff elsewhere in the country. For the no-shows, on the other hand, civil rights activity almost always took the form of on-campus fund-raising or educational programs.

When it was no longer comfortable or politically correct for whites to remain in the civil rights movement, some percentage of the volunteers and no-shows moved on to other struggles. Chief among these were the three movements discussed earlier in the chapter. Nearly half of the Mississippi veterans report being "very involved" in the antiwar movement, as compared to 30 percent of the no-shows. Among those who did return to school in the fall, twice the percentage of volunteers as no-shows were "very involved" in the student movement. Forty percent of the female volunteers, but only a quarter of the no-shows report this same level of involvement in the women's liberation movement. When each subject's total movement involvements for the years 1964–1970 are combined into a single "activism scale," the volunteers' scores on the scale average 75 percent higher than the no-shows.[39]

Other bits of information drawn from the questionnaires merely confirm this general portrait. For the period from 1964 to 1970, the volunteers list twice as many memberships in political organizations as the no-shows. For their part, the no-shows are three times as likely as the volunteers to report no such memberships during these years. Finally, an amazing 40 percent of the volunteers count some form of activist employment as part of their work history during the Sixties. The comparable figure for the no-shows is 25 percent.

What all of these figures leave unanswered is the question of causality. *Why* were the volunteers so much more active following the summer than the no-shows? Was it really the result of their experiences in Mississippi? Given the similarity between the two groups going into the summer, this is a tempting explanation. But there is another possibility as well. It may be that whatever factors account for the volunteers' going in the first place also explains their higher levels of activism following the summer.

The analysis reported in Appendix F allows for a choice between these two explanations. The technical details of the analysis are outlined in the appendix. Here we are only concerned with the basic logic of the analysis and its results: the analysis makes it possible to assess the influence that each of fifteen factors had on the applicants' level of activism following Freedom Summer. Six of these factors predate the summer, and four focus on the summer itself, allowing for a clear answer to the question of whether participation in the project resulted from prior differences between the volunteers and no-shows or from the volunteers' experiences in Mississippi.

The results reported in Appendix F clearly support the latter interpretation. Only one of the six pre-summer factors—number of organizational memberships on the eve of the project—bore any significant relationship to the applicant's level of activism in the late Sixties. In contrast, three of the four factors that relate most directly to the summer were significantly related to the same variable. Indeed, the single best predictor of the applicant's subsequent activism was his or her status in the Summer

Project—that is, high levels of activism between 1964 and 1970 were clearly related to, and presumably a function of, the volunteers' involvement in the Freedom Summer campaign.

What was it about Freedom Summer that encouraged the volunteers' later activism? Two other variables included in Appendix F may suggest some answers to this question. One of those variables is the applicant's own estimate of the change in his or her "political stance" before and after Freedom Summer. Political stance was measured by means of a ten-point scale ranging from "1" for radical left to "10" for radical right. The results reported in Appendix F indicate that a leftward shift in the applicant's political orientation following Freedom Summer is significantly related to level of Sixties activism. One can read this result as suggesting that participation in the Summer Project radicalized the volunteers, thereby encouraging higher levels of activism for the rest of the decade.

A second variable to bear a strong relationship to the activism measure is the applicant's estimate of the number of Freedom Summer volunteers he or she remained in contact with in 1970. The greater the number of ties, the higher the level of activism. Freedom Summer did more than simply radicalize the volunteers. It also put them in contact with any number of other like-minded young people. Thus, the volunteers left Mississippi not only more disposed toward activism, but in a better structural position, by virtue of their links to one another, to act on these inclinations. But whatever the specific effects of Freedom Summer, its overall impact is clear. Building on the experiences and contacts gained in Mississippi, the volunteers went on to engage in much higher levels of activism in the late Sixties than did the no-shows.

Personal Differences

To this point the focus of the chapter has been narrowly political. But the political impact of Freedom Summer was anything but narrow. The Summer Project foreshadowed the central message of the women's movement by making the volunteers aware of the political significance of their personal lives. As a result, many project veterans left Mississippi with a political perspective on aspects of their lives they had previously regarded as private and nonpolitical. They looked at their families, personal relationships, and intended career choices in a new and often jaundiced light. The immediate effect of this rethinking was the type of "reentry crisis" described in the previous chapter. Some volunteers failed to return to school. Others broke off relationships—even engagements—they had been involved in prior to the summer. Relations with parents were often strained. Obviously, the no-shows experienced none of these problems, at least not as a function of the project. The question is, were these difficulties only temporary or did they presage more enduring differences in the personal lives of the two groups? The answer is clearly the latter. Especially in the areas of work and marriage, the volunteers were to make significantly different choices than the no-shows; and, once again, those differences appear to be rooted in the volunteers' experiences in Mississippi.

Choices about Work   Having decided to organize their lives around the Movement, it was only logical that the volunteers choose jobs that reflected their politics. In some cases, those choices betray a direct connection to Freedom Summer. For example, two of the volunteers interviewed attribute their decisions to go into law to the respect they gained for the civil rights lawyers they met in Mississippi. Linda Davis described the impact of her experiences in Mississippi this way:

> [M]y decision to be a lawyer . . . was very much influenced [by Freedom Summer] . . . I mean, there is nothing so wonderful when you are in jail and see your lawyer drive up and get you out . . . I still love the 1964 Chevy Impala because that was what all those guys drove . . . I do think it was a car with a very pretty line, but it just, oh boy . . . it really was the white steed to carry us away. . . . [But] also . . . I did see . . . in that year I stayed down [in Mississippi], Arthur Kinoy and his friends [bring] a law suit against the Mississippi Democratic Party. . . . That was a brilliant move. It put us on the offensive. It put the black citizens of Mississippi as plaintiffs. . . . And then the depositions were taken throughout the state and that also was a wonderful process. . . . Psychologically, it was so important and I just saw people come alive. . . . [So] I really was excited . . . [by] what I saw the lawyers able to do.[40]

In a biographical retrospective written ten years after Freedom Summer, Bryan Dunlap offered a similar account of his choice to go to law school:

> I'd been impressed with the Lawyers Guild people in Jackson during my stay. They made no excuses for being middle-class professionals . . . yet they could help people concretely at exactly the moments when the people most needed help. They were the single best example of how to connect idealism with social reality I had seen in Miss. I wanted to follow their example.[41]

In similar fashion, other volunteers switched to careers in education because of their teaching experiences in Mississippi.[42] Perhaps the most noteworthy example of one who did was Stephen Blum, a graduate student in philosophy, who returned from Mississippi to help establish, at Northwestern University, one of the nation's first Upward Bound programs. It is hard not to read the influence of Freedom Summer into Blum's pioneering involvement in the program. Upward Bound was designed to offset the inferior educational backgrounds of disadvantaged—and generally minority—students as a way of preparing them for college. Aside from the exclusive focus on preparation for college, this would also serve as a perfect description of the Freedom Schools in which Blum taught.[43]

More important than any specific link between Freedom Summer and later jobs, however, was the way the Summer Project changed the criteria by which the volunteers evaluated the attractiveness or worth of any job. Said Gren Whitman, "After that summer I never would have taken a job unless it had some social value . . . served some political end."[44] Another elaborated on this idea:

> I don't think I was that different [from other students] before I went to Mississippi. I mean there were lots of jobs I wouldn't have taken no matter how well they were paying me. . . . [But] I wanted to make money basically or at least live comfortably. I also remember saying on my college application that I was interested in nuclear physics because I had read someplace that it was the highest prestige job . . . . so I was into that too. . . . But Mississippi really changed all that. I went from looking at jobs from what was in it for me to . . . [weighing] their political value for others.[45]

This last quote is probably a bit ingenuous. Instead of abandoning self-interest as a criteria for job selection, it is probably more accurate to say that this volunteer came, as a result of his experiences in Mississippi, to look for different things in a job. Having defined himself as an activist, he became more (self) interested in confirming that identity through work rather than simply making money. Nonetheless, the shift he describes, from a monetary to a political valuation of work, is a significant one and apparently one shared by many of the volunteers. On the follow-up questionnaires, nearly half of the volunteers indicated "strong agreement" with the statement: "My participation in social movements affected my choices about work." Less than a third of the no-shows responded the same way. Even more impressive from a behavioral standpoint is the fact that a third of the volunteers were employed as full-time activists some time between 1964 and 1970. The comparable figure for the no-shows is less than 20 percent. For a large percentage of the volunteers, then, political considerations weighed heavily in the work they chose to do.

The greater weight given to the politics of the job by the volunteers may also help to account for one other difference in the work histories of the two groups. The volunteers changed jobs much more frequently during the late Sixties than the no-shows. Project veterans reported holding almost twice as many full-time jobs as the no-shows. In his interview, one of the volunteers offered a possible explanation for this difference. Said the volunteer, "I've never really pursued a 'career' in any conventional sense. I've either worked doing social action or at ordinary jobs that supported my politics . . . but [work] as something to organize my life around? Never."[46] Contrast that attitude with the explanation offered by one of the no-shows to account for her relatively low level of involvement in the women's movement: "I certainly supported what was going on [in the women's movement], but I was in a work setting where lots of men made cracks about bra-burners, you know, the whole bit . . . so I kept a fairly low profile."[47] The difference in the attitudes is in the relative priorities accorded politics and career. Like the volunteer quoted above, a substantial minority of the project veterans reversed the conventional emphasis and subordinated career to activism. Therefore, as their political commitments changed, so oftentimes did their jobs. Sometimes the change was precipitated by a geographic move that was connected to a new political involvement. One volunteer, for example, described a change in jobs necessitated by a move to California:

> I guess my first real job was in New York . . . [working] as a project director in a Head Start office. . . . That lasted just about a year. . . . While I was doing that I got involved in some boycott work [related to the farmworkers strike in California] . . . so involved that I eventually moved out there [California] and got a job as a mechanic, if you can believe that, while I was doing . . . work for the UFW [United Farm Workers].[48]

This account nicely captures the episodic, politically motivated quality of many a volunteer's work life during the late Sixties. The following three work histories taken directly from the questionnaires provide additional examples of this pattern:

CASE 1

1965–1967	Southern Student Organizing Committee (SSOC)
1967–1968	Charlotte Labor Council
1968	U.S. National Student Association Southern Project
1968–1973	*Great Speckled Bird* (underground newspaper)

Case 2

1964–1965	COFO/CORE
1965–1967	Reporter and Editor, *Southern Courier* newspaper
1968	Protective Service Worker, Connecticut Department of Welfare
1969–1970	LSCRRC [Law Students Civil Rights Research Committee]; worked on trials of Black Panther members

Case 3

1964–1965	High School Teacher, Montpelier, Vermont
1965–1966	Director, Vermont in Mississippi, Inc. (VIM), Jackson, Mississippi; "VIM . . . was the first state licensed and supported integrated day-care center in the state."
1966–1967	Director, Community Development Agency, Jackson, Mississippi
1968–1971	Center Worker, then Assistant Director, Inner City Development Project, Milwaukee, Wisconsin[49]

By contrast, the work histories of the no-shows are much more conventional. While the no-shows tend to be overrepresented in the same fields as the volunteers—especially education, law, and social service—their careers are more linear, less episodic than the volunteers. They make fewer job changes; and when they do change jobs, the change usually corresponds to the normal advancement sequence in their field. One of the no-shows accounted for the stability of his work history in the following way. He said that early in his career he had "thought about changing jobs or maybe getting out of the field altogether. But I figured I had already invested a lot and you don't want to waste that."[50] The investment he spoke of was to his *career*. For many of the volunteers, however, the commitment was to a larger political struggle.

Choices about Marriage   The preeminent position of politics in the lives of the volunteers is also strongly reflected in their marital histories during the late Sixties. However, the form that that political influence took is a little suprising. Given the critique of marriage and traditional monogamous relationships voiced by many radical feminists in the late Sixties, one would expect fewer volunteers than no-shows to have ever married. While this proved to be the case, the percentage difference (84 percent to 82 percent) was small and statistically insignificant. Moreover, it was the male volunteers who were responsible for this difference. The female volunteers were actually more likely to marry than the female no-shows.

Does this mean that the volunteers exempted their personal relationships—especially marriage—from political scrutiny? Hardly. What it means is that the volunteers were born a little too early to have their chances of getting married affected by radical feminism. As one female volunteer wryly observed, "the really strong anti-male, anti-marriage thing came along after I was married . . . in those days you took a lot of heat for it [being married]. . . . It may have helped end my marriage, but it didn't stop it from starting (laughing)!"[51]

It must be remembered that the volunteers averaged nearly twenty-four years of age at the beginning of the summer. That meant that the majority of them had grown up in the Fifties and early Sixties, during one of the more romanticized and conservative eras of gender socialization in this country's history. Even as they were challenging much of this socialization, the volunteers couldn't help but be affected by it as well. One of the volunteers acknowledged these contradictory influences:

> You know . . . we're always depicted as this angry, rebellious generation. What never gets asked is "where did this anger come from?" The answer, it seems to me, . . . has to do . . . with the incredibly romantic myths we were raiesd to believe [in]; America as a chosen people, the Horatio Alger business . . . and . . . this whole idea that some white knight would come along and sweep you off your feet . . . and I just kind of . . . laid my politics on top of this [image] . . . my white knight turned into a committed comrade with the correct political analysis. . . . [But] I don't remember being critical of marriage per se until much later.[52]

This description nicely captures the view of many volunteers coming out of the summer. They were no less interested in getting married than their peers, but their vision of Mr. or Mrs. Right had been altered by their experiences in Mississippi. They were now looking for a partner who shared their commitment to the struggle. Given this criteria, it is not surprising that many of the Mississippi veterans found their partner among the other volunteers. Within three years of the summer, there had been at least thirty-one marriages between two project veterans. Indeed, the first of these "movement marriages" took place during the summer. Bill Hodes included the following account of the wedding in a letter home:

> Here's that bit of local color you've all been waiting for. Two [volunteers] just got married a few minutes ago—guess we have to call it a Freedom Wedding, to keep the nomenclature straight.
> The brief service was held in a little chapel on the ground floor of the office. Flowers were scotch-taped to the wall. Strings were hung from wall to wall; sprigs of spruce alternating with Mississippi Free-

dom Summer leaflets hung along the way. Up front where Christ
should be was the poster of two Negro kids sitting on a porch with
the words: *Give them a future in Mississippi.* . . .

When it was all over, Jim Forman stood up and yelled in that
wonderful booming voice of his: "ONE MAN—ONE WOMAN—
TWO VOTES." This was the signal for a fierce rice-pelting scene,
and much was the merriment thereof. We sang WE SHALL OVER-
COME, with Jim calling the verses.[53]

As the letter suggests, the wedding was as much a celebration of a
political union as anything else. In describing his own marriage to a
volunteer, Ken Scudder acknowledged the central role Freedom Summer
played in the union. "We were a political marriage; a product of that
time . . . a product of this very fragile thing . . . of being on the battle lines together."[54] Even for those volunteers who chose not to marry
fellow volunteers their images of marriage and ideal partners were affected by the project. Two, in particular, recalled wrestling for the first
time with the question of interracial marriage and, in the face of their
doubts about such unions, questioning their commitment to the movement.[55] Once again, Freedom Summer had served to politicize their personal lives. The whole question of mate selection took on a political
significance it had previously lacked. Eventually both of these volunteers
resolved their doubts by marrying black men they had met in the movement.

For other volunteers, the effect of the summer was more general,
serving simply to increase the importance of political compatibility in
their choice of partners. For example, Judy Michalowski couldn't remember making any conscious political decisions about dating, "but
even if I didn't . . . people who came in contact with me were screened
out. . . . That summer helped solidify an identity that tended to screen
some people or make it more likely to get involved with some people
than others."[56] It also made it more likely that relationships established
before the summer would be subjected to political scrutiny upon the
volunteers' return home. Len Edwards provided the following account
of this process in his description of what proved to be a painful transition year out of Mississippi:

> [It was a] very tough year . . . I wasn't very social at all and didn't
> really have . . . nice relationship[s] with people I would say for a
> whole year; and my friends had to put up with me . . . I broke
> up with a girlfriend that I'd had before I went down to Mississippi
> and it was clear that what happened down there . . . made it im-

possible for me to relate to her. I mean I think I loved her—she was
a wonderful girl—we just, . . . it wasn't her fault, you know.[57]

Even more painful was the case of the young teacher who divorced
his wife shortly after returning from Mississippi. He explains:

> It probably wasn't just the summer; we were headed in different
> directions anyway . . . but the summer certainly brought things to
> a head. . . . I came back feeling very much a part of this larger
> movement and I want [sic] to keep doing stuff; marches, demon-
> strations, the whole smear . . . and she . . . was freaked by all
> this. . . . She kept saying, "you're not the person I married," . . .
> and she was right, I *wasn't* the person she married. *I had gotten
> much more political.*[58] (Emphasis added)

Like a good many of the volunteers, these two had been politicized
by the events of the summer. No aspect of their lives was exempt from
political examination. Politics or the movement now loomed as the central organizing principle of their lives. The no-shows, on the other hand,
had experienced no such dramatic political radicalization. What differentiated their orientation to work from that of the volunteers applies as
well to marriage and personal relationships. While political compatibility
was important to them, their overriding goal in getting married was not
to affect political union with another person. While not irrelevant, the
political values of their mates were clearly secondary to other considerations.[59] Several remarks made by no-shows nicely capture this difference
in emphasis. Said one, "Look, I was very [politically] active at that
time . . . it was very important to me . . . [but] my wife was fundamentally apolitical. It would have been nice if it were otherwise, *but I
didn't marry her for her politics"* (emphasis added).[60] Another expressed
it this way:

> We were both marginally active in the [antiwar] movement; on the
> fringes really. And I liked that about her; I mean the fact that it
> wasn't her whole life. . . . There was a certain obsessive quality
> about the "movement chicks"—that's what they were called; it's not
> my term—that for me anyway was a real turn-off . . . I mean they
> just lived and breathed politics.[61]

Once again, then, there is a more conventional quality to the lives
of the no-shows than the volunteers. Without the radicalizing influence
of Freedom Summer, most of the no-shows were never willing to accord
politics and the movement the central place in their lives that the volun-

teers did. In this sense, a great many of the project veterans were like
the "movement chicks" described above. They were obsessive about their
politics. And like any true obsession, their commitment to the Movement permeated every aspect of their lives. David Harris (1982: 224)
might as well have been describing the volunteers as himself when he
penned the following words:

> Perhaps only a Sixties veteran who had intense politics and an in-
> tense relationship going at the same time can understand. There was
> an overwhelming urge to get all parts of my life stacked up on top of
> my political base. Somehow, anything less felt like abandoning the
> cause. It was a hard, if not impossible, balancing act to sustain.

The volunteers would find it difficult as well. As long as the political
and cultural wave known as the Sixties continued to wash forward, the
balancing act remained possible. As that wave began to recede in the
early Seventies, it became an increasingly tough act to pull off.

6

The Morning After
THE SEVENTIES AND BEYOND

THE MISSISSIPPI veterans were among the first to catch the political and cultural wave of the Sixties. Indeed, they had as much to do with shaping the chronological and substantive character of that wave as anyone else. Nor did their commitment to the wave begin and end with the Summer Project. As detailed in Chapter 5, many of the volunteers continued to organize their lives around the movement long after the summer ended. Jobs were taken as a means of furthering the struggle. Marriages were conceived of as political partnerships. Decisions about where to live often turned on which cities were viewed as the most politically progressive; for example, by 1970 nearly 40 percent of the volunteers were living in California's Bay Area.

As long as the Sixties wave continued to wash forward, the volunteers' efforts to build their lives upon a progressive political base proved largely successful. No matter what frustrations or political setbacks the New Left suffered, it was able, for a time, to reassure itself that it remained the political wave of the future. As Breines (1982: xi) put it:

> [W]e believed that we could achieve an egalitarian, free, and participatory society. And, immodestly, we thought that we glimpsed its beginnings in our own political activity. We believed that we were going to make a revolution. We were convinced that we could transform America through our political activity and insights.

As especially committed and influential members of the New Left, the volunteers shared in the sense of destiny and political mission implied in this vision. Riding any wave is an enjoyable experience; riding one the size and significance of the Sixties was especially exhilarating.

One volunteer groped to capture the feeling. "It was incredible," he said. "We were it! We were at the center of everything! We were making history all the while flying by the seat of our collective pants. What a rush! Were we full of ourselves? You bet. Did it feel great? Fuck, yes!"[1]

At some point, however, the wave crested and began inexorably to wash backward. Exactly when this occurred is a matter of opinion. The 1968 Democratic Convention in Chicago, Nixon's first term election as President, the shooting of students at Kent State—all have been mentioned as the symbolic high-water mark of the New Left. But if the point at which the political tide turned is uncertain, the fact that it did so is not. Nor is there any doubt about the direction the tide has been running for the past fifteen or so years. The same volunteer quoted above described the early Seventies as

> a very confusing, kind of aimless period . . . depressing really.
> . . . Looking back it seems incredible that we ever thought we
> could really pull off a revolution. That's how far we've retreated
> since then. . . . At the time, though, [we] were riding such a high
> and then, WHAM, all of a sudden the party was over. . . . I sup-
> pose the ending was inevitable. It's the fifteen-year morning after
> that's been the real bummer.[2]

Many of the volunteers interviewed echoed these sentiments. They too had experienced the early Seventies as discontinuous with the previous five to seven years of their lives. Almost all of them, but especially the males, had a "morning after" story of their own to tell. Finally, the volunteers were nearly unanimous in seeing the last fifteen years as a period of political and cultural retrenchment in American society.

But what of their lives during this period? While there exists a voluminous literature on activists during the Sixties, the trail grows cold as we enter the Seventies. Apparently, like old soldiers, old radicals "just fade away." Or, if we are to believe the popular media accounts, become stockbrokers or born-again Christians. Judging from the questionnaires and interviews, the truth is neither as simple nor as reassuring as these accounts suggest. The volunteers did not "fade away" or "sell out." Instead, they struggled through the Seventies to reconcile the personal and political lessons of Mississippi with an America that was increasingly apolitical and individually oriented. Their efforts to do so mark their lives during the Seventies as much more continuous with the Sixties than the popular accounts suggest. While they made accommodations to a changing America, their first allegiance still seems to have been to the conceptions of politics and self formed in Mississippi.

Politics as Usual

We tend to stereotype decades in the same way we stereotype people. Whatever factual base the stereotype rests on is soon overwhelmed by the stereotype itself. So the Fifties were "quiet and conformist" even though the decade also saw the rise of the civil rights movement and rock and roll. Though the overwhelming majority of people—including students—remained apathetic and uninvolved during the Sixties, the decade is remembered as "raucous and rebellious." In similar fashion, the Seventies will always be remembered as the "Me Decade," supposedly because personal concerns replaced social activism as the defining quality of the era. There are three distortions in this characterization. First, "personal concerns" (or self-interest) have probably always functioned as the dominant motivation underlying social life. Second, the roots of the "Me Decade's" preoccupation with self are to be found in the Sixties, not the Seventies. It was the twin emphases on personal liberation and social action that marked the late Sixties as distinctive. Initially, the two were joined, as the concern with personal liberation was intended to encourage people to overcome the vestiges of racism or sexism that hampered social action. Over time, however, the rhetoric of personal liberation fostered forms of behavior (e.g., drug usage, sexual experimentation) whose connection to social action was tangential at best. Thus, the focus on self that we have come to associate with the Seventies did not so much arise, then, as represent a depoliticized holdover from the Sixties.[3]

Finally, while activism may have declined in the Seventies, it certainly did not disappear. The women's, environmental, and antinuclear movements grew stronger, not weaker, during the decade. The Seventies also saw the proliferation of local neighborhood movements throughout the country.[4] The volunteers were active in all of these efforts. One volunteer spoke for many of the project veterans when she said: "I've never been a fair-weather activist. I got into the Movement when it wasn't the thing to do and I stayed in while lots of people were dropping out in the early Seventies. . . . I'm in for the long haul."[5]

This quote also highlights an important process that served to change the nature of the activist experience for the volunteers during the Seventies—that is, the collapse of the New Left and the many organizational vehicles (e.g., SDS, Resistance) that had sustained mass activism in the late Sixties. Without these vehicles, many "fair-weather" activists *did* succumb to the general societal decline in movement activity. With the political tide now ebbing, the volunteers found themselves transformed from a political vanguard into a rear guard. They received less support for their activism, and the activist subcultures that did survive became smaller and smaller. Where once they had been "at the center of everything," the volunteers grew increasingly marginal to the dominant political and cultural trends in American society.

The female volunteers were less affected by these processes than were the males. The reason is simple: the women's movement grew stronger during the period, affording the female volunteers a vehicle to sustain their activism as well as a community to support a more general feminist lifestyle. The role of the women's movement in sustaining the activism of the female volunteers was acknowledged by two of them in their interviews. Their comments follow:

> I actually came to the [women's] movement late, '71 or '72, somewhere around there. . . . Before that I was doing draft counseling . . . then they ended it [the draft] and . . . the whole [antiwar] movement . . . kind of lost its focus. I joined a CR [consciousness raising] group at this point [and] . . . didn't really a miss a beat. . . .[6]

> New Left history is a bit sexist if you want my opinion. The rap is always that the Movement collapsed after '68 or '69. But what movement are they talking about?! The women's movement was going great guns at that point. . . . I probably was at my activest [sic] between '70 and '72. . . . *It's only the guys who didn't know what to do with themselves*.[7] (Emphasis added)

In contrast, the collapse of the antiwar movement early in the decade deprived the male volunteers of the cause and the community around which they had organized their activism and, quite often, their lives. To the extent that the male volunteers did remain active, their energies tended to be absorbed by the three movements noted earlier. Table 6.1 reports the levels of involvement of the volunteers in the environmental, antinuclear and local neighborhood movements. Having granted activism a central place in their lives, many volunteers were determined to find new issues around which to organize. The environment, the growing nuclear power industry, and a myriad of other issues afforded them the vehicles to do so. Increasingly, however, the focus of organizing efforts was at the local, rather than national, level. Even in the case of the environmental and antinuclear movements, most organizing was directed at local environmental conditions or nuclear plants, respectively. There would appear to be three reasons for this shift in focus. First, the divisive splintering of the New Left at the close of the Sixties deprived the left

Table 6.1   Percentage of Volunteer's Reporting That They Were "Very," "Moderately," or "Somewhat" Involved in the Environmental, Antinuclear, and Local Neighborhood Movements

Level of Involvement	Environmental		Antinuclear		Local Neighborhood	
	%	No.	%	No.	%	No.
Very involved	11	(21)	12	(24)	18	(36)
Moderately involved	14	(27)	18	(36)	17	(34)
Somewhat involved	33	(65)	31	(62)	24	(48)
Total	58	(113)	61	(122)	59	(118)

of the national organizations that might have coordinated widespread protest activities. Second, the antibureaucracy, antileader ethic within the New Left encouraged local organizing. Finally, the Sixties veterans were themselves settling down and increasingly turning their attention to issues and conditions in their immediate environment. The volunteers were very much a part of this trend. The following "activist profiles" drawn from the interviews and questionnaires illustrate the diversity and local character of much of the organizing the volunteers engaged in during this period:

CASE 1: GREN WHITMAN

1968–1971   Whitman became very involved during this period in the antiwar movement, especially around Baltimore. His antiwar activities included:
- His work with and on behalf of the Berrigan brothers, two Catholic priests who gained widespread notoriety for their antiwar activities
- His work with the Baltimore Interfaith Peace Mission
- His work for the Baltimore Defense Committee which defended antiwar demonstrators and draft resistors
- His work for the Peace Action Center in Baltimore, for which he served as director in 1968

1971–1978   Increasingly after 1971, however, Whitman's political energies were absorbed by local political and especially neighborhood issues. These involvements had two principal components:
1. At the formal political level he twice ran unsuccessfully for local public office and worked on a good many other campaigns
2. At the grass roots level, he helped organize his immediate neighborhood around a variety of issues. These included efforts to:

- Block construction of a high-rise hotel several blocks from his home (successful)
- Preserve "open space" in the form of a kind of people's park in the neighborhood (successful)
- Establish a free clinic in the neighborhood
- Establish a food coop in the neighborhood

The principal vehicles through which these local efforts were coordinated were the Abell Improvement Association and the Greater Homewood Community Corporation.

CASE 2: DEBRA ELLIS[9]

1967–1971	Was involved in the early women's movement in NYC.
1968–1971	Entered law school, where "we terrorized the law school." At that point the school was beginning to admit larger numbers of women—about 20 percent—to cover their admissions against the likely possibility of male students being drafted. The women founded a group of women law students which pressed for:

- More equitable treatment of women in law school
- Greater equality in employment opportunities

1971–1976	Moved to an Indian reservation, where she worked for a legal services program. Describes this period as "intense, but wonderful." Loved the "purity of the existence," the simple way of life.
1977–1981	Moved to Albuquerque where she got involved in a local environmental movement which "a bunch of old radicals basically put together." The centerpiece of the movement was the effort to keep uranium mining out of the county.

CASE 3: HEATHER TOBIS BOOTH[10]

1967–1970	Active as one of the central figures in the burgeoning women's liberation movement in Chicago. Active in both WRAP (Women's Radical Action Project) and Chicago Women's Liberation Union.
1969–1971	As an offshoot of her feminist activities, she got "very involved in the day care movement in Chicago."
1971–1972	Got involved in "a community organization started in Chicago by the [Saul] Alinsky group" aimed at combating environmental pollution.
1972–1973	While working as an editor for a Chicago publishing firm, Booth initiated efforts to improve the working conditions of the firm's secretaries. The company responded by laying her off. She countered by filing a grievance with the National Labor Relations Board. Eventually she and several others

won a judgment against the company and were awarded back pay.

1973–1980   With the money from the settlement, Booth founded the Midwest Academy, a training school for organizers. She served as its director until 1978.

1977–1980   Founded the Citizen Labor Energy Commission to work on energy and related issues. She served as director of the organization until 1980.

These cases illustrate the changing nature of the volunteers' activism during the Seventies. As the volunteers graduated from college and entered the labor force, they used the organizing techniques learned in Mississippi (and subsequent campaigns) to protest objectionable working conditions. As they moved from the university into homes or apartments of their own, they applied their organizing skills to issues at the neighborhood level. In so doing, they enjoyed considerable success. The cases cited above are only a small fraction of those described by the volunteers in their interviews and questionnaires. Of the forty project veterans interviewed, nine others had activist histories during the Seventies just as impressive as the three volunteers spotlighted here. Many others who were less active also drew upon their activist training when the need arose, applying their well-honed skills at home and work alike. For example, Miriam Cohen Glickman described how she helped

> organize a group in our neighborhood to get stop signs; and we used the community organizing skills that I had learned in Mississippi. And we were the only group for . . . a huge number of months that got stop signs because the city had a policy against them. . . . So you take your skills to the suburbs.[11]

With each passing year, however, fewer of their age peers were inclined to join them in these struggles. As the Sixties receded into nostalgia, people whose commitment to the politics of the era had been less deep-seated, dropped by the wayside. The activist subculture was slowly disintegrating, leaving the volunteers who remained active more and more isolated as the decade wore on. The shifting political tide would also have a personal impact on many of the volunteers during the Seventies.

The Personal Remains Political

In the Rosellen Brown novel, *Civil Wars*, the marriage of two Freedom Summer veterans disintegrates as the political conditions that gave rise to the union dissolve. Brown (1984: 44–45) captures the pain and inevitability of the dissolution in the following passage:

> [H]e had had everything: experience, courage, pain, openness, and that infinitely touching grown boy's body she could never have enough of. But were those two who spoke and held each other without breath and finally pronounced themselves in love only their own ideals for which they had found a willing embodiment? Were they stand-ins for real people who were somewhere else, like those paste diamonds some women wear while their priceless diamonds doze on velvet in a safe? If Teddy was only the hero and Jessie the groupie, *who* had married that afternoon in Tolewood in white Mexican wedding shirts and dungarees under a sign that substituted for a wedding canopy: ONE MAN + ONE WOMAN = TWO VOTES? And what if one ideal accidentally marries one real person? One round and one flat—she remembered something from a college class on the novel—didn't Dickens make flat characters? It had begun to occur to her early on, and she suppressed it, that when she looked at Teddy in a group or even alone, at rest, what she was seeing was really a painting, or a photograph of a generic Early Movement Hero, the shadows his nose and his eyelashes cast altogether hypothetical. Was he shallow, or only grandly deluded to think that where he lived now, in 1979, could make a difference to anyone? Sometimes she thought of the animals who'd survived in the thickets of genetics, the first mutant long-necked giraffes who didn't starve because they could eat from the tops of the trees, who miraculously had the qualities they needed for one time, one place. Teddy, perhaps, had such qualities.

Before the Seventies ended, many of the volunteers would know the pain and sense of dislocation Brown is describing. Following the activist imperative to treat the personal as political, the Mississippi veterans had chosen mates and jobs on the basis of their politics. But they had done so when the radical tide was running high. Between the Sixties and late Seventies the political and cultural context changed dramatically. Nineteen seventy-nine was light years and worlds away from 1964. To the extent that the volunteers had hitched their marital or occupational dreams to the political visions of 1964, they were in for a rough ride.

Political Marriages in an Apolitical Era

Marriages fail for a variety of reasons. One of the chief culprits, however, is change (c.f. Houseknecht, Vaughan, and Macke, 1984; Scanzoni, 1978). Marriages are partnerships founded on certain assumptions about the world and the partners themselves. Should these assumptions be rendered obsolete, the likely result is a marital crisis. The marriage need not dissolve, but the terms of the partnership will certainly have to be renegotiated if it is to survive. As we have seen, political assumptions were as important as any in the marriages of many project veterans. For some, like the heroine of *Civil Wars*, it was the political status of their spouse that cemented the relationship. David Harris (1982: 224) has said as much about his marriage to Joan Baez:

> Ten years after it ended, David Harris' romance with Joan Baez is, for me, indistinguishable from the politics of the moment. We were public creatures. Sweet-voiced heroine of a generation joins with young knight advancing in the battle for peace in our time. Without the intoxication of those roles and the image they fostered, I doubt whether the relationship would ever have come off.

For others, the political assumptions underlying their union had less to do with the stature of their mate than a common analysis of the present and a shared vision of the future. But in an era of change, nothing changed quite as quickly or dramatically as the radical left's prescription for a just and egalitarian society. What was cutting edge analysis one year was bourgeois reactionism the next.

Since the volunteers typically wed in the late Sixties, it was inevitable that their marriages would be affected by the ever-changing currents of New Left politics. Judging from the interviews with the volunteers, the effect was usually for the worse. Several volunteers explicitly acknowledged the role of changing political circumstances in the dissolution of their marriages. One white woman who had wed a black activist in 1965 recounted the growing marital strains that accompanied the subtle, but dramatic, political redefinition of interracial unions:

> When we married, it was like, you know, we were the . . . living embodiment of "black and white together." . . . We couldn't have been more politically correct . . . than we were. Then came . . . [black power] and the whole separatist thing. . . . He just caught hell . . . from other [blacks] . . . you know, he was insulting his race, his black sisters [by] being with me. . . . Later I caught a lot of flack from feminist friends [because] . . . I was in this really macho culture. . . . Who could bear up under those pressures?[12]

Another volunteer recalled how his marital fortunes seemed to parallel the collapse of the New Left:

> [W]e were both very politically active. This is the height of my political existence . . . in SDS . . . We met during [a] . . . strike.

We got married. . . . I don't know why we got married . . . here
we were in a movement where marriage seemed totally beside the
point . . . and yet we went ahead and got married at a fairly young
age . . . very strange, and I remember . . . we got married . . .
in the middle of a faction fight and we ran out to City Hall and got
married in the middle of the day, ran back to the faction meeting,
you know, as if almost . . . [to] say, "Oh, this wasn't anything."
. . . I mean the marriage never should have happened and I think
part of the putrefaction of the marriage was symptomatic of the
putrefaction of politics. . . . [It] was a disintegrating world. So
long as that world was around the marriage . . . had a context . . .
but when [the collapse of the Movement] . . . forced us to turn
inward . . . there were no barriers, no insulation, no other diver-
sions, [no] other involvements really.[13]

Ken Scudder put it more succinctly. He said, "we were a political
marriage—a product of that time. We never would have gotten married, we never would have done anything, if it weren't for the movement. . . . And when that began to wind down, you know, the contradictions began to surface and we had a miserable . . . time of it."[14]

A comparison of the marital histories of the volunteers and no-shows
is certainly consistent with the general picture being painted here. Nearly
half (47 percent) of all the volunteers who married following the summer were divorced sometime between 1970 and 1979. Among the no-
shows, the comparable figure was under 30 percent. Without knowing
the reasons for divorce, it is impossible to say with certainty that it was
political pressures that account for the difference in divorce rates between the two groups. At the same time, the central importance accorded politics by the volunteers, combined with the dramatic and generally depressing direction of political change during the Seventies,
makes this a likely possibility.

Whether casually related or not, the personal continued to reflect the
political in the lives of the volunteers. The collapse of the New Left
and the activist community that had sustained them through the Sixties
was mirrored on the home front. As activism waned in American life,
the volunteers paid for their ongoing commitment to political struggle
with a certain increase in social marginality. A similar dynamic appears
to have also been at work in the volunteers' employment histories.

Change and Marginality: Making a Career of It

It is hard to characterize the work histories of the volunteers during the
Seventies without comparing them to the no-shows. That comparison

clearly reveals a continuation of the very different employment patterns shown by the two groups in the late Sixties. The volunteers' work histories remain less traditional and more episodic than the no-shows. The volunteers changed jobs far more often during the decade than the no-shows. Thirty percent of all no-shows held a single job through the Seventies. Only 9 percent of the volunteers did so. At the other extreme, twice as many volunteers as no-shows (16 percent to 8 percent) held five or more jobs. Moreover, there are likely to be significant gaps, years of unemployment or underemployment, in the work histories of the volunteers. As a result, the average number of years of full-time, non-activist employment during the Seventies is nearly a year-and-a-half more for the no-shows than the volunteers.[15]

What accounts for these differences? The likely answer is the continuing desire of many of the volunteers to subordinate career to politics. Describing this period in her life, one female volunteer said she was "looking for something [political] to be involved in, and that . . . became . . . a way of organizing my life, of finding meaning in my life, you know, as opposed to . . . a career or a house . . . [or] economic advantages . . . ."[16] Eventually, she satisfied her desire for political involvement by joining and working full-time for the Communist Labor Party. Another volunteer described his attitude toward a conventional career during this period as one of "repulsion." The very idea of organizing one's life around anything other than politics seemed almost immoral to him. Consequently, he attended school and worked at various jobs as "a kind of incidental nuisance" to his involvement in a string of radical leftist groups including Progressive Labor, the SDS Labor Committee, and the Socialist Labor Committee.[17]

Indeed, many of the volunteers evidenced more political than occupational continuity in their lives, at least through the early Seventies. After 1973 or 1974, however, it grew more and more difficult to sustain the life of the free-lance activist. For one thing, the leftist subculture that had supported this lifestyle was rapidly disintegrating. Just as important, economic recession and political backlash were drying up the monies that had been available in the late Sixties to subsidize life as a subsistence radical (McCarthy and Zald, 1973). At least two of the volunteers cited these trends as partial explanations for their declining activism *and* the onset of more conventional work histories. One put it this way:

> Hard times played a hand in it [her declining activism]. . . . There always seemed to be money around—I'm talking about during the Sixties now—to live off of. You didn't live well, maybe, but you

could survive. Some of it was liberal guilt money . . . but . . . there was also . . . War on Poverty [funds], research grants, money from parents . . . you didn't seem to need as much money, either . . . there was this community, you could always count on housing and feeding you . . . [but] it seemed to evaporate . . . when the money started drying up. At that point [1973], I was pretty much forced to get some sort of "straight" job. . . . But between school and various part-time or movement jobs, I made it nearly ten years without really working.[18]

Despite their best efforts, then, most of the volunteers were forced by changing political and economic circumstances to rethink their orientation to work. Those who had managed, like the volunteer quoted above, to subordinate work to politics began to reverse the emphasis. While still applying political criteria to their work choices, the volunteers also began to evidence a greater concern for the security and stability of a traditional career. As it came to be more and more obvious that they were not going to be able to organize their lives around the movement, the volunteers looked to structure their lives in other ways. For many, work served as the new anchor. One for whom it did explained the circumstances surrounding his new-found interest in work:

I'm always reading in the paper how . . . some Sixties radical is now selling stocks or something, and there is always this sort of critical tone [to the story]; you know, this guy "sold out" or something. . . . But to sell out implies a choice . . . I mean, you have to sell out something. But at some point there really wasn't anything to sell out. I mean I didn't *choose* nursing home administration over the Movement. . . . The Movement was dead. So you plow your energies into something else. I got into work.[19]

By contrast, very few of the no-shows experienced this kind of disjuncture in their lives in the early to mid-Seventies. Especially as regards work, most of the no-shows were already settled into conventional career tracks by this period. One no-show spoke for many in responding to a question on the "collapse of the movement" in the early Seventies. She said, "it didn't really affect me. . . . As the war wound down, things just seemed to die. After that there really weren't . . . [issues] that I identified with. Besides, I had my hands full with work and two children."[20]

By the mid-Seventies, then, many of the no-shows were settled comfortably into fairly conventional work and family histories. Their lives were not noticeably affected by the shifting political tide of the era. However, for those volunteers who had organized their work and family lives around their politics, it was inevitable that they would bear the costs of political retrenchment. On the personal front, these costs were reflected in the high divorce rate experienced by the volunteers in the Seventies.

On the job front, too, the project veterans appear to have paid a price for their politics. Having, in effect, postponed the start of their careers, the volunteers had sacrificed the market advantage they should have enjoyed as babies born during World War II or the early postwar years. Had the volunteers entered the work force on schedule in the mid to late Sixties, they would have benefited not only from a boom economy, but the relative paucity of competitors for an expanding number of jobs. Instead, by waiting until the early Seventies, the volunteers found themselves confronting the same stagnant, overly competitive job market as their younger brothers and sisters. Excluding those who were employed prior to Freedom Summer, the modal years for entrance into full-time, nonactivist employment was 1969 for the no-shows and 1972 for the volunteers. Though only a scant three years, the difference was a highly significant one. Landon Jones (1980: 178, 180–181) explains why:

> With the track to the top greased by the absence of a large generation ahead of them, [the earliest] baby boomers began to move into the system in the late Sixties. The median age of partners began to drop in law firms. Companies were so eager for the services of young business school graduates, attuned to the youth market, that they bid up starting salaries faster than oil-lease rights. Teaching jobs were easy to get, especially for the oldest members of the baby boom, who were desperately needed to teach their younger brothers and sisters. . . . [But] the economic position of the boom generation was being reversed. Once our affluent generation, it was economically disadvantaged by the competition of its own numbers. . . . The . . . problem was that demand dried up long before the supply did. The Bureau of Labor Statistics reported that the first employment difficulties among college graduates started developing after 1969. Soon, more than 11 percent of the class that graduated in June of 1972 had not found jobs they wanted by October. . . . During the years from 1969 until 1976, some 2 million baby-boom graduates—twice the number of the preceding seven years—entered the labor force. More than 2.1 million of them, or 27 percent were forced to take jobs they had not been trained for . . . or were unable to find work at all. (By comparison, only 7 percent of the graduates of the earlier period suffered that fate.)

For a time, then, the baby boom created unprecedented employment opportunities as virtually all fields expanded to satisfy the increased demand for goods and services occasioned by the rapidly expanding population. Over time, however, the boom came to exert a negative effect on employment chances simply by increasing to prohibitive levels the numbers of young people looking for jobs. Both the volunteers and the no-shows found themselves on the cusp of this economic transition. By entering the labor market sooner, the no-shows tended to benefit from the opportunities created by the baby boom. The volunteers, on the other hand, appear to have suffered the fate of the later baby boom cohorts. Not only did they have more trouble finding jobs initially, but they are more likely to have reported being unemployed or underemployed at some point during the Seventies. Because of these difficulties, it seems reasonable to assume that the volunteers earned less money per year on the average than the no-shows. Moreover, many of these job-related deficits have persisted until the present. Indeed, it may well be that the personal and occupational costs borne by the volunteers have increased since the Seventies.

The Volunteers Today

The closest thing we have to an explanation of what happened to the Sixties radicals is a popular media account stressing wholesale generational sell-out as a general response to the collapse of the movement.[21] The contemporary lives of former activist "stars" such as Jerry Rubin and Eldridge Cleaver are routinely offered up as "evidence" to support this "explanation." Rubin, now a stockbroker, and Cleaver, the born-again clothier, represent reassuring symbols of a kind of moral and political repentance claimed to be typical of many Sixties radicals. The following excerpt from a story in *In These Times* (Neumann, 1982: 24) captures the flavor of the contemporary depiction of the Sixties radical.

> Studio 54, with all its overteched mirror-plated sheen, has faded a bit. It is no longer the absolute definition of hip. Discos come and go, and while "Studio" remains glitzy as can be, one senses that the truly hip—the Brookes and Warhols and Laurens of this city—are quaffing Perrier elsewhere. But it retains a certain charm nonetheless.
>
> The bartenders, each one a young Adonis, still strip to the waist and get sweaty serving drinks. The darkened gray men's room boasts an attendant who looks like he stepped off the set of *Brideshead Revisited*. The young women in the hat check room are model pretty—it's a privilege to have them handle your worn woolens.

Yep, it's a far cry from the park in 1968, a long toss from scattering dollar bills on the floor of the stock exchange or getting banned on college campuses by provoking the young innocents to revolution against the established order.

But for $8 on Wednesday nights, you can combine the two, after a fashion, and attend Jerry Rubin's Business Networking Salon. Jerry has resurfaced with a vengeance and is now ready to do for Manhattan's single professionals what he once did for the disaffected students of the '60s: get them high on his version of the latest thing.

For all this supposed typicality, Rubin, along with Cleaver, are virtually the only former radicals proffered by the press as examples of this pattern. In contrast, the few systematic follow-up studies of the Sixties activists have produced findings exactly opposite of the popular account.[22] Briefly, these studies have found former activists to be more likely than nonactivists to define themselves as politically "radical," espouse leftist political attitudes, eschew traditional career and family commitments, and remain active in movement politics.

In the face of this evidence and the relative dearth of examples of those who repented their activism, why does the myth of generational sell-out persist? The answer to this question may lie in the larger depoliticizing function of the myth. If, as the account suggests, most of the Sixties radicals grew up to become Yuppies, then we can chalk up their earlier radicalism to immaturity or so much faddishness. In this view, Sixties radicalism looms as little more than the hula hoop of its era. By growing up to espouse mainstream values and hold conventional jobs, figures like Rubin and Cleaver reassure us that we need not take the politics of the era seriously. The "kids" were just sowing a few wild oats before they settled down. Properly chastened, the Sixties radicals are now finding fulfillment in commodity futures and reclaimed urban housing. The lie in all this, of course, is that with few exceptions, today's Yuppies have not been drawn from the ranks of yesterday's radicals. Information from the questionnaires support this conclusion. The volunteers have not spent the last fifteen years embracing the stereotypic Yuppie lifestyle. Instead, they struggle today, even as they struggled through the Seventies, to reconcile the personal and political lessons of Mississippi with an America grown increasingly conservative and self-absorbed.

Keeping the (Political) Faith

There is very little in the contemporary lives of the volunteers to support the popular image of the Sixties radical renouncing his or her earlier political leanings. Although some of the volunteers have grown pessimistic about the prospects for political and economic change, their collective commitment to the politics they practiced fifteen or twenty years ago remains strong. Of the forty volunteers interviewed, only nine thought their political orientations had changed significantly since Freedom Summer. Eight of the nine saw themselves as having grown essentially apolitical in the intervening years. The remaining volunteer professed to being fundamentally more conservative than he was in the late Sixties. Thus, the volunteers display a great deal more continuity than discontinuity in their politics post-Freedom Summer. This continuity is evident in both the current attitudes and political involvements of the project veterans.

Attitudinally, the volunteers remain overwhelming leftist in political orientation. Two-thirds of the Mississippi veterans, but only 40 percent of the no-shows, place themselves on the "leftist" end—that is numbers 1, 2, and 3—of a ten-point scale intended to measure their "present political stance." In defining themselves this way, most of the volunteers are merely confirming a political identity forged twenty years ago during Freedom Summer. Said one simply, "I don't think my political thinking has changed a helluva lot since then [Freedom Summer]. I steered clear of the . . . really radical stuff in the late Sixties/early Seventies. . . . The project has always been my political barometer."[23] Much the same connection between current values and the summer project was asserted by several other volunteers. Jan Hillegas saw the connection as bound up with the fundamental question of participatory democracy.

> One of the phrases that was used a lot in Mississippi around the Summer Project was "Let the people decide." . . . I've been wrapped up in a lot of issues—Central America, nuclear power, civil rights, a lot of things. And they're all important. But it seems to me that the basic thing that I keep getting back to . . . is the question of "Who decides?" and "What does it mean to let the people decide?"[24]

Another defined the political thread linking Freedom Summer to her present as "twenty years of coalition building . . . creating new 'beloved communities' as a basis for political struggle."[25] Whatever the nature of the connection, the attitudinal continuity between the past and present is clear for most of the volunteers.

Nor is it only in their current attitudes that the volunteers betray allegiance to their political pasts. Their present political activities make them as anomalous today as they were in 1964. Like then, they are a decidedly activist group in a nonactivist era. Nearly half of all the volunteers (46 percent) report being currently active in at least one social movement. Only a third of the no-shows make the same claim. Seventy percent of the volunteers, but only half of the no-shows report membership in at least one political organization. To get an idea of how unusual these figures are, consider that in a group of 117 adults matched to the volunteers on the basis of age and education, only 6 percent claimed to be currently active in a social movement. Less than two in ten reported being a member of any political group.[26] When compared to this matched group, both the no-shows and volunteers emerge as exceptionally active politically. But the levels of political involvement remain significantly greater among the volunteers. As Robbie Osman put it, "I've found I can't stop playing a political role. I have to prove that I will continue to play a political role. I sometimes wish to hell it would go away so I could . . . do something else . . . it's like this compulsive energy in my life."[27]

The exercise of this "compulsive energy" takes nearly as many forms as there are volunteers who remain active. For example, in 1984 Osman co-produced an album of antinuclear songs entitled, "Out of Darkness." Featuring artists such as Pete Seeger, Holly Near, and Sweet Honey in the Rock, the album afforded Osman and his co-producer "a way to work together on a project that reflected our values as cultural and political activists . . . and a way to help anti-nuclear organizations earn desperately needed funds."[28] However, in the early Eighties the lion's share of Osman's political energies were devoted to the Livermore Action Group, a California-based group that had hoped through direct action to force the Lawrence-Livermore Laboratory—one of two facilities in the United States where nuclear weapons are designed—to shut down. As an important force in the project, Osman drew extensively on his experiences during Freedom Summer. As in Mississippi, building a close-knit community of activists absorbed as much of his and the project's energies as concrete actions against the lab. Moreover, many of the techniques used in Mississippi were employed in the Livermore project. These included the extensive use of "movement songs" as well as attempts to develop solidarity through mass civil disobedience. Indeed, in describing the project, Osman consciously used Freedom Summer as a standard against which to measure the Livermore experience.

> We were onto something that was very exciting. The energy was electric in a way that nothing's been for me since Mississippi or [the strike at Columbia University in] '68, and in some ways better than Mississippi or '68. . . . [W]e're wiser and . . . we've learned a lot of lessons and we have a lot more resources.[29]

The Livermore project also illustrates an interesting dynamic that further underscores the ongoing political significance of Freedom Summer. Osman was not the only Mississippi veteran included in the ranks of the Livermore activists. In part because of Osman, another volunteer had been attracted to work on the project.

In accounting for some current political involvement, several other volunteers ascribed a similar role to friendships established in Mississippi. In Michigan, a volunteer became heavily involved in the state-wide nuclear freeze campaign at the urging of another project veteran she hadn't spoken to in "at least ten years."[30] In California, Annie Popkin was inspired to organize "Unlearning Racism" workshops after participating in one conducted by another Mississippi veteran, Ricky Sherover-Marcuse.[31] All told, nearly half (44 percent) of all the volunteers returning questionnaires report that they remain in contact with at least one other project participant.[32] Apparently, then, we can still speak, in a limited sense, of a Freedom Summer community and its role in encouraging activism.

The examples cited above also attest to the variety of vehicles that have absorbed the political energies of the volunteers. They hardly exhaust those vehicles, however. Another volunteer, David Chadwick, founded Defuser, an organization "dedicated to rock and roll and the elimination of nuclear weapons." Besides music—Defuser has thus far released one album—the group's principal weapon has been a kind of gallows humor intended to outrage as it mobilizes. To dramatize the imminent dangers of nuclear destruction, Defuser has disseminated information on an organization, the World Suicide Club, that is every bit as outrageous as it is fictitious. Described as "the largest and most effective organization on earth working toward global thermonuclear war," the World Suicide Club engages in a wide variety of activities ranging from conventional lobbying for nuclear weapons in space—"the ultimate in light shows"—to rating relevant movies—"War Games" was awarded Four Mushroom Clouds.[33] Add gallows humor to the list of weapons employed by the volunteers.

Other volunteers are engaged in more conventional political activities. One, Barney Frank, is currently serving as a Democratic Congressman from Massachusetts. Corinne Freeman Barnwell has been employed since 1980 as the Human Rights Coordinator for the City of New Orleans. Heather Tobis Booth is serving as the national co-director of Citizen Action, a progressive national political organization with 1.5 million members active in twenty states. She reports that in 1984 the organization raised more than 30 million dollars to tackle a variety of problems. "If you want a term for our movement," she said, "it would be 'democratic populism.' We're involved in a wide range of issues—crime control, campaigns against toxic waste and high utility rates and for health protection for senior citizens" (quoted in the *Chicago Tribune*, February 14, 1985).

Continuing a trend that began in the mid-Seventies, other volunteers have eschewed national issues for local politics. Andy Schiffrin, who has been active in a progressive coalition in Santa Cruz, California, explains his preference for local movements this way:

> I feel so powerless about affecting . . . [national issues] in the kind
> of world that I live in and I feel in the local . . . issues I'm able to
> have effects. . . . I grew up losing . . . or the victories were mini-
> mal. . . . I got to feel very powerless . . . one of the things that's
> really good about Santa Cruz is that we've been able to win on a lot
> of important issues. . . . We are successful. We may not be for
> long, but we have been and we are now and . . . that's very nur-
> turing in a political sense.[34]

But the political legacy of the project veterans is not simply a litany of political victories. For every volunteer who continues to fight the good fight, another has left the activist fold. Half of all the volunteers are uninvolved in social movements. Thirty percent belong to no political organizations. Those who have grown more pessimistic about the prospects for social change outnumber optimists nearly two to one.[35] The interesting question, of course, is how to account for these very different patterns of contemporary activism. Why have some of the volunteers remained so involved while others have abandoned their earlier activism? By using the same statistical technique employed in Appendix F, we can begin to answer this question. Appendix G reports the results of a similar analysis intended to assess the strength of the relationship between the applicant's current level of activism—as measured by several items on the follow-up questionnaire—and seventeen possible explanatory factors.[36]

The results of this analysis mirror those reported earlier in the book. Much like the volunteers on the eve of Freedom Summer or those applicants who were most involved in the late Sixties, those who remain active today can be distinguished from the less active by virtue of their stronger ties to an activist subculture. The best predictors of contemporary activism among the applicants are the number of political organizations they belong to and their level of activism during the Sixties. The first of these variables may be the more important of the two. The variable can be seen as a proxy for the level of social support the applicants continue to receive for their activism. To the extent that one remains embedded in a political community, as represented by the applicants' ties to formal political organizations, they are likely to feel some pressure to be active and also to feel more optimistic about the effectiveness of their activism. Psychologically, at least, there *is* strength in numbers.

By contrast, those who are currently isolated from either organizational or individual sources of support for activism express a great deal of pessimism about the utility of social action. Much of this ·pessimism seems to have developed in the last five years. One admitted "giving up when Reagan was elected. You can only beat your head against the wall so much."[37] Another recalled "calling a meeting to protest . . . [a school closing]—this is a year ago now—and being the only one who showed up." So disheartened was the volunteer by the experience that she has since "withdrawn from politics completely."[38] Finally, a third volunteer confessed to feeling "guilty about not being more active, but to be involved you've got to feel your actions . . . are likely to make a difference . . . or be effective in some way. . . . In this country at this time [1985] I just don't have that feeling."[39]

The above quotes indicate that these are not the self-centered, opportunistic, political drop-outs that the popular press is so fond of portraying. These are not individuals who remained active only as long as it was stylish to do so and now embrace Yuppiedom with the same enthusiasm they once reserved for the movement. Instead, theirs is a reluctant withdrawal tinged with guilt and sadness at the loss of political purpose and personal connection their lives once had. Later in his interview, the volunteer quoted above added that his lack of political involvements "saddens me a lot, not just 'cause I feel I should be out there doing something, but because I feel like I've lost touch with the best part of myself."[40] Another volunteer expressed the same feelings even more poignantly when asked to describe his current political life.

> I was afraid you were going to ask that. I don't know, I feel that in a way I'm more profoundly disaffected and that my radicalism is so deep I can't find the words for it . . . but . . . I have no political affiliations; I'm not politically active except for the occasional demonstrations . . . and I feel in consequence a . . . great loss, a kind of rootlessness, a lack of real orientation and identity in the world . . . because of the loss of that political anchor . . . I cannot in good conscience any longer make that identification [as an activist] in my own head, and that's profoundly troubling and disorienting . . . if you've lived for so many years bound up in that world . . . and felt that you knew what your life was about.[41]

To the same question, another of the volunteers replied simply that her present political life was "a totally unresolved tragedy!"[42] Having recently severed her affiliation with the Communist Labor Party after twelve years, she felt uprooted and at loose ends personally and politically. Later while discussing her years with the Party, she began to cry. My field notes describe the rest of the interview:

> I turned the tape off. We continued to talk for another 35–45 minutes, with the central topic of discussion being the extreme loneliness and lack of purpose in her life. At various points she compared her present state of affairs to the sense of political purpose and community she felt both in Mississippi and the Communist Labor Party. . . . One thing she said sticks in my mind as especially poignant. She said, "I'm living a lie and I just don't know how to undo it!" Very tough![43]

It is difficult to reconcile these anguished feelings with the popular image of the opportunistic radical-turned-Yuppie. Instead of easily changing with the times, the volunteers have resisted the general drift of political and cultural change over the last fifteen years. Even those who are not presently active seem still to be attuned to a political vision and way of life glimpsed in Mississippi and nurtured in succeeding years. Their principled allegiance to this vision has, as these quotes suggest, cost them dearly in personal as well as political terms.

The Personal Costs of Keeping the Faith

There is a faintly anachronistic sense about the volunteers that is at once admirable and poignant; admirable because of the volunteers' stubborn refusal to abandon political ideals, and poignant because of the isolating effects of this refusal. This isolation is clearly evident in the personal lives of the volunteers.

Going it Alone   One of the most surprising findings to come out of this study concerns the current marital status of the volunteers. Only half of the project veterans are presently married. This compared to 72 percent of the no-shows, and 79 percent of a comparison group of nonactivists who share the same age and educational characteristics as the volunteers.[44] What accounts for this striking difference? The answer to this question would seem, once again, to lie in the volunteers' continuing allegiance to a politicized view of the world.

Marriage is a kind of reciprocal matching process with each spouse selecting the other on the basis of whatever characteristics they deem desirable in a mate. In an era such as our own, those who continue to accord politics a high priority are likely to find themselves dissatisfied with most of the potential mates available to them. At the same time, their continuing preoccupation with politics is likely to make them less attractive to others who might be looking for a partner. Without information on how the volunteers are seen by their age peers, it is impossible to know for sure whether this latter dynamic applies to the volunteers. However, judging from the interviews, it would seem as if the volunteers were not overly thrilled by the singles they were meeting. The reason: they did not fit the *political* criteria the volunteer brought to the mate selection process. When asked what she was looking for in a mate, one volunteer replied that she "still hold[s] out hope for . . . [a political partner]. You know, I tell myself it doesn't matter, 'don't be so critical, or you'll never find anyone,' and then I go out with someone and . . . they don't seem to have a political bone in their body . . . and I'm just not interested."[45] Another said that, "the number one thing is a good comrade; someone who shares my politics and need to be involved."[46] Unfortunately, the number of single people around who share the volunteers' politics would seem to be very limited. "A good comrade," would not appear to be the number one criteria most forty-five-year-old singles are looking for in a mate.

The personal costs of political radicalism have been especially high for the female volunteers. Table 6.2 compares the gender differences in marital status between the volunteers, no-shows, and the comparison group described earlier. Table 6.2 confirms what was noted above. Irrespective of gender, the volunteers are much less likely to be married than are the no-shows. But it is the female volunteers who are especially likely to be single. This difference cannot be accounted for by any marked preference on the part of the female veterans for being single. Of the sixteen female volunteers interviewed, eight were single; and of those eight, only one could *perhaps* be described as preferring life as a single woman. The other seven were clear in stating their preference for a mate.

But if simple preference does not account for this "marital gap," what does? Given the historically strong connection between the lesbian community and the women's liberation movement, it is tempting to attribute some of the disparity to differences in sexual preference. Though this cannot be ruled out conclusively, the questionnaires and interviews produced little evidence to support this proposition. The issue was too personal and potentially sensitive to ask about explicitly on the questionnaire. One question, however, did ask the respondents to report their level of involvement in a variety of movements, including gay rights.

Table 6.2   Marital Status of the Volunteers, No-Shows,
and a Matched Comparison Group,[a] by Gender[b]

	Volunteers		No-Shows		Comparison Group	
	%	No.	%	No.	%	No.
			Females			
Married	42	(21)	64	(30)	74	(1370)
Unmarried	58	(29)	36	(17)	26	(483)
Total	100	(50)	100	(47)	100	(1853)
			Males			
Married	54	(60)	77	(48)	82	(1979)
Unmarried	46	(52)	23	(14)	18	(432)
Total	100	(112)	100	(62)	100	(2411)

[a] The comparison group is composed of all subjects from the Census Bureau's 1984 Current Population Survey Annual Demographic File who share the same age and general educational level as the volunteers.
[b] The marital status of an additional forty-two subjects could not be determined or was unreported on the questionnaires.

Given the central importance of politics in the lives of the volunteers and their demonstrated willingness to organize against their own oppression, it is not unreasonable to assume that most gay volunteers would have been active in the gay rights movement. If this assumption has any merit, we would be justified in concluding that very few of the volunteers are gay. Only twelve of 205 volunteers described themselves as either "very" or "moderately" involved in the gay rights movement. More important for our purposes is the gender breakdown of those who were involved. The final tally shows seven men and only five women.

The interviews conveyed much the same impression as the questionnaires. Faced with several direct questions concerning their present "personal life" and/or "lifestyle preferences," only two of sixteen females and one of the twenty-four male volunteers made mention of romantic or sexual relations with members of the same sex. And of the three who did so, only two—the male and one of the females—defined themselves as gay. The other female saw herself as primarily heterosexual and her same-sex relations as simply an expression of her more general political solidarity with women. Consistent with this view, she described herself as looking to establish a permanent relationship with a man.

Given these findings, it is hard to account for the gap in current marital status between male and female volunteers on the basis of differences in sexual preferences. Instead, gender differences in the current political values and activities of the volunteers would appear to be the answer. The female volunteers have remained more radical in their politics than have their male counterparts. The female volunteers are more likely to report being involved in contemporary social movements.[47] They belong to more political organizations than the male volunteers.[48] Finally, they define themselves as consistently more leftist in political orientation than do the males.[49] If, in fact, leftist politics has the isolating effect ascribed to it earlier, then these findings may account for the marital gap between the male and female volunteers. By virtue of their greater adherence to leftist politics, the female project veterans loom as that much more marginal than the male volunteers.

Underlying the greater contemporary radicalism of the female volunteers and, by implication, the isolation it has fostered, is the women's movement. The movement is implicated in the marginality of the female volunteers in at least two ways. First of all, the vitality of the movement throughout the Seventies allowed the female volunteers to distance themselves from the general swing to the right in American life and politics. This enabled them to remain more leftist in political orientation than the male volunteers who had no comparable movement to insulate them from conservative political influences. Second, the enduring strength of the women's community during the Seventies provided support for alternative conceptions of family life and personal relationships. The female volunteers participated in a number of these arrangements. As we have seen a few of them were involved in relationships with other women. Several others lived in communal houses with from two to six other feminists. Finally, at least three of the volunteers had children by male friends and proceeded to raise them on their own. Virtually all of these lifestyle experiments occurred after 1973, during a period in which the male volunteers were being forced to adjust to a personal life organized outside of the movement. The female volunteers, on the other hand, were able to make the women's movement their family, often obviating the need for other relationships. This arrangement worked as long as the women's community remained alive and well. In recent years, however, that community has been weakened by the defeat of the Equal Rights Amendment, numerous factional quarrels, and its failure to attract younger recruits. Increasingly, it has become less a large and growing family and more an island cut off from the rest of society by a unique combination of gender, generation, and politics. Moreover, it is, in the words of one of the volunteers, an island

> that is shrinking. . . . As the [women's] movement becomes more
> institutionalized and less into the small group thing, you see lots of
> women on the Left getting scared and jumping at the first chance to

marry. . . . [This] probably also explains the whole rediscovery and romanticizing of family by women who only a few years ago were . . . so down on the family. . . . The ranks are thinning to be sure.[50]

To the extent that the female volunteers have continued to identify with the women's community, they have been very affected by this dynamic. They have found themselves feeling more isolated and more alone than at any time in the recent past. Three of the volunteers explicitly acknowledged these feelings and linked them to a strong desire to either start a family or a lasting relationship. One volunteer said simply, "the movement always was my family . . . now that it's disappearing, I feel I need something else to hold on to."[51] Annie Popkin offered a more subtle account of her new-found maternal desires:

> During the women's movement I never really wanted to be a wife. And I never really thought about being a mother. . . . [Now] it's something I might want to do, but I want to do it in the context of a . . . family. . . . I think several things . . . [explain] this change. For one thing, the context of the movement has been very different. . . . It gives people a lot more chance to be internal. I was always at a meeting before. . . . Recently I have wanted to go inward . . . I want to have more of a domestic life, a quieter life, than I ever had before. . . . Maybe I'm just feeling some of that traditional socialization as I approach 40. . . . I don't feel that urgent, but definitely more than I ever did before.[52]

Several other volunteers expressed these same desires but felt they were too old to act on them. For them, sadness at the disintegration of the women's movement has not been offset by the anticipated joys of a more traditional domestic existence. Instead they feel they sacrificed these desires in the service of the movement. Two women in particular expressed strong regret at what they saw as the personal costs of their politics. One of them remarked that she had subordinated her

> personal life to this very public movement existence. I mean, I really didn't have a personal life at all. . . . Then there was the whole anti-male, anti-family thing and that didn't exactly encourage [a personal life]. And, in a way, you didn't really miss it because the movement almost substituted for it. . . . But now I regret the fact that I never married or have [sic] a family. . . . I'm very aware of being alone these days.[53]

My edited field notes from the session with the second woman capture the social isolation and marginality she feels in her life:

Would have liked to have had a baby and family, but knows it's too late for her. Real sense of melancholy about this. *Sees many women of her age and politics in the same boat.* . . . After feeling she had "found a home in the movement," she once again is marginal. "Most of my close friends are either Native Americans or high school dropouts." For a while she lived with and still has a close relationship with a 24-year old high school dropout who she described as "punk." Those, like herself, she describes as "the dispossessed."[54] (Emphasis added)

Even by the standards of the volunteers, these two women represent extreme cases of alienation and social marginality. But it is only the extent and not the fact of their isolation that marks them as unusual. To a greater or lesser extent, many of the volunteers have been "dispossessed" by the political and cultural changes of the last fifteen years. The costs of this dispossession have been economic as well as social.

Settling for Less   One of the principal images associated with the myth of the activist-turned-Yuppie is that of the former radical pursuing fame and fortune in some decidedly mainstream career. With the project veterans, however, one finds far more political continuity than discontinuity in their current work choices. Less than 10 percent of the volunteers hold jobs in the business world. Among the no-shows, the percentage is twice as high. Apparently, the image of the radical-turned-capitalist has more appeal for reporters and editors than for the former activists themselves.

On the other hand, just as many volunteers continue to work as full-time paid activists as hold business jobs (7 percent in each case). Even more—8 percent—are unemployed.[55] Another 2 percent are currently living and working in religious or secular communes. Only 2 percent of all the no-shows fall into these latter two categories combined. In their work profiles, then, the volunteers betray much the same type of political imprint that characterizes their personal lives. Not only are the volunteers four times more likely to be unemployed than the no-shows, but they also make less money per year than those applicants who did *not* go to Mississippi. Better than a quarter of the no-shows but less than 20 percent of the volunteers report incomes exceeding $40,000. At the other end of the scale, 21 percent of the volunteers average less than $10,000 per year as compared to 14 percent of the no-shows. That these differences bear the imprint of the volunteers' politics is suggested by a number of separate findings.

Perhaps the most straightforward of these findings is the significant negative relationship between income and current activism reported in Appendix G. The finding is clear. Those applicants who have remained politically active earn less money on the average than do those who are relatively less active. Part of this disparity may reflect the ongoing effects of the volunteer's later entrance into a career. But some of the difference can probably also be attributed to the clear political, as opposed to monetary, criteria many of the volunteers apply to their jobs. This was certainly the impression conveyed by the interviews. Far more of the volunteers than no-shows took pains to describe the political and social values that underlie the work they do. One noted that "money and status have never been important to me in my work. First off, I have to enjoy what I'm doing. . . . Secondly, it has to have . . . a progressive political element to it."[56] Ken Scudder said that he "simply could not ever again do something that wasn't . . . socially relevant. . . . I work as a paralegal. . . . I am relatively underemployed although this has its advantages. It leaves me a certain amount of time to . . . run marathons and do political work."[57] Annie Popkin admitted that she didn't "make . . . much money, but I'm not afraid of starving. And I still prefer to take a job that [enhances] . . . me or contributes to the world than one that makes more money."[58]

Judging from the jobs actually held by the volunteers, it seems clear that the majority of them agree with Popkin's sentiment. It would otherwise be hard to account for the narrow concentration of volunteers in the relatively few job titles represented in Table 6.3. One can see that the volunteers are disproportionately concentrated in the so-called "helping professions," principally education, social service, and the law. While also overrepresented in these fields, the no-shows display a somewhat broader occupational profile than the volunteers. The job distribution for those in the comparison group is broader still.

Besides being narrowly concentrated in the helping professions, the jobs taken by the volunteers share something else in common. They are not as high paying as the occupations held by the no-shows. Even in the case of the legal profession, one finds the volunteers disproportionately concentrated in the lowest-paid positions within the field. So the volunteers are more likely to be working as public defenders or in the fields of poverty or consumer law rather than serving as legal counsel for private corporations. This politically motivated job selectivity helps explain the significantly lower incomes of the volunteers. Add to that their relatively late entrance into the job market and generally episodic work histories, and the income gap between the volunteers and no-shows becomes entirely understandable.

A bit more puzzling is the greater income disparity between the male volunteers and no-shows as opposed to the females in these groups. While the female volunteers bear more of the marital costs of participa-

Table 6.3   Percentage of Volunteers, No-Shows, and Comparison
Group[a] in Selected Occupational Groups

	Volunteers		No-Shows		Comparison Group	
	%	No.	%	No.	%	No.
Selected professional occupations						
College professors	17	(34)	18	(18)	3	(108)
Lawyers or judges	8	(16)	12	(12)	2	(83)
Teachers (except college)	7	(15)	5	(5)	11	(465)
Health practitioners	3	(6)	0	(0)	0	(4)
Social workers	2	(5)	4	(4)	1	(40)
Clergy	2	(4)	2	(2)	1	(29)
Physicians and dentists	2	(4)	1	(1)	2	(91)
Nurses	1	(3)	2	(2)	2	(64)
Psychologists	1	(2)	4	(4)	0	(13)
Engineers	0	(0)	0	(0)	3	(115)
Accountants	0	(0)	0	(0)	2	(78)
Writers, artists, entertainers, athletes	11	(22)	7	(7)	2	(106)
Executive, managerial, administrative occupations	15	(30)	21	(21)	17	(723)
Other professionals (including technicians)	10	(21)	5	(5)	7	(316)
Sales occupations	2	(4)	3	(3)	9	(395)
Administrative, support occupations, including clerical	1	(2)	4	(4)	7	(283)
Service occupations	1	(3)	0	(0)	5	(229)
Farming, forestry, fishing occupations	0	(0)	1	(1)	2	(90)
Precision production, craft, and repair occupations	1	(3)	3	(3)	4	(178)
Operators, applicators, and laborers	1	(3)	1	(1)	8	(320)
Unemployed or not employed	12	(25)	8	(8)	13	(534)
	97	(202)	101	(101)	101	(4264)

[a] The comparison group is composed of all subjects from the Census Bureau's 1984 Current Population Survey Annual Demographic File who share the same age and general educational level as the volunteers.

Table 6.4 Annual Income for the Volunteers, No-Shows,
and a Matched Comparison Group,ᵃ by Gender

	Volunteers		No-Shows		Comparison Group	
	%	No.	%	No.	%	No.
Females						
40,000+	8	(5)	8	(4)	4	(68)
30,000–39,999	15	(10)	12	(6)	5	(90)
20,000–29,999	24	(16)	27	(13)	18	(331)
10,000–19,999	23	(15)	27	(13)	24	(448)
5,000–9,999	11	(7)	6	(3)	15	(282)
0–4,999	20	(13)	19	(9)	34	(634)
Total	101	(66)	99	(48)	100	(1853)
Males						
40,000+	25	(34)	40	(24)	30	(720)
30,000–39,999	16	(22)	17	(10)	19	(454)
20,000–29,999	28	(38)	23	(14)	22	(532)
10,000–19,999	13	(18)	13	(8)	17	(409)
5,000–9,999	7	(9)	5	(3)	7	(161)
0–4,999	10	(14)	2	(1)	6	(135)
Total	99	(135)	100	(60)	101	(2411)

ᵃ The comparison group is composed of all subjects from the Census Bureau's 1984 Current Population Survey Annual Demographic File who share the same age and general educational level as the volunteers.

tion, it is the male project veterans who suffer disproportionately the income gap between volunteers and no-shows. In fact, as Table 6.4 shows, the difference in income for females in these two groups is negligible. Moreover, both the female volunteers and no-shows have much higher annual incomes than a matched sample of women drawn from the Census Bureau's Current Population Survey for 1984. By contrast, the income distribution for the male volunteers is significantly lower than that for the no-shows or the males in the matched sample.[59]

The explanation for this difference is not entirely clear. One possibility is that the Summer Project was more subversive of traditional male career plans than it was those of the female volunteers. That is, to the extent that the project increased the importance of "working with people" and "serving others" as job criteria, it probably served to differentiate the male volunteers from the male no-shows far more than it did the women who went to Mississippi from those who did not. Women, to the extent they were encouraged to pursue careers at all, were geared in this era to take jobs in the helping professions. Men were not. It may be, then, that the project served to change the career plans of the male volunteers while merely reinforcing those of the female participants. If this interpretation is correct, the male volunteers would have gravitated toward lower paying careers in teaching, social service, and the like, while a larger percentage of the no-shows would have gone on to land higher paying jobs in such traditionally male-dominated fields as business and administration.

Whatever the explanation for the difference, it is clear that the male volunteers have paid a price for their participation in the project. So too, in a personal sense, have the female volunteers.[60] It is hard to reconcile these costs with the popular image of "the Sixties radicals today." Instead, one is struck by the degree to which the volunteers have remained true to the vision of life and politics glimpsed in Mississippi. The personal and career costs they have been willing to bear attest to their faithfulness to this vision. So, too, do their present lives and the many poignant and inspiring ways in which they continue to pursue the essential elements of the Freedom Summer experience.

Freedom High: The Search Continues

The power of the Freedom Summer experience owed to a number of elements. There was, first of all, the strong sense of mission and moral purpose that "fighting the good fight" afforded the volunteers. There was also the overwhelming feeling of ecstasy that came from their stepping out of traditional roles and the lives they had led prior to Freedom Summer. Finally, underlying it all, was the intoxicating sense of connection and acceptance that followed from membership in the "beloved community." Above all else, it is the ongoing importance of these elements that distinguishes the volunteers from the no-shows. This is not to say that the no-shows don't also want to experience ecstasy, moral purpose, and community in their lives. But having never experienced these feelings as intensely as the volunteers did, they do not seem as focused on their attainment. It is not hard, on the other hand, to see the ongoing pursuit of these feelings and experiences as deeply etched into the current lives of the volunteers. Perhaps the best way to capture this emphasis is through a series of profiles of the volunteers today.

Stuart Rawlings[61]   Stuart was a sophomore at Stanford when he went South for Freedom Summer. He stayed the entire summer, clearly counting the experience as one of the most important of his life. As he put it:

Whenever I think about Mississippi, I feel so lucky that I was able to . . . do that . . . it worked out perfectly for me and [it was] a wonderful . . . experience and I feel like I accomplished something very important. It's all just fond memories, but I have a lot of fond memories . . . I just moved from one Mississippi to another and, unlike a lot of the volunteers, I kept seeking out similar experiences.

Among the other experiences Rawlings had in the years following Freedom Summer were a six-month trip to Brazil, an extended visit to an Israeli kibbutz, and a tour of duty in Vietnam, courtesy of International Voluntary Services. In all of these cases, Freedom Summer served as both an impetus to action and as a standard for evaluating the experience. Commenting on his time in Vietnam, Rawlings said:

It was a lot like Mississippi . . . it wasn't quite [as intense] for the whole time because . . . we sort of settled down into a peaceful lifestyle for part of that period but a lot of it was . . . [just as intense]. The similarities were that Vietnam, like Mississippi, was top billing on Cronkite every night and, . . . like Mississippi, you didn't know whether you were going to live through the night or not.

Nor did Rawlings abandon this adventurous, episodic lifestyle once the Sixties were over. Instead, he has continued to treat life as a series of experiential episodes right up to the present. Two of his more recent adventures include an eighteen-month exploration of Africa and a two-month journey through Nicaragua, Honduras, and El Salvador. When I interviewed Stuart, he was living in Palo Alto, California, and working at the Sleep Disorders Center at Stanford. His thoughts, however, were very much on his next adventure, "the ultimate Mississippi," as he called it. His plan is to spend one to two years traveling to seven different countries in the world in search of orphans to adopt. The end result would be an international family of underprivileged children. Rawlings' description of his plan manages to evoke both the idealism that is still so characteristic of the volunteers as well as the hunger for a cause and a community one senses in talking with so many of the Mississippi veterans:

My love of kids [is] a very strong factor in my life and there's nothing that I would love more . . . than to have the richness of coming home to a Somali girl and . . . an Afghani boy, maybe a Cambodian boy or a Bolivian girl. . . . I'd pull all of my life together in this thing . . . I know that this would bring out love in me . . . and I would grow tremendously feeling part of these cultures on a daily basis.

Rawlings' description recalls the essence of Freedom Summer as expressed by another volunteer in a remark quoted earlier. That volunteer noted that while in Mississippi, he felt "utterly selfless and yet found" himself at the same time.[62] It is this desire for personal fulfillment and connection through service to others that comes through so clearly in Rawlings' remarks. Can one envision a more dramatic evocation of the "beloved community" than Rawlings' dream of an international family of orphans? Yet he is hardly the only volunteer to give voice to these desires.

Chude Pamela (Parker) Allen[63]   Like Rawlings, Chude had just finished her junior year in college when she went to Mississippi. The experience, in combination with her year as a visiting student at Spelman College in Atlanta, changed her life. Both in Mississippi and Atlanta, Chude embraced the vision of the "beloved community" as intensely as any volunteer I spoke with. Through that community, she found love, acceptance, and a purpose in life that was as personally liberating as it was politically satisfying. The experience was not without cost, however.

Chude returned North, clearly alienated from white society. In 1965 she virtually insured her marginality by marrying the black activist, Robert Allen. They remained together until 1977. Together they weathered the volatile social and political crosscurrents of the late Sixties and early Seventies, but in a way that denied her the sense of belonging and community she had felt in Mississippi. Her involvement in the antiwar movement was centered around a group of black draft resisters that included her husband. Both her race and sex necessarily limited her role and the degree to which she was accepted by the group. Nor did the women's movement provide a wholly comfortable "home" for Chude. Though a pioneering activist in the movement, her marriage and strong identification with the black community tended to isolate her from other white feminists. Chude describes this process:

> [T]here was a way in which the women's movement was supposed to be about . . . sharing our pain and opening up, but . . . I was with white women and I was married to a black man and there were some things I wouldn't share . . . some struggles and some . . . aspects of myself that I would not open up because I was in a room full of white faces.

While certainly understandable, Chude's protective instincts prevented her from giving herself emotionally to the women's movement the way other feminists did and the way she had been able to in Mississippi. "What I lost," she said, "was my ability to stand there and just absolutely share my heart and soul . . . share your heart and your guts and your soul and . . . to be willing to go to the . . . most raw part of how you experience life, which is where you're most alive." Along with the sense of community she felt in Mississippi, it is this quality of the Freedom Summer experience that remains so powerful and so attractive to Chude today. Indeed, when I interviewed her, she had recently left a spiritual community, which she had joined in hopes of reclaiming these aspects of her Freedom Summer experience. Though not without problems, she felt the experience had accomplished what she had hoped it would. It allowed her much the same intensity of experience and absorption into a close-knit community that she had experienced in Mississippi. The end result was a "freeing [up] of a kind of spontaneity" and a reconnection with a self she clearly associates with Freedom Summer.

Neil McCarthy[64]　　Neil graduated from college the week before he left for the orientation session in Oxford, Ohio. His plan was to work in Mississippi for four weeks and then join his family for a vacation on Lake Michigan. He never made it. In fact, he stayed in Mississippi until December of 1964. He describes his time in Mississippi as "the most frightening and rewarding thing I've done in my life . . . the richest part . . . [of the experience] was the bond you felt with everyone on the project. We really were a family."

By his own admission, Freedom Summer set in motion a lifelong search for political community. After a two-year hitch in the Peace Corps "to refine my organizing skills," McCarthy returned to the States and threw himself into the antiwar movement. In doing so, though, he avoided "mass organizations such as SDS in favor of smaller, more democratic groups." His longest stint was with a Resistance chapter in Madison, Wisconsin, which he described as "feeling as much like the Greenwood [Mississippi] project as anything I've experienced since." Not that he gave up looking.

In 1972 Neil entered graduate school in history. Over the next eight years, he was involved in literally dozens of organizing efforts, both on and off campus. The common thread in all these efforts was participatory democracy. Said McCarthy:

> You've got to build community above all else. If you give people a taste of it, there's nothing you can't do. It's that rich and, I should add, that rare an experience in our society. I never had it till I went South and I . . . *haven't been able to live without it since.*
> (Emphasis added)

It is tempting to see the importance he continues to attach to community as growing out of the nomadic life he has led as a visting professor over the last six years. Forced by an extremely depressed job market to take a string of one-year appointments, McCarthy hasn't lived anywhere for more than a year since graduate school. This makes him personally—he was divorced in 1977—as well as professionally marginal. But it has not kept him from seeking out or building political community wherever he has gone. In fact, his personal isolation has only intensified his need to do so. The by now familiar refrain of self through collective action can once again be heard in McCarthy's account of his gypsy life-style.

> The first thing I do when I get into a new town is find out what's going on [politically] . . . try to connect with the local movement people . . . if nothing much is happening, I'll try to get something going . . . [I'll] run off a leaflet and put a couple hundred out; try to get a vigil or a meeting going . . . partly just to meet people. . . . If I had a family I probably wouldn't have that much time and energy. *But really the Movement always has been my family.* (Emphasis added)

Neil, Chude, and Stuart are only three of the forty volunteers I interviewed for this project. I would never pretend they were typical of those forty, let alone the approximately 250 Mississippi veterans with whom I have had contact. But they do highlight, in rather stark terms, two qualities that, in varying degrees, set the volunteers apart from the no-shows and the rest of their age peers. First, to a remarkable extent, they have remained faithful to the political vision that drew them to Mississippi nearly a quarter century ago. Second, they have paid for this lifelong commitment with a degree of alienation and social isolation that has only increased with time. The political and cultural wave that once carried them forward so prominently continues to recede, putting more and more distance between them and mainstream society with each passing day. In a sense, the volunteers are anachronisms. They have remained idealists in a cynical age. They continue to tout community in a society seemingly antagonistic to the idea. They are, for the most part, unrepentant leftists in an era dominated by the right. If, however, these qualities make the volunteers anachronistic, it is more a comment on contemporary America than on the volunteers themselves. In their view, it is they who have kept the faith while America has lost it. If this study is any indication, we can count on the volunteers being around for a long time reminding us of that fact. As Mario Savio put it not long ago, "we've lost very few sheep from this fold. The rest of us are bleating just as before. And I think we'll go on for the rest of our lives."[65]

Let It Shine

I began this book by stressing the importance of the intersection of history and biography in the telling of the Freedom Summer story. As that story draws to a close, it is only appropriate that I return to that theme.

The more I talked with the Mississippi veterans, the more I came to see the Summer Project as a kind of prism, refracting not only the biographies of its white and black participants, but American history as well. All who took part in the project did so based on understandings and motivations that were rooted in their earlier biographies. The SNCC veterans were drawn from the generation of blacks who had grown up amid the rising optimism of the Fifties and early Sixties. They were old enough to remember the joy that greeted the 1954 Supreme Court school desegregation decision. They had been inspired by the courage and charisma of Martin Luther King, Jr., and the success of the Montgomery Bus Boycott. But most important, they had shared in the excitement and exhilaration of the sit-in movement as it swept through the South. It was those sit-ins and the sense of momentum and optimism they inspired that brought the SNCC veterans to Mississippi in 1961. There they encountered savage brutality, frustration, failure. Yet the nightmare of Mississippi had not been able to fully extinguish the idealism and optimism the veterans had brought to the state. In its basic conception, the Summer Project was a testament to the enduring faith and optimism of those who had conceived it. The hopes of the planners rested on little more than the effectiveness of moral suasion and the power of the beloved community.

For their part, the white volunteers were just as optimistic and idealistic as the SNCC veterans. Mississippi had not yet tempered the privilege and sense of potency most had known since birth. Their biographies had prepared them well for the ascendant liberalism and shining promise of the early Sixties. They responded to the challenge of existential theology and Kennedy's call to public service. For them, going to Mississippi reflected the same motives that would later prompt many of them to enter the Peace Corps. For the most part, theirs was an idealism not yet tainted by cynicism or revolutionary rhetoric.

In true before-and-after fashion, both the SNCC veterans and the white volunteers were changed by their experiences in Mississippi. For the SNCC veterans, the changes were not rooted exclusively in Freedom Summer. Rather, the project marked the end of a long process of radicalization that had begun with Bob Moses' entrance into the state three years earlier. In this sense, Freedom Summer and the MFDP challenge was, for many of the SNCC veterans, simply the last of many straws. But it was one that was to have important and enduring consequences for the organization. The lack of tangible results from the campaign, coupled with the defeat of the MFDP convention challenge, precipitated a crisis within SNCC from which the organization never really recovered. In the wake of this crisis, consensus regarding the very premises upon which SNCC had been founded collapsed. Among the casualties of this process was the image of the beloved community; of black and white working together for a just and interracial society. The hostility toward whites in SNCC increased noticeably, as did the calls for whites to leave the movement.

These calls deprived the white volunteers of a home in the black movement, at precisely the moment when many were prepared to commit to it. For their part, the volunteers emerged from Mississippi profoundly radicalized in both personal and political terms. Given the intensity of their experiences in Mississippi as well as the education they had received at the hands of the SNCC staff, their political radicalization was hardly surprising. It was the personal lessons learned in Mississippi that were somewhat unexpected and were to prove especially significant in shaping the character of the "Sixties experience." What the volunteers had discovered in Mississippi was nothing less than the political significance of the personal. Encoded in this discovery was an ideology and rhetoric of personal liberation that, when fused with the earlier emphasis on political change, were to give the Sixties their distinctive cast. Over time, changing oneself came to be seen as synonymous with changing society. This dual emphasis ushered in an era in which sexual experimentation, drug usage, and attempts to build alternative forms of community were seen as every bit as much a part of the movement as conventional political protest.

What makes Freedom Summer so significant in this regard is that it seems to have marked a crucial stage in the process by which these two emphases were fused. Never before had so many put the ideology of personal politics into practice for such an extended period of time. In addition, the project represented an important early exposure to the type of tight-knit, politically based community that would figure so prominently in the ideology and practice of the New Left. It is hard not to see the imprint of the Freedom Summer project on any number of other New Left "experiments," ranging from the SDS-organized Economic Research and Action Projects (ERAP), to the CR groups of the women's movement, to the countless politically based communal houses that sprang up throughout the country.

The significance of the Summer Project does not derive simply from its role in shaping some of the basic elements of New Left culture. Without some means of disseminating those elements, the project would likely have had little impact outside of the South. The volunteers provided one such means. Along with the early SDS, Friends of SNCC groups, and the Northern Student Movement, the volunteers brought the lessons of the Southern civil rights movement to the North. Through these groups, the ideological and material elements of the movement were passed, baton-style, to the population—white college students—that would dominate the New Left for the remainder of the era. Thus, not only did the Summer Project give early expression to elements central to the emerging counterculture, but it also provided a crucial means by which those elements could be diffused to a much larger population. For these reasons, a case can be made for Freedom Summer as among the seminal events in the coalescence of the "Sixties experience."

The historical significance of the Mississippi volunteers may not, however, have ended with the close of the Sixties. They may yet play a role in the resurgence of leftist activism in this country. This prediction rests on speculation, but speculation that is based on ample historical precedent. It is only in popular parlance that social movements "die" or political eras "come to a close." The finality of these phrases is rarely borne out in reality. Movements do not so much die as survive on a much smaller scale. More often than not, it is the media's interest in the movement that lapses, creating the impression that the movement has died. But rarely is this the case. Instead, movements retrench, scale down, and adapt to changing political climates. We think of the Prohibition Movement as having died long ago, but, in fact, the Women's Christian Temperance Union survives to this day. So too does the Ku Klux Klan, though we tend to associate it more with an older, more virulently racist South than with the New South of the 1980s. At the height of McCarthyism, the American Left survived in lonely Greenwich Village cell meetings, isolated pacifist groups, and the haunted (and hunted) specter of the American Communist Party.

In similar fashion, the New Left lives on in contemporary America in the lives and political involvements of people like the Freedom Summer veterans. They are the keepers of the leftist flame, nurturing the ideological and organizational remnants of what was once a proud and thriving movement. Theirs is not simply a nostalgic holding action, however. To survive, movements must be able to maintain themselves during otherwise hostile eras. The left has always been able to do this, surviving the collapse of Populism in the 1890s, the Red Scare following World War I, and the political witch-hunts of the early Fifties. It will withstand the Reagan revolution and the rise of the Moral Majority as well. It will do so because the likes of the Freedom Summer veterans will have constructed ideological and organizational bridges linking the New (by then Old) Left to the next major upsurge in leftist activism.

The volunteers and others of their ilk will not lead the new movement any more than the survivors of the Old Left led the rise of the New Left. Then, as now, popular consciousness in America had been purged of any real awareness of its recent leftist past. So Sixties youth knew too little about their leftist elders to grant them much credibility and status other than as nostalgic curiosities. In truth, the New Left drew heavily on the sources of ideological and organizational continuity provided by these "curiosities." SDS developed within the supportive, if ultimately constraining, context of the League for Industrial Democracy. SNCC benefited from the resources and ideological direction afforded by two organizations—the Highlander Folk School and the Southern Conference Educational Fund—with roots in the Old Left. Specific individuals whose activism dated to the Thirties also played key roles in ushering in the New Left. It would be hard to overstate the contributions of such Old Leftists as Ella Baker, Glenn Smiley, Bayard Rustin, Anne and Carl Braden, Michael Harrington, and others in the resurgence of the Left during the Sixties.

It is very likely that some of the Freedom Summer veterans will play a similar role in the next upsurge of leftist activism in this country. As demoralized and isolated as they are at present, any significant swing of the political pendulum could well elevate the volunteers and the organizations they steward to positions of prominence in a resurgent left. Who is to say that Heather Tobis Booth's Midwest Academy won't play the same role in the 1990s that the Highlander Folk School did in the Fifties and Sixties? How do we know that out of Ricky Sherover-Marcuse's Unlearning Racism workshops there won't come the individuals who will catalyze a new wave of leftist organizing in the Bay Area? We don't. From just as humble beginnings did the New Left arise. In all likelihood, the origins of the next major movement of the left will be just as modest and draw just as heavily on the ideological and organizational legacy of the recent past.

Certainly this prediction accords well with the central empirical theme of this study. Activism depends on more than just idealism. It is not enough that people be attitudinally inclined toward activism. There must also exist formal organizations or informal social networks that structure and sustain collective action. The volunteers were not appreciably more committed to Freedom Summer than the no-shows. Their closer ties to the project, however, left them in a better position to act on their commitment. Those volunteers who remain active today are distinguished from those who are not by virtue of their stronger organizational affiliations and continued ties to other activists. Attitudes dispose people to action; social structures enable them to act on these dispositions. Thus by sustaining political organizations and maintaining links to others, the volunteers are preserving the social contexts out of which movements have typically emerged. As a result, they may yet enjoy another turn on the historical stage. Nearly two decades ago, Michael Harrington (1972) speculated that the Sixties radicals might have an even greater impact on the Eighties than the Sixties. Harrington's prediction may yet prove prophetic.

So much for the history side of the history-biography equation. But what of the lives of the history-makers? Is it possible now to characterize the biographical impact of the project on the volunteers? I think so. The volunteers were among the very first to recognize and climb aboard the Sixties wave. Indeed, it was their climbing aboard that gave the wave much of its initial shape and momentum. As long as that wave washed forward, the volunteers enjoyed a high that few of us will ever know. Biography and history meshed in a way that only those on the cutting edge of social and political change can ever appreciate. It is clear from their accounts that it was an exhilarating experience, affording them an intoxicating sense of purpose, potency, and personal promise.

But the wave receded and continues, as of 1988, in recession. It is not simply the ongoing political dominance of conservatives that marks this recession, but the general societal backlash against most of the major elements of the Sixties counterculture. Although studies indicate that most forms of illegal drug use have actually declined since the early Seventies, the hue and cry over the problem is more strident and moralistic than ever before. Congressional wives have spearheaded efforts to clean up rock music lyrics. There are even those who privately welcome the recent AIDS epidemic as a regrettable, but just, antidote to the excesses of a sexual revolution rooted in the Sixties. In so many ways, it is very much an era of reaction.

How have the volunteers fared in the face of the backlash? The popular view would have us believe that the Sixties radicals have accommodated, perhaps even embraced, the Eighties lifestyle. For those who climbed aboard the Sixties wave late or whose commitment to it was not particularly strong, there may be some truth to this view. However, when applied to the volunteers, the popular account is demonstrably false. Anyone whose commitment to the movement was as thoroughgoing as was many of the volunteers' does not easily forsake the political vision and sense of self on which such a commitment was based. As attractive as the image of the radical-turned-Yuppie may be as a legitimation for today's politics, it is not borne out in the contemporary lives of the volunteers. To an extraordinary extent, the Mississippi veterans still bear quiet allegiance to the politics they espoused twenty-five years ago. If measured only in conventional terms, this allegiance has cost the volunteers dearly. To hold firm in the face of a political and cultural pendulum swing, the likes of which we've experienced in this country over the past two decades, is to learn a great deal about alienation and political marginality. One volunteer compared his plight to that of a beleaguered leftist at the height of the McCarthy era.[1] The analogy is certainly apt. In that case too, individuals paid dearly for the consistency of their political convictions. Political values and personal identities, once honored as the wave of the future, came to be stigmatized. Once synchronized, history and biography diverged with occasionally tragic consequences.

The red-baiting and witch-hunts of the McCarthy era cost many their careers, their families, and, on occasion, their lives. The volunteers have known their share of tragedy as well. There is the sad case of Dennis Sweeney, once one of the most honored of the volunteers. After years of searching for the proper follow-up to Freedom Summer, Sweeney dropped from sight sometime in the early Seventies. Those who saw him over the next few years told bizarre stories of Sweeney's preoccupation with an alleged CIA plot to drive him crazy by means of electrodes implanted in his body. Sweeney came to see his former mentor and onetime Freedom Summer strategist, Allard Lowenstein, as central to the plot. The grisly denouement to the story came on March 14, 1980 when Sweeney met Lowenstein at the latter's New York City law office and emptied a handgun into him. Lowenstein died a short while later.

Another volunteer, Stephen Bingham, spent thirteen years living underground as a political fugitive. He had gone underground on August

21, 1971, just hours after the charismatic black activist, George Jackson, and five others—three guards and two white trustees—had been killed in an alleged uprising at Soledad Prison in California. Bingham, a radical lawyer working in the prison movement, had visited Jackson that day and was wanted for questioning in the case. He was suspected of having smuggled in the gun that Jackson used to kill the others. Though professing innocence, that night Bingham left the home he shared with several other lawyers and promptly dropped out of sight. He did not resurface until July 9, 1984, when he faced a crowd of reporters in Glide Memorial Church in San Francisco to announce his return and intention to fight the charges outstanding against him. He has since been acquitted of any criminal role in the Soledad shoot-out; but only at the cost of thirteen years of his life, the interruption of his career, and a "permanent homesickness for my family and friends which you can never imagine."[2]

During the course of my research, I learned of at least one other volunteer who had killed himself for what others described as political reasons. Besides Sweeney, three other volunteers are presently confined to mental institutions. These dramatic instances are over and above the numerous cases of divorce or job loss that are attributable to the political commitments of the Mississippi veterans.

Still, for the volunteers, the biographical legacy of the project has not been entirely negative. The political pendulum has indeed swung far from its position during Freedom Summer. For the volunteers, the exhilarating fit between biography and history is only a memory. But memories are not without their own reward. There is a pride and a strength to the volunteers that owes a great deal to their memories of that summer nearly a quarter century ago. The simple fact is that they were tried and not found wanting. That is more of an affirmation of self than most of the rest of us will ever know. That knowledge has been a source of strength for the volunteers for a long time. They continue to draw upon it today.

> [T]he thing I remember most is . . . the courage of the Mississippi citizens that we were working with. . . . They were a great source of inspiration for me then and they are still a great source of inspiration to me now. I mean, when I get into a really bad situation or . . [when] I'm real worried about my internal fortitude, I . . . dip back into that time and . . . my knowledge of what I saw those people doing.[3]

> The memories of that summer are very important to me because they . . . redeem me personally. . . . [They serve] as a reminder to me

that there are qualities in me that are worth . . . something and that people are capable of quite remarkable things. It's the single most enduring . . . moment of my life. I believe in it beyond anything.[4]

I know that I exaggerate the importance of that summer . . . and especially my role in it. But those memories have served me well. The . . . purest moment of my life was in that little church in Hattiesburg, sweating like a pig and crying like a baby, singing, "This Little Light of Mine." Do you know the words? One part goes:

> The light that shines is the light of love,
> lights the darkness from above.
> It shines on me and it shines on you,
> shows what the power of love can do.
> This little light of mine, I'm gonna let it shine,
> Let it shine, let it shine, let it shine.

[Beginning to cry] Somehow the fact that I once had that experience is very important to me. . . . It's like that little light still shines in my life a bit.[5]

Let it shine, let it shine, let it shine.

Appendix A

Questionnaires Sent to Freedom Summer Volunteers and Applicants

THE UNIVERSITY OF ARIZONA
TUCSON, ARIZONA 85721

COLLEGE OF ARTS AND SCIENCES
FACULTY OF SOCIAL AND BEHAVIORAL SCIENCES
DEPARTMENT OF SOCIOLOGY

Dear Mississippi Freedom Summer Applicant:

I am a sociologist contacting you through your alumni office to ask your help in completing a major national study of activism in the United States in the 1960's. The study seeks to establish the extent of such activism as well as its causes and consequences. My interest in social movements stems from both research and personal involvement in a number of movements past and present. My experiences have led me to conclude that, as important a political and social phenomenon as 60's activism was, it remains only poorly understood by scholars and the general public alike.

At this point you may be wondering how your name was obtained in connection with this research. Simple. In a search of the Martin Luther King, Jr. Center Archives in Atlanta your name turned up on a list of Freedom Summer applicants who subsequently withdrew from the project. This double status marks you as someone whose answers to the attached questions are especially crucial to the success of this study.

The questionaire is neither long nor painful to complete. In fact, other applicants who have filled it out report the 15-25 minute experience to be a rather engaging exercise in personal recollection. I would like to be able to say that grave psychic consequences await those who fail to complete the questionaire. But, of course, that is not the case. I can only hope that you will take a few minutes and contribute to a study that promises to be politically as well as sociologically significant. Thank you very much.

Sincerely,

Doug McAdam

Doug McAdam

> Born: 1952, Pasadena, CA. Schools:
> B.A. Occidental, 1973; M.A. and Ph.D.,
> SUNY Stony Brook, 1979. Publications:
> Political Process and the Development
> of Black Insurgency, 1982. With James
> Rule, et. al., The Politics of Privacy,
> 1980. "The Decline of the Black Move-
> ment," in Jo Freeman (ed.) Social Move-
> ments of the 60's and 70's, 1982.

ENDORSEMENT

After looking over your previous published work (Politcal Process and the Development of Black Insurgency) I feel good about endorsing your planned survey of former Mississippi Freedom Summer applicants. I am confident that this will not be another of those traditional academic surveys which are unrelated to the real world and social action. You are clearly a committed and serious person whose work is intended to help in the promotion of social change, and I am happy to see that you give assurance you will not publish individual names without permission and will refuse to give information you collect to government authorities. I would therefore encourage people to cooperate with your project and I look forward to seeing the results of your work.

Sincerely,

Howard Zinn

Howard Zinn
Professor of Political Science
Boston University

INSTRUCTIONS

I would be grateful in you would take the 15-25 minutes necessary to complete this questionaire. I know it is difficult to fit complex life experiences into questionaire categories, but I have tried to design questions that are easy to answer yet capture essential aspects of the activist experience. Please feel free to add comments wherever you wish. Your answers will remain absolutely confidential. I want to assure you that I will not respond to any government request for information I collect.

I would be happy to send you a summary of my findings. If you would like a summary, please write your name and address on the return envelope. If you have any questions at all, please feel free to contact me by phone and I will return your call. My number is (602) 626-3889.

I hope that you will enjoy participating in the study and would appreciate it if you would return your completed questionaire in the envelope provided within the next five days if possible. Thanks again for all your help.

1. Were you attending college during the spring immediately preceding Freedom Summer?

    no _____   yes _____

2. Please check the activities listed below you were involved in prior to Freedom Summer.

    A. <u>On Campus</u>: (go to B if you were <u>not</u> attending college immediately prior to Freedom Summer)

    1) performing arts _____
    2) National Student Association _____
    3) student government _____
    4) fraternity/sorority _____
    5) academic clubs or honor societies _____
    6) religious groups or activities _____
    7) school newspaper _____
    8) athletics _____
    9) tutorial program _____
    10) SDS _____
    11) peace organizations or activities _____
    12) civil rights organizations or activities _____
    13) other political organizations (e.g. Young Democrats, etc.) _____
    14) others (please describe) _____
    _____

    B. <u>In the Community</u>:

    1) religious groups or activities _____
    2) civil rights organizations or activities _____
    3) peace organizations or activities _____
    4) volunteer work _____
    5) others (please describe) _____
    _____
    _____

3. How did you first learn about the 1964 Mississippi Freedom Summer project?

4. Please <u>rank</u> the following in terms of their importance in influencing your decision to apply to the Freedom Summer project:

    parents _____
    friends or acquaintances _____
    minister or rabbi _____
    movement literature _____
    spokespersons for movement groups _____
    organizations of which you were a member _____
    religious groups or organizations _____
    other (please describe) _____

5. What factors influenced your decision to withdraw from participation in the Freedom Summer project? (Be as specific as possible)

6. Did any of your <u>close</u> friends subsequently participate in Freedom Summer?

    yes _____   no _____

7. Please check the statement(s) listed below which best describes your activity <u>immediately</u> following Freedom Summer.

    I returned to the same school I had been previously attending _____
    I transfered to another undergraduate school _____
    I dropped out of school _____
    I went South to work in the civil rights movement _____
    I got a job _____
    I remained in the North and did full-time organizing or related movement work _____
    I entered graduate school at another institution _____
    Other (please describe) _____

Appendix

8. Please check the activities you were involved in following Freedom Summer:

    A. <u>On Campus</u>: (go to B if you were not enrolled in college following Freedom Summer)

1) performing arts _____	10) SDS _____
2) National Student Association _____	11) peace organizations or activities _____
3) student government _____	12) civil rights organizations
4) fraternity/sorority _____	or activities _____
5) academic clubs or honor societies _____	13) other political organizations
6) religious groups or activities _____	(e.g. Young Democrats, etc.) _____
7) school newspaper _____	14) others (please describe) _____
8) athletics _____	
9) tutorial program _____	_____

    B. <u>In the Community</u>:

1) religious groups or activities _____	4) volunteer work _____
2) civil rights organizations or activities _____	5) others (please describe) _____
3) peace organizations or activities _____	_____

9. Please list all of the colleges you've attended since the fall of 1964 and the dates of your enrollment at each.

School	Enrolled	
	From	To

10. Were you active in the civil rights movement after Freedom Summer?

    no _____ (if no, skip to question 11)   yes _____ (if yes, in what ways were you active?)

    1) joined the staff of one of the major civil rights organizations _____
    2) returned to school and was active in civil rights activities on campus _____
    3) was active in direct action projects in my local community _____
    4) participated in community organizing _____
    5) joined or organized a local chapter of one of the major civil rights groups _____
    6) was active in civil rights related fundraising activities _____
    7) participated in mass marches or demonstrations _____
    8) participated in voter registration activities _____
    9) participated in or helped organized rent strikes _____
    10) participated in public forums on civil rights issues
       (e.g. interracial workshops, human relations commissions, etc.) _____
    11) worked tutoring inner-city children _____
    12) other (please describe) _____

    _____

11. Please list all the political or movement organizations, including local groups, you belonged to from the end of Freedom Summer through the time of the killings at Kent State in May of 1970. (Include any nonpolitical organizations through which you participated in political activities; e.g. churches.)

12. Did you have contact after the summer with any persons who had participated in Freedom Summer?

    no _____ (if no, please go on to question 14)
    yes _____ (if yes, please estimate the number of such persons you had contact with: _____.

13. Please estimate the number of Freedom Summer participants you remained in contact with in:

    1966 _____   1970 _____   1980 _____   the present _____

14. Please check the appropriate space to indicate your level of involvement in the
    following movements or political activities since Mississippi Freedom Summer.

	very involved	moderately involved	somewhat involved	not involved
1) Vietnam Antiwar Movement	____	____	____	____
2) Student Movement	____	____	____	____
3) Women's Movement	____	____	____	____
4) Farm Workers Movement	____	____	____	____
5) Gay Rights	____	____	____	____
6) Pro-Abortion	____	____	____	____
7) Right to Life	____	____	____	____
8) Common Cause	____	____	____	____
9) Environmental Movement	____	____	____	____
10) Labor Organizing	____	____	____	____
11) Local Community Organizing	____	____	____	____
12) Contemporary Draft Resistance	____	____	____	____
13) Anti-Nuclear Movement	____	____	____	____
14) Nuclear Freeze	____	____	____	____
15) Contemporary Peace Movement	____	____	____	____
16) Moral Majority	____	____	____	____
17) Socialist Movement	____	____	____	____
18) Libertarian Party	____	____	____	____
19) Democratic Party	____	____	____	____
20) Republican Party	____	____	____	____
21) Local Electoral Campaigns	____	____	____	____
22) State Electoral Campaigns	____	____	____	____
23) National Electoral Campaigns	____	____	____	____
24) Other (please describe				

_____ ____ ____ ____ ____

_____ ____ ____ ____ ____

15. Are you presently employed?   no ____   yes ____   (if yes, please list your job below)

16. Please list the __major__ jobs you've had from the present back to 1964.

	Years of Employment	
Job	From:	To:

17. Please check the category which best describes your gross individual income last year.

0-$4,999 ____	$10,000-$19,999 ____	$30,000-$39,999 ____
$5,000-$9,999 ____	$20,000-$29,999 ____	$40,000 and over ____

18. Sex: Male ____   Female ____

19. Race: Black ____   White ____   Other ____

20. Have you ever been married?

    no ____ (if no, please go to question 23)   yes ____

21. How many times have you been married?   ____

22. Please list the date(s) of your marriage(s): _____

_____

23. If you have had children, please list the year(s) of birth.

Appendix

24. Please check the statement that best describes your reaction to the following items.

	strongly agree	agree	disagree	strongly disagree	don't know	not applicable
My participation in social movements affected my choice of mate(s).						
My participation in social movements affected my choices about work.						
My participation in social movements affected my choices about having children.						
In the 1960's social movements were very effective vehicles of social change.						
Social movements are potentially effective vehicles of social change in contemporary America.						
Religious beliefs are an important influence in my life.						
The tax structure should be modified to reduce the income differences between the rich and the poor.						
Environmental standards should be reduced to aid in stimulating the economy.						

25. Please circle the number which best characterizes your political stance:

	Radical Left			Moderate				Radical Right		
1) Before Freedom Summer	1	2	3	4	5	6	7	8	9	10
2) Immediately After Freedom Summer	1	2	3	4	5	6	7	8	9	10

26. Please circle the number which best characterizes your present political stance:

Radical Left			Moderate				Radical Right		
1	2	3	4	5	6	7	8	9	10

27. Place a check beside those institutions you are presently participating in:

third political party	_____	commune	_____
neighborhood movement or tenant group	_____	daycare	
reform wing of political party	_____	alternative school	
progressive caucus in profession	_____	other(s) (please list)	
consciousness-raising group	_____		
self-help group	_____	_____	
food coop	_____		
work coop	_____		

28. Please list all political or movement organizations, including local groups, you currently belong to. (Please include any ostensibly nonpolitical organizations through which you participate in political activities, e.g. churches.)

29. Are you currently involved in any social movements?

no _____ yes _____ (if yes, which ones?)

245

GEORGE MASON UNIVERSITY

THE STATE UNIVERSITY IN NORTHERN VIRGINIA ■ 4400 UNIVERSITY DRIVE ■ FAIRFAX ■ VIRGINIA ■ 22030

Department of Sociology
Anthropology

Dear Mississippi Freedom Summer Volunteer:

We are three sociologists contacting you through your undergraduate alumni office to ask for help with a study of the 1964 Mississippi Freedom Summer. Our interest in social movements stems from both our research and personal involvements in a number of social movements past and present. That experience has led us to believe that Freedom Summer was a significant event in the larger protest era of the 1960's.

We are looking at documents of the period and at what has been written since that time by participants and social scientists. To find out more from those who took part in it, we will be interviewing some participants and sending questionnaires to as many volunteers as we can locate.

As you can see from our questions, we are interested in more than simply reconstructing Freedom Summer. We want to place this complex experience in the larger context of the social activism of this whole era. We want to explore how people became involved, the connections between Freedom Summer and subsequent political action, and the personal and social forces that influenced activism over time. We think these questions are relevant today and that understanding past successful social action can contribute to social change in the present.

Sincerely,

Lois Horton   *Doug McAdam*   *Victoria Rader*
Lois Horton   Doug McAdam   Victoria Rader

ENDORSEMENTS

As I understand the hypothesis on which Lois Horton, Doug McAdam, and Victoria Rader plan to proceed, it is that to some extent Mississippi Freedom Summer created a "Class of 1964" which fanned out into a variety of movement projects in the later 1960's.

This makes sense in my own experience. For instance, I know that the nucleus of persons who created the draft resistance movement to the Vietnam War had been in Mississippi together and deliberately sought a peace movement equivalent. I find, as I am sure you have, that on meeting someone who was in Mississippi and who later went into some other movement venture, one felt less need to "check them out" than might have been the case otherwise.

So I am cautiously optimistic about this research and hope that you will cooperate with it, as I plan to. An important kind of cooperation each of us might provide, beyond doing the questionnaire, is to jot down current addresses of Freedom Summer alumni we happen to have kept in touch with. Also, at least in my own case, there is a stack of letters somewhere in the house which I wrote in the summer of 1964 and never found their way into Elizabeth Sutherland's book, and I think it would help if each of us tried to unearth such private archives and make available those portions which are of general interest.

Incidentally, this gives me a way to say an impersonal Hello to some persons I haven't seen in a long time. Hello. We shall overcome, I still believe.

Staughton   1694 Timbers Court
Staughton Lynd   Niles, Ohio 44446

After looking over your previous published work (<u>Political Process and the Development of Black Insurgency</u>; <u>Black Bostonians</u>) I feel good about endorsing your planned survey of former Mississippi Freedom Summer volunteers. I am confident that this will not be another of those traditional academic surveys which are unrelated to the real world and social action. You are clearly committed and serious people whose work is intended to help in the promotion of social change, and I am happy to see that you give assurance you will not publish individual names without permission and will refuse to give information you collect to government authorities. I would therefore encourage people to cooperate with your project and I look forward to seeing the results of your work.

Sincerely,

Howard Zinn
Howard Zinn
Professor of Political Science
Boston University

Appendix

Lois Horton

Born 1942, Buffalo, N.Y.
Schools: B.A. SUNY at
Buffalo, 1964; M.A. Univ. of
Hawaii; PhD. Brandeis, 1977.
Published: with James O.
Horton, Black Bostonians:
Family Life and Community
Struggle in the Antebellum
North. "Race and the Class
Issue in Contemporary
America," American Quarterly,
Win/Spg, 1982-83, forthcoming.

Doug McAdam

Born 1952, Pasadena, Cal.
Schools: B.A. Occidental, 1973;
M.A. and PhD. SUNY Stony Brook,
1979. Published: Political
Process and the Black Protest
Movement, 1982. With J. Rule,
Linda Stearns and D. Uglow,
The Politics of Privacy, 1980.
"The Decline of Social Insur-
gency," in Jo Freeman (ed.),
The Politics of Social
Movements, 1982.

Victoria Rader

Born 1944, Phoenix, Ariz.
Schools: B.A. U. of Calif.
at Berkeley, 1966; M.A. and
PhD. Univ. of Chicago, 1973.
Published: "Student Influence
on the Changing Character of
Federal City College," Urban
Education, Winter, 1978; "The
Social Construction of Ages
and the Ideology of Stages,"
Humanity and Society, Fall,
1981.

INSTRUCTIONS

We would be grateful if you would take the 30-40 minutes necessary to answer this questionnaire. We know it is difficult to fit such an experience into questionnaire categories, but we have tried to design questions that are easy to answer yet capture essential aspects of the activist experience. Please add comments whenever you wish. Your answers will remain absolutely confidential. We want to assure you that we will not respond to any government requests for information we collect.

We would be happy to send you a summary of our findings. If you would like a summary, please write your name and address on the return envelope. If you have any questions at all, please feel free to call and leave your name and phone number or write to us and we will call you. (Our number is (703) 323-2900.) Also, we do not have current addresses for many volunteers, and would greatly appreciate any addresses you might send us.

We hope that you will enjoy participating in the study, and would appreciate it if you would return the completed questionnaire within five days, if that is possible.

1. Please provide the approximate dates of your arrival in and departure from Mississippi during the summer of 1964.

    arrival _____

    departure _____

2. Were you attending college during the spring immediately preceding Freedom Summer?

    no ____   yes ____

3. Please check those activities you were involved in prior to Freedom Summer.

    On Campus:

    1) performing arts ____
    2) National Student Association ____
    3) student government ____
    4) fraternity/sorority ____
    5) academic clubs or honor societies ____
    6) religious groups or activities ____
    7) school newspaper ____
    8) athletics ____
    9) tutorial program ____
    10) SDS ____
    11) peace organizations or activities ____
    12) civil rights organizations or activities ____
    13) other political organizations (e.g. Young Democrats, Friends of SNCC) ____
    14) others (please describe) ____
    _____

    In the Community:

    1) religious groups or activities ____
    2) civil rights organizations or activities ____
    3) peace organizations or activities ____
    4) volunteer work ____
    5) others (please describe) ____
    _____

4. How did you first learn about the 1964 Mississippi Freedom Summer Project?

5. Please _rank_ any of the following which influenced your decision to participate in the Freedom Summer Project in terms of their importance.

parents	____	spokespersons for movement groups (which ones?) ____
friends or acquaintances	____	_____
minister or rabbi	____	movement literature (which?) ____
organizations of which you were a member	____	_____
religious groups or organizations	____	other (please describe) ____ _____

6. Was your perception of the major news media (for example, mass news magazines, major metropolitan dailies and network television news) changed as a result of your summer experience?

no ____   yes ____   (If yes, please describe)

7. Please check the response that best describes the effect of your summer experience on your perception of:

	Lowered my Estimate	Raised my Estimate	Perception Unchanged
1) The President	____	____	____
2) Congress	____	____	____
3) The Supreme Court	____	____	____
4) The Justice Department	____	____	____
5) The FBI	____	____	____
6) Federal Courts	____	____	____

8. Please check the statement below which best describes your activity _immediately_ following Freedom Summer.

I returned to the same school I had been attending. ____
I transferred to another undergraduate school. ____
I graduated the previous spring. ____
I dropped out. ____
I stayed in the South to continue work in the movement. ____
I got a job. ____
I returned to the North to do organizing or related movement work there. ____
I entered graduate school at another institution. ____
Other (please describe). ____

_____

9. If you returned to any college, please check the activities you were involved in after Freedom Summer.

On Campus:

1) performing arts	____	10) SDS	____
2) National Student Association	____	11) peace organizations or activities	____
3) student government	____	12) civil rights organizations or activities	____
4) fraternity/sorority	____		
5) academic clubs or honor societies	____	13) other political organizations (e.g. Young Democrats, Friends of SNCC)	____
6) religious groups or activities	____	14) others (please describe)	____
7) school newspaper	____		
8) athletics	____	_____	
9) tutorial program	____		

In the Community:

1) religious groups or activities	____	5) others (please describe)	____
2) civil rights organizations or activities	____		
3) peace organizations or activities	____	_____	
4) volunteer work	____		

10. Please list any colleges you've attended since Freedom Summer and the dates of your enrollment.

From   To

11. Did you remain active in the civil rights movement after the summer?

no ____ (If no, please go to question 13.) yes ____ (If yes, in which of the following ways?)

1) joined the staff of one of the major civil rights organizations ____
2) returned to school and was active in civil rights related activities on campus ____
3) was active in direct action projects in my local community ____
4) participated in community organizing ____
5) joined or organized a local chapter of one of the major civil rights organizations ____
6) was active in civil rights related fundraising ____
7) participated in mass marches or demonstrations ____
8) participated in voter registration activities ____
9) participated in or helped organize rent strikes ____
10) participated in public forums on civil rights issues (for example, interracial workshops, human relations commissions, encounter groups, public speaking)
11) worked tutoring inner-city children ____
12) other (please describe) ____

12. Immediately following Freedom Summer, were your civil rights activities:

1) confined to the North ____
2) confined to the South ____
3) in both regions? ____

13. If you did NOT remain active after the summer, please describe why you were less active.

14. Please list all political or movement organizations, including local groups, you belonged to from Freedom Summer through the time of the killings at Kent State in May, 1970. (Include any nonpolitical organizations through which you participated in political activities, e.g. churches.)

15. Did you read alternative sources of political information following Freedom Summer?

no ____ yes ____ (If yes, please list those you read regularly, e.g. The Student Voice, SDS Bulletin, National Guardian, Berkeley Barb.)

16. Did you maintain contact after the summer with any people you were associated with in Freedom Summer?

    no ____ (If no, please go to question 19.)
    yes ____ (If yes, please describe the nature of these contacts, e.g. occasional letter writing, long-term friendship. <u>Also</u>, please indicate their role in Freedom Summer, e.g. trainer, resident, COFE staff, SNCC staff, volunteer.)

    1) _____
    2) _____
    3) _____
    4) _____
    5) _____
    6) _____
    7) _____

17. Did any of these contacts influence your decision as to whether or not to remain active in the civil rights movement?

    no ____ yes ____ (If yes, in what ways?)

18. Please estimate the number of volunteers you remain(ed) in contact with in:

    1966 ____ 1970 ____ 1980 ____ the present ____

19. Please check the appropriate space to indicate your level of involvement in the following movements or political activities since the Mississippi Freedom Summer.

	very involved	moderately involved	somewhat involved	not involved
1) Vietnam Antiwar Movement	___	___	___	___
2) Student Movement	___	___	___	___
3) Women's Movement	___	___	___	___
4) Farm Workers	___	___	___	___
5) Gay Rights	___	___	___	___
6) Pro-Abortion	___	___	___	___
7) Right to Life	___	___	___	___
8) Common Cause	___	___	___	___
9) Environmental Movement	___	___	___	___
10) Labor Organizing	___	___	___	___
11) Local Community Organizing	___	___	___	___
12) Contemporary Draft Resistance	___	___	___	___
13) Anti-Nuclear	___	___	___	___
14) Nuclear Freeze	___	___	___	___
15) Contemporary Peace Movement	___	___	___	___
16) Moral Majority	___	___	___	___
17) Socialist Movement	___	___	___	___
18) Libertarian Party	___	___	___	___
19) Democratic Party	___	___	___	___
20) Republican Party	___	___	___	___
21) Local Electoral Campaigns	___	___	___	___
22) State Electoral Campaigns	___	___	___	___
23) National Electoral Campaigns	___	___	___	___
24) Other (please describe)	___	___	___	___

_____
_____

250

Appendix

20. Please give approximate dates for the periods since 1964 when you were:

   More active in social movements _____

   Less active in social movements _____

   Were there factors which accounted for your:

        more active times? _____

        less active times? _____

21. Were any of the personal contacts or friendships you established during Mississippi Freedom Summer influential in your deciding whether or not to become involved in any of the other movements or political activities listed above?

   don't know ____ no ____ yes ____ (If yes, in what ways?)

22. Please check any statement below which describes your family experience <u>before</u> Freedom Summer.

   Part of my family environment included:
   1) a very active commitment to moral or ethical principles. ____
   2) a serious commitment to religious principles. ____
   3) very active conservative political involvements. ____
   4) a tradition of radical activism. ____

23. Are you presently employed? no ____ yes ____ (If yes, what do you do?)

24. Please list the <u>major</u> jobs you've had from the present back to 1964.

                  <u>Job</u>   <u>Year(s)</u>

APPENDIX

25. Please check the category which best describes your gross __individual__ income last year.

    0-$4,999 ____ $10,000-$19,999 ____ $30,000-$39,999 ____
    $5,000-$9,999 ____ $20,000-$29,999 ____ $40,000 and over ____

26. Sex   Male ____   Female ____

27. Race   Black ____   White ____   Other ____

28. Have you ever been married?

        no ____ (If no, please go to question 31.)   yes ____

29. How many times have you been married?   ____

30. Please list the dates of your marriage(s). _____

31. If you have had children, please give their years of birth.

32. Please check the column which best describes your reaction to the following statements.

	Strongly Agree	Agree	Disagree	Strongly Disagree	Don't Know	Not Applicable
My participation in social movements affected my choice of mate(s).						
My participation in social movements affected by choices about work.						
My participation in social movements affected my choices about having children.						
In the 1960's social movements were very effective vehicles of social change.						
Social movements are potentially effective vehicles of social change in contemporary America.						
Religious beliefs are an important influence in my life.						
The tax structure should be modified to reduce the income differences between the rich and the poor.						
Environmental standards should be reduced to aid in stimulating the economy.						

33. Please __circle__ the number which best characterizes your political stance:

	Radical Left			Moderate				Radical Right	
Before Freedom Summer	1	2	3	4	5	6	7	8	9	10
Immediately After Freedom Summer	1	2	3	4	5	6	7	8	9	10

34. Please circle the number which best characterizes your __present__ political stance.

Radical Left			Moderate				Radical Right	
1	2	3	4	5	6	7	8	9	10

35. Please check the institutions, if any, you are presently participating in:

third political party ____
neighborhood, movement or tenant group ____
reform wing of political party ____
progressive caucus in profession ____
consciousness-raising group ____
self-help group ____
food coop ____
work coop ____

commune ____
daycare ____
alternative schools ____
others (please list) ____

_____
_____

Appendix

36. Please list all political or movement organizations, including local groups, you <u>currently</u> belong to. (Please include any nonpolitical organizations through which you participate in political activities, e.g. churches.)

37. Are you currently involved in any social movements?

    no ____   yes ____   (If yes, which ones?)

38. Which sources of political information do you currently refer to regularly?

    1) daily newspaper(s)   ____   (which ones?) _____
                                                        _____

    2) weekly news magazine(s)   ____   (which ones?) _____
                                                        _____

    3) network television news   ____   (which?)   _____
    4) national political publications
       (e.g. The Progressive, Common
       Cause Newsletter)   ____   (which ones?) _____
                                                        _____

    5) local organizational newsletters____
    6) other (please list)   ____   _____

THANK YOU VERY MUCH FOR COMPLETING THE QUESTIONNAIRE.

Again, any help you could provide in locating other volunteers would be greatly appreciated. Please list any addresses you can give us.

_____
_____
_____

Appendix B

Results of Logit Regression Assessing the Effect of Various Independent Variables on Participation in the Freedom Summer Project

Independent Variable	Dependent Variable b	Summer Status SE(b)
Sum of personal constraints	−.011	.090
Level of prior activism	.032	.018
Integration measures		
Number of organizational affiliations	.194[b]	.059
Categories of interpersonal contact		
Strong tie to participant or known activist	.604[b]	.144
Weak tie to participant or known activist	.259	.149
Strong tie to withdrawal	−.395[c]	.201
Major		
Social science	−.258	.158
Other majors	−.140	.158
Home region		
West North Central	.236	.298
New England	.065	.257
Mid-Atlantic	.063	.218
East North Central	.011	.226
West	.444	.311
South	.008	.263
College region		
West North Central	−.340	.288
New England	−.245	.203
Mid-Atlantic	−.364	.193
East North Central	−.469[c]	.200
West	−.395	.216
South	−.029	.257
Race—white	.063	.108
Gender—female	−.206[c]	.089
Age	.315[c]	.142
Highest grade completed	.030	.076
Distance from home to Mississippi	.0001	.0003
Constant	−.348	1.12

$N = 794$.

[a] Summer status: $0 =$ withdrawals; $1 =$ participants.

[b] $p < .01$.

[c] $p < .05$.

Source: Doug McAdam, 1986, "Recruitment to High-Risk Activism: The Case of Freedom Summer," *American Journal of Sociology* 92: 64–90.

Appendix C
Accounting of All Projects at Summer's End

Location	Voter Registration	Community Center	Freedom School	Number of Students	Funds Expended[a]
Aberdeen	X				$ 75.00
Batesville	X	X			244.00
Belzoni	X	X			1017.00
Benton County	X		X	60[b]	[i]
Biloxi	X	X	X	35[c]–70[b]	875.00
Canton	X	X	X	107[b]–110[c]	2164.60
Carthage	X	X	X	75[c]–85[b]	[i]
Charleston	[d]	[d]	[d]	[d]	[i]
Clarksdale	X	X	X	60[c]–75[b]	885.00
Cleveland	X	X		[b]	125.00
Columbus	X		X	45[b]–60[c]	2157.13
Flora	X[e]	X[e]	X	75[b]	[i]
Gluckstadt	X[e]	X[e]	X	65[b]	[i]
Greenville	X	X	X	35[c]–125[b]	505.00
Greenwood	X	X	X	60[c]–100[b]	2613.00
Gulfport	X	X	X	75[c]	724.00
Harmony	X	X	X	35[b]	[i]
Hattiesburg	X	X	X	650[b]–675[c]	1640.00
Hollandale	X				[i]
Holly Springs	X	X	X	70[b]–155[c]	2752.79
Indianola	X	X	X	70[b]	[i]
Itta Bena	X				539.70
Jackson	X		X	375[b]	40695.62[f]
Laurel	X	X	X	60[b]–65[c]	1273.00
Leake County	[d]	[d]	[c]	[d]	5.00
Magdalene	X		X	53[b]	[i]
Marks	X				75.00
McComb	X		X	11[b]–75[c]	2195.00
Meridian	X	X	X	150[c]	465.00
Moss Point	X	X	X	40[c]	565.00
Mound Bayou	X	X	X	30[c]	300.00
Mount Olive			X	105[c]	325.00
Natchez	X				770.00
Pascagoula	[d]	[d]	[d]	[d]	[i]
Philadelphia	X		X	45[b]	200.00
Ruleville	X	X	X	50[c]–60[b]	570.00
Shaw	X	X	X	25[c]	935.00
Tallahatchie	[d]	[d]	[d]	[d]	260.00
Tchula	X	X	X	80[b]	[g]
Tupelo	X				600.00
Valley View	X	X	X	200[b]	238.62

Appendix C (*Cont.*)

Location	Voter Regis- tration	Com- munity Center	Freedom School	Number of Students	Funds Expended[a]
Vicksburg	X	X	X	60[b]	2225.00
West Point	X		X	10[b]	[i]
Yazoo City	X				560.32
Totals	38	23	30	3,036–3,433	$68,897.59[h]

[a] Expenditures taken from monthly accounts (June–August) found in papers donated to SHSW by Martin and Victoria Nicholaus (hereinafter Nicholaus papers).

[b] Estimate of students taken from press release issued by communications, Jackson, Mississippi, August 25, 1964; in archives of the Freedom Information Service, Jackson, Mississippi.

[c] Estimate of students taken from a second internal project talley found in the archives of the Freedom Information Service.

[d] Information not available.

[e] Flora and Gluckstadt shared voter registration and community center projects.

[f] Figure includes funds dispersed from central project office, Jackson.

[g] Included in figure for Mount Olive.

[h] Figure includes an additional expenditure of $322.81 in support of the White Community Project.

[i] No expenses listed.

Appendix D
Mississippi Summer Project Running Summary of Incidents

MISSISSIPPI SUMMER PROJECT
RUNNING SUMMARY OF INCIDENTS

JUNE 16: Philadelphia: Mt. Zion Baptist Church burns to ground. Fire starts soon after Negro mass meeting adjourns. Three Negroes beaten by whites. Church was freedom school site.

State-wide: Negroes attempt to attend Democratic Party precinct conventions for the first time in this century. Results vary. Two Negroes, two whites elected in Jackson.

JUNE 17: Vicksburg: Summer volunteer arrested for driving while intoxicated. Not allowed phone call. Held overnight. Aquitted at trial next day.

JUNE 20: Fayette: Police, citizens order SNCC worker out of his house. He flees, but when car recovered two days later his camera, food, and personal documents are missing.

JUNE 21: Brandon (Rankin Co.) Molotov cocktail explodes in basement of Sweet Rest Church of Christ Holiness. Fire; minor damage.

McComb: Homes of two civil rights workers planning to house summer volunteers bombed. One damaged extensively. Seven dynamite sticks left on lawn of third home with no civil rights ties

Meridian: Three civil rights workers missing after short trip to Philadelphia.

JUNE 22: Clarksdale: Four volunteers arrested on vagrancy charges while engaged in voter registration work. Held 3-1/2 hours, released.

Brandon: Negro youth killed in hit-and-run accident.

JUNE 23: Philadelphia: Missing car found burned; no sign of three workers. Car was on list circulated state-wide by Canton White Citizens Council.

Jackson: Shots fired at home of Rev. R.L.T. Smith. White man escapes on foot, reportedly picked up by a city truck. (Smith's home is under 24-hour guard.)

Moss Point: Knights of Pythias Hall firebombed. Arson attempt on side of building. Damage slight. Used for voter rallies.

Moss Point: Two summer volunteers picked up as they leave cafe, relax on private lawn. Taken by police at 85 m.p.h. without lights at night to Pascagoula jail. Held in "protective custody" overnight, then released.

Jackson: Civil rights worker held eight hours after receiving $5 change for a $20 bill.

Jackson: White car fires shot at Henderson's cafe. Negroes pursue. Three shots fired, hitting one Negro in head twice.

Clarksdale: Local pastor, a civil rights leader, arrested for reckless and drunk driving. He is a total abstainer.

State-wide: Negroes try to attend Democratic Party county conventions. Participation systematically discouraged.

Ruleville: LOOK, TIME reporters covering voter rally at Williams chapel, chased out of town by car at speeds up to 85 m.p.h. Early next morning, nine Negro homes, cars hit by bottles thrown from similar car.

JUNE 24: Meridian: Threat: "You G. D. people are going to get bombed."

Hollandale: Police, mayor tell summer volunteer he can't live in Negro section of town and register voters.

(over)

257

2-2-2

JUNE 24: Drew: Thirty volunteers, staff workers engaged in voter registration meet open hostility from whites. Weapons shown.

Canton: Civil rights car hit by bullet.

Collins: 40 M-1 rifles, 1,000 rounds of ammunition stolen from National Guard armory.

JUNE 25: Ruleville: Williams Chapel firebombed. Damage slight. Eight plastic bags with gasoline found later outside building.

Jackson: Two separate arrests of volunteers on minor traffic charges. Seven questioned in one case; charges dropped in other. (Law student presented his own case.)

Philadelphia: Southern newsman's car deliberately rammed by local citizen. Newsman gets two tickets.

Itta Bena: Two volunteers working with local Negro, handing out literature for voter registration rally, taken to gas station-bus stop by four white men who tell them: "If you speak in town tonight, you'll never leave here."

Greenville: Federal building demonstration. No harassment.

Durant: Civil rights worker's car stopped on highway for repairs. Driver charged with illegal parking. $60 bond paid.

JUNE 26: Hattiesburg: Hate literature from whites: "Beware, good Negro citizens. When we come to get the agitators, stay away."

Columbus: Seven voter registration workers arrested for distributing literature without a city permit. Bond: $400 each.

Itta Bena: FBI arrests three local residents for June 25 incident. Two are released on $2,000 bail, one on $1,000.

Clinton: Church of Holy Ghost arson. Kerosene spilled on floor, lit after local white pastor speaks to Negro Bible class. (Fifth firebombing in 10 days.)

Holmes County: Two staffers detained for illegal parking, no Mississippi permit. One arrested. Bond $60.

Holly Springs: Harassment: beer cans tossed at volunteers, car tires slashed.

Greenwood: Freedom House call: "You'd better not go to sleep or you won't get up."

Greenwood: Voter registration worker picked up by police, released after questioning.

Jackson: CORE field secretary beaten at Hinds County jail while a federal prisoner. Third beating of a civil rights worker at same jail in two months, second of federal prisoner.

Canton: Two volunteers picked up by police, told all out-of-town visitors must register with them. Registered, released.

Belzoni: Three arrested for disturbing the peace. Two released without charges, third held on $100 bond.

JUNE 27: Batesville: Local person helping voter registration gets obvious harassment ticket for illegal parking outside courthouse.

Vicksburg: Threatening call: "We're going to get you."

Philadelphia: Local Negro contact has bottle thrown through window of home. Threatening note attached.

(more)

Appendix

3-3-3

JUNE 27: <u>Greenwood:</u> Several phone harassments; bomb threat.

<u>Doddsville:</u> Highway Patrol kills 34-year-old Negro with history of mental illness. Local deputy who knew Negro with patrolman. Mother asks to see body. Police reply: "Get that hollering woman away." Ruled "justifiable homicide" in 17 hours.

<u>Jackson:</u> Two phone threats: "We're going to kill you white SOBs."

JUNE 28: <u>Jackson:</u> Civil rights worker held 8-1/2 hours without charges; stopped for no reason while driving near COFO office. (Mississippi law permits holding for 72 hours "for investigation.")

<u>Vicksburg:</u> High school girl tells friends COFO "going to get it."

<u>Canton:</u> Threatening calls throughout the night.

<u>Ruleville:</u> Mayor tells visiting white Methodist chaplain he cannot attend white Methodist services: "You came here to live with Negroes, so you can go to church with them, too." He does, with three volunteers.

<u>Batesville:</u> Report local Negro man beaten, missing.

<u>Jackson:</u> "Hospitality Month" in Mississippi: white volunteer kicked over from behind, slugged on arrival from Oxford at local train station.

JUNE 29: <u>Hattiesburg:</u> Two cars owned by volunteers shot by four whites in pickup truck at 1:00 a.m. No injuries, $100 damage to each car. Three witnesses. (Owners were sleeping two blocks away.)

<u>Columbus:</u> Six carloads of whites drive up on lawn of Freedom House. Five flee before police arrive. Police question, release two men in sixth car.

<u>Hattiesburg:</u> Civil rights worker charged with reckless driving, failure to give proper signal. Held overnight, paid fine.

<u>Biloxi:</u> Volunteers in White Community Program turned away from hotel.

<u>Hattiesburg:</u> Phone rings. Volunteers hears tape recording of last 20 seconds of his previous conversation. Someone goofed!

<u>Columbus:</u> Restaurants serving volunteers threatened.

JUNE 30: <u>Vicksburg:</u> Negro woman threatened for registering to vote.

<u>Ruleville:</u> Man loses job for housing white volunteers.

<u>Jackson:</u> Car circles office with gun, threatens teen-ager: "Want to shoot some pool, nigger?"

<u>Jackson:</u> Volunteer charged with reckless driving. Fine $34. (He moved from one traffic lane to another in integrated car.)

<u>Holly Springs:</u> White teen-agers scream profanities, throw rocks at office from passing car.

<u>Hattiesburg:</u> Whites in pickup truck with guns visible drive past office several times. FBI checks June 29 car shooting.

<u>Holly Springs:</u> SNCC staff worker jumped by local white who threatens to shoot both him and his office with 12-gauge shotgun.

<u>Harmony:</u> Freedom School teachers arrive. School superintendent announces first Negro summer school in memory of local residents.

<u>Tchula:</u> Two carloads of highway patrolmen start excessively close watch on volunteer. Ended 48 hours later.

(over)

4-4-4

JUNE 30: <u>Oakland</u>: Police find body of white man, badly mangled by hit-run driver, no identification at all. (Later found no civil rights tie.)

<u>Greenville</u>: Report that on June 19 a Negro porter at Greenville General Hospital was beaten by policeman with billy club there. Porter charged with resisting arrest and disturbing the peace.

JULY 1: <u>Holly Springs</u>: Justice of Peace (and Mayor) has local farmer arrested on assault and battery charges in June 30 incident. Bail set at $1,000.

<u>Clarksdale</u>: Pickup truck tries to run down SNCC worker and volunteer. License plates hidden.

<u>Gulfport</u>: Police threaten to hurt children of lady housing civil rights workers. Workers plan to move elsewhere.

JULY 2: <u>Harmony</u>: Sheriff, school superintendent tell community abandoned buildings may not be used for freedom school. Cross burned, tacks strewn in Negro community.

<u>Vicksburg</u>: Whites chase, shoot at Negro on motorcycle.

<u>Hattiesburg</u>: Two voter registration canvassers followed and questioned by men describing themselves as state officials.

<u>Hattiesburg</u>: School superintendent threatens all janitors who participate in civil rights activity. Ditto at Holiday Inn.

<u>Hattiesburg</u>: Local police stop Negro girl, five white boys en route home. Policeman curses, threatens arrest, slaps one boy.

<u>Batesville</u>: Panola County Sheriff Carl Hubbard detains several persons housing civil rights workers, spends most of night in courtyard where many workers are living.

<u>Meridian</u>: White teen-age girl throws bottle at civil rights group outside church, cuts leg of local Negro girl.

<u>Canton</u>: Local police turn on sirens, play music on loudspeaker near COFO office, fail to answer phone calls.

<u>Gulfport</u>: Two voter registration workers threatened: "Things are fine around here; we don't want them to change." Man grabs volunteer's shirt: "I'm going to whip your ass." Workers run.

JULY 3: <u>Meridian</u>: Volunteer's car goes through green light, hits local station wagon. Volunteer charged with running light, reckless driving. Bond $122.

<u>So So</u>: The "Greasy Spoon," a Negro grocery and teen spot, is bombed. Damage minor. Sheriff's deputy says there is no civil rights motive for the bombing, calls it "senseless."

<u>Greenwood</u>: Three visiting Congressmen witness voter registration, call it discriminatory.

<u>Tougaloo</u>: En route to Canton, four civil rights girls are chased by two cars driven by whites. They decide to stop here (in Jackson) for safety.

<u>Jackson</u>: Lots of phone harassment. WATS line goes dead, then rings--a technical impossibility.

<u>Columbus</u>: Police impound volunteer's car---claim it's stolen because transfer papers are not notarized.

<u>Itta Bena</u>: Police question two volunteers about robbery, say they were only ones in vicinity. No charges filed.

<u>Greenwood</u>: Two tagless cars drive continually past office.

<u>Moss Point</u>: Police, white citizens pressure Negro cafe owners not to serve civil rights workers.

(more)

Appendix

Policeman says white racist in town has gun on his person, grenade in a satchel.

JULY 3: **Harmony:** Sheriff, superintendent post "no trespassing" sign at abandoned school. Local citizens move books, other materials to Negro church. Police flash lights on homes.

JULY 4: **Laurel:** Police barely prevent large racial clash after two Negroes, two whites injured in attempt to integrate drive-in. Police fail to respond to calls for help from injured Negroes.

Clarksdale: Local manager says Negroes going to courthouse will be discharged: "I have a large contract with the head of the White Citizens Council, and I'm not going to lose thousands of dollars for one of you."

Batesville: Volunteer, local worker chased 30 miles by car.

JULY 5: **Greenville:** Local citizens test several restaurants. The eating places are closed either before or after testing.

Ruleville: Local segregationist visits COFO office, has a very friendly argument with civil rights workers. Police ask him to leave. He refuses. Charged with disorderly conduct. Fined.

Laurel: Civil rights worker who witnessed and reported the July 4 incident is arrested. Police say he has 4-6 months left to serve on previous sentence.

Columbus: St. Louis (Mo.) Negro beaten by whites who mistake him for a "Freedom Rider." En route to a funeral, he's fined $75.

Laurel: Two volunteers questioned by police who stop their integrated car as it leaves Sunday school. Charges dropped against driver, but passenger arrested on vagrancy charge. She left pocketbook in car at police station, gets 10 days suspended sentence.

Jackson: NAACP integrates local hotels without major incident. Individuals integrate many other places on their own.

Jackson: Local woman's leg cut by bottle thrown at COFO office.

JULY 6: **Jackson:** Voter registration group harassed by police who say "One man, one vote" sticker has been found on city car. They threaten arrest for trespassing if anyone will sign charge.

Jackson: McCraven-Hill Missionary Baptist Church damaged by kerosene fire. Church has no ties to civil rights movement.

Clarksdale: Station wagon plays "chicken" with civil rights workers going home.

Jackson: Negro youth slugged by white who flees in truck.

Moss Point: Negro woman shot twice at voter rally, singing "We Shall Overcome." Three Negroes arrested when they pursue car from which they believe shots were fired. White car not checked.

Greenwood: Harassment call: "I just shot one of your workers..."

Itta Bena: Local Police, sheriff hold civil rights worker incommunicado, trigger wide search by federal authorities, SNCC.

Hattiesburg: Owner's wife pulls pistol as 15-25 youngsters try to integrate drive-in. Youngsters run, are arrested and put in drunk tank by police. Three are roughed up.

Raleigh: Methodist and Baptist churches burned to ground.

JULY 7: **Shaw:** Stores refuse to cash volunteer's travelers check.

Shaw: Police ask all volunteers to register. Only four do not.

(.over)

6-6-6

JULY 7:   Clarksdale: Sheriff asks white minister driving integrated car: "Are you married to them niggers? You ain't no minister, you're a SOB trouble maker...I'm gonna stay on your back until I get you."

Vicksburg: White boys throw bottle, break windshield of car waiting to pick up freedom school student.

Greenwood: Six young students picketing jailhouse ("Stop Police Brutality," "One Man, One Vote") arrested. So are three others with them.

JULY 8:   McComb: SNCC Freedom House bombed; two injured. Despite numerous requests by Congressmen, attorneys, pastors (and a personal visit with the mayor—who also heads the White Citizens Council), no local police were seen in the area prior to the bombing. 15 FBI agents, several packing pistols, show up during day. 150 local citizens attend rally same night.

Hattiesburg: Rev. Robert Beech of National Council of Churches arrested on false pretense charge after allegedly overdrawing his bank account $70. Bail set at $2000.

Ruleville: Volunteer bodily ejected from county circuit clerk's office for accompanying local woman to voter registration.

Columbus: Three volunteers arrested on trespass charges after stopping at a gas station for a soft drink. Friendly conversation there until attendant says, "You boys should be on the road." They leave immediately. He files charges. Bail $500 to $1000 each.

Clarksdale: Bomb threat.

Hattiesburg: Bottle thrown at picnic by passing car. No plates.

Holly Springs: Civil rights worker arrested. Reckless driving. $250.

Clarksdale: Police chief in Lafayette tells Negro cafes not to serve volunteers.

Vicksburg: Bomb threat.

JULY 9:   Greenwood: Local insurance salesman slugs volunteer during voter canvas. Follows in car and rebeats.

Yazoo City: Folk singer arrested for reckless driving. Quick fine.

Clarksdale: Volunteer arrested for taking pictures in court room. Photos taken in hall after police chief sprayed room deodorant on two girls.

Gulfport: Four arrested for refusing to leave local people and cross street on police orders as they near court house. Held on $500 bond for violating anti-picketing law.

Vicksburg: Freedom school students stoned en route to class.

Moss Point: Five Negroes fired from jobs for attending mass rally. Woman fired from work for housing two volunteers.

Clarksdale: Police chief visits office when another white man comes to turn off electricity.

Gulfport: Police urge volunteer to leave for his own protection, or face charges of inciting to riot.

JULY 10: Clarksdale: Chairs removed from libraries. NAACP youths refused service at two restaurants.

Hattiesburg: Rabbi, two volunteers, two local teen-agers attacked by two men as they walked in uninhabited area. Assailants escape after attacking three men. On emerging from hospital, rabbi says Jews in Mississippi should "stand up for decency and freedom with all risks involved" or leave the state.

(more)

Appendix

JULY 10: Vicksburg: Four civil rights workers chased by two cars, one of which has a man with revolver.

Jackson: J. Edgar Hoover opens Jackson FBI office, first statewide center since 1946. Cites efficiency as reason. Says 153 agents now in state. Says FBI can give civil rights workers "no protection" (beyond reports based on complaints and directions for investigation from civil rights division of Justice Department).

Greenwood: SNCC staff member arrested on public profanity charge. Policeman overheard him say, "We've got to get some damn organization in our office." Bail: $15.

Moss Point: Howard Kirschenbaum, only volunteer to leave the MSP because of arrests and harassment, returns with $2000 in gifts from New York.

JULY 11: Shaw: Local Negro offered $400 by five whites to bomb SNCC Freedom House, $40 for list of residents' home addresses.

Laurel: Four young Negroes injured during and after attempts to integrate Kresses lunch counter, where Negroes had eaten earlier.

Canton: Small firebomb thrown at Freedom House lawn.

Vicksburg: Amateur bomb thrown through window of Negro cafe.

Canton: Volunteer arrested on traffic charges while delivering freedom school books.

Browning: Pleasant Plan Missionary Baptist Church burns to ground. Whites sought to buy it, Negroes would not sell.

Laurel: Local NAACP president received two death threats both for July 19.

Holly Springs: Integrated staff picnic broken up by police.

Clarksdale: NAACP member testing barber shop driven out at gun point.

Harmony: Police visit local Negroes who have had contact with COFO volunteers, staff, forcing them to sign peace bonds. Police come armed with a warrant to search for liquor.

Greenwood: Local Negro woman hit in chest by white man, while accompanied by two volunteers. No police cooperation in getting assailants.

JULY 12: Canton: Two summer volunteers, visitor refused admission to First Methodist Church. Volunteers had been welcomed a week earlier.

Greenwood: Bomb threat.

Jackson: Half-body found in Mississippi identified as Charles Moore, former Alcorn A&M student. Second half-body found in river. (In mid-April, more than 700 students, all Negroes, were summarily dismissed from Alcorn after a non-violent general grievance demonstration)

Jackson: White teen-agers slash Negro woman's tires, spit in face of volunteer co-ed after integrated group eats at drive-in.

Jackson: Elderly man attacks Negro woman at Greyhound coffee shop. She is treated for cut head, hand, then charged with disturbing the peace. Out on $50 bond. Assailant escapes.

Biloxi: Volunteer picked up while canvassing, informed of complaints by local residents, released.

Itta Bena: Local woman attacked by two white boys while baby sitting. Both her arms cut.

Natchez: Jerusalem Baptist and Bethel Methodist Churches burned to ground. Home of Negro contractor in Natchez firebombed.

(:over)

8-8-8

JULY 13: Clarksdale: Negro volunteer chased out of white laundromat, picked up by police for failure to signal turn, taken to jail and beaten. Sheriff says: "You're a nigger and you're going to stay a nigger." Charged with resisting arrest, out on $64 bond.

Clarksdale: Chief voter registrar closes courthouse for next few days. Stated reason: court in session, no time for registration.

Clarksdale: Owner of electric company has project leader pointed out to him, then fingers knife in his presence.

JULY 14: Canton: Man threatened with job loss if youngster continues in Freedom School. Youngster stays.

Drew: Police chief, local citizens protest Albuquerque Journal article based on volunteer's letter home. Volunteer says letter was edited.

Hattiesburg: State Sovereignty Commission visits office.

Vicksburg: Milkman's assistant loses job because he attends the Freedom School.

Vicksburg: SNCC team confirms burning of Bovina Community Center July 7.

Drew: Police pick up James Dann for distributing literature without permit. Later, seven people arrested for distributing literature without a permit and blocking the sidewalk. $100-$200 bond.

Holly Springs: Oxford police chief told civil rights worker he should not come back to town. Chief threatened to hit Negro over head, especially if he did not speak to others with proper respect. (No major changes.)

Laurel: Gas bomb thrown at local Negro's home.

Batesville: Movie which had upstairs for Negroes now offers admission only to whites.

Canton: Three white men pursue five civil rights workers in car en route home.

JULY 15: Biloxi: Two arrested in traffic harassment case.

Clarksdale: Another traffic arrest: improper turn.

McComb: Freedom School enrolls 35 here.

Drew: 25 arrested for willfully and unlawfully using the sidewalks and the streets during voter registration rally. Citizens Council met at 9 a.m.

Gulfport: Civil rights worker arrested for putting posters on a telephone pole. City ordinance. Bond $50.

JULY 16: Canton: Volunteers report they were beaten by police last night following arrest with truck carrying freedom registration supplies, books, miscellany. Bond set at $150 each.

Greenwood: Freedom Day -- 111 arrests, including 13 juveniles. Group includes 98 adults, of whom 9 were SNCC staff and 13 volunteers.

Vicksburg: White man comes to door of home where volunteer staying. Has pistol showing in holster. Asks to see owner of house. At another home housing workers, car circles block 10-15 minutes.

Greenwood: Silas McGhee, local resident, picked up by three whites, forced to enter cab of their pickup truck at gunpoint, then beaten with pipe and plank. Incident occurs just after he leaves FBI office. He returns there ; agents take him to hospital. He has been active in attempts to integrate theatre.

(more)

Appendix

9-9-9

JULY 16: <u>Greenville:</u> Freedom Day: 101 people took test, 100 more came too late. No arrests.

Hattiesburg: Two voter canvassers stopped by police.

Hattiesburg: Police question those who complain about inadequate protection for those going to Freedom School may charge them with threatening mayor.

Indianola: Of those arrested in Drew July 15, 10 women are being held at county jail and 15 men at county farm near here. Superintendent of farm tells lawyer he can't guarantee safety of those at the farm. FBI advised.

Laurel: Volunteer canvassing accosted by two white boys who accuse him of not being from Mississippi, knock materials from hand and run.

Cleveland: Freedom Day: 25 to 30 picket without incident. About 20 of 25 from Shaw group register. More than 50 from other communities came, of whom 30 registered. Process slow but polite. Ten regular and 45 auxiliary police allow only those registering or picketing on courthouse grounds.

JULY 17: McComb: Mount Zion Hill Baptist Church in Pike County bombed or burned to ground. Pastor of this church had let Project use his McComb Church, St. Mary's.

Philadelphia: Columbia law student and a writer beaten with chain by two middle-aged white men in early afternoon.

Greenwood: 15 staff and volunteers on hunger strike until let out of jail after being brought in during massive freedom-day arrests.

Greenwood: Greenwood and Drew mass arrest cases have been removed to Federal court and bonds reduced to $200 out of state, $100 for residents.

Yazoo: Three Negro men, late teens or early twenties, arrested for looking at a white girl.

Greenshaw: White summer volunteer harassed by three white men while putting up voter registration poster.

JULY 18: Lauderdale: Two summer volunteers arrested for willful trespass while discussing voter registration on front porch of two Negro women; no complaint made by women.

Hattiesburg: Kilmer Estus Keyes, white, of Collins, Mississippi, turned self in to local police in connection with beating of Rabbi and two workers last week. Charged with assault; out on $2500 property bond. (Eventually fined $500 and given 90-day suspended sentence.)

Batesville: 8 people detained one and one-half hours by sheriff who was "trying to see if there is a state ordinance against the passing out of leaflets." Statute not found; released into crowd of whites standing about. Local volunteer hit hard in jaw by white man.

Starkville: Police Chief followed two volunteers to various stops in Negro cafes, delivered lengthy "anti-agitator" speech directed at local Negroes talking to volunteers. Lengthy verbal abuse by police chief, directed to the voter-registration workers.

JULY 19: Columbus: Two voter registration workers detained in jail in Aberdeen for four hours after being picked up as suspicious strangers and refusing to be driven out of town and left on highway by police.

Greenwood: Mass arrest victims still at city jail and county farm. No visiting privileges at Farm--among those there is a 78 year-old man who is in need of medicine which no one has been able to bring to him.

(over)

JULY 19: <u>Oxford</u>: An Ole Miss student who has contacts at Rust College (Negro) had his seat covers slashed while car parked outside faculty home, threatening note left. He has had much harassment before, but cannot get administration to act.

<u>Biloxi</u>: Voter registration worker chased, threatened by two men in pick-up truck;

<u>Biloxi</u>: White Community Project worker arrested for trespass in white restaurant where he had worked for one day until owner discovered he was a civil rights worker. Owner turned him into police when he went back to restaurant.

<u>Batesville</u>: Town marshals threatened volunteers at mass meeting in Crowder (13-15 miles away). Said "Lucky I have no gun in here...wish I didn't have my badge on..."

JULY 20: <u>Greenville</u>: Nine shots fired at car workers went to mass meeting in. Two workers threatened that white mob would form at place where they were staying.

<u>Hattiesburg</u>: White volunteer beaten downtown as left bank with two other freedom school teachers. Assailant hit from behind. No words exchanged. Volunteers and attacker charged with assault.

<u>Ruleville</u>: Two workers ordered out of cafe. Doors locked with people inside.

<u>Greenwood</u>: Both barrels of shotgun fired at worker's car.

<u>Greenwood</u>: Trial of mass arrest victims held despite filing of petition to remove case to federal courts. Defendants remained mute on basis of violation of constitutional rights. Convicted of violation of picket law--30 days, $100 fine.

<u>Clarksdale</u>: Three workers (girls) of newly formed Clarksdale Youth Action Group arrested for trespass outside local cafe in Negro section.

<u>McComb</u>: SNCC field secretary hit on side of head by white man as both stopped their cars for red light at intersection of two state roads and federal highway_{while}

JULY 21: <u>Lexington</u>: Volunteer hit in face and body with fists by white man/waiting outside courthouse to take part in voter registration campaign.

<u>Laurel</u>: Rights workers believe the second ouster of summer project workers from a rented office here this summer is due to "intimidation" of local Negro realtors by white persons opposed to the Project.

<u>Clarksdale</u>: Volunteer arrested for running red light, paid fine.

<u>Holly Springs</u>: $200 bond levied on volunteer for failure to have a car inspection sticker.

<u>McComb</u>: Freedom School enrollment reaches 75 in this "hard core" area.

<u>Greenwood</u>: Windows of three Negro cafes broken. Windows of volunteer's car also broken.

<u>Natchez</u>: Within 45 minutes after 3 SNCC workers arrived in this area to set up a Summer Project office, one is arrested for failure to stop at stop sign. Police Chief tells him police knew of their movements "every minute of the day." Continual following by police.

<u>Doodleville</u>: Three Negro youths in company of white volunteer picked up and held for "investigation" at Club 400 by police. Volunteer later arrested for "improper tags." Negro youths released on bond; amount not known.

<u>Clarksdale</u>: Two precinct meetings of the Mississippi Freedom Democratic Party attracted 160 persons here.

JULY 22: <u>Jackson</u>: Volunteer beaten with billy clubs by two whites at a major downtown intersection. Police officer who returned the beaten volunteer and two colleagues to the COFO office indicated that a complaint had been filled out and a pick-up call had been issued for any cars matching the assailants!

<u>McComb</u>: Mt. Vernon Missionary Baptist Church, organized more than 80 years ago, found burned. FBI, sheriff, and police uncovered no clues. Fire officially listed as "of undetermined origin." Neither the pastor nor his church is in any way affiliated with the civil rights movement.

(more)

-11-11

JLY 22: **Tchula:** Driver of car carrying man who attacked volunteer here yesterday reportedly arrested.

Natchez: Local Negro taken into police custody today while walking along street with two SNCC field secretaries.

Greenville: Local Negro arrested for forgery while passing out voter registration leaflets with several other local citizens. After being questioned about civil rights activity here released for lack of evidence on forgery charge.

Natchez: Mayor tells SNCC field secretary that most of the nationally publicized shipment of arms to white terrorist groups in this area has been done in Adams Co., as opposed to the city. Police continue to follow the SNCC workers "every minute."

JLY 23: **Tchula:** SNCC staff member followed out of Jackson, arrested by police on speeding charge

Canton: White volunteer and Negro CORE staff member harassed by a group of white men while canvassing for voter registration. CORE staffer struck five times with wooden cane by one of the whites. The workers were on porch of some potential Negro registrants when white drove up.

Moss Pt.: Volunteer arrested today for improper turning, released on $40 bond.

Durant: Volunteer assailed today while canvassing for voter registration. Two white men approached him and asked what it would take to get him out of town; volunteer replied he was not quite ready to leave. After approximately 10 minutes of talk, one man began to punch him, then left after several minutes of blows.

Granada: SNCC staff member arrested for speeding.

Moss Pt.: At mass meeting last night, $33 was collected for a woman who lost her job two weeks ago for housing COFO volunteers. Several people pledge to give 50¢ a week indefinitely to help pay hospital expenses of local resident who received back and side wounds when shots were fired into voter registration mass meeting July 6.

Shaw: Local white woman tells local Negro woman that she plans to watch mail and those Negroes who get letters from "freedom riders" (presumably Summer Project volunteers) would "get hell after they leave." Mail is picked up at a post office box.

Jackson: Surprise—police court acquits three local youths on public drunk charges. Trio were arrested July 21 in Club 400 at Doodleville.

Harmony: Local residents plan to start construction of a wooden frame building for use as a permanent Community Center to be staffed by Project volunteers.

Meridian: Hearing continued to July 30 for omnibus suit filed against Ku Klux Klan, Sheriff Rainey, Deputy Sheriff Price, the White Citizens Council, and others in attempt to enjoin acts of violence on the part of defendants and the classes of officials and citizens they represent. This hearing is the first of its kind in Mississippi.

LY 24: **Holly Springs:** Voter registration worker arrested for "disturbing the public peace" at a Holly Springs Freedom Day, is being held on $500 bond. Volunteer charged with "using profanity in front of more than two people" after using two-way radio to inform office of profanities local policeman told potential Negro registrants on court house steps. Police insisted that the 40-50 potential registrants walk to the courthouse steps one by one, eight feet apart, and have a police escort from steps to registrar's office. Approximately 55 helmeted highway patrolmen and 35 helmeted local police were stationed at the courthouse for Freedom Day. Their presence in such numbers prompted cancellation of planned integrated picketing of the courthouse.

McComb: Amite County's Rose Hill Church reported burned last night. Owner of a local Negro club near Freedom House arrested and beaten. Officer tells owner "Now that you've got white folks in here, you're getting uppity."

Ruleville: A Negro woman ordered off the bus and handled roughly by driver when she sat down next to white man. All but two passengers got off.

Ruleville: Rabbi and Summer volunteer are "forcibly ejected" from office of Drew City attorney where they had gone to attend a meeting of the parents of children detained and then released July 15. (over)

12-12-12

JULY 24: <u>Jackson</u>, <u>Meridian</u>: FDP holds precinct meetings.

JULY 25: <u>Greenwood:</u> Ten to 15 workers handing out Freedom Registration forms prompt at least three incidents: 1) SNCC worker Eli Zeretsky approached by three whites who took his clip board from him and tore up forms. Police stood by, refused to act unless Zeretsky knew assailants' names and filed complaint with a judge; 2) white volunteer Adam Kline was jumped from behind and hit on head, police refused aid; 3) volunteer William Hodes, white, threatened by local whites in presence of police who refused to make arrest and refused to give name of citizen involved so that complaint could be filed.

<u>Greenwood:</u> Shot fired at home of Silas McGhee, the young man whose beating in local movie theater prompted first arrests under the 1964 Civil Rights Act.

<u>Canton</u>: First FDP county convention adopted resolution of loyalty to principles of National Democratic Party for strong and enforceable civil rights plank in platform. Approximately 300 people attend, of whom 102 wer voting delegates elected by precincts.

<u>Hattiesburg</u>: Home of two local FDP leaders bombed between 1 and 4 a.m. Broken whiskey bottle found indicated "molotov cocktail" type of device. Used on home of Mr. and Mrs. Boyd, FDP temporary chairman and secretary.

<u>Ruleville</u>: Rock smashed windshield of local Negro housing civil rights workers; car parked in his yard.

<u>Drew</u>: Affidavit received from parent of one of Negro children arrested after July 15 rally: mayor and city attorney called meeting of parents, told them defense would not be provided unless children signed statement disavowing association with "the communists coming into town." According to affidavit, city attorney called Congressman Don Edwards (D-Cal) a communist and said Edwards has been "Castro's secretary." Summer volunteer and rabbi were forcibly ejected from room when they tried to attend the meeting yesterday.

<u>Clarksdale</u>: Bottle thrown through office window last night.

(more)

268

13-13-13

JULY 26: <u>McComb</u>: Two bombs were thrown at the home of a local civil rights leader. As the first bomb was thrown, leader's wife fired at car with shotgun. When car's lights were seen approaching again, her husband ran outside but was knocked to ground by second explosion before he had time to fire. About 50 people attended a voter registration meeting at this home today.

<u>Batesville</u>: Tear gas bomb explodes behind home in which five civil rights workers are living, forcing occupants to leave. Sheriff and deputy arrived approximately 30 minutes later, found grenade still hot, handled it a good deal so that FBI found it covered with police fingerprints.

<u>Mileston</u>: SNCC car burned outside home housing volunteers.

<u>Mileston</u>: Volunteer approached in store by two whites who ask where he lived. He pointed to Community Center. They go to their car, take a pistol each from trunk, put them in their belts, come back and tell volunteer they would "find out what was going on" when they "came back."

<u>Canton</u>: Church Council of Canton voted in June to keep all summer civil rights workers from attending services. One Presbyterian church took exception and admitted volunteers until today, when two white volunteers were turned away by three white men who told them they had "caused too much dissension in church." At a Methodist Church, four white volunteers were refused attendance for third week in row. As they left church, a group assembled around their car, shoved them into the car, and slammed the door with such force the window cracked. Their car was followed to its destination by pick-up truck.

<u>Greenwood</u>: Silas McGee, the young man whose July 16 beating led to first arrests under civil rights act, and his brother Jake are mobbed by 150-200 whites as they leave theater after they walked from theater to car. Jake hit repeatedly by whites. Both receive cuts and abrasions of face and shoulders and glass in eyes when a coke bottle is thrown through car window. Both treated at LeFlore Co. Hospital, then trapped there with SNCC staff members until 1 a.m. as cars of armed whites blocked all roads leading out of hospital. FBI, local police, highway patrol, and sheriff refuse protection out of hospital, until 1 a.m. After more than three hours of waiting behind locked doors, the sheriff followed SNCC staff and McGee car to their destinations.

JULY 27: <u>Jackson</u>: Aaron Henry, Ed King, Mrs. Victoria Gray replied publicly to Sen. Douglas' (D-Ill.) "conciliatory suggestion" that no Mississippians be seated at convention or the delegation be half Dixiecrat, half Democratic: "we are dubious of value of delegation that is half-slave, half-free."

<u>Canton</u>: On arrival at bus station, five NCC ministers are threatened by seven local whites. When ministers try to leave station in car with two local Negro housewives, their car is trapped in narrow, one-way alley for two hours. One local white stops his car in front of them, the other stops in rear. Separate crowds of 100 whites, 50 Negroes gather. Local Negro alerts CORE staff, who send pick-up truck to scene and persuade local sheriff to let ministers drive out of alley.

<u>Greenwood</u>: Brick thrown through window of Negro barbershop in neighborhood where Freedom Registration was held.

<u>McComb</u>: White volunteer arrested for "failure to yield the right of way" as he drives a group of local Negro children for voter registration canvassing and leaflet distribution for an FDP precinct meeting. Fined $16.50.

<u>Mayersville</u>: Precinct meeting held in Moon Lake Baptist Church. Owner of plantation across street threatened to burn the church if any more civil rights meetings were held there. (2,399 Negroes here out of total population of 3,576.)

<u>Batesville and Holly Springs</u>: Precinct and county meetings.

<u>Gulfport</u>: Precinct meetings.

JULY 28: <u>Itta Bena</u>: Voter registration house broken into during night. Front porch supports broken, leaving badly sagging roof. Door half torn off, all windows broken. Posters urging citizens to vote for Fannie Lou Hamer in Democratic primary ripped off. Volunteers have received several threatening phone calls about the house and voter registration activities there.

<u>Holly Springs</u>: Police cars surrounding school where FDP precinct meeting was being held are themselves surrounded by approximately 200 Negro FDP participants singing freedom songs. Participants gathered around cars as they left school late at night. Police record license of every car at school, stop about 70 drivers to check licenses, arrest five on various traffic charges. School superintendent said he would burn or tear down school if meeting were held there.

<u>Vicksburg</u>: Precinct meetings--FDP <u>Clarksdale</u>: FDP county meeting. (over)

14-14-14

JULY 29: <u>Hollandale</u>: A Negro SNCC staff member chased from a traditionally white barber shop by a razor-wielding barber: "If you don't get out of here, I'll kill you."

<u>Ruleville</u>: A plantation worker fired for being a freedom registrant and attending two voter registration rallies. Plantation renter tells Negro: "get off the place and don't come back. You're messed up in the voter registration and I don't want to have anything to do with you." (This type of incident occurs often; it is seldom reported in detail.)

<u>Greenville</u>: FDP precinct meetings. <u>Gulfport</u>: County meeting—FDP.

JULY 30: <u>Meridian</u>: The Mount Moriah Baptist Church, a Negro church located in a completely white neighborhood, burned to ground last night. Although many homes are located close to the site, the fire department was not notified until too late to halt the fire.

<u>Gulfport</u>: Local Negro volunteer forced into car at gunpoint last night, blindfolded, and taken into a room at a location he guessed to be Biloxi. Five men question him at length about COFO activities. They offer to pay him well for information about people and organizations who contact COFO. He was not injured or molested, except for one man repeatedly poking him with a gun. FBI investigating.

<u>Drew</u>: Negro SNCC volunteer and Ruleville Negro volunteer arrested in Drew for distributing leaflets for FDP on public property without permit. Total bond for two: $600.

<u>Meridian</u>: County meeting. <u>Laurel</u>: Precinct and county meetings.

JULY 31: <u>Brandon</u>: Pleasant Grove Missionary Baptist Church burned to ground last night. Fire department came to scene, left before fire put out, stating they had "been called too late." A butane tank was buried next to church. FBI investigating.

<u>Carthage</u>: Rev. Edward K. Heininger, NCC volunteer, and John Polacheck, summer volunteer, brutally beaten in office of Dr. Thaggard Sr. in Madden today. Polacheck had gone to clinic yesterday for medical treatment, but left when he was told to go to Negro waiting room (he is white). He came back today with minister, and both were met in waiting room by doctor who began berating Heininger for his civil rights work. While they were talking, Heininger was hit from behind. Polacheck estimates that between 5 and 10 men beat them for approximately 5 minutes. Heininger reported that the doctor pushed him from the front into the punches of his assailants. Heininger was knocked unconscious, suffered severe injury to the left eye with possible internal injury to the eye, severe lacerations of scalp and face, contusions on back of neck, bad cut on left ear, and swelling of mouth and lips with possible injury to gums. Polacheck got to their car parked outside clinic and pulled in the minister who was on his back outside the car. One of several whites standing around car grabbed keys. A deputy sheriff arrived, handcuffed Heininger and Polacheck and jailed them for disturbing peace: the doctor had reported they had used profanity. They were released on cash bond of $100 each after being brought to station in a nonofficially marked pick-up truck and car. Trial set for Sug. 27.

<u>Meridian</u>: White summer volunteer arrested for reckless driving and speeding. He was not informed of charges until after being held at police station under arrest. At station, he was asked whether he was "sure" what his race is, and was hit on hand when reached for ticket to see what charges were being placed against him.

<u>Greenwood</u>: Silas McGhee and a summer volunteer arrested for driving with improper vehicle license. Both cars had temporary 7-day Tennessee license tags. Negro SNCC worker reported the arrests to Greenwood office over car radio, then was arrested for resisting arrest. Total bond: $200.

<u>Batesville</u>: Three shots fired late last night past Negro home where five volunteers stay. July 26 the same home was tear gas bombed. A local white reportedly has threatened to kill the home owner if he does not oust the volunteers.

<u>Shaw</u>: Three white volunteers made to leave Negro high school cafeteria where they had been invite to a fund-raising supper. They were warmly received by students and supervising teacher, but were told by principal they must first secure permission of superintendent to enter school. One volunteer called this an "excellent demonstration of the fact that not only Negroes but whites also are not free in Mississippi."

<u>Ruleville</u>: Precinct meetings.

(more)

5-15-15

AUG. 1: Holly Springs: Wayne Yancy, 21-year-old volunteer from Chicago, killed in head-on collision here today. He was passenger in car driven by SNCC worker Charles Scales. Both are Negro. Highway patrol claimed Scales passed another car near hill crest, crossed yellow line, hit oncoming car. He was charged with manslaughter, hospitalized with injuries. SNCC staffer and summer volunteer nurse who tried to visit him were bodily thrown out of hospital in Memphis, Tenn.

Greenwood: Two local Negro volunteers arrested for disorderly conduct in front of store belonging to police officer Henderson, who dragged a pregnant Negro woman on pavement during Freedom Day demonstration. At police station, officers twisted one volunteer's arms behind him, kicked him, shoved his head three times against a concrete wall, hit him in mouth with stick, shoved and kicked him into cell, kicked him 7 more times after he fell to floor--and then refused him a doctor. Bail originally set at $50 each. White volunteer arrested same night on Negro business street. He was treated roughly by police during arrest. Officers pushed, kicked and stamped on his feet at station. FBI visited him within minutes of his confinement to ask if he had been beaten. Bond originally set at $100. When SNCC workers arrived to bail out all three, they discovered bond had been raised to $200 each. All three were bailed out.

Canton: Six civil rights workers--five white, one Negro--handing out Freedom Registration forms in downtown Canton jailed.

Vicksburg: FDP county meeting held at Courthouse, first FDP meeting to be held in govt. building.

Ruleville, Moss Pt., Jackson: County meetings.

McComb: "In White America" production at Freedom School.

AUG. 2: Greenwood: Summer volunteer arrested on Justice of Peace warrant for assault with deadly weapon. Arrest apparently connected with breaking of window in store owned by police officer Henderson. Volunteer not near store, but had been calling jail all night to obtain information on other arrests. She was held for four hours and released on $1,000 bond.

Greenwood: Annie Lee Turner, the pregnant 15-year-old Greenwood Negro whom officer Henderson reportedly dragged across the pavement during Freedom Day, arrested today while among group of local youth gathered in front of Henderson's store. Henderson came, ordered them to disperse, then reportedly dragged Mrs. Turner to waiting police car. She was held on $50 bond for disturbing the peace. A police blockade, with tear gas equipment, was maintained at Henderson's store for 2 hours.

Greenwood: Local resident arrested today while in his front yard. He reported that police car drove by, an officer made obscene gestures, the Negro laughed, the car backed up, and the Negro was arrested for profanity. Bond: $50.

Greenwood: Shortly after midnight four shots were fired at SNCC office from passing car.

Jackson: Report of local Negro man beaten very badly after being arrested for an accident.

Natchez: Passing car fires shots at Archie Curtis Funeral Home. Curtis was beaten last Feb. by hooded men on desolate road outside city. He was lured to spot by unidentified caller who told him a woman was dying of heart attack. Earlier, Curtis had participated in vote drive.

Canton: Shot fired from car passing approximately 50 feet from Freedom House.

Greenville: County meeting, FDP.

Hattiesburg: "In White America" tours Freedom Schools.

AUG. 3: Columbus: Police arrest Negro volunteer for driving without a license and charge SNCC project director with allowing him to do so. Bail set at $300 and $100, respectively.

Batesville: SNCC project director Charles Weaver and summer volunteer Benjamin Graham arrested while trying to get names of 25 potential Negro voter registrants lined up outside courthouse. Weaver arrested while talking with another volunteer, who had been ordered out of courthouse by registrar. Graham arrested when he inquired what police were doing to Weaver. Both charged with interfering with officer. (The registrar is under federal injunction to facilitate registration.)

Greenwood: White volunteer arrested on John Doe warrant for assault and battery. Arrest stems from his participation in Freedom Registration Drive. Elderly white man with limp came up while volunteer was distributing FDP registration forms Aug. 1 and stepped on his foot. He asked if volunteer wanted

(over)

16-16-16

to "punch me in the face." Volunteer did not reply. Today he was picked up from across the street from Greenwood SNCC office. Two police, one with club, served warrant and grabbed him. He is held on $100 bond. (This is 8th arrest in Greenwood this weekend. At least three of previous arrests involved extensive police brutality at jail.)

Jackson: Local Negro volunteer arrested for vagrancy in front of drugstore near his home. He had an SNCC button on his shirt, reportedly did not have his draft card with him. He is held on $225 property bond.

Clarksdale: White Church of Christ minister and white summer volunteer refused admission to white Church of Christ. Church members felt they were "exploiting the church."

AUG. 4: Washington, D.C.: FBI announces that two of three bodies found near Philadelphia last night have been identified as Andrew Goodman and Michael Schwerner. (Third subsequently identified as James Chaney.)

Shaw: Negro schools closed indefinitely following student boycott. This was triggered by Negro principal's request that three white volunteers leave cafeteria where they'd been invited for school fund-raising dinner last Friday. Students declared boycott of cafeteria, asked Student Union to assemble their grievances, then called a general boycott of the schools which was supported by 75 per cent of students. The Union called the boycott "because of the inadequate education we're getting." Its demands included up-to-date texts, a well-stocked library with Negro history materials, workshops and laboratories, foreign languages and other courses needed for college entrance. Principal relayed these requests to white school superintendent, then notified students schools would be closed. Heavily armed sheriff's deputies in helmets soon arrived on scene.

Moss Pt.: Approximately 62 people arrested during voter registration meeting held on front lawn of SNCC office. Five were civil rights workers, rest local Negro citizens. The orderly meeting had been in process for 15 minutes when an assistant deputy sheriff gave the group 5 minutes to disperse. Group stayed. Within minutes 18 helmeted policemen with guns, bayonets, and clubs surrounded them; 15 minutes later a prison bus drove up. Ten police cars and two motorcycles--total of 40 officers--accumulated. All at meeting were put in bus and taken to jail. They were held for breach of the peace on $300 cash or $600 property bond each.

Cleveland: Fifty potential Negro registrants lined up at courthouse this morning, accompanied by 13 civil rights workers. Negroes were admitted one by one at 45 minute intervals. Leaflets were given them without incident. But when civil rights workers moved across street, all 13 arrested for distributing pamphlets among pedestrians. Charges based on anti-litter ordinance. Bond: $300 each.

Marks: LCDC attorney received head injuries, including large gash over one eye, when he was thrown against police car by city marshal. Attorney arrested for "obstructing officer in performance of duties" and held on $200 bail. He had gone to Marks to check detention of voter registration worker, when he saw marshal had stopped car filled with civil rights workers. He went over to investigate and the incident followed.

Jackson: After being refused service at small cafe, local volunteer chased by white man in pick-up truck who fired two shots at him.

McComb: Pete Seeger held folk music workshops at McComb Freedom School this morning following evening concert last night.

Hattiesburg: Seeger conducted folk music workshops in two Freedom Schools this afternoon. "In White America" at the Freedom Schools here.

Meridian: Community concert by Seeger in support of Summer Project. Four people refused service at supposedly integrated "Dairy Queen." Bus driver refused to pick up person wearing CORE shirt.

Cleveland: Car with 3 or 4 armed whites circled house of local volunteer between midnight and 1 a.m., parked briefly about 100 yards from her home.

AUG..5: McComb: Two teen-age Negro boys, students at McComb Freedom School, have received harassing phone calls from two white girls. Boys were arrested few days ago, and yesterday were sentenced to year in jail each under Mississippi's recent phone harassment law.

Natchez: Mt. Pilgrim Baptist church in Finwick reported burned last night.

(more)

G. 5: <u>Shaw</u>: Thirty-five parents are organizing association to meet with school board and high school
17-17 faculty. In addition to students' demands which led to boycott and closing of schools, parents
will take action against inadequate school lunch program, problems of split session and mechanics
of desegregation in school system there.

<u>Jackson</u>: Community concert by Pete Seeger. <u>Gulfport</u>: Free Southern Theater production of
"In White America."

JG. 6: <u>Jackson</u>: Approximately 300 delegates from precinct meetings and county conventions attended
first State Convention of the Mississippi Freedom Democratic Party. Alternates and observers
bring total attendance to 1,000. Slate of 68 delegates and alternates was elected to represent
Mississippi at National Democratic Convention. Hattiesburg housewife Mrs. Victoria Gray
elected National Committeewoman, and Rev. Ed King, white chaplain of Mississippi's private,
interrracial Tougaloo College elected National Committeeman. Dr. Aaron Henry, Clarksdale
pharmacist and president of state NAACP, named permanent chairman of Convention, and
chairman of National Convention delegation. After Convention, newly elected State Executive
Committee named Pass Christian resident Laurence Guyot chairman and Hattiesburg resident
Mrs. Peggy J. Connor secretary of Party. Mrs. Fannie Lou Hamer, candidate for Congress in
Mississippi's 2nd District, named vice-chairman of delegation and Mrs. Annie Devine of
Canton, secretary. Address of keynoter Miss Ella J. Baker, currently coordinator of Washington
office of FDP, received standing ovation and sparked spontaneous marching and Freedom song in hall.
Among resolutions adopted were statement of loyalty to Natl. Democratic Party platform & candidates.

<u>Gulfport</u>: "In White America," Free Southern Theater production, at Freedom Schools.

JG. 7: <u>Meridian</u>: Over 200 persons gathered at four churches to take part in memorial procession for slain
civil rights worker James Chaney. Walking in silence, two abreast, in somber dress, the mourners
joined approximately 400 others for memorial service at First Union Church. Procession and service
followed private burial of Chaney in Meridian. Immediately following service, Free Southern
Theater production of "In White America" was presented at church in conjunction with Freedom
School convention which began here tonight.

<u>Jackson</u>: A. Phillip Randolf, president of American Negro Labor Council and longtime head of
Brotherhood of Sleeping Car Porters, addressed mass meeting of students and parents of Jackson
Freedom schools which opened this week.

<u>Aberdeen</u>: Integrated group refused service at Tom Restaurant and Elkin Theater.

<u>Jackson</u>: SNCC staffer Ivanhoe Donaldson arrested for improper driver's license. He was not in
car at time of arrest. There were four integrated cars in front of house at which he was picked up.
Bond: $50

<u>Jackson</u>: White co-ed volunteer Mary Zeno and local Negro volunteer Rommie Drain chased by
white man with pistol in belt as they canvassed for voter registration.   lane.

<u>Jackson</u>: Freedom School coordinator Tom Wahman arrested and fined $17 for failing to yield proper/

G. 8: <u>Jackson</u>: N.Y. pathologist David M. Spain, M.D., reported today after post-mortem examination
of body of James Chaney, "in lay terminology--the jaw was shattered, the left shoulder and upper
arm were reduced to a pulp; the right forearm was broken completely across at several points, and
the skull bones were broken and pushed in toward the brain. Under the circumstances, these injuries
could only be the result of an extemely severe beating with either a blunt instrument or chain. The
other fractures of the skull and ribs were the result of bullet wounds. It is impossible to determine
whether the deceased died from the beating before the bullet wounds were inflicted. In my extensive
experience of 25 years as a pathologist and as a medical examiner, I have never witnessed bones so
severely shattered, except in tremendously high speed accidents such as airplane crashes."

<u>Hattiesburg</u>: Two men, Clifton Archie Keys, 51, and his nephew Estus Keys, 31, were tried today
for the July 10 beating of Rabbi Arthur Lelyveld, 51, of Cleveland, Ohio. Pair pleaded nolo
contendre, waived arraignment, and paid fines of $500 each. They also received 90 day suspended
sentences on condition of good behavior. The charge was changed by District Attorney James
Finch from assault and battery with intent to maim to simple assault and battery.

<u>Meridian</u>: Approximately 150 outstanding students from throughout state gathered for Freedom School
Convention here today. Resolutions brought by student delegates from their community Freedom
Schools were divided into four groups: Foreign Relations, Medical Care, Education, and Public
Accommodations, and workshops held in each area. "Seeds of Freedom," a Holly Springs Freedom
School production based on life and death of Medgar Evers, was performed during evening, as well
as Free Southern Theater production of "In White America."   (over)

AUG. 8: **Tallahatchie**: Four members of a local family--the first Negro family to attempt to register to vote
18-18-18 from this county in several decades--have been steadily harassed since they attempted to register last
Tuesday. On Tuesday night two truckloads of whites with guns came by at 6 p.m., 10 p.m., and
3 a.m. shouting obscenities and threats. They have been back several times, and the family is
now afraid to go to work in the fields. The County Registrar is currently under a court injunction to
determine the qualification of Negro registrants by the same standards as whites, not to limit Negro
registrants to coming in one at a time, and not to use the constitutional interpretation section of
the registration form. Approximately 70 per cent of the county's population is Negro. SNCC voter
registration activity began here two weeks ago.

> **Shaw**: Two cross burnings here were reported night of Aug. 6-7. Both were apparently intended
> to frighten local families involved in civil rights work.

AUG. 9: **Mileston**: Shortly after midnight a bomb was thrown in road approximately 40 yards from new Freedom
Center. Thrown by whites from passing car, the bomb left a hole approximately one foot deep and
5 or 6 feet wide in road. There were no injuries.

> **Aberdeen**: Two or three cannisters of tear gas were found on lawn of Freedom House here. Local
> police arrived and removed cannisters before FBI could take fingerprints.

> **Canton**: "In White America" produced here tonight.

AUG. 10: **Marigold**: An elderly Negro man was shot to death in a gas station here this morning. Although
reports vary, it seems confirmed that the man ordered gas and either had forgotten his billfold and
could not pay, or received more gas than he had ordered and refused to pay for the extra. The
gas station attendant began to beat him. A local policeman shot and killed the Negro who was unarmed

> **Aberdeen**: Two local Negro voter registration workers were stopped and given speeding tickets here
> after they and approximately 20 other Negroes attempted to integrate the downstairs section of the
> Elkins movie theater. CDC lawyer Abe Weitzman and law student Richard Wheelock were harassed
> as they observed the integration attempt. Their car was kicked by local white citizen, and they were
> stopped and questioned by police. They were followed back to Columbus by police car and carload
> of whites. The two given speeding tickets were driving 25 mph in a 30 mph zone. A third local
> Negro who participated in integration attempt was ticketed for improper lights. His lights were in o

> **Canton**: "In White America" presented here tonight.

AUG. 11: **Glucksdadt**: Mt. Pleasant Church in Gluckstadt burned to ground last night. It had been used daily
as Freedom School site. Within minutes after leaving site, white volunteer Jim Ohls arrested for
reckless driving.

> **Aberdeen**: White volunteer Joel Bernard attacked by local white man today while engaged in voter
> registration canvassing. Volunteer was with local Negro filling out Freedom Registration form when
> white man drove up in pick-up truck, questioned him about what he was doing, struck him to ground
> and punched him several times. Bernard managed to break away, and was searching for telephone
> when police car passed by. White he was explaining incident to police, his attacker--who had been
> following in his truck--came out and began threatening once again. Bernard taken to station for
> questioning, was refused use of telephone, and was refused protection back to office. He sustained
> bruises and grazed arm.

> **Ruleville**: Mrs. Fannie Lou Hamer, candidate for Congress suffered brutal beating in County jail in
> Winona for her voter registration activities, is again being theatened. One of men involved in her
> earlier beating has been passing by her home today in pick-up truck, pointing her out to a series of
> companions. Mrs. Hamer, who suffered a permanent back injury from her earlier beating, states
> she feels the man "is up to something drastic."

> **Cleveland**: Preliminary hearing held this morning on fatal shooting yesterday of 60-year-old Negro
> Neimiah Montgomery by police officer Leonard Yarborrow of Marigold force. Witnesses testified
> that Montgomery went berserk soon after he drove into station, when attendant asked to be paid.
> Montgomery reportedly ran across highway to trailer and got hammer, then threatened to kill woman
> Service station attendant got an axe handle and he and Montgomery struggled for it. Officer
> Yarborrow arrived and reportedly tried to subdue Montgomery. Officer shot him twice, both bullets
> going into heart. This was viewed at hearing as justifiable homicide while acting in line of duty.

> **Anguilla**: Two local Negro civil rights workers, Louis Grant and Bob Wright, arrested this evening
> while handing out leaflets advertising Freedom Day in Rolling Fork. Leaflets urged voter registratio
> (Bond set later at $200 on anti-littering charge.)   (more)

Appendix

UG. 12: Aberdeen: Potential Negro registrants taken to Courthouse today found it closed. Officials there said registrar was sick. There is no deputy registrar.

Greenwood: Six local Negro youths arrested today while standing in front of Doris' store in Baptist Town, singing. At least one beaten. Doctor and nurse dispatched to jail. Charges unknown.

Charleston: 24 Negro citizens attempted to register at Tallahatchie Co. Courthouse here yesterday. Approximately 93 armed whites gathered. Cars and trucks with guns prominently displayed were double- and triple-parked in front of courthouse. Potential registrants were able to take test quickly as registrar is under Federal injunction to cease discrimination. Sheriff also under Federal injunction restraining him from intimidating Negro applicants.

Ruleville: Students at local Negro school organizing to force teachers to register to vote. Only one is registered. They are also pressing to improve school conditions, and to stop practice of students financing school's operations. Classes reportedly have class field days when students go out in field and pick cotton to raise money for school.

Ruleville: Mrs. Hamer threatened with murder in telephone call to her home tonight.

Oak Ridge (near Vicksburg): Three people who have supported FDP beaten and shot at last night by men with hoods over their heads and in robes. Henry Ollins, his wife Lucy, and their next door neighbor Thomas Hick attacked by three carloads of men. Attackers broke doors of both houses and fired high-powered rifle at Hick's house. Both Mr. and Mrs. Ollins beaten; she sustained damaged hip, while he suffered rather severe beating, according to Vicksburg hospital. Hick managed to wrest hodd off one of men, and has delivered it to sheriff. According to MSP spokesman, "Warren Co. prides itself on not having a White Citizens Council, let alone a KKK."

Ocean Springs (near Gulfport): In two separate incidents, two local Negro men shot at here today. 19-year-old city employe Calvin Galloway cutting grass near beach when three white men drove by and fired pistol shots. Second incident involved man about 50, Barney Brooks. His attackers may have been same as those of Galloway. Neither was hit by shots.

Biloxi: Rental of local store for precinct meeting cancelled by owner today when SNCC poster put up. Local people reportedly told him they feared he was going to "move the nigras in."

Brandon: St. Matthews Baptist Church here burned to ground last night. Fire department spokesman told AP that department was unable to stop the fire.

Hattiesburg: Mrs. Dorethea Jackson, local Negro woman, arrested yesterday when she would not give her seat to white woman on bus. Mrs. Jackson reportedly was pulled off bus by policeman. She asserted that knife was planted in her purse. Charges as yet unkown.

Lexington: "In White America" produced here.

UG. 13: Canton: 18-year-old Gluckstadt Freedom school student, whose school site was burned to ground two days ago, arrested today for alleged reckless driving and attempting to run Constable Bruno Holly off road.

Ocean Springs: Report here of third shooting in 24 hours at local Negro citizens, none hit. Also here last night, three white women in pick-up truck attempted to run over local Negro woman.

Cleveland: Local Negro reported that Willie Carter, another Negro Cleveland resident, offered $200 by Shaw chief of police W.H. Griffin "to get rid of" three local Negroes--Elijah Smith, Aaron German, and Charles Bond--who are active in voter registration activity. Carter reportedly accepted offer, but second man reported it to COFO.

Columbus: Summer volunteer Ron Bridgeforth jailed at Starkville today on charges of refusing to be fingerprinted and photographed. He had gone to courthouse to pay parking fine. Bond: $500.

Ruleville: 19-year-old white volunteer Joseph Smith arrested this evening in Drew on charges of "conduct tending to incite a breach of peace" while passing high school campus. He is in Drew City jail; bond not set.

Greenwood: Production of "In White America."

UG. 14: McComb: Supermarket across street from church site of McComb Freedom School bombed before 1 a.m. today. All windows shattered and walls and roofing damaged. Blast, which left large hole in ground, almost knocked down voter registration worker in Freedom House two blocks away. (over)

20-20-20

AUG. 14 (Cont.): Immediately after explosion, white SNCC staffer Mendy Samstein ran outside, jumped into car, passed by car with two white men in it, followed car until he could record license; he had seen car before and found it listed on McComb SNCC's "suspicious car" list. Law student Clint Hopson arrested for interfering with officer as he worked his way through crowd at bomb site and spoke with one of officers there. He was released on $52.50 bail. Local voter registration worker Roy Lee arrested when he returned to scene of bombing and charged with inciting to riot, threatening life of policeman, cursing, and disorderly conduct. Being held on $900 bond. McComb SNCC spokesmen stated he was arrested for no apparent reason.

Natchez: Tavern next door to Freedom House here bombed tonight. Owners of tavern, an integrated couple, live in home attached to it. Tavern owned by Jake Fisherman and Evangeline Thronton. He is white, she, negro. Natchez SNCC spokesmen report that police were circulating through crowd of several hundred spectators, stating that "the wrong place" had been bombed. Firemen told one of voter registration workers there (whom they did not recognize) "those outside agitators are in that house. The bomb was set for that house. They're here to stir up trouble. George Greene rents that place." Greene is 20-year-old SNCC staff member working in Natchez.

Aberdeen: Elkins theater closed down today rather than integrate. There have been two integration attempts at theater Aug. 6 and 11.

Aberdeen: 24 voter registration workers had to wait outside courthouse here last night as local Negro volunteer Leon Smith tried for traffic violation. When Smith's lawyer inquired why workers were not permitted in courtroom, judge said, "I don't hold trials for monkeys." As workers waited outside, large group of whites gathered, many with baseball bats. This morning local volunteer Sammy Bets, who tried to attend trial, fired without being given any reason by his white employer, one of white crowd outside courthouse last night.

Aberdeen: Three local voter registration workers given traffic tickets as they drove home from registration meeting last night. This is third time this week that this form of harassment used by police.

Hattiesburg: Local Negro citizen Willie Mae Martin re-arrested last night in connection with charge of resisting arrest and interfering with police officer last March. Billy McDonald, another Hattiesburg Negro resident, and FDP chairman Lawrence Guyot arrested at same time, McDonald on same charge as Miss Martin and Guyot solely for interfering. Because of legal misunderstandings, three did not know they were scheduled to appear for hearing to be held six months after their charge. Miss Martin and McDonald assigned $200 bond and 30 days imprisonment, and Guyot $100 and 30 days. It is doubtful that Guyot will be released before the Democratic National Convention.

Ruleville: Local attorney has informed voter registration workers here that any white volunteer staying overnight in Negro section of Drew, a small town near here, would be arrested.

Columbus: Local voter registration volunteer John Luther Bell jailed at nearby West Point today on charges of larceny and disturbing peace. He was arrested while canvassing for potential Negro registrants. Bell was one of three outstanding students selected as delegate to Freedom School convention in Meridian Aug. 8-10.

Hattiesburg: Freedom School teacher Sandra Adickes, UFT volunteer, arrested today when she attempted to have six of her students check out books from public library deemed for whites only. After they were refused applications for cards, they sat down at tables to read magazines. Short time later police chief Hugh Herrin walked in and announced library was being closed. Everyone made to leave library, which Mayor Claude F. Pittman now states was closed for inventory. This is second time this year it has closed for inventory. Miss Adickes and students were followed by police from time they left library. They went to integrated lunch counter, where waitress said she would serve only Negroes. UFT volunteer arrested outside lunch counter and released under $100 bond on a vagrancy charge.

Greenwood: White women owners of grocery store here fired with shotguns on crowd of 75-100 Negro pickets today. Their "Happy Day" store has been object of civil rights boycott for past several days. There were no injuries reported. Police arrived shortly after shooting and dispersed pickets.

Columbus: LCDC Attorney Tom Connelly arrested on charges of reckless driving today after pick-up truck rammed into his parked car. Local white citizen Travis Hamilton ran his truck into Connelly's car, smashing door, shattering window, and injuring passenger and law student Richard Wheeler (cut on arm by flying glass). Connelly released after several hours on $110 bond.   (more)

21-21-21

AUG. 14 (cont.): As Connelly was being driven home from District Attorney's office by summer volunteer Steve Fraser, their car was met by highway patrol roadblock. Fraser was given ticket for improper license. Roadblock then ended.

Canton: Bullet fired at Freedom House at approximately 10 p.m. from passing car. No injuries or apparent damage. Police came immediately upon being informed and were cooperative.

Indianola: Local white resident Joe Hopkins today drove to Freedom School while classes in session, questioned volunteer about presence of NY reporter and Attorney Andrew Goldman, fumbled with rifle, drove off. Earlier, Hopkins told Negro family living next door to Freedom School site that civil rights workers "better get out of there." He said, "I'm going to blow up that place." Two Negro citizens also told summer volunteer that several white men planned to "shoot up the place" tonight. Local police stated they would patrol area all night.

AUG. 15: Jackson: Between 10:30 p.m. and 12:30 a.m., voter registration worker beaten over head with baseball bat outside COFO office, carload of one white and four local Negro voter registration workers was shot at 8 to 10 times, four crosses were burned simultaneously, and local student shot by white man: white volunteer Philip Hocker working on pick-up truck across street from COFO office as three other workers--two Negro, one white--sat in car behind him lighting his work with headlights. Another car doubleparked beside car and truck. Young white man wearing bermuda shorts went up to Hocker, hit him on back of head with bat, and continued to hit him after he fell to street. At 10:45 Hocker taken from office to Baptist hospital, still bleeding about the head. At 11 crosses burning at Lynch St. and Terry Rd. approximately three blocks from COFO office; at Sun-n-Sands Hotel, where many Project lawyers, doctors, ministers, and national press correspondents stay; at Millsaps College; and at Valley Rd. and Hwy.80, site of soon-to-be-integrated public school. White summer volunteer and four local Negro voter registration workers shot at 8 to 10 times by two white men in car as they drove through Jackson. Civil rights workers stopped when they saw parked police car. Officer, after hearing Smith's statement, sent out report over radio that "we got some colored people who say some niggers were shooting at them." As soon as Oldsmobile containing attackers came close, police drove off. Investigating plainclothesman found 5 bullets in the car. Willie Gynes was shot in leg by white man in car passing a teen dance here. Gynes is in the Emergency ward of University Hospital.

Meridian: Two local Negro voter registration volunteers, Sam Brown and David McClinton, and SNCC staffer Preston Ponder fired upon today while driving Hwy 11 in Jasper Co. Shot hit and cracked front window of trio's car as they returned from investigating beating several weeks ago of school teacher and her mother.

Greenwood: SNCC staffer Jesse Harris arrested today for disturbing peace. Arrest made under warrant, presumably in connection with boycott currently in operation against several stores here.

Greenwood: Silas McGhee, young man whose brutal beating led to first arrests under 1964 Civil Rights Act, shot in face tonight as he sat in car outside Lulu's restaurant. McGhee alone in car when shot fired by white man in passing car. He was rushed to University Hospital in Jackson in critical condition. McGhee initially brought to Leflore Hospital here. Staff reportedly unable to remove bullet which entered through left side of face near temple and lodged near left side throat. Two SNCC staffers refused admittance to hospital because they were not wearing shirts; they had taken off their shirts to help stop McGhee's bleeding.

Laurel: Volunteer and three local Negro voter registration workers beaten today after sitting down for service at theoretically integrated Kress' department store lunch counter. Ten whites approached as Levelle Keys, James House, Larry McGill and Ben Hartfield being served. Two of whites beat group with baseball bats. Hartfield knocked unconscious. Woman pulled pistol on McGill. His mother yelled "Don't kill my son" to woman who pulled pistol. For this remark, McGill's assailant reportedly filed assault charge against his mother. SNCC staffer Fred Richardson entered store earlier, was asked to leave because he had a camera. Richardson outside Kress' when incident occurred and was himself beaten by whites who gathered at scene when he called police. His camera taken by one of his attackers. Police arrived and warrants were sworn out against several of the attackers.

AUG. 16: McComb: McComb office raided at 1:30 a.m. by 24 policemen in five cars, representing city police, sheriffs and deputies, and highway patrol. Warrants were for illegal liquor. None was found, but officers spent good deal of time reading letters and literature found in office. (over)

277

22-22-22

AUG. 16 (cont.): The workers had just returned from an evening of canvassing bars and restaurants in McComb area, announcing rallies and Freedom Days. These were planned in response to a period of increased violence and harassment by local white community.

Greenwood: Several hundred local Negro citizens gathered at Friendship Baptist Church here to protest shooting of McGhee. Approximately 100 of those who had gathered in church came to SNCC office after meeting. Police in full riot garb, with tear gas equipment, blocked off both ends of street on which office is located until angry crowd dispersed.

Philadelphia: Memorial service held today for civil rights workers James Chaney, Michael Schwerner, and Andrew Goodman who were slain here June 21 after inspecting burned-out church site of a Freedom School.

Laurel: White volunteer David Goodyear beaten unconscious at gas station here today, and his companion, white volunteer Linnelle Barrett, was kicked and stepped upon. They were outside their car when two white men approached and asked if they were civil rights workers. When they replied "yes," several whites milling around closed in and began beating them. Police came in three cars immediately after being notified. Within an hour after incident, police--on basis of license number--picked up assailants' car. Gas station attendant closed station and left before police arrived. Two of Goodyear's teeth were loosened.

AUG. 17: Four voter registration workers, 3 white and 1 Negro, arrested on vagrancy charges here as they left public library which had refused them service. Susan Patterson, Ben Achtenburg, Tom Edwards, and Bill Jones held on $100 cash bond or $250 property bond. (Hattiesburg)

Ruleville: Three local Negro youths picked up by police here and held for half an hour for distributing announcements of tonight's production of "In White America."

Laurel: Anthony Lynn hit twice by passing white citizen as he stood on street corner here today. Lynn was with local Negro citizen whom he had just accompanied to courthouse to take voter registration test. Lynn called police and pointed out his assailant to them. Assailant denied everything; police had both file affidavits.

Gulfport: Volunteer Steve Miller badly beaten today by passing white man as he left Carnegie Library. Miller sustained severe bruises on jaw, right temple, and head, and is suffering from amnesia. County police officer arrived at scene, but left without providing any aid. Taxi then refused to take him to hospital. Civil rights workers arrived at hospital with Miller about one hour after beating. They were made to wait another two hours for doctor. Assailant walked by police officer and commented "I got me one." Workers went to city police, who refused to take action for lack of complaint. Warrant filed by one of witnesses at whom assailant had swung but not hit. Miller not capable of filing warrant. Sheriff is investigating.

Indianola: Approximately 25 white citizens, some of whom were reportedly White Citizen's Council members, attended this evening's performance of "In White America." Eight to 10 helmeted police arrived in two cars, said there would be no trouble. Play features integrated cast of 8; it describes suppressions and victories of American Negro in his own country.

Winona Co.: White volunteer Tim Morrison arrested here for faulty driver's license and fined $18.

Clarksdale: Franklin Delano Roosevelt III arrested and fined for speeding while going 25 mph in 35 mph zone. Roosevelt has been doing research on project to bring aid to civil rights workers.

AUG. 18: McComb: After series of bombings and intimidation, first Southwest Mississippi Freedom Day was peacefully conducted here today. 25 potential Negro registrants went to courthouse, 23 of whom permitted to take test. Registrar processed one applicant every 40 minutes. Police and FBI agents were at Pike Co. courthouse in Magnolia throughout day. (Of Pike Co.'s 35,063 Negro voting-age citizens, 207 (3%) registered, as contrasted to 9,989 registered whites representing 82.1%.) Over 200 local Negro citizens attended mass meeting here last night to protest terrorist activities brought against Negro citizens and voter registration workers in this hardcore area.

McComb: Attempted house-burning reported by SNCC spokesmen today. At 1:30 a.m. local Negro resident Vera Brown, whose daughter is active in civil rights movement here, woke up to smell of smoke. Gasoline-filled jar found smoking under house. Conflagration was smothered with little damage. Mrs. Brown plans to attempt to register as part of Freedom Day.

(more)

23-23

G. 18: <u>Philadelphia</u>: Shortly before 11 p.m., Aug. 15, cdr stopped across street from Freedom School head-quarters here and driver kept single-barreled shotgun pointed at office for about 5 minutes, left, and returned second time. When two Freedom School teachers filed warrant about incident with district attorney, official put on it that party was COFO worker who made $9.64 a week, "lives off people in community, and has no other visible means of support." Freedom School cordinator Ralph Featherstone refused to sign affidavit with this addition. His companion, volunteer Walter Kaufman, did sign complaint. Name of man with gun is known; action on case is awaited. Aug. 16 a rumor began spreading that office and motel across street from it, where workers eat, would be bombed. By Aug. 17 rumor was widespread--woman at motel was threatened and told workers she could not feed them any more. FBI watched office all night; local police took no action. This morning Deputy Sheriff Price, officer who arrested James Chaney, Michael Schwerner, and Andrew Goodman, came to office and took films of all workers. He came by three times. He reportedly has been questioning local Negro citizens as to the workers' activities. Today local Negro citizen beaten by white man when he went into store with Negro girl. Philadelphia staff reports man could be taken for white and was probably thought to be project worker. He came to office after leaving doctor's office. He was frightened and refused to contact local police. FBI contacted, and man questioned for about ½ hour. One agent reportedly was "very hostile."

<u>Greenwood</u>: Jake McGhee, younger brother of Silas, arrested here this morning for traffic violation. His mother, Mrs. Laura McGhee, hit in chest by desk sergeant when she went to pay fine. Mrs. McGhee hit officer in nose; officer went for gun. Greenwood staff members George Greene and Ed Rudd held policeman's hand til another officer came in and calmed him down. Jake fined $100 for improper license and impersonation. Warrant issued for Mrs. McGhee's arrest for assaulting office

<u>Jackson</u>: 17-year-old Negro from Columbus formally announced plans today to seek state charter for Mississippi Young Democrat Club. Melvin L. Whitfield assumed presidency of new Young Democratic group at their Aug. 10 convention in Meridian, which included representatives from about 25 Mississippi communities. He will represent body, along with 9 other Mississippi officers, at meeting of National Committee of Young Democratic Clubs of America Aug. 21-23 in Atlantic City. Group, thus far all-Negro, learned few weeks ago that existing Young Democratic organization in Mississippi has never been granted charter by national body. Spokesman noted, "Our organization, in keeping with principles stated in constitution of Young Democratic Clubs of America, is open to anyone who is between ages of 16 and 40 who 'professes and demonstrates allegiance to principles of National Democratic Party,' regardless of race or creed."

<u>Gulfport</u>: Man who yesterday beat volunteer Steve Miller today was arrested and charged with assault. Gulfport resident James Robert Thomas released on $200 bond. Thomas has only been charged with assault as warrant against him was filed by Miller's companion Charles Wheeler, who was not hit. Miller will swear out warrant when able.

<u>Vicksburg</u>: Early this morning, bottle hurled through window of barbershop owned by Mr. Eddie Thomas, Warren Co. FDP delegate.

<u>McComb</u>: As white volunteer Marshall Ganz drove back from Pike Co. courthouse in Magnolia to transport potential Negro registrants, he was followed by four men in unmarked pick-up truck. When he stopped at red light, one man quickly got out of truck and began running at him. Ganz quickly drove off and was followed by truck back to McComb. Passenger in truck threw bottle which narrowly missed going through window of Ganz' car.

<u>Natchez</u>: Five-gallon can of gasoline, a bomb-like apparatus, found under Blue Moon bar here. Bar belongs to Jake Fisher, whose brother's bar was found bombed in Louisiana over the weekend.

<u>Yazoo City</u>: Two local Negro citizens today filed applications for cards at local library here without incident. Police talked with two "politely" and later contacted mother of one.

<u>Shaw</u>: Three Negro members of Shaw Mississippi Student Union entered town library today and successfully registered for cards. When Eddie Short, James Johnson Jr., and Willie Wright left, they were followed by four police officers and watched by a number of bystanders.

G. 19: <u>Jackson</u>: Three busloads of FDP delegates and alternates to National Convention, as well as FDP staff members, left from Jackson amidst hundreds of well-wishers late this evening.

(over)

24-24-24

AUG. 19: <u>Jackson:</u> At conclusion of 3½-day staff meeting at Tougaloo College this weekend, Dir. Robert M announced that Mississippi Summer Project would not end. Speaking at press conference, Moses sa 200 of volunteers now in state plus 65 SNCC staff and about 30 CORE staff would stay in state throughout year. This figure does not include those who will come down for minimum stay of three months who have been applying for work during year since Summer Project began. Moses also note that medical, legal, and ministerial groups have announced plans to place Mississippi operations on a permanent basis.

<u>Natchez:</u> Owner of house rented by SNCC workers here has indicated he does not want to rent it civil rights workers for fear of bombing. Company holding house's insurance indicated it does not want to continue the policy on the house.

<u>Meridian:</u> Church burning reported in Collinsville.

<u>McComb:</u> Three potential Negro registrants in front of Pike Co. courthouse in Magnolia told they would be arrested if they did not move. Three sat in car for 30 minutes. Ten minutes later white volunteer Dave Gerber arrested for speeding enroute from courthouse to McComb. Bond: $22.50.

<u>Meridian:</u> Local Negro voter registration worker Sam Brown arrested on charges of disorderly conduct and resisting arrest tonight. Released on $50 bond.

<u>Philadelphia:</u> Increased harassment and intimidation efforts continue at Evers Motel headquarters c Neshoba Co. mobile Freedom School here. Between 8:55 and 9:15 p.m. two carloads and one tru of white men with rifles visible parked outside headquarters on outskirts of Philadelphia. Deputy Price observed smiling as one carload of whites told him, "We're gonna get the job done tonight." While carloads of whites parked or occupants milled about in front of office and other cars cruised in area, threatening phone calls received at approximate intervals of 5 minutes stating "Your time up." Calls continued til 4 a.m. New office opened Aug. 14 with 11 workers, four of them staff.

<u>Jackson:</u> At press conference, Project Dir. Robert Moses said "Voter registration drives will be increased across state. Campaigns will be intensified in Panola and Tallahatchie Co.'s, where recent court orders have opened new possibilities for work, and in other counties where legal relie appears imminent. Also under consideration are such new efforts as mobile libraries in rural areas, strengthening of citizens band radio security system, development of permanent community center facilities, and an adult literacy program specially designed by SNCC for the Black Belt."

AUG. 20: <u>Canton:</u> At 1:30 a.m. pick-up truck drove into driveway of Freedom House. Local Negro citize saw "third light" inside truck, in addition to two headlights. When truck's occupants noticed all observers they quickly drove off, and were reportedly observed trying to put out fire in bed of truc When witnesses got to street, they found gallon jug, broken, with oily rags sticking out at top.

<u>Philadelphia:</u> Neshoba Co. law enforcement has used questionable building lease to try to evict COFO workers from their newly opened office. At about 11 a.m. Deputy Cecil Price, Sheriff Rainey, and District Attorney Walter Jones presented an eviction notice, indicating that six COF workers then in office would be arrested if they had not left premises by 1 p.m. The law officers claimed the building lease was invalid, and that old tenants still held lease. Police, both city an county, appeared frequently at office from about 1 to 3 or 4 p.m. with warrants for arrest of six o trespass charges. Former occupant of building came to office late this afternoon and agreed to terminate his hold on building and to have all his property moved out within five days. COFO workers indicated their determination to stay in Philadelphia despite legal or other types of pressu Local Negro woman told one of workers this morning: "If you leave us now, they'll kill us. They pile our bodies one on top of the other." Additional staff was moved into Philadelphia by late af noon, and more will be sent as soon as needed, "to keep our pledge to the local people," a Jackson office spokesman said. Today's legal harassment followed several tense hours last night a Philadelphia office surrounded by carloads of armed whites. Following eviction notice, local Ne citizens came to office and provided "a fabulous dinner for us all."

<u>Shaw:</u> Herman Perry, Negro cotton farmer, elected president of the Bolivar Improvement Assn. a mass meeting here Wed. night. More than 100 attended. Assn. plans to organize Negro farmers and others for community planning and improvement. With widespread Negro unemployment and poverty in area, group hopes to become eligible for federal aid. To avoid complete economic dep dence, group needs some kind of industry to employ Negroes. Assn. grew out of Freedom School class in politics. Mass meeting scheduled for tomorrow evening in Shaw, to make plans for school boycott and integration of public schools here. (more)

Appendix

AUG. 20: <u>Clarksdale:</u> Medical Committee for Human Rights physicians Richard Moore and Les Hoffman arrested for loitering while in their car outside Freedom House here. Released on $16 bond each; trial Aug.21.

UG. 21: <u>Belzoni:</u> ~~Police cars follow voter registration workers here~~ continuously, surrounding them at every house at which they stop. Four to five cars of local white citizens also follow. This morning, police chief Nichols reportedly told workers to get out of town, that he was planning to bomb house. Yesterday Nichols entered house for second time without warrant. He said house is public place, and that warrant is unnecessary. House located about one block outside city limits. This evening three voter registration workers surrounded for several hours by 12 truckloads of armed whites as they sat in Wimpy's Cafe here. Crowd gathered as workers stopped at filling station just inside city limits. They entered cafe to report situation to Greenwood SNCC office. Sheriff closed cafe by saying to owner, "Close that place down, nigger." Local Negro citizen reportedly hit on side of head with blackjack.

<u>Gulfport:</u> Local Negro Aaron Jones today was arrested while handing out leaflets here announcing performance by Caravan of Music folksinger. Jones now in Juvenile Court custody on delinquency charge.

<u>Itta Bena:</u> Perry's Chapel burned to ground late this evening. Wood frame building deemed to be out of jurisdiction of Itta Bena fire department.

UG. 22: <u>McComb:</u> Local voter registration worker Percy McGhee arrested for "loitering" inside courthouse near here today. Being held on $60 bail. McComb police officer pulled gun on SNCC staff member Seephus Hugh who went to post bond for McGhee. Four more workers went to jail and successfully bonded out McGhee.

<u>Jackson:</u> As two Freedom School teachers, one white and one Negro, walked along street here today, car with two white passengers doubled back, drove by slowly, and took their picture.

<u>Laurel:</u> A going-away picnic given by local Negroes for three white voter registration workers was broken up today by an estimated 15 white men who beat one volunteer, reportedly with sticks and chains, and shot at two others. As group sat around private lake on Negro-owned farm near here, six white men approached and asked if group knew "Dixie." When one student began to play the song, a white man grabbed his guitar and threw it in lake. About 9 other white men came out of bushes surrounding lake site. White volunteer Willard Hayden saw at least two weapons among men: a club and a chain. Weapon brought down on his head; he and local voter registration worker Robert Morgan plunged into lake to head back to farmhouse. Shots, probably from pistol, aimed at them. White volunteer David Gelfand was severely beaten by white assailants. He sustained sprained--possibly broken--wrists, and bruises and lacerations of the back. His assailant has been tentatively identified as R.V. Lee, the man who is to stand trial Friday for beating white volunteer Anthony Lynn in front of Laurel Courthouse last Monday.

UG. 23: <u>Tupelo:</u> Voter registration headquarters here were object of arson early this morning. Damage was moderate. Workers arrived at office today to find attic gutted, all windows in rear part of building broken, and door burned. Neighbors reported fire department had put fire out at about 3 a.m. City investigators said there was evidence of arson. Tupelo has been the scene of FDP organizing involving 20 to 30 local workers, as well as three staff workers. Office was opened six weeks ago.

<u>McComb:</u> Local white citizen held for 3 hours last night by five heavily armed, hooded white men. He is described by McComb SNCC spokesmen as "poor; his friends are all Negroes and he lives in Negro neighborhood."

UG. 24: <u>Columbus:</u> Rev. Cluke Arden and white volunteer Bruce Amundson were turned away yesterday from Lutheran Church here after being questioned at length by minister and church elders. Amundson was asked to apologize for having brought a Negro to the church last Sunday.

<u>Greenville:</u> Law student Len Edwards and three LCDC lawyers were refused a room after having made prior reservation at Holiday Inn here, when manager saw a Negro in their car.

<u>Holly Springs:</u> Local Negro sharecropper Mr. J.T. Dean, turned off his land for no apparent reason. This is latest in series of economic actions taken against Dean since he applied to register to vote during Marshall Co. Freedom Day Aug. 15. Aug. 16 Dean's credit cut off. He was told by land owner he was no longer needed to work the land. His water supply was also cut off. Today Howard Jones, local Negro citizen who made application to register during Holly Springs Freedom Day July 24, told at courthouse that his test has not yet been graded. So far, none of more than 200 local Negro citizens who took voter registration test this summer has been notified as to whether or not he passed.

(over)

26-26-26

AUG. 24: Gulfport: Local Negro voter registration worker John Handy arrested here for disturbing peace and held on $300 bond. Arrest came few hours after Handy talked with Negroes outside Henderson's store in Greenwood, which has been boycotted for more than six weeks. Owner, Greenwood police officer, dragged young, pregnant Negro woman across pavement Freedom Day. When Handy stopped outside store, Henderson told him warrant would be issued for his arrest. (Charges dropped Aug. 25.)

Gulfport: Four local Negro voter registration workers, Luther Adams, Clifton Johnson, Jonnie Campbell, and Charles Wheeler, today were refused service at Albrught and Wood Drug store counter. They were served water, then asked to leave. Adams went back to store and asked if it were segregated; waitress replied, "You were served water, weren't you?"

Moss Pt.: Negro citizens here have decided to boycott nearby laundromat after young Negro girl arrested for attempting to wash clothes in "white section." Petition will be presented to laundry's owner tomorrow morning by boycotting citizens demanding that discrimination there be ended.

AUG. 25: Amory: Three young Negro voter registration workers, Adair Howell, Andrew Moore and Essie Carr, arrested today as they canvassed for potential registrants. Trio saw police coming and went to Negro home. Police entered home and arrested workers, charging them with disturbing peace and "forcing" Negro woman to sign form. Local officials denied knowledge of whereabouts of workers after their arrest. Howell and Moore located by FBI last this evening in Amory City jail. They are being held under $100 bond each. Miss Carr released to custody of her parents.

Drew: Law student Len Edwards arrested for reckless driving after being followed by local police chief. He made U-turn at speed of 5 miles per hour.

Moss Pt.: Owner of local laundromat here refused to desegregate facilities when presented with petition by local Negro citizens. He reportedly stated that he realized Negroes constituted 80% of his business, but that whites would refuse to wash there if partition removed. He reportedly told Negroes that "Communists are behind this whole thing," and that "Negroes and whites had a good relationship in Moss Pt. until few months ago when COFO workers came in." (On Aug. 26, six Negroes arrested for urging fellow citizens not to patronize the laundromat.)

Mound Bayou: Seven young Negro members of Mississippi Student Union arrested today for allegedly chasing white salesman out of town. Man shot at students. Although the seven, Henry Martin, Wendel Ishman, Herbert Battle, Oliver Know, James McKay, Walter Ricket, and Gary Dillen are being held in jail, no charges have been placed against them yet.

Columbus: Group of 30 Negro high school students followed by six police cars, one containing sheriff and police dog, as they walked to voter registration meeting last night. Police remained outside meeting for over ½ hour and later returned to cafe where group had first gathered. Police entered cafe and told students who had just returned from meeting that they were to go home.

AUG. 26: Canton: George Johnson, registration worker, was shot at three times on his way to Freedom House early this morning. He was approximately three blocks from the house when car pulled up from behind and fired three shots from approximately 500 feet away. Johnson identified car as police car since it was equipped with searchlight and red warning light on top. Johnson, who both heard the shots and saw the flash of the bullets, ducked into nearby bushes and sought shelter in a local house. Approximately 10 minutes later he started back to Freedom House down another street and stated that he saw "the same police car which came past me at 50 or 60 miles per hour, shining its spotlight on me." Johnson entered another local home for refuge. Late last week, Johnson, in response to Canton CORE office policies, registered with the police as a civil rights worker and gave the Freedom House as his home address.

Appendix E

Papers of the Parents Mississippi Emergency Committee

PARENTS MISSISSIPPI EMERGENCY COMMITTEE
604 G Street, SE
Washington, D.C.
202 547-8522
or   547-8524

Dear Parents:

We who send you this letter, like you, are parents of young people participating in COFO's Mississippi Summer Project. Proud as we are of our sons and daughters, we are nevertheless concerned about their safety and the safety of the citizens of Mississippi with whom they are working this summer. We are sure that you have already taken action, as we have, to secure protection for them, but we would like to report to you our activities up to date.

1. We are enclosing a copy of our press release and a letter from Boston legal authorities, presented at a press conference in Washington on June 24, for which we received national TV, radio and newspaper coverage. This conference was arranged with the help of the Washington Human Rights Project, and we have been assured that groups of parents will have no difficulty in arranging local press conferences. If you need guidance, contact your local Civil Rights organizations or Mr. Tom Leatherwood or Mr. Ron Wilmore at 202-547-8522 or 8524.

2. Since we have been in Washington this week (we are parents from New York, New Jersey, Maryland, Massachusetts and Washington, D.C.), we have been successful in arranging interviews with Nicholas Katzenbach, Deputy Attorney General of the U.S., Lee White, Assistant to President Johnson, Senators Keating and Javits of N.Y., Speaker of the House John McCormack, Representatives Redd and Ryan of N.Y., as well as assistants of Senators Case and Williams of N.J., Senator Saltonstall of Mass., Senator Humphrey of Minn., Sen. Brewster of Maryland, and Rep. Osmers of N.J. IT IS MOST URGENT THAT CONGRESSMEN RECEIVE DELEGATIONS FROM THEIR CONSTITUENTS, as well as concerned citizens who feel that all Congressmen represent all the people of the United States. NOTE: In the event that your son or daught is arrested, notify your Senator and Congressman immediately and ask them to telephone the jail. We have been advised on Capitol Hill that such a phone call from Washington is effective.

3. Fortunately, the NAACP National Convention is now in progress in Washington and we have talked with many leaders of that organization. Their members are enthusiastically supporting us and already many, many telegrams have gone to the President asking for Federal Marshals to be sent to Mississippi.

4. By means of this letter, we are contacting parents nationally. Enclosed is a list of participants in your state. Will you take the responsibiity of contacting other parents immediately to organize group action? This is a MUST! The White House and Capitol Hill must know that large numbers of people want them to act before any other tragedies occur. Tuesday, Wednesday, and Thursday (June 30, July 1 and 2) are vitally important. We need more people to bring the necessary pressure and it is most urgent that parents and friends from every state converge on Washington to lobby for all avaialble protection immediately.

We are certain that your emphasis, as is ours, will be that the Federal Government can and must assume responsibility for the protection of its citizens anyplace in the Union. We have asked for Federal Marshals to be sent to Mississippi. If you have any additional ideas or suggestions, please let us know.

> Yours in freedom,
> Parents Mississippi Emergency Committee

THINGS TO DO IN YOUR COMMUNITY

1. Call all other parents in your area and organize. <u>Please</u> sent us a corrected list of participants and parents as soon as <u>possible</u>.
2. Arrange a press conference. (If you need help, let us know.)
3. Letters and wires to the President, Attorney General, Congressmen, Senators, and local officials urging that Federal powers be used to protect the people in Mississippi.
4. Ask your friends, neighbors, community leaders and clergy to ACT.
5. Begin to arrange for trip to Washington -- together if possible. We have found that it is very easy to organize parents around this matter.
<u>NOTE</u>: Make sure Congress is in session on the day you plan to come.
6. Raise funds to support your activities and ours.

THINGS TO DO IN WASHINGTON

1. Check in with Tom Leatherwood or Ron Wilmore at the above address.
2. See <u>your</u> Congressman and all other Congressmen from your state. See your Sena<u>tors</u>.
3. Demand an interview with top officials of the Justice Department.
4. Since the Federal Government has clear powers to act, insist on a meeting at the White House.
5. We can help to arrange a press conference in Washington if you come with a state delegation.
6. Bring letters or other material from your son and daughter about what is happening in Mississippi to use in your interview.

Appendix

(Personally delivered to the White House on June 9, 1964)

Mr. President:

You are undoubtedly aware that this summer almost 1,000 Americans are traveling to Mississippi under the auspices of the Council of Federated Organizations in that state. The purpose of their trip will be to carry on educational activities, community center programs, and voter registration work, in order to insure equal opportunity for all. Among these volunteer workers will be forty-five students from Harvard, Brandeis, Radcliffe, and Boston Universities, whose names are appended to this appeal.

As you know, the record of the past several years indicates that the liberties, and the lives of these people will be in jeopardy this summer. That record is full of intimidations, arrests, beatings, shootings and even murder, inflicted upon Negro and white citizens. It is clear beyond doubt that they cannot depend upon the State of Mississippi for protection.

The Constitution of the United States vests responsibility in you, Mr. President, to enforce the laws of the nation. For this purpose you have both inherent and statutory powers. We urge you, in the name of that humanity which the nation espouses and that equality of rights to which you have pledged support, to use the plenitude of your Presidential authority to take preventive and collective measures to protect the life and the constitutional liberties of all persons within the State of Mississippi. We ask that you station in Mississippi, in advance of trouble, Federal Marshals sufficient to deter, prevent, or immediately suppress actions which would deprive Americans of their constitutional rights.

The eyes of the nation, and of the world, will be on Mississippi this summer. Let them see right and justice prevail in that State through the authority and dignity of the Executive of our nation.

Mark DeWolfe Howe, Professor of Constitutional Law,
    Harvard University Law School
Rev. Robert F. Drinan, S.J., Dean, Boston College Law School
Prof. Joseph T. Witherspoon, Jr., Univ. of Texas Law School
Albert O. Beisel, Boston University Law School
Prof. Sanford J. Fox, Boston College Law School
Prof. Robert G. Haber, Boston College Law School
Rev. Wm. J. Kenealy, S.J., Boston College Law School
Prof. John D. O'Reilly, Jr., Boston College Law School
Prof. Robert S. Sullivan, Boston College Law School

(over)

Professor Kenneth T. Bainbridge, Harvard University
Edmond C. Berkeley, Editor, <u>Computers & Automation</u>
Dr. Ruth Berman
Right Rev. John M. Burgess, Suffragan Bishop Episcopal
 Diocese of Massachusetts
Dr. Ross Cannon
Dr. Robert Coles, Harvard University
Prof. Paul Deats, Jr., Boston University
Rabbi Roland B. Gittlesohn
Mr. & Mrs. John Chipman Gray
Rabbi Albert I. Gordon
Mrs. Melvin Gordon
Prof. Oscar Handlin, Winthrop Prof. of History,
 Harvard University
Mary Howe
Kivie Kaplan
Prof. Leonard W. Levy, Dean of Faculty, Brandeis Univ.
Dr. Bernard Lown
Mrs. Herbert Marcuse
Prof. Barnard McCabe, Tufts University
Drs. Wm. & Ruth Murphy
Mrs. John B. Paine
Mrs. Malcolm E. Peabody
Rabbi Samuel Perlman, Hillel House, Boston Univ.
Katherine B. Perlman
Prof. Douglas Reynolds, Tufts University
Mrs. David Riesman
Mr. & Mrs. Edward Ryerson
Arthur Schlesinger, Prof. Emeritus, Harvard University
Rabbi Steven J. Schwartzchild, Chairman, Social Action
 Comm., New England Region, United Synagogue
Dr. Bradbury Seasholes, Tufts University
Dr. Alfred Stenton, Director McLean Hospital
Rev. Francis W. Sweeney, S.J., Boston College
Rev. Richard L. Twomey, S.J., Boston College
Mr. & Mrs. Robert C. Webb
Prof. Harold Weisberg, Dean, Graduate School,
 Brandeis University
Prof. Victor Weisskopf, M.I.T.
Rabbi Leonard Zion, Associate Dean, Student Affairs,
 Brandeis University
Prof. Howard Zinn, Boston University

Affiliation of the signers of this appeal are for the purpose of
identification only.

cc: Attorney General Robert Kennedy

(List of 45 students attached)

Appendix

FOR IMMEDIATE RELEASE
June 25, 1964

As a group of parents representing the mothers and father of nearly 1000 young people now actively engaged in the Mississippi Summer Project we wish to express our deepest gratitude to President Lyndon B. Johnson for his thorough and untiring efforts in behalf of James Cheney, Andrew Goodman and Michael Schwerner immediately following their tragic disappearance in Philadelphia, Mississippi. It is our most fervent hope that in order to prevent further tragedy befalling any of the people of Mississippi or the brave students helping in the struggle for freedom, the President will do everything in his power immediately to provide every measure of federal protection, particularly the assignment to that troubled area of federal marshals in a number sufficient to deter further lawlessness.

We were shocked by the statement (made yesterday by Attorney General Robert Kennedy), as reported in The New York Times, that the federal government cold not take "preventive" police action. The hesitant position of the Justice Department is directly challenged by some of the most eminent legal and historical authorities in the country, including Professor Mark DeWolfe Howe of Harvard Law School; the Reverend Robert F. Drinan, Dean of Boston University Law School, and Professor Leonard Levy, Dean of Faculty, Brandeis University. We concur with the position of these authorities and it is our firm opinion that more than sufficiently strong powers rest within the government to enable it to provide exactly the protection for which we ask. The attached letter to the President, outlining this position, was personally delivered to the White House on June ninth, and copy sent to Mr. Kennedy.

APPENDIX

We have come to Washington to plead for the oppressed people of Mississippi and for our sons and daughters, young people of forty states who care so deeply for our democratic ideals that they have put their very lives in jeopardy. Soon we will return to our homes, still standing firmly behind our children and supporting them in their efforts. We will continue our appeal to the federal government and . will enlist in our communities across the nation the assistance of all who share the conviction that the moral fiber of our nation is at stake. We trust that it will not be necessary for us to go to Mississippi to defend the ideals of our Republic.

Appendix F

Results of Regression Analysis Assessing the Effect of Various Independent Variables on Level of Activism between 1964 and 1970

Independent Variable	Dependent Variable Level of Activism b	SE(b)
Number of volunteers in contact with		
In 1966	.201	.212
In 1970	1.476[a]	.632
Political orientation prior to Freedom Summer	− .935	.683
Change in orientation pre- and post-Freedom Summer	.534[b]	.223
Participation in Freedom Summer? (yes/no)	5.008[a]	1.848
Gender	1.787	1.885
Age	.139	.238
Family income prior to Freedom Summer	.0002	.0003
Level of activism prior to Freedom Summer	.213	.136
Number of organizational affiliations prior to Freedom Summer	1.306[b]	.575
Number of years married during the Sixties	− .106	.403
Number of years as parent during the Sixties	− .326	.606
Number of years employed full time during the Sixties	−1.136[a]	.440
Number of years in college during the Sixties	− .708	.448
Attend college post-Freedom Summer? (yes/no)	2.452	1.965
Constant	10.263	8.431

$N = 189$.

[a] $p < .01$.

[b] $p < .05$.

Appendix G

Results of Regression Analysis Assessing the Effect of Various Independent Variables on Current Level of Activism

Independent Variable	Dependent Variable b	Level of Current Activism SE(b)
Number of volunteers presently in contact with	.126	.283
Present political orientation	− .771[b]	.318
Political orientation prior to Freedom Summer	− .821[b]	.340
Participation in Freedom Summer? (yes/no)	− .702	.756
Presently married? (yes/no)	.274	.791
Presently employed full-time? (yes/no)	2.762	1.413
Gender	− .189	.223
Age	− .117	.872
Income	−1.071[a]	.319
Family income prior to Freedom Summer	.00005	.0001
Level of activism prior to Freedom Summer	− .715	.664
Level of political activism between 1964 and 1970	.294[a]	.054
Number of current organizational affiliations	1.098[a]	.195
Number of organizational affiliations between 1964 and 1970	− .269	.264
Number of years of college attendance	− .472[a]	.158
Number of years of full time employment since Freedom Summer	.079	.010
Held activist job? (yes/no)	1.729[b]	.696
Constant	10.985[a]	3.416

$N = 221$.

[a] $p < .01$.

[b] $p < .05$.

Notes

Prologue

1. Interview with an anonymous Freedom Summer volunteer, August 14, 1984.
2. Interview with an anonymous Freedom Summer volunteer, April 22, 1985.
3. Interview with Len Edwards, August 17, 1984.
4. Interview with Linda Davis, April 18, 1984.
5. Interview with Marion Davidson, March 21, 1985.
6. The "Scottsboro boys" were nine black teenagers brought to trial in 1931 and convicted on trumped up rape charges in a case involving a white woman. The name "Scottsboro boys" comes from the small town in northern Alabama where the trial took place. Eventually the convictions were reversed due to the legal efforts of lawyers representing the American Communist Party and the national attention they succeeded in focusing on the case.
7. Of the 556 addresses I know to be current, 465 were supplied by college and university alumni associations.
8. Two questionnaires were actually produced during this phase of the project: one tailored to the experiences of the volunteers, and the other geared to the lives of the no-shows. A copy of each of these questionnaires is included as Appendix A of the book.
9. By the strictest methodological canons, only 90 percent of the interviews were truly random. What enabled me to travel around the country interviewing the former applicants was receipt of a Guggenheim Fellowship. Before learning of this award, I had been content simply to interview any volunteer I came in contact with. In July of 1984 I was lucky enough to attend a reunion of Bay Area volunteers held in Oakland. While there, I arranged to interview ten of those in attendance on a return trip in August. Upon receipt of the Guggenheim award, I drew the names of forty volunteers at random. Reflecting their disproportionate concentration in the Bay Area, fifteen of the names drawn were those of volunteers who lived in and around San Fran-

cisco. Two of these were volunteers I had already interviewed. Rather than discard the other eight interviews I had already done, I merely substituted them for eight of the names I had drawn. So strictly speaking, eight of the eighty interviews conducted were not random.

Chapter 1

1. Interview with Gren Whitman, April 18, 1985.

2. Interview with an anonymous Freedom Summer volunteer, February 5, 1985.

3. There was no official poverty level in 1960. However, in 1976 the Census Bureau devised an estimated 1959 poverty standard to enable policymakers to make historical comparisons. According to the Census Bureau, a reasonable estimate of the poverty level for a family of four in 1959 was $2,973 (U.S. Bureau of the Census, 1976: 143). By this standard, 85.8 percent of all non-white and 43.3 percent of all white families in Mississippi in 1959 had incomes below the official poverty level (U.S. Bureau of the Census, 1963). If one defines family more restrictively as a husband and wife and two children under the age of 18, the figures change somewhat. Using this more restrictive definition, only 18.8 percent of white, but 77.3 percent of nonwhite families in Mississippi fall below the poverty level (U.S. Bureau of the Census, 1963).

4. McCord (1965: 35).

5. Holt (1965: 102).

6. McCord (1965: 152).

7. Shown below are the 1960 infant-mortality rates for Mississippi and the United States:

Number of Deaths, under 1 Year, per 1,000 Live Births

	Mississippi	United States
Total	41.6	26.0
White	26.6	22.9
Non-white	54.3	43.2

Sources: U.S. Department of Health, Education and Welfare 1963 *Vital Statistics of the United States 1960*. Volume II–Mortality Part B. Washington, D.C.: U.S. Government Printing Office; U.S. Bureau of the Census, 1964 Statistical Abstract of the United States: 1964 (Eighty-Fifth Edition). Washington, D.C.: U.S. Government Printing Office.

Chapter 2

1. It is difficult to pinpoint the exact number of persons who made formal application to the Summer Project. Various authors have hazarded a wide range of guesses as to the total number of people who participated in the project. Demerath, Marwell, and Aiken (1971: xvii) place the number at around 500. Both Elizabeth Sutherland (1965) and Mary Aiken Rothschild

(1982: 31) estimate the total number of volunteers to have been closer to 650. My own research, however, suggests that the number was closer to Sellers and Terrell's (1973) figure of 900 than to either of the lower estimates. I am physically in possession of 720 applications from persons who went to Mississippi and an additional 239 applications from project no-shows. In addition, there is an alphabetic gap in both sets of applications between the letters I and N. That is, the applications for all persons in both groups with last names beginning with the letters, J, K, L, M, and N are missing. Correcting for this alphabetic gap, I would place the total number of applicants in the two groups to be roughly 900 for the volunteers and 300 for the no-shows.

2. The estimates of the number of students who worked in the Freedom Vote campaign are almost as varied as those for Freedom Summer. Matusow (1971: 140) places the number at 80. The better estimate, however, is 100 students. That figure has been put forth by Carson (1981: 98) and McLemore (1971: 102). In addition, the SNCC veteran Mendy Samstein included the figure in his unpublished "Notes on Mississippi," written shortly after the conclusion of the Freedom Vote campaign (Samstein Papers, State Historical Society of Wisconsin archives—hereinafter SHSW—Madison, Wisconsin).

3. Mendy Samstein, "Notes on Mississippi," p. 4 in Samstein Papers, SHSW.

4. This account is confirmed in Carson, 1981: 98–99, and Samstein's "Notes on Mississippi," p. 5, in Samstein Papers, SHSW.

5. Samstein, "Notes on Mississippi," p. 6, in Samstein Papers, SHSW.

6. This account is taken from Carson, 1981: 100.

7. Quoted in James Atwater, "'If We Can Crack Mississippi . . .'," *Saturday Evening Post,* July 25, 1964, p. 16.

8. Interview with James Forman, August 29, 1985.

9. See Holt, 1965: 157.

10. Minutes of SNCC Executive Committee Meeting, May 10, 1964, p. 10.

11. U.S. Department of Health, Education and Welfare, Office of Education, *Digest of Educational Statistics,* p. 84, Table 62. Washington, D.C.: U.S. Government Printing Office, 1965.

12. Ibid, p. 73.

13. Summer Project applications; from the author's collection.

14. Summer Project applications.

15. Summer Project applications.

16. Interview with Elinor Tideman Aurthur, June 12, 1985.

17. Interview with an anonymous Freedom Summer volunteer, June 20, 1985.

18. Summer Project applications.

19. Summer Project applications.

20. Summer Project applications.

21. Summer Project applications.

22. Interview with Judy Michalowski, August 10, 1984.

23. Interview with Chude Pamela Allen, August 14, 1984.

24. Interview with an anonymous Freedom Summer volunteer, April 22, 1985.

25. Interview with an anonymous Freedom Summer volunteer, August 14, 1984.

26. Interviews with two anonymous Freedom Summer volunteers, August 10, 1984 and March 29, 1985.

27. Interview with an anonymous Freedom Summer volunteer, August 14, 1984.

28. Ibid.

29. Memo included in Robert Saul Starobin papers, SHSW; hereinafter Starobin Papers.

30. Only fifty-five of the applicants for whom I have applications were rejected by the Project staff. Correcting for the applications that are missing from my collection, I place the number of applicants rejected at no more than seventy.

31. Interview with an anonymous Freedom Summer applicant, November 17, 1984.

32. Volunteers averaged 23.6 years of age and no-shows 21.8.

33. Interview with an anonymous Freedom Summer volunteer, March 20, 1985.

34. Letter written by Mrs. Jeanette Parker; included in papers given to the author by Chude Pamela Allen (hereinafter cited as Allen papers).

35. Interview with Judy Michalowski, August 10, 1984.

36. Those I have obtained came from three sources; the Archives of the Martin Luther King, Jr. Center in Atlanta, Georgia; the Freedom Information Service collection in Jackson, Mississippi; and the State Historical Society of Wisconsin archives in Madison.

37. Interviewer report form; from the author's collection.

38. Interviewer report form.

39. Interviewer report form.

40. Interview with an anonymous Freedom Summer applicant, June 6, 1985.

41. An open-ended list of seventeen motivational "themes" were used to capture the applicants reason(s) for applying to the project. In addition, a single dichotomous code was used to distinguish between answers that reflected either "self-interested" or "other-oriented" motives for participating. Statements that stressed the *personal* challenge of the campaign or the *individual* benefits of the experience (e.g., teaching experience), were coded as "self-interested" motives. Those that reflected more general, "selfless" concerns were categorized as "other-oriented" motives. However, neither of the above code dimensions captured any significant distinctions between participants and withdrawals. The average number of motives ascribed to both groups that were categorized as "self-interested" or "other-oriented" were not statistically different. Nor did the seventeen thematic code categories produce a characteristic motivational "profile" for participants distinct from that of the

no-shows. Both groups tended to rely upon the same mix of themes in explaining their reasons for participating.

42. Summer Project applications.

43. Of the 202 ties to other applicants listed by the volunteers, only twenty-five were to persons who later withdrew from the Project. This is a withdrawal rate of 12 percent, as compared to the 25 percent rate for all applicants. By contrast 30 percent (twelve of forty) of the no-shows' ties to other applicants were to other no-shows.

44. In coding these activities, I assigned a numeric value to each activity based on its intensity relative to all other forms of civil rights activism. So, for example, participation in the Freedom Rides was assigned a score of "7," while contributing money to a civil rights organization had a point value of only "1." Each subject then received a final score computed as the sum of the point totals for the activities reported on their applications.

45. Interview with an anonymous Freedom Summer volunteer, June 20, 1985.

46. This conclusion accords with a growing number of systematic studies of recruitment into political or religious movements. See, for example, the work of Bibby and Brinkerhoff, 1974; Bolton, 1972; McAdam, 1986; Orum, 1972; Rosenthal, et al., 1985; and Snow, Zurcher, and Ekland-Olson, 1980.

Chapter 3

1. Letter written by Margaret Aley, June 23, 1964; included in papers given to the author by Margaret Aley Chavez (hereinafter cited as Chavez papers).

2. Letter written by Ruth Steward to her parents; included in Elizabeth Sutherland papers, State Historical Society of Wisconsin archives (hereinafter SHSW), Madison, Wisconsin (hereinafter cited as Sutherland papers).

3. Entry in Margaret Rose Beernink's journal dated June 17, 1964; in author's possession (hereinafter cited as Beernink journal).

4. For a comprehensive account of the events leading up to the triple murder, see Lomax, Griffith, and Gregory, 1964.

5. Entry in Stuart Rawlings' journal dated June 26, 1964 (hereinafter cited as Rawlings journal); in author's possession.

6. Letter written by Margaret Aley, June 23, 1964; Chavez papers.

7. Rawlings journal, June 25, 1964.

8. Letter written by Ellen Lake to her parents, June 20, 1964; included in papers (hereinafter cited as Lake papers) on file SHSW.

9. Letter written by Pam Parker to her parents, June 30, 1964; Allen papers.

10. Within a year, the phrase "freedom high" had come to be used derisively by one faction within SNCC to refer to those it regarded as not sufficiently concerned with issues of organization and structure. But throughout the summer, the phrase retained a generally positive connotation.

11. Interview with an anonymous Freedom Summer volunteer, August 16, 1984.

12. Quoted in *Esquire* Magazine, June 1983, p. 239.

13. Interview with an anonymous Freedom Summer volunteer, April 6, 1985.

14. Letter written by Margaret Rose, August 9, 1964; Beernink papers.

15. Rawlings journal, July 4, 1964.

16. In an interview on April 22, 1985, one volunteer described how, after working for several weeks on a large project in Columbus, Mississippi, "me and one other guy were assigned to go to Starkville where no one had ever been . . . we *were* the project in Starkville . . . that was a scary thing."

17. The procedures for processing, training, and assigning late arrivals is spelled out in a letter dated July 18, 1964, from Mrs. Ruth Schein, Secretary, Summer Project, to a woman who had applied to work in Mississippi in August. The letter is contained in papers copied by the author from the originals which are stored in the Martin Luther King, Jr. Center in Atlanta (hereinafter cited as King Center papers).

18. This accounting was copied from the original contained in the archives of the Freedom Information Service, Jackson, Mississippi. The archives have been maintained since the conclusion of the Summer Project by Ms. Jan Hillegas, who came to Mississippi as a volunteer in the summer of 1964 and never left. The accounting has been used as the basis for Appendix C.

19. "The Mississippi Freedom Democratic Party: Background and Recent Developments," unpublished paper, Student Non-Violent Coordinating Committee, 1965, p. 2.

20. Letter written by Les Johnson; included in papers donated by Sandra Hard to SHSW (hereinafter cited as Hard papers).

21. Letter written by Robert Feinglass to his father; included in papers (hereinafter cited as Feinglass papers) on file SHSW.

22. Letter written by Ellen Lake to her parents, July 4, 1964; Lake papers.

23. Rawlings journal, p. 91.

24. Entry in Ronald de Sousa's journal dated July 20, 1964; in author's possession (hereinafter cited as de Sousa journal).

25. Background materials on the Freedom Schools were prepared by several SNCC staffers prior to the summer for distribution to the volunteer teachers. These materials are reproduced in Holt, 1965: 324–330.

26. In a letter dated August 23, 1964, one volunteer teacher, Robert Popkin, described the "typical Freedom School day" as being divided into three general parts:

9–10	Freedom Songs (recreation and cultural activities)
10–11	Negro History (leadership development)
1– 3	academic subjects (academic work)

This letter was contained in papers (hereinafter cited as R. Popkin papers) given to the author by Robert Popkin.

27. Among the projects producing student newspapers were Holly Springs ("The Freedom News"), McComb ("Freedom Journal") and Benton County ("The Benton County Freedom Train") (copies in author's possession).

28. See Appendix C for enrollment estimates.

29. de Sousa journal, July 23, 1964.

30. Undated letter written by Pam Parker; Allen papers.

31. This percentage reflects the number of volunteers who reported some prior civil rights activity on their applications.

32. Letter written by Matthew Zwerling to his parents, June 30, 1964; contained in papers (hereinafter cited as Zwerling papers) on file SHSW.

33. From Don Hamer, "Special Report: The Plantation of Mr. John Aket Hayes," contained in papers donated by Michael Kenney (hereinafter cited as Kenney papers) to the Wilson Library, University of North Carolina at Chapel Hill and currently comprising Appendix B of Records of Student Non-violent Coordinating Committee.

34. Interview with an anonymous Freedom Summer volunteer, May 27, 1985.

35. Letter from Pam Parker; Allen papers.

36. Interview with Elinor Tideman Aurthur, June 12, 1985.

37. Interview with David Gelfand, February 7, 1985.

38. Entry in Gren Whitman's journal, dated July 31, 1964; in author's possession (hereinafter cited as Whitman journal).

39. In their interviews (dates: 8/10/84; 8/22/84; 2/7/85; 3/29/85; 4/6/85; 6/20/85) six former volunteers told stories similar to that recorded in Gren Whitman's journal.

40. Letter from Betty Carstens dated July 6, 1964; contained in papers donated by Christopher Wilson (hereinafter cited as Wilson papers) to the SHSW.

41. Interview with an anonymous Freedom Summer volunteer, May 28, 1985.

42. Ibid.

43. Interview with an anonymous Freedom Summer volunteer, August 9, 1984.

44. Interview with an anonymous Freedom Summer volunteer, April 22, 1985.

45. Interview with Ken Scudder, August 23, 1984.

46. During interviews at least six of the former volunteers acknowledged a high frequency of sexual behavior on their projects (dates of interviews: 8/9/84; 8/22/84; 8/23/84; 2/5/85; 4/17/85; 4/22/85).

47. Interview with an anonymous Freedom Summer volunteer, June 20, 1985.

48. Interview with an anonymous Freedom Summer volunteer, May 9, 1985.

49. Interview with an anonymous Freedom Summer volunteer, April 22, 1985.

50. Rawlings journal, July 22, 1964.

51. Interview with an anonymous Freedom Summer volunteer, April 6, 1985.

52. The summary is from Rothschild (1982: 58).

53. Letter written by Michael Kenney, July 15, 1964; Kenney papers.

54. This incident is described in detail in Belfrage, 1965: 222–223. An anonymous volunteer also provided an eyewitness account of the incident in an interview on August 14, 1984.

55. For an account of the dynamite attack, see Harris, 1982: 62.

56. The incident is described in detail in a letter written by Larry Spears, one of the victims of the July 10 attack. The letter is included as pp. 73–76 of Stuart Rawlings' journal.

57. This is an excerpt from page 10 of a collection of affidavits compiled at the end of the summer by the Communications Section of the Summer Project; contained in Allen papers.

58. Excerpt from an unpublished anonymous article entitled "The Mississippi Summer Project" (pp. 13–14); found in the archives of the Freedom Information Service, Jackson, Mississippi.

59. Letter written by William Hodes to his parents, August 2, 1964; included in papers (hereinafter cited as Hodes papers) on file SHSW.

60. Letter written by Pam Parker to her parents, August 6, 1964; Allen papers.

61. Entry in Jo Ann Ooiman Robinson's journal, dated June 23, 1964; journal on file SHSW (hereinafter cited as Robinson journal).

62. Letter written by Matthew Zwerling to his parents, June 30, 1964; Zwerling papers.

63. Interview with an anonymous Freedom Summer volunteer, May 30, 1985.

64. Interview with Barry Clemson, April 17, 1985.

65. de Sousa journal; in author's possession.

66. Interview with Jan Hillegas, March 26, 1985.

67. Interview with an anonymous Freedom Summer volunteer, March 21, 1985.

68. Two volunteers recounted such incidents in their interviews (dates: 8/23/84; 6/12/85), while a third described a similar case in his journal (de Sousa journal; in author's possession).

69. de Sousa journal; in author's possession.

70. Interview with Miriam Cohen Glickman, June 1, 1985.

71. Interview with Barry Clemson, April 17, 1985.

72. Letter written by Pam Parker; Allen papers.

73. Interview with Stuart Rawlings, August 22, 1964.

74. Interview with Linda Davis, April 18, 1985.

75. Letter written by William Hodes to his parents, July 26–27, 1964; Hodes papers.

76. Rawlings journal, July 10, 1964.

77. Interview with Elinor Tideman Aurthur, June 12, 1985.

78. This number is based on several estimates including Evans' (1980: 94)

as well as one based on my own data. Twenty-four of the volunteers who returned my questionnaire reported that they stayed in Mississippi beyond the summer. Given that I have questionnaires from roughly 30 percent of the volunteers, a simple extrapolation from my data would place the number of volunteers who remained in Mississippi at around 80.

79. Letter written by Ellen Lake to her parents, August 12, 1964; Lake papers.

80. Letter written by Pam Parker to her parents, August 6, 1964; Allen papers.

81. Letter written by Pam Parker to her parents, August 27, 1964; Allen papers.

Chapter 4

1. Perhaps the best account of the convention challenge is provided by Clay Carson in his book, *In Struggle: SNCC and the Black Awakening of the 1960's* (1981: 123–128).

2. These figures are reported in Holt (1965: 167).

3. U.S., Congress, Senate, Select Committee to Study Governmental Operations with Respect to Intelligence Activities, *Intelligence Activities: Hearings on Senate Resolution 21*, 94th Congress, 1st session, volume 6, pp. 174–177, 495–510.

4. This account is reported by David Harris in his book, *Dreams Die Hard* (1982: 74).

5. Thirteen of the twenty-four volunteers who reported on their questionnaires that they remained in Mississippi following the summer were white females.

6. Interview with an anonymous Freedom Summer volunteer, August 18, 1984.

7. This phrase has long been attributed to Moses. Whether he actually said it, or it is apocryphal, is not clear.

8. Interview with Heather Tobis Booth, May 7, 1985.

9. Interview with an anonymous Freedom Summer volunteer, April 18, 1985.

10. Interview with an anonymous Freedom Summer volunteer, August 19, 1985.

11. This excerpt is taken from an unpublished essay entitled, "Thoughts about Mississippi," written by Brian Peterson; included in papers (hereinafter cited as Peterson papers) on file, SHSW.

12. Interview with David Gelfand, February 7, 1985.

13. Interview with an anonymous Freedom Summer volunteer, June 8, 1985.

14. Interview with Marion Davidson, March 21, 1985.

15. See U.S., Congress, Senate, Select Committee to Study Governmental Operations with Respect to Intelligence Activities, *Final Report—Book III, Supplementary Detailed Staff Reports on Intelligence Activities and the*

Rights of Americans, 94th Congress, 2d session, 1976. Kennedy's role in authorizing the wiretaps on King are also carefully documented in David Garrow's excellent book, *The FBI and Martin Luther King, Jr.* (1981: 64–65, 72–73, 91–95, 201–202).

16. Interview with an anonymous Freedom Summer volunteer, April 22, 1985.

17. The following table shows that those volunteers who described themselves—using the ten-point scale described in Chapter 2—as more politically moderate prior to Freedom Summer were also more likely to report a drop in their estimate of federal officials as a result of their experiences in Mississippi.

Percent of the Volunteers Reporting a Lowered Estimate of Various
Branches or Agencies of Government, by Political Orientation
Prior to Freedom Summer

Orientation Prior to Summer	President		Congress		Justice Dept.		FBI	
	%	No.	%	No.	%	No.	%	No.
Radical (1–3)	34	(34)	28	(28)	47	(48)	64	(65)
All other (4–10)	51	(47)	53	(49)	54	(50)	82	(78)

18. Interview with an anonymous Freedom Summer volunteer, April 28, 1985.

19. Interview with an anonymous Freedom Summer volunteer, May 9, 1985.

20. Interview with an anonymous Freedom Summer volunteer, June 8, 1985.

21. Interview with Heather Tobis Booth, May 7, 1985.

22. Interview with an anonymous Freedom Summer volunteer, April 12, 1985.

23. Interview with Robbie Osman, August 13, 1984.

24. Letter written by Ellen Lake to her parents, August 12, 1964; Lake papers, SHSW.

25. Interview with Chude Pamela Allen, August 14, 1984.

26. From a taped transcript of the voice-over narration of the television show in question; in author's possession.

27. Interview with Len Edwards, August 17, 1984.

28. Letter written by Pam Parker to a friend, August 30, 1964; Allen papers.

29. The interviews in question took place on: 8/14/84; 2/5/85; 3/21/85 and 6/6/85.

30. Letter written by Len Edwards; included in papers given to the author by Len Edwards (hereinafter cited as Edwards papers).

31. Letter written by Mrs. Jeannette Parker; Allen papers.

32. Interview with an anonymous Freedom Summer volunteer, August 14, 1984.

33. Interview with an anonymous Freedom Summer volunteer, April 28, 1985.

34. de Sousa journal, June 30, 1964.

35. Interview with an anonymous Freedom Summer volunteer, May 22, 1985.

36. Interview with an anonymous Freedom Summer volunteer, April 22, 1985.

37. Interview with Marion Davidson, March 21, 1985.

38. Interview with an anonymous Freedom Summer volunteer, April 22, 1985.

39. Letter written by Margaret Aley, June 23, 1964; included in papers given to the author by Margaret Aley Chavez (hereinafter cited as Chavez papers).

40. Interview with an anonymous Freedom Summer volunteer, May 22, 1985.

41. Excerpt from an anonymous journal entry dated June 23, 1964; found in the archives of the Freedom Information Service, Jackson, Mississippi.

42. Letter written by William Hodes to his parents; Hodes papers, SHSW.

43. Interview with an anonymous Freedom Summer volunteer, August 10, 1984.

44. Interview with Barry Clemson, April 17, 1985.

45. Interview with an anonymous Freedom Summer volunteer, April 20, 1985.

46. Editorial in the *Jackson Clarion-Ledger*, July 30, 1964.

47. Letter written by Charles J. Benner to John Lewis, June 16, 1964; included in Allen papers.

48. Included as part of Rawlings' journal; column dated June 25, 1964.

49. Summer Project application.

50. Interview with Robert Beyers, February 4, 1985.

51. Article in the *San Francisco Chronicle*, July 22, 1964, p. 7.

52. Interview with Andrew Schiffrin, August 15, 1984.

53. This figure is given in Holt (1965: 85).

54. Elizabeth Sutherland, "The Cat and Mouse Game," in *The Nation* (September 14, 1964), pg. 2.

55. This figure is given in Holt (1965: 78).

56. This excerpt is from a letter written by Larry Spears and included as pp. 73–76 of Rawlings' journal.

57. Included as page 184 of Rawlings' journal.

58. Interview with an anonymous Freedom Summer volunteer, June 20, 1985.

59. Memo included in Popkin papers.

60. Ibid.

61. Information on these groups came from materials included in the

Hodes papers and from minutes, newsletters, and announcements contained in papers (hereinafter cited as Parents' Mississippi Freedom Association papers) donated by the Parents Mississippi Freedom Association to SHSW.

62. Minutes, Parents' Mississippi Freedom Association papers.

63. Ibid.

64. Interview with Len Edwards, August 17, 1984.

65. Interview with Stuart Rawlings, August 22, 1984.

66. Excerpt quoted in materials contained in Hodes papers, SHSW.

Chapter 5

1. Of those volunteers who reported on their questionnaires that they returned to school in the fall, 62 percent re-enrolled at schools that had at least five other returning volunteers.

2. There have been many books written about the Free Speech Movement at Berkeley. Among the most noteworthy are Draper, 1965; Feuer, 1969; Heirich, 1968: Lipset and Wolin, 1965; and Miller and Gilmore, 1965.

3. The names of all 783 arrested in the sit-in remain on file at the state Court of Appeals. The list of those who returned to Berkeley in the fall was compiled from information provided by the volunteers on the follow-up questionnaires and from subsequent interviews with two of the Berkeley returnees.

4. Weissman does not appear as an "official" Freedom Summer volunteer on the project rosters I have been able to obtain. However, in a six-part retrospective on the Free Speech Movement that appeared in the *San Francisco Examiner,* he is described as a participant in the Summer Project.

5. Art Goldberg served as the president of SLATE, the leftist student political party on campus. The founder of SLATE, Mike Miller, remained an active force in Bay Area civil rights activities during the 1963–1964 academic year. Malcolm Zaretsky and Betty Garman were perhaps the central figures in the UC Berkeley Friends of SNCC chapter while Robert Wolfson served as president of the campus chapter of CORE. These brief thumbnail sketches are based on information recorded on the original project applications as well as in Heirich, 1968.

6. This excerpt is taken from the interviewer report form on Mario Savio on file at the Martin Luther King, Jr. Center, Atlanta, Georgia.

7. Interview with an anonymous Freedom Summer volunteer, August 19, 1984.

8. Evans (1980: 157) reports that Yale, Ohio State, Kansas, Brooklyn College, Michigan State, and St. Johns all experienced student demonstrations in the winter and spring of 1965.

9. Two of the volunteers I interviewed claim to have been involved in campus demonstrations at Yale and Brooklyn College the same year as the FSM. In addition, Rothschild (1982: 181) reports that "former . . . volunteers took part in demonstrations at Harvard, Yale, Stanford, San Francisco State, Columbia, and the University of Washington over the next four years."

10. Interview with an anonymous Freedom Summer volunteer, March 26, 1985.

11. Interview with an anonymous Freedom Summer applicant, September 12, 1984.

12. Interview with Elinor Tideman Aurthur, June 12, 1985.

13. Interview with an anonymous Freedom Summer volunteer, August 13, 1984.

14. Interview with Barry Clemson, May 17, 1985.

15. When Kennedy assumed office there were no more than 500 military personnel in Vietnam. A month before his assassination the number stood at 16,732 (Boettcher, 1985: 182).

16. Letter written by Ellen Lake to her parents, August 12, 1964; Lake papers.

17. Interview with an anonymous Freedom Summer volunteer, February 5, 1985. The individual the volunteer is referring to is almost certainly Clarence Robinson, a half-brother of Silas McGhee. Robinson, a paratrooper, was on furlough from the Army for at least part of the summer and figured prominently in several incidents in Greenwood (c.f. Belfrage, 1965: 170–171).

18. Interview with an anonymous Freedom Summer volunteer, April 18, 1985.

19. Letter written by Bruce Maxwell, May 8, 1965; included in papers (hereinafter cited as Maxwell papers) on file at SHSW.

20. At least three volunteers reported during their interviews that they were actively involved in planning teach-ins at their schools. The interviews took place 3/26/85, 4/20/85, and 5/22/85.

21. A copy of the ad is included in papers donated by Sandra Adickes to SHSW (hereinafter cited as Adickes papers).

22. The ongoing activities of the committee were described by Adickes on pages 5–6 of an unpublished paper included in her collection at SHSW. The paper is entitled, "My Seven Year (H)itch: A Rambling, Discursive, Anecdotal History of the Evolution of a Radical Teacher."

23. Whitman's account is taken from a letter he wrote to the author on July 9, 1985; in author's possession.

24. A copy of the statement was enclosed with the July 9, 1985 letter sent to the author by Gren Whitman; in author's possession.

25. The forty-six groups or individuals are listed in a two-page directory released by Resistance in December, 1967. A copy of the directory is on file at SHSW.

26. Interview with an anonymous Freedom Summer volunteer, November 17, 1984.

27. The original memo was never published. It was, however, reprinted under the title, "Chicago Women Form Liberation Group," in the November 13, 1967 issue of New Left Notes.

28. Jo Freeman participated in the smaller 1965 Summer Project after applying but deciding not to go South for Freedom Summer.

29. Interview with Miriam Cohen Glickman, June 1, 1985.

30. Interview with an anonymous Freedom Summer volunteer, August 18, 1984.

31. Interview with Annie Popkin, February 9, 1985.

32. This quote was taken from a transcript of a taped session of shared reminiscences offered by some thirty Bay Area volunteers gathered together for a twenty-year reunion. Organized by Annie Popkin and Robbie Osman, the reunion was held on July 14, 1984; tapes in author's possession.

33. The following table reports the volunteers' and the no-shows' estimates of their pre- and post-summer political orientations on a 1–10 scale, with 1 representing "radical left" and 10 "radical right":

	Pre-Summer	Post-Summer
No-Shows	3.48	3.27
Volunteers	3.57	2.63

34. Interview with an anonymous Freedom Summer volunteer, April 22, 1985.

35. Interview with an anonymous Freedom Summer applicant, July 29, 1985.

36. Interview with an anonymous Freedom Summer volunteer, April 12, 1985.

37. Interview with an anonymous Freedom Summer volunteer, March 20, 1985.

38. Interview with Jan Hillegas, March 26, 1985.

39. The activism scale was constructed using four questionnaire items. The first asked the respondent to report the forms of civil rights activism, if any, they were involved in *following* the summer. A numeric value was then assigned to each of these forms of activity based on its intensity relative to all others. So, for example, joining the staff of one of the major civil rights organizations earned a numeric value of 5. Participating in civil rights fund-raising was accorded a value of 1. A second item asked the subject to "list all the political or movement organizations" they belonged to "from Freedom Summer through the time of the killings at Kent State in May 1970." All organizations listed—except for SDS and SNCC—were assigned a point value of 1. Membership in either SNCC or SDS was worth 2 points. Third, all subjects were asked to indicate their level of involvement in the major movements of the period. These included the antiwar, student, and women's liberation movements, among others. Defining oneself as "very involved" in any of these movements carried with it a point value of 3. To have been "moderately" or "somewhat involved" counted for 2 and 1 points, respectively. Finally, all instances of full-time paid activist employment were assigned a point value of 5. The individual's score on the activism scale was simply the sum total of the points they received on these four items. Not surprisingly, the mean "activism score" for the volunteers (24.4) was significantly higher than the comparable figure for the no-shows (15.4).

40. Interview with Linda Davis, April 18, 1985.

41. This excerpt was taken from a letter written by Bryan Dunlap on August 26, 1974. The letter was prompted by former volunteer Jan Hillegas' efforts to find out what the project veterans were up to ten years after Freedom Summer. The letter was copied from the original which remains in Hillegas' possession.

42. Interviews with anonymous Freedom Summer volunteers, August 13, 1984 and June 6, 1985.

43. Interview with Stephen Blum, August 13, 1984.

44. Interview with Gren Whitman, April 18, 1985.

45. Interview with an anonymous Freedom Summer volunteer, April 12, 1985.

46. Interview with an anonymous Freedom Summer volunteer, April 6, 1985.

47. Interview with an anonymous Freedom Summer applicant, August 31, 1984.

48. Interview with an anonymous Freedom Summer volunteer, June 8, 1985.

49. These work histories were taken verbatim from three follow-up questionnaires completed by Freedom Summer volunteers.

50. Interview with an anonymous Freedom Summer applicant, May 9, 1985.

51. Interview with an anonymous Freedom Summer volunteer, March 29, 1985.

52. Interview with an anonymous Freedom Summer volunteer, April 20, 1985.

53. Letter written by Bill Hodes to his parents, July 13, 1964; in Hodes papers.

54. Interview with Ken Scudder, August 23, 1984.

55. Interviews with Chude Pamela Allen and an anonymous Freedom Summer volunteer, both on August 14, 1984.

56. Interview with Judy Michalowski, August 10, 1984.

57. Interview with Len Edwards, August 17, 1984.

58. Interview with an anonymous Freedom Summer volunteer, May 22, 1985.

59. Support for the claim that political considerations played more of a role in the volunteers' selection of mates than was true for the no-shows comes in the form of a comparison of the two groups' answers to a single questionnaire item. All subjects were asked to respond to the following statement: "My participation in social movements affected my choice of mate(s)." Thirty percent of the volunteers "strongly agreed" with this statement as compared to slightly more than 20 percent of the no-shows.

60. Interview with an anonymous Freedom Summer applicant, August 7, 1984.

61. Interview with an anonymous Freedom Summer applicant, June 30, 1985.

Chapter 6

1. Interview with an anonymous Freedom Summer volunteer, May 22, 1985.

2. Ibid.

3. Indeed, it can be argued that this concern with self, however politically motivated it may have been at the outset, proved in the end to be a major factor contributing to the demise of the New Left. Quite simply, the narcissism and self-absorption fostered by this concern for self-awareness eventually proved incompatible with the needs for self-denial and sacrifice required of any successful social movement.

4. For an interesting account of these movements, see Boyte, 1980.

5. Interview with an anonymous Freedom Summer volunteer, February 5, 1985.

6. Interview with an anonymous Freedom Summer volunteer, November 17, 1984.

7. Interview with an anonymous Freedom Summer volunteer, August 18, 1984.

8. Case #1 was compiled from information provided by Gren Whitman on his questionnaire and during an April 18, 1985 interview.

9. Case #2 is based on a questionnaire as well as an interview conducted in March of 1985. The volunteer in question requested anonymity. I have referred to her here as Debra Ellis.

10. Case #3 draws on three sources of information: (1) a completed questionnaire from Heather Tobis Booth, (2) an interview with her conducted May 7, 1985, and (3) a profile of Ms. Booth entitled, "A Woman Born to be Riled," in the February 14, 1985 *Chicago Tribune*.

11. Interview with Miriam Cohen Glickman, June 1, 1985.

12. Interview with an anonymous Freedom Summer volunteer, July 29, 1985.

13. Interview with an anonymous Freedom Summer volunteer, April 22, 1984.

14. Interview with Ken Scudder, August 23, 1984.

15. The volunteers average just 4.7 years of full-time employment during the decade as compared to 6.0 years for the no-shows.

16. Interview with an anonymous Freedom Summer volunteer, June 12, 1985.

17. Interview with an anonymous Freedom Summer volunteer, April 22, 1985.

18. Interview with an anonymous Freedom Summer volunteer, June 20, 1985.

19. Interview with an anonymous Freedom Summer volunteer, April 12, 1985.

20. Interview with an anonymous Freedom Summer applicant, October 13, 1984.

21. Certain scholars have also interpreted various forms of evidence as supporting conclusions consistent with the popular media account (c.f. Foss and Larkin, 1976).

22. Among the best follow-up studies of the Sixties activists are: Abramowitz and Nassi, 1981; Braungart and Braungart, 1980; DeMartini, 1983; Fendrich, 1974, 1976, 1977; Fendrich and Krauss, 1978; Fendrich and Tarleau, 1973; Nassi and Abramowitz, 1979; Whalen and Flacks, 1980.

23. Interview with an anonymous Freedom Summer volunteer, November 17, 1984.

24. Quote taken from the transcript of a speech given by Jan Hillegas, April 5, 1984, at Jackson State University, Jackson, Mississippi, to commemorate the twentieth anniversary of the Summer Project.

25. Interview with an anonymous Freedom Summer volunteer, June 6, 1985.

26. The matched comparison group was created by asking the parents of students in Introductory Sociology courses at George Mason University and the University of Arizona to fill out a modified version of the questionnaires completed by the volunteers and no-shows. Questionnaires were solicited from parents in a total of five courses during the 1982–1983 and 1983–1984 academic years. In all, a total of 1,073 questionnaires were collected. Of these, 117 were filled out by parents whose age and educational background matched that of the volunteers. Given the way the comparison group was created, care should be exercised in interpreting the results of the survey. Obviously, the comparison group is not a representative sample of the United States as a whole.

27. Interview with Robbie Osman, August 13, 1985.

28. *Out of the Darkness*. Fire on the Mountain, 4001. The quote is from the album's liner notes written by Robbie Osman and Linn Shapiro.

29. Ibid.

30. Interview with an anonymous Freedom Summer volunteer, March 20, 1985.

31. Interview with Annie Popkin, June 6, 1985.

32. It is interesting to note that the female volunteers are much better linked to other project veterans than are the males. Only 37 percent of the male volunteers, but 55 percent of the females, report having contact with another volunteer. Given the role of such ties in encouraging activism, the more extensive nature of the ties for female volunteers may help explain why they remain more politically active than their male counterparts.

33. The profile of Defuser and The World Suicide Club was compiled from written materials and information obtained from David Chadwick during an interview on June 8, 1985.

34. Interview with Andrew Schiffrin, August 15, 1984.

35. To measure whether the volunteers had grown more optimistic or pessimistic about the use of social movements as a means of affecting social change, they were asked on the questionnaire to respond to the following two statements:

> In the 1960s social movements were very effective
> vehicles of social change.
>
> Social movements are potentially effective vehi-
> cles of social change in contemporary America.

In responding, the volunteers were to check any one of five response categories: (1) strongly agree; (2) agree; (3) don't know; (4) disagree; (5)
strongly disagree. Seventeen percent of the volunteers responded more posi-
tively to the first statement than the second. Only 9 percent saw social movements as potentially more effective today than in the Sixties.

36. The applicants' current level of political activism was measured by a
scale constructed from their responses to four items on the follow-up questionnaire. First, they received one point for answering "yes" to the question
of whether they were currently involved in any social movement. For all social
movements they claimed to be involved in, they received three additional
points. Each political organization they were currently a member of netted
them an additional point. Finally, if they were currently employed full-time
in an activist capacity, they received five more points. The person's score on
the contemporary activism scale was simply the sum of these points totals.

37. Interview with an anonymous Freedom Summer volunteer, August 18,
1984.

38. Interview with an anonymous Freedom Summer volunteer, August 10,
1984.

39. Interview with an anonymous Freedom Summer volunteer, April 18,
1985.

40. Ibid.

41. Interview with an anonymous Freedom Summer volunteer, April 22,
1985.

42. Interview with an anonymous Freedom Summer volunteer, June 12,
1985.

43. Field notes from interview with an anonymous Freedom Summer volunteer, June 12, 1985.

44. The comparison group consists of 4,264 people, sharing the same age
and general educational level as the Freedom Summer applicants, drawn from
the Census Bureau's Current Population Survey Annual Demographic File
for 1984.

45. Interview with an anonymous Freedom Summer volunteer, April 20,
1985.

46. Interview with Annie Popkin, June 6, 1986.

47. Fifty-six percent of the female and 41 percent of the male volunteers report being currently involved in at least one social movement.

48. The female volunteers report an average of 2.5 memberships in political
organizations. The comparable figure for the male project veterans is 1.8.

49. On their questionnaires, 72 percent of the female and 61 percent of the
male volunteers placed themselves at the "leftist" end (1–3) of the ten-point
scale intended to measure their "current political stance."

50. Interview with an anonymous Freedom Summer volunteer, April 28, 1985.

51. Interview with an anonymous Freedom Summer volunteer, July 29, 1985. Of late, feminist scholars have begun to acknowledge just how widespread the feelings voiced by this volunteer are. In a recent paper, Deborah Rosenfelt and Judith Stacey (1987: 348) have noted that

> In the early days of the women's movement, we felt ourselves part of a supportive feminist community whose bonds and beliefs made finding a mate seem far less imperative than it does for many women now. . . . Many of us now find ourselves aging in a period in which our old communities have become fragile and fragmented. This loss deepens the desire for committed partnerships to meet our needs for intimacy, for continuity, for reliable interdependence.

52. Interview with Annie Popkin, June 6, 1985.

53. Interview with an anonymous Freedom Summer volunteer, July 29, 1985.

54. Field notes from an interview with an anonymous Freedom Summer volunteer, March 21, 1985.

55. Also included in the unemployment category are those volunteers who are either imprisoned or institutionalized.

56. Interview with an anonymous Freedom Summer volunteer, March 26, 1985.

57. Interview with Ken Scudder, August 23, 1984.

58. Interview with Annie Popkin, June 6, 1985.

59. Even this comparison understates the degree to which the male volunteers are underpaid relative to their counterparts in the comparison group. The fact is the latter group is not strictly comparable to the volunteers. While the two groups were matched on *level* of education, it was impossible to also control for the quality or nature of that education. In light of the highly skewed, elite nature of the education enjoyed by most of the volunteers, the income advantage of those in the comparison group is even more significant, given their less advantaged educational backgrounds.

60. In distinguishing between the personal costs borne by the female volunteers and the professional or financial costs of the male volunteers, it is important to keep in mind two important qualifiers. First, the male volunteers have suffered financially only in relation to the no-shows and the matched group of males drawn from the 1984 Current Population Survey. Relative to all males in the United States, the volunteers are clearly better paid and, in all respects, better off occupationally. Secondly, the characterization of the female volunteers as occupationally advantaged is again a relative, rather than an absolute, one. It is only in relation to their female counterparts in the comparison group and among the no-shows that the women volunteers have done well. An absolute comparison of the incomes of the male and female volunteers shows the females lagging well behind the males.

61. This profile is based upon various forms of information supplied by

Stuart Rawlings. These included: (1) a completed questionnaire; (2) an interview conducted August 22, 1984 and, (3) various reports compiled by Stuart describing the various trips and experiences touched on in the profile. All materials in author's possession.

62. Interview with an anonymous Freedom Summer volunteer, April 22, 1985.

63. The profile of Chude Pamela Allen is based on her questionnaire, an Aug. 14, 1984 interview with her, and several subsequent phone calls and letters.

64. This final profile draws upon a completed questionnaire and an interview conducted August 19, 1984. Neil McCarthy is not the volunteer's real name. The volunteer in question requested anonymity.

65. Interview with Mario Savio in the *Washington Post*, Sunday, October 21, 1984, Section C, p. 3.

Epilogue

1. Interview with an anonymous Freedom Summer volunteer, March 20, 1985.

2. Quoted in "The Last One Home," by Jo Durden-Smith in the January, 1985, issue of *California Monthly*, p. 95.

3. Interview with Linda Davis, April 18, 1985.

4. Interview with an anonymous Freedom Summer volunteer, April 22, 1985.

5. Interview with an anonymous Freedom Summer volunteer, May 22, 1985.

Bibliography

Scholarly Books and Articles

Abramowitz, Stephen I. and Alberta J. Nassi
  1981 "Keeping the Faith: Psychological Correlates of Activism Persistence into Middle Adulthood," *Journal of Youth and Adolescence* 10: 507–523.
Adams, Jane
  1967 "People's Power: On Equality for Women," *New Left Notes* (January 20).
Adickes, Sandra
  1967 "My Seven Year (H)itch: A Rambling, Discursive, Anecdotal History of the Evolution of a Radical Teacher," paper presented at Conference on Radicals in the Professions, July 14–17, 1967, Ann Arbor, Michigan.
Belfrage, Sally
  1965 *Freedom Summer*. New York: Viking Press.
Bem, Daryl J.
  1972 "Self-perception Theory," in Leonard Berkowitz (ed.) *Advances in Experimental Social Psychology*, Vol. 6. New York: Academic Press, pp. 1–62.
Berger, Peter
  1963 *Invitation to Sociology*. Garden City, NY: Doubleday & Company.
Bibby, Reginald W., and Merlin B. Brinkerhoff
  1974 "When Proselytizing Fails: An Organizational Analysis," *Sociological Analysis* 35: 189–200.
Block, J. H., N. Hann, and B. M. Smith
  1969 "Socialization Correlates of Student Activism," *Journal of Social Issues* 25: 143–178.
Boettcher, Thomas D.
  1985 *Vietnam: The Valor and the Sorrow*. Boston and Toronto: Little, Brown and Company.

Bolton, Charles D.
    1972 "Alienation and Action: A Study of Peace Group Members,"
          American Journal of Sociology 78: 537–561.
Boyte, Harry C.
    1980 *The Backyard Revolution*. Philadelphia: Temple University Press.
Braungart Richard G. and Margaret M. Braungart
    1980 "Political Career Patterns of Radical Activists in the 1960s and
          1970s: Some Historical Comparisons," *Sociological Focus* 13: 237–
          254.
Breines, Wini
    1982 *Community and Organization in the New Left: 1962–1968*. South
          Hadley, MA: J. F. Bergin Publishers, Inc.
Brown, Rosellen
    1984 *Civil Wars*. New York: Penguin Books.
Carden, Maren Lockwood
    1974 *The New Feminist Movement*. New York: Russell Sage Foundation.
Carson, Clayborne
    1981 *In Struggle: SNCC and the Black Awakening of the 1960s*. Cam-
          bridge: Harvard University Press.
Coles, Robert
    1964 "Social Struggle and Weariness," *Psychiatry* 27 (no. 4): 305–315.
Cottle, Tomas J.
    1971 *Time's Children*. Boston: Little, Brown and Company.
DeMartini, Joseph R.
    1983 "Social Movement Participation: Political Socialization, Genera-
          tional Consciousness, and Lasting Effects," *Youth and Society* 15:
          195–233.
Demerath III, N. J., Gerald Marwell, and Michael T. Aiken
    1971 *Dynamics of Idealism*. San Francisco: Jossey-Bass Inc.
Dillard, J. L.
    1977 *A Lexicon of Black English, The Words the Slaves Made*. New
          York: Continuum Books.
    1972 *Black English, Its History and Usage in the United States*. New
          York: Random House.
Draper, Hal
    1965 *Berkeley: The New Student Revolt*. New York: Grove Press, Inc.
Easterlin, Richard A.
    1980 *Birth and Fortune*. New York: Basic Books.
Erskine, Hazel
    1969 "The Polls: Negro Philosophies of Life," *Public Opinion Quarterly*
          33 (no. 1): 147–58.
Evans, Sarah
    1980 *Personal Politics*. New York: Vintage Books.
Fendrich, James M.
    1977 "Keeping the Faith or Pursuing the Good Life: A Study of the

Consequences of Participation in the Civil Rights Movement," *American Sociological Review* 42: 144–157.

1976 "Black and White Activists Ten Years Later: Political Socialization and Adult Left-wing Politics," *Youth and Society* 8: 81–104.

1974 "Activists Ten Years Later: A Test of Generational Unit Continuity," *Journal of Social Issues* 30: 95–118.

Fendrich, James M. and Ellis S. Krauss

1978 "Student Activism and Adult Left-wing Politics: A Causal Model of Political Socialization for Black, White and Japanese Students of the 1960's Generation," in Lewis Kriesberg (ed.) *Research in Social Movements, Conflicts and Change*, Vol. 1: 231–255, Greenwich, CT: JAI Press.

Fendrich, James M. and Alison T. Tarleau

1973 "Marching to a Different Drummer: Occupational and Political Correlates of Former Student Activists," *Social Forces* 52: 245–253.

Feuer, Lewis Samuel

1969 *The Conflict of Generations*. New York: Basic Books.

Flacks, Richard

1971 *Youth and Social Change*. Chicago: Markam.

Fligstein, Neil

1981 *Going North*. New York: Academic Press.

Forman, James

1972 *The Making of Black Revolutionaries*. New York: Macmillan.

Foss, Daniel A. and Ralph W. Larkin

1976 "From 'The Gates of Eden' to 'The Day of the Locust': An Analysis of the Dissident Youth Movement of the 1960's and Its Heirs of the Early 1970's . . . The Post Movement Groups," *Theory and Society* 3: 45–64.

Gallup, George H.

1972 *The Gallup Poll: Public Opinion, 1935–1971*. Vol. 3. New York: Random House.

Garrow, David J.

1981 *The FBI and Martin Luther King, Jr*. New York: Penguin Books.

1978 *Protest at Selma*. New Haven: Yale University Press.

Gitlin, Todd

1987 *The Sixties: Years of Hope, Days of Rage*. New York: Bantam Books.

Harris, David

1982 *Dreams Die Hard*. New York: St. Martins.

Harrington, Michael

1972 *Fragments of the Century*. New York: Saturday Review Press/ E. P. Dutton & Company.

1962 *The Other America: Poverty in the United States*. New York: Macmillan.

Hayden, Casey and Mary King
1966 "Sex and Caste: A Kind of Memo." *Liberation* 10 (April): 35–36.
Heirich, Max
1968 *The Beginning, Berkeley 1964.* New York: Columbia University Press.
Hewlett, Sylvia
1986 *A Lesser Life: The Myth of Women's Liberation in America.* New York: William Morrow.
Holt, Len
1965 *The Summer That Didn't End.* New York: William Morrow.
Houseknecht, Sharon, Suzanne Vaughan, and Anne S. Macke
1984 "Marital Disruption Among Professional Women: The Timing of Career and Family Events." *Social Problems* 31: 273–84.
Hubbard, Howard
1968 "Five Long Hot Summers and How They Grew," *Public Interest* No. 12: 3–34.
Hyman, Herbert H. and Paul B. Sheatsley
1964 "Attitudes Toward Desegregation," *Scientific American* 211 (no. 1): 16–23.
Isserman, Maurice
1987 *If I Had a Hammer: The Death of the Old Left and the Birth of the New Left.* New York: Basic Books.
Jones, Landon
1980 *Great Expectations.* New York: Ballantine Books.
Keniston, Kenneth
1968 *Young Radicals.* New York: Harcourt, Brace and World, Inc.
King, Mary
1987 *Freedom Song: A Personal Story of the 1960s Civil Rights Movement.* New York: William Morrow.
Kluger, Richard
1975 *Simple Justice,* Volumes I and II. New York: Alfred A. Knopf.
Lewis, Steven H. and Robert E. Kraut
1972 "Correlates of Student Political Activism and Ideology," *Journal of Social Issues* 28: 131–149.
Lipset, Seymour M. and Sheldon S. Wolin (eds.)
1965 *The Berkeley Student Revolt: Facts and Interpretations.* Garden City, NY: Doubleday & Company.
Lomax, Louis E., John Howard Griffith, and Dick Gregory
1964 *Mississippi Eyewitness.* Menlo Park, CA: E. M. Keating.
Louis, Debbie
1970 *And We Are Not Saved: A History of the Movement as People.* Garden City, NY: Doubleday.
Matusow, Allen J.
1971 "From Civil Rights to Black Power: The Case of SNCC, 1960–1966," in John H. Bracey, Jr., August Meier, and Elliott Rudwick (eds.) *Conflict and Competition: Studies in the Recent Black Pro-*

test Movement. Belmont, CA: Wadsworth Publishing Company, Inc.

McAdam, Doug.
1986 "Recruitment to High-Risk Activism: The Case of Freedom Summer," *American Journal of Sociology* 92: 64–90.
1982 *Political Process and the Development of Black Insurgency, 1930–1970.* Chicago: The University of Chicago Press.

McCarthy, John and Mayer Zald
1973 *The Trend of Social Movements in America: Professionalization and Resource Mobilization.* Morristown, NJ: General Learning Press.

McCord, William
1965 *Mississippi: The Long, Hot Summer.* New York: W. W. Norton & Company.

McLemore, Leslie Burl
1971 "The Mississippi Freedom Democratic Party: A Case Study of Grass-Roots Politics." Ph.D. dissertation, University of Massachusetts.

Miller, James
1987 *'Democracy is in the Streets': From Port Huron to the Siege of Chicago.* New York: Simon and Schuster.

Miller, Michael V. and Susan Gilmore
1965 *Revolution at Berkeley.* New York: Dell Publishing Company.

Mills, C. Wright
1959 *The Sociological Imagination.* New York: Oxford University Press.

Moody, Anne
1968 *Coming of Age in Mississippi.* New York: Dell Publishing Company.

Nassi, Alberta J. and Stephen I. Abramowitz
1979 "Transition or Transformation? Personal and Political Development of Former Berkeley Free Speech Movement Activists," *Journal of Youth and Adolescence* 8: 21–35.

Orum, Anthony
1972 *Black Students in Protest.* Washington, DC: American Sociological Association.

Pettigrew, Thomas F.
1964 *A Profile of the Negro American.* Princeton, NJ: D. Van Nostrand.

Ploski, Harry A., and Warren Marr II (eds.)
1976 *The Afro American.* New York: The Bellwether Company.

Pouissant, Alvin F.
1966 "The Stresses of the White Female Worker in the Civil Rights Movement in the South," *American Journal of Psychiatry* 123 (No. 4): 401–407.

Price, Daniel O.
1969 *Changing Characteristics of the Negro Population.* Washington, DC: U.S. Government Printing Office.

Raines, Howell
  1983   *My Soul Is Rested*. New York: Penguin Books.
Romaine, Anne Cook
  1970   "The Mississippi Freedom Democratic Party through August, 1964,"
         Masters' thesis, University of Virginia.
Rosenfelt, Deborah and Judith Stacey
  1987   "Second Thoughts on the Second Wave," *Feminist Studies* 13
         (No. 2): 341–61.
Rosenthal, Naomi, M. Fingrutd, M. Ethier, R. Karant, and D. McDonald
  1985   "Social Movements and Network Analysis: A Case of Nineteenth
         Century Women's Reform in New York State," *American Journal
         of Sociology* 90: 1022–1054.
Rothschild, Mary Aiken
  1982   *A Case of Black and White: Northern Volunteers and the Southern
         Freedom Summers, 1964–1965*. Westport, CT: Greenwood Press.
  1979   "White Women Volunteers in the Freedom Summers: Their Life
         and Work in a Movement for Social Change." *Feminist Studies* 5:
         466–495.
Sale, Kirkpatrick
  1973   *SDS*. New York: Random House.
Scanzoni, John
  1978   *Sex Roles, Women's Work, and Marital Conflict*. Lexington, MA:
         Lexington Books.
Schwartz, Michael
  1976   *Radical Protest and Social Structure*. New York: Academic Press.
Sellers, Cleveland, with Robert Terrell
  1973   *The River of No Return: The Autobiography of a Black Militant*.
         New York: William Morrow.
Silver, James W.
  1963   *Mississippi: The Closed Society*. New York: Harcourt, Brace and
         World, Inc.
Sinsheimer, Joe
  1983   *Bringing the Country to White Heat: The 1964 Mississippi Project
         and Its Volunteers*. Duke University. Unpublished manuscript.
Skocpol, Theda
  1979   *States and Social Revolutions*. New York: Cambridge University
         Press.
Smith, Lillian
  1964   *Our Faces, Our Words*. New York: W. W. Norton & Company.
Snow, David, E. Burke Rochford, Jr., Steven K. Warden, and Robert D.
Benford
  1986   "Frame Alignment Processes, Micromobilization, and Movement
         Participation," *American Sociological Review* 51: 464–481.
Snow, David A., Louis A. Zurcher Jr., and Sheldon Ekland-Olson
  1980   "Social Networks and Social Movements: A Microstructural Ap-

proach to Differential Recruitment," *American Sociological Review* 45: 787–801.

Spain, David
1964 "Mississippi Autopsy," in *Mississippi Eyewitness*. Menlo Park, CA: E. M. Keating, pp. 43–49.

Stouffer, Samuel
1955 *Communism, Conformity and Civil Liberties*. New York: Doubleday & Co.

Student Non-Violent Coordinating Committee
1965 "The Mississippi Freedom Democratic Party: Background and Recent Developments," unpublished paper.

Sugarman, Tracy
1966 *Stranger at the Gates*. New York: Hill and Wang.

Sutherland, Elizabeth (ed.)
1965 *Letters from Mississippi*. New York: McGraw-Hill Book Company.

Watters, Pat
1971 *Down to Now: Reflections on the Southern Civil Rights Movement*. New York: Pantheon Books.

Whalen, Jack and Richard Flacks
1980 "The Isla Vista 'Bank Burners' Ten Years Later: Notes on the Fate of Student Activists," *Sociological Focus* 13: 215–236.

White, Theodore H.
1965 *The Making of the President, 1964*. New York: Atheneum Publishers.

Wofford, Harrison
1980 *Of Kennedys and Kings: Making Sense of the Sixties*. New York: Farrar, Straus and Giroux.

Zinn, Howard
1965 *SNCC, The New Abolitionists*. Boston: Beacon Press.

Newspaper and Magazine Articles

Atwater, James
1964 "If We Can Crack Mississippi . . .", *Saturday Evening Post*, July 25, 1964.

Barker, Karlyn
1984 "The Outlook Interview," *The Washington Post* (October 21, 1984).

Cowan, Paul and Geoffrey Cowan
1983 "Letters from Mississippi," *Esquire* (June): 237–240.

Dellabough, Robin
1984 "A Conversation with Mario Savio and Bettina Aptheker," in *California Monthly* (December).

Durden-Smith, Jo
1985 "The Last One Home," *California Monthly* (January), pp. 84–87.

Fortune
  1951   (April) "More Booms Ahead."
Galloway, Paul
  1985   "A Woman Born to Be Riled," *Chicago Tribune* (February 14, 1985).
Maidenburg, Michael and Philip Meyer
  1970   "The Berkeley Rebels Five Years Later: Has Age Mellowed the Pioneer Radicals?" Detroit Free Press, seven-part series, February 1–7, 1970.
Neumann, A. Lin
  1982   "Do It with a Business Card." *In These Times* (December 8–14), p. 24.
Newsweek
  1964   "Allen's Army." February 24, 1964.
San Francisco Examiner
  1984   The Free Speech Movement 20 Years Later (special reprint of a six-part series that appeared in the paper).

Government Publications

Council of Economic Advisers
  1987   *The Annual Report of the Council of Economic Advisers.* Appendix B, Statistical Tables Relating to Income, Employment and Production. Washington, DC: U.S. Government Printing Office.
U.S. Bureau of the Census
  1976   *Current Population Reports,* Series P-60, No. 102. "Characteristics of the Population Below the Poverty Level: 1974." Washington, DC: U.S. Government Printing Office.
  1975   *Historical Statistics of the United States, Colonial Times to 1970.* Bicentennial Edition, Parts 1 and 2. Washington, DC: U.S. Government Printing Office.
  1964   *Statistical Abstract of the United States: 1964* (Eighty-Fifth Edition). Washington, DC: U.S. Government Printing Office.
  1963   *U.S. Census of the Population: 1960.* Vol. I. *Characteristics of the Population.* Part 26, "Mississippi." Washington, DC: U.S. Government Printing Office.
  1962   *U.S. Census of the Agriculture, 1959.* "Color, Race and Tenure of Farm Operator." Vol. 2, Chapter 10. Washington, DC: U.S. Government Printing Office.
  1961   *U.S. Census of the Population, 1960. General Population Characteristics, U.S. Summary.* Final Report PC (1)-1B. Washington, DC: U.S. Government Printing Office.
  1961   *U.S. Census 1960,* Volume 1. Washington, DC: U.S. Government Printing Office.

U.S. Congress, Senate Committee to Study Government Operations with Respect to Intelligence Activities

    1975 *Intelligence Activities: Hearings on Senate Resolution 21*, 94th Congress, First Session, Volume 6. Washington, DC: U.S. Government Printing Office.

    1976 *Final Report—Book III, Supplementary Detailed Staff Reports on Intelligence Activities and the Rights of Americans*. 94th Congress, Second Session. Washington, DC: U.S. Government Printing Office.

U.S. Department of Health, Education and Welfare, Office of Education

    1965 *Digest of Educational Statistics*. Washington, DC: U.S. Government Printing Office.

    1963 *Vital Statistics of the United States, 1960*. Volume II, "Mortality," Part B. Washington DC: U.S. Government Printing Office.

Manuscript Collections

Public Collections

State Historical Society of Wisconsin Archives

Stephen Bingham Papers
Robert Feinglass Papers
Susan Gladstone Papers
Richard Gould Papers
Dale Gronemeier Papers
Sandra Hard Papers
Christopher Hexter Papers
William Hodes Papers
Eugene Hunn Papers
James Kates Papers
Ellen Lake Papers
Charles Miller Papers
Eugene Nelson Papers
Martin and Victoria Nicholaus Papers
Jo Ann Ooiman Robinson Papers
Parents Mississippi Freedom Association of California Papers
Brian Peterson Papers
Mendy Samstein Papers
Robert Saul Starobin Papers
Elizabeth Sutherland Papers
Patrick Thomas Papers
Lise Vogel Papers
Christopher Wilson Papers
Matthew Zwerling Papers

Other Public Collections

Freedom Information Service, Jackson, Mississippi—miscellaneous materials

Martin Luther King, Jr. Center Archives and Library, Atlanta, Georgia—Freedom Summer Collection

State of Mississippi Archives, Jackson, Mississippi—miscellaneous materials

Wilson Library, University of North Carolina at Chapel Hill—Michael Kenney Papers

Materials in the Author's Possession

Journals

Margaret Rose Beernink
Ronald de Sousa
Stuart Rawlings
Grenville Whitman

Letters

Chude Pamela Allen
Margaret Rose Beernink
Margaret Aley Chavez
Marion Davidson
Len Edwards
Robert Popkin

Miscellaneous Materials

Chude Pamela Allen
Robert Beyers
Clayborne Carson
Margaret Aley Chavez
Marion Davidson
Jan Hillegas
Annie Popkin
Robert Popkin
Stuart Rawlings
Grenville Whitman

Interviews

Freedom Summer Volunteers

Chude Pamela Allen, August 14, 1984
Robert Beyers, February 4, 1985
Stephen Blum, August 13, 1984
Heather Tobis Booth, May 7, 1985

David Chadwick, June 8, 1985
Barry Clemson, April 17, 1985
Marion Davidson, March 21, 1985
Linda Davis, April 18, 1985
Len Edwards, August 17, 1984
James Forman, August 29, 1985
Corrine Barnwell Freeman, March 28, 1985
David Gelfand, February 7, 1985
Miriam Cohen Glickman, June 1, 1985
Jan Hillegas, March 26, 1985
Heidi Dole Howell, November 12, 1984
Linda Wetmore King, August 14, 1984
Judy Michalowski, August 10, 1984
Rob Osman, June 14, 1984
Annie Popkin, February 9, 1985
Stuart Rawlings, August 22, 1984
Andy Schiffrin, August 15, 1984
Ken Scudder, August 23, 1984
Elinor Tideman Aurthur, June 12, 1985
Gren Whitman, April 18, 1985
Fred Winyard, August 16, 1984
Anonymous male, February 5, 1985
Anonymous male, April 22, 1985
Anonymous male, June 20, 1985
Anonymous female, August 10, 1984
Anonymous female, March 29, 1985
Anonymous male, March 20, 1985
Anonymous female, June 6, 1985
Anonymous male, April 6, 1985
Anonymous male, April 12, 1985
Anonymous female, August 18, 1984
Anonymous male, August 19, 1984
Anonymous male, June 8, 1985
Anonymous female, June 28, 1985
Anonymous male, May 9, 1985
Anonymous male, May 22, 1985
Anonymous female, April 20, 1985
Anonymous male, March 26, 1985

Freedom Summer Applicants*

Male, August 17, 1984
Male, August 18, 1984
Male, August 27, 1984

* In advance of doing the interviews, I decided to treat all of the Freedom Summer applicants (no-shows) anonymously.

Female, August 28, 1984
Female, August 31, 1984
Male, September 2, 1984
Male, September 12, 1984
Female, October 13, 1984
Female, November 17, 1984
Male, March 22, 1985
Female, March 30, 1985
Male, April 4, 1985
Female, April 4, 1985
Male, April 11, 1985
Female, April 17, 1985
Male, April 18, 1985
Male, April 26, 1985
Female, April 27, 1985
Male, April 29, 1985
Female, April 30, 1985
Female, April 30, 1985
Female, May 3, 1985
Male, May 4, 1985
Male, May 9, 1985
Female, May 17, 1985
Male, May 21, 1985
Male, May 23, 1985
Male, May 30, 1985
Female, May 31, 1985
Male, June 4, 1985
Female, June 6, 1985
Female, June 7, 1985
Female, June 10, 1985
Male, June 11, 1985
Male, June 26, 1985
Female, June 29, 1985
Male, June 30, 1985
Male, July 27, 1985
Male, July 28, 1985
Female, July 29, 1985

Index

Sellers, Cleveland, 3, 29, 96, 142, 293*n*
Selma to Montgomery March, 116
Sexism in the Freedom Summer project:
sexual relations during the summer
and, 105–7; work assignments and,
107–10, 179
Sexual preferences, of the volunteers,
220–21
Sexual relations during Freedom Summer:
as an influence upon the volunteers'
later patterns and conceptions of
sexuality, 4, 13, 93, 143–45; inter-
racial relationships as a component
of, 4, 93–95, 144–45, 196; general
descriptions of, 93–96, 297*n*. *See also*
Sexism in the Freedom Summer
project
Shapiro, Linn, 307*n*
Shaw, Mississippi, 88, 255
Sheatsley, Paul B., 20
Sherover-Marcuse, Ricky, 216, 236
Silver, James W., 26
Sinsheimer, Joe, 131
Sit-in movement: 20, 233; "sympathy
demonstrations" in support of, 21
Skocpol, Theda, 145
SLATE, 302*n*
Sleep Disorders Center, 229
Smiley, Glenn, 7, 236
Smith, B. M., 44
Smith, Lillian, 32
Snow, David A., 46, 295*n*
Social class: the volunteers and, 12, 13–
14, 17, 39–43, 56, 65, 87, 88, 133,
142, 159, 233; feelings of efficacy
and, 13, 233
Social networks: importance in sustaining
subsequent activism among the volun-
teers, 5, 161, 169, 176–77, 182–83,
190, 216, 217–18, 237, 289, 290,
302*n*, 307*n*; role in mediating re-
cruitment to the Freedom Summer
project, 63–65, 237, 254, 295*n*
Socialist Labor Committee, 209
Sociology, 167, 173, 180
Sociology of women, 180
Soledad Prison, 239
South Africa, 175
South Vietnam, 171
Southeast Asia, 171, 172, 174
Southern Christian Leadership Confer-
ence, 39, 40, 130, 151
Southern Conference Educational Fund,
236
Southern Courier, 194
Southern Student Organizing Committee,
193
Spain, David, 155
Spears, Larry, 298*n*, 301*n*
Spelman College, 72, 83, 230

Sproul Hall Administration Building,
163–64, 166, 168
Stacey, Judith, 309*n*
Stanford University, 37, 38, 40, 42, 53,
151, 152, 161, 228, 302*n*
Starkville, Mississippi, 265, 275, 296*n*
Starobin, Robert Saul, 294*n*
State Historical Society of Wisconsin, 256,
293–303*n*
Steward, Ruth, 68, 295*n*
Stouffer, Samuel, 29
Strickland, John, 69
Strong, Edward, 164
Student movement: role of the Freedom
Summer volunteers in, 5, 132, 163–
66, 169–70, 180, 188, 189, 302*n*,
303*n*; the early sixties resurgence of,
21–22, 132; impact of Freedom
Summer upon, 117, 126, 132, 161–
62, 166–69; Free Speech Movement
as a model for, 162, 166, 169 (*see
also* Free Speech Movement); the
anti-war movement and, 173–74
Student Non-violent Coordinating Committee: early history in Mississippi
of, 26–27, 29, 35–36; as driving
force behind the Freedom Summer
project, 28–29, 32, 35–42, 75, 77,
83, 154, 296*n*; origins of, 29–31,
236; impact of early years in Mississippi upon, 31–32, 103, 233; growing divisions over issue of nonviolence within, 32, 120, 122–23,
125; growing divisions over the role
of whites within, 32–33, 38, 103,
117, 120, 123–25, 234; growing
distrust of the federal government
within, 32, 121, 122, 175–76; Executive Committee of, 38, 40, 293*n*;
financial straits of, 39–40; impact of
on the Freedom Summer volunteers,
67–68, 131, 142–43, 234; role in the
Mississippi Freedom Democratic
Party, 77–78, 81, 118–20, 121, 234,
296*n*, 299*n*; interracial sex as a source
of tension within, 95, 106, 123–24;
influence of on the New Left, 111,
126, 166, 169–70, 171, 177, 185;
and the staff retreat at Waveland,
Mississippi, 111, 126, 178–79;
charges of sexism within, 111, 126;
retention of some of the Freedom
Summer volunteers as field secretaries
by, 112–13, 123–24, 188, 231, 298–
99*n*, 304*n*; the debilitating effect of
Freedom Summer on, 117, 120, 121–
26, 234; factional conflict within,
117, 125–26, 295*n*; opposition to the
Vietnam War by, 175–76; expulsion
of whites from, 180, 188, 234; the

CPSIA information can be obtained at www.ICGtesting.com
Printed in the USA
LVOW11s0331090814

398055LV00001B/21/P